D0294754

'UNSINKABLE'

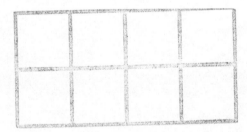

'UNSINKABLE'

CHURCHILL AND THE
FIRST WORLD WAR

RICHARD FREEMAN

Churchill was dubbed 'the unsinkable politician' by
the *Morning Post* when he returned to office in 1917.

First published 2013

The History Press
The Mill, Brimscombe Port
Stroud, Gloucestershire, GL5 2QG
www.thehistorypress.co.uk

© Richard Freeman, 2013

The right of Richard Freeman to be identified as the Author
of this work has been asserted in accordance with the
Copyright, Designs and Patents Act 1988.

British Library Cataloguing in Publication Data.
A catalogue record for this book is available from the British Library.

ISBN 978 0 7524 9889 8

Typesetting and origination by The History Press
Printed in Great Britain

CONTENTS

ACKNOWLEDGEMENTS

Extracts from the following are reproduced with permission of Curtis Brown Ltd., London on behalf of the Estate of Sir Winston Churchill: *The World Crisis 1915*; *The World Crisis 1911-1914*; *The World Crisis 1916-1918*; *Thoughts and Adventures*; *Great Contemporaries*; *Painting as a Pastime*. All Copyright © Winston S. Churchill.

The following are reproduced with permission of Curtis Brown Ltd., London on behalf of C&T Publications: *Winston S. Churchill Volume III: Companion Volume 2* by Martin Gilbert; *Winston S. Churchill Volume III* by Martin Gilbert; *Winston S. Churchill Volume III: Companion Volume 1* by Martin Gilbert; *Winston S. Churchill Volume IV: Companion Volume 1* by Martin Gilbert.

The following are reproduced with permission of Curtis Brown Group Ltd: Soames *Clementine Churchill* and Soames *Speaking for Themselves*.

Material from *From Dreadnought to Scapa Flow Volume 2* by Marder (1956) is reproduced by permission of Oxford University Press.

Material from *Fear God and Dread Nought Volume II* by Arthur Marder published by Jonathan Cape is reproduced with the permission of The Random House Group Ltd.

Attempts to trace the copyright owners of *Memories and Reflections* by H.H. Asquith have proved unsuccessful. The publishers undertake to correct any omissions on reprint.

I am most grateful for the help of the Parliamentary Archives in tracing the three wartime Acts of Parliament relating to the suspension of the rule regarding the re-election of ministers on assuming office.

Battle diagrams: Marcus Freeman.

PRELUDE

On 11 November 1918, Lloyd George, the Prime Minister, called a meeting of his Cabinet. Of those ministers who had gone to war on 4 August 1914, only two were at the Cabinet table to savour the fruits of victory: Lloyd George and Winston Churchill.

They had survived for two reasons: they were the only two senior politicians who understood war and the only two who had the courage to wage it. They were fearless, ruthless and determined.

Lloyd George's role in the war was uncomplicated. He was one of the few strategic thinkers in the Cabinet. Free of any connections with the army or the aristocracy, he was able to bring a fresh, pragmatic eye to the problems of the war. His innate cunning enabled him to outmanoeuvre anyone who was less committed. Alien as war was to his character, to him defeat was inconceivable.

As to Churchill, he was born for war and from early childhood had been enthralled by the stories of battles fought by his famous ancestor, the Duke of Marlborough, in the War of the Spanish Succession (1701–14). In 1893, Churchill entered Sandhurst Military College and was commissioned as a cavalry officer in 1895. He then served in India and the Sudan before becoming a war correspondent at the time of the Second Boer War (1899–1902). By then, he had published two books on his soldiering – both huge commercial successes – as well as a novel. His time in South Africa resulted in a stream of newspaper reports on the war as well as two further books. Ten years later, Churchill was appointed First Lord of the Admiralty.[1] By 1914, he had the perfect qualifications for a war minister.

And yet it all went so badly wrong. Not because Churchill failed as a minister, but because he had enemies. In particular, he had made an enemy of the Tory Party when he crossed the floor of the House, in 1904, to join the Liberals. His meteoric rise through a series of ministerial posts only served to deepen the hostility of his former colleagues. As a result, the Tory Party spent the early part of the war seeking to get Churchill out of office – they succeeded in May 1915. They then spent two years keeping him out until his dramatic return in July 1917.

Although no other senior politician was more suited to run the 1914–18 war, no one was more obstructed in that task. This book tells the story of how, almost from the first month of the war, Churchill became the victim of false stories, libellous innuendoes and malicious attacks as his enemies sought to remove him from power. His heroic action at Antwerp was presented as a fool's errand. He was made the scapegoat for the bungled Dardanelles campaign. He was kept out of the 1915 coalition by men of less than half his stature. He was denied a brigade command in 1916 for purely political reasons. His return to power was blocked time and again by his old party.

But when, finally, Lloyd George found the courage to face down Churchill's denigrators, the fallen politician came back as Minister of Munitions. From July 1917, to the day of victory, the war belonged to Lloyd George and Churchill.

The story of Churchill and the First World War is one of a country that foolishly denied itself the services of one of the two greatest war ministers of the twentieth century. Fortunately, Lloyd George was big enough to recognise Churchill's talents. And Churchill was big enough to rise to every challenge posed by the war.

CHAPTER I

IN A BELGIAN FIELD

'A desperate expedient to meet a desperate situation.'[1]

In a field outside Antwerp stands a man in a flowing cape, sporting a yachting cap and puffing on a huge cigar. Behind him are 400,000 terrified citizens, who have been under siege for weeks. He looks into the distance from where the thundering noise of German heavy guns can be heard. This man is the Allies' last hope and his name is Winston Spencer-Churchill, the First Lord of the Admiralty. He has been despatched to Belgium in a last desperate effort to stem the advancing Germany armies.

Two days earlier, on 2 October 1914, Churchill had been on a train to Dover. His mission – to consult with the Belgians – was important but not pressing. But when he stepped off the train at Dover he was handed a telegram which urgently recalled him to London. Around midnight, he was back in Lord Kitchener's London house and there he found three despairing men: Kitchener (War Minister), Sir Edward Grey (Foreign Secretary) and Sir William Tyrrell (Grey's Private Secretary). What had brought them together was a telegram from Sir Francis Villiers, the British Envoy Extraordinary to Belgium. His message had been blunt: the Belgians were abandoning Antwerp.

Even Field Marshal Lord Kitchener, hero of the Sudan and architect of victory in the Second Boer War, reeled under the news. If Antwerp fell, the German armies would have a clear route through to France. The small British army of six divisions, sent to war with such high hopes, had been in retreat almost from the day that it met the advancing Germans. The French were also in retreat.

Britain and France faced defeat within days, yet Kitchener had no suggestions to make and all that he and Grey could do was to wring their hands. Then Churchill spoke up. True, it might be impossible to hold on to Antwerp, but what about delaying the German advance? Every day of delay was one more to bring forward reinforcements. Kitchener and Grey seized on the plan and soon Churchill was once more speeding towards Dover.

The official naval historian of the First World War described this mission as a 'desperate expedient to meet a desperate situation'.[2] Churchill was to offer the Belgians huge reinforcements if they would hold out for just a few more days.

At home, the War Office and the Admiralty set to work that night to find men and guns to send to Antwerp. Meanwhile, an empty-handed Churchill reached the city at 3.00 p.m. on 3 October, where he met the King of the Belgians and the Belgian Prime Minister. By early evening, he had an agreement. The Belgians would hold on in return for the promise of large-scale support. In a long telegram to London Churchill reported that the Belgians were sure that they could hold the city for at least three days.

Churchill then went to inspect the lines. There were no trenches – the land had been defensively flooded – and every building of any size was a target for the German artillery. Meanwhile, armed only with rifles, the defenders crouched behind bushes. Beyond the lines, German forces were steadily destroying the outer defensive forts using enormous howitzers before turning their artillery on the inner forts. The dispirited Belgian soldiers became spectators as they watched the mighty defence works being destroyed.

The next day, Kitchener was able to telegraph details of the 53,000 men he was to send to Belgium, commencing with Churchill's very own Naval Brigades that he had created in August.

Churchill set up his headquarters in the city and directed the laying of new defensive positions and, despite heavy shellfire, toured the front line and oversaw dispositions. His calm courage reinvigorated the dispirited Belgians and they returned to their guns and defences. Late at night on 4 October, Churchill reported progress to Kitchener and sent him a long list of urgently needed supplies. Meanwhile, the newly revitalised Belgian Prime Minister told him that Antwerp had to be defended at any price. Churchill's marines had now arrived and the Naval Brigades were expected that evening. By this time, Churchill had become so involved in the battle that he telegraphed to Asquith to offer his resignation from the Cabinet in exchange for a high military rank.

The situation was stable on 5 October, as the Belgians had even succeeded in repulsing a German attack and, by the end of the day, held the whole line of the River Nethe, with casualties not exceeding 150 men. Once more, Churchill set forth to tour the lines and to hand over the command of the Naval Brigades to Major General Archibald Paris of the marines. They met in a cottage, which shook with the explosions as German shells fell nearby. Later, Churchill narrowly missed being a casualty as a shell landed close by when he was getting out of his car. That night he retired to bed at 2.00 a.m. in an optimistic mood. The Belgian troops had held their ground and, even as he slept, a large British force was moving on Antwerp.

When Churchill woke the next day all was confusion, but he set about positioning the newly arrived Naval Brigades into the battlefront, insisting that they be dug-in since none had been trained for manoeuvre. In fact, the brigades were never close to the action. Watching wounded soldiers retreating from the battle area and the masses of refugees fleeing from the city, Churchill realised that the Germans were inexorably gaining ground.

The next day, General Henry Rawlinson arrived to take over from Churchill. Before departing, Churchill joined Rawlinson in a Council of War at the Belgian Royal Palace. Both men were ready to fight on, but the Belgians feared that their lines of retreat would soon be cut and could only accept that nothing more could be done. As Rawlinson took over, Churchill left to return to his less exciting duties at the Admiralty. On 9 October, German forces entered Antwerp. Churchill's bold intervention had bought the Allies five precious days.

No operation in the First World War better illustrates Churchill's incomparable capacity for war. He never accepted that nothing could be done. Even in a situation as desperate as Antwerp, he could see how some purpose could be achieved by continuing to fight as he was always able to apply imagination to an apparently doomed scenario; always ready to find another way when everything seemed lost. And most of all, he had high courage as he neither experienced fear nor shrank from death. These qualities will come to the fore again and again in the story of Churchill in the First World War.

CHAPTER 2

FROM SANDCASTLES TO STEEL CASTLES

The wars of peoples will be more terrible than those of kings.[1]

THE ROAD TO WAR

When the Archduke Franz Ferdinand of Austria was assassinated at Sarajevo on 28 June 1914, *The Times* wrote that 'The political effects of the tragedy of Sarajevo can only be broadly surmised.'[2] But during that long, hot summer, Britain had no intention of allowing events in remote Serbia to impinge on daily life. In early July, the new passenger liner MS *Akaroa* left on her maiden voyage to Australia – she was to return as a troop ship; a Mr F.V.A. Smith of the Burton-upon-Trent Amateur Radio Club received his licence to transmit; a new park was opened at Wembley; and a new library was opened at Thornton Heath. Life continued as usual.

The Permanent Secretary in the Foreign Office, Sir Arthur Nicolson, hoped that events in Sarajevo would not 'lead to any further complications'.[3] Churchill, also, took little notice of the assassination. On that day he was indulging in one of the privileges of his post, touring the home ports and naval bases on the Admiralty yacht HMS *Enchantress*. Never one to deny himself luxury, he had the vessel turned into the combination of floating office and relaxing salon. Wherever he went, the daily work of the Admiralty was efficiently carried out in the comfortable cabins. When administration work was finished, Churchill entertained naval officers, politicians, businessmen and friends in style.

Churchill arrived on HMS *Enchantress* for his first major public duty after the assassination: the Fleet Review, held in mid-July, at Portland on the Channel coast. By now, there had been threatening diplomatic exchanges between Austria-Hungary and Serbia, but Russia and Germany had taken no steps to calm the ever increasing tension on the Continent. Churchill had announced the Fleet Review in the spring, so it was pure coincidence that it was to take place when a Continental war was imminent. The Liberal government, ever hostile to defence expenditure, had limited the review to ships positioned in British waters. Even so, the Royal Navy was still able to assemble a total of 460 warships and support vessels for King George V to review.

Churchill had been First Lord of the Admiralty since 1911. Henry Asquith, the Prime Minister, had appointed him at a time when there was widespread public concern over the ever-growing German navy, which had been building warships at a rapid pace since 1898. Although Germany protested that the ships were required to help build an empire, the British public was not convinced. Each new keel laid down brought a fresh wave of panic from a fractious electorate.

At the Admiralty, Churchill had laboured night and day to build a navy that could answer the German challenge. Not that he had started from scratch as he had inherited 'the fleet that Jack built'. This was a popular reference to Admiral of the Fleet Lord John 'Jacky' Fisher, who was First Sea Lord in the period 1904–10 and almost certainly the greatest reforming admiral of all time. Fisher had turned a dormant fleet, obsessed with spit and polish and sailing in parade-perfect formations, into a war-ready machine mounting the greatest firepower ever seen. Churchill had a very high opinion – too high, many said – of the ageing admiral and regularly sought his advice on ships and men.

On the morning of 20 July, it was a proud and enthusiastic Churchill who presented the results of his labours to King George V. After a night of rain, the skies were heavy with cloud and a cold easterly wind blew over the sea. As the two men looked across the grey waters they saw the towering bulk of the battleship HMS *Iron Duke*, leading the First and Second Fleets for the approval of His Majesty. The *Iron Duke* was the flagship of the Commander-in-Chief, Admiral Sir George Callaghan, the man who was to command Britain's first line of defence if war were ever to come. Not that the spectators had any expectation of war, as that was something they left to the Continental powers who were inextricably tied together in a web of alliances. Britain had no formal alliance with any power. Even the famous *Entente Cordiale* of 1904 did no more than oblige Britain to leave France a free hand in Morocco, in return for France keeping out of Egyptian affairs.

The twenty-two-mile-long parade of ships from the Royal Navy was an expression of a self-confident empire at the height of its powers. The fleet comprised fifty-five battleships, four battlecruisers, twenty-seven cruisers, twenty-eight light cruisers and seventy-eight destroyers, not to mention vast numbers of minelayers, minesweeping gunboats, repair ships and depot ships for torpedo craft.

As if the gods wished to bless the review, the sun broke through as the first ships began to pass the royal yacht. The King observed the thin scarlet line of the marines standing to attention around the forecastle of each warship. As each vessel passed His Majesty, a band thundered out triumphal music and the sailors gave three cheers for their sovereign. It took an hour for the First Fleet to pass, by which time the leading vessels were disappearing over the horizon. The Second and Third Fleets, which had been mobilised purposely for the occasion, followed, being led by the older but still powerful pre-dreadnought battleships and their cruisers and auxiliaries.

Years later, Winston Churchill was to recall that 'One after another the ships melted out of sight beyond the Nab [lighthouse]. They were going on a longer voyage than any of us would know.'[4]

—————————⊰⊱—————————

As the fleet disappeared from view, the King and Churchill made a hasty departure. They were to return to London to deal with a most pressing matter: Ireland. The country was on the brink of civil war over the Irish Home Rule impasse. On 12 April 1912, Asquith had introduced the Liberal Party's third attempt at a Home Rule Bill for Ireland. Whereas Prime Minister William Gladstone's two earlier attempts (in 1886 and 1893) had both failed, Asquith could confidently expect to put his Act on the Statute Book. He could be equally certain that, if the Act came into force, the Protestant counties of Ireland (known as Ulster) would rise in arms against the British government. This was not some wild prediction. Under the leadership of the brilliant and unscrupulous lawyer Sir Edward Carson, 500,000 Ulster people had signed his 1912 'Covenant', which committed them to use 'all means which may be found necessary' to prevent the Bill becoming law. A provisional government was established, thousands of Ulster Volunteers were recruited and 100,000 rifles had been imported. As the Cabinet contemplated the rebellious Ulster threat, the British army base at the Curragh was never far from their minds.

In March 1914, the government had faced an increasing threat of violence in Ireland from the Ulster Volunteers. Orders were prepared for troops to protect military sites and public buildings. The army officers at the Curragh base wrongly assumed that they were about to be ordered into action against the volunteers. General Sir Arthur Paget, Commander-in-Chief in Ireland, was called to London, where he was briefed on the government's limited precautions. When he returned to Ireland, Paget woefully misrepresented what he had been told at the briefing. More convinced than ever that they were to be ordered into action, seventy officers resigned their commissions. The War Minister responsible for this farce – Colonel J.E.B. 'Jack' Seely – was forced to resign. But the real casualty was the government, which had now lost control of its own armed forces in Ireland.

All this explains how it was that, while half of Europe was on the brink of war, the British Cabinet met day in, day out to discuss Ulster. The Home Rule conference finally sat from 21 July to 24 July, and Churchill was there to record its dismal progress. On the second day he told his wife, Clementine, that it was 'in extremis'.[5] On the fourth day the conference broke up in total disarray. And so it was that until the end of July, the British Cabinet had never for one moment discussed the threatening developments on the Continent. Ultimatums, threats to mobilise, mobilisations came and went, but Ulster was the only cloud on the Liberal government's horizon. Asquith described the Cabinet's mood when he wrote to his epistolary 'lover' Venetia Stanley: 'Happily there seems to be no reason why we should be anything more than spectators.'[6] (Venetia was a close friend of Asquith's daughter Violet and had been his intimate correspondent since 1910.)

On 23 July, at 6.00 p.m. – the penultimate day of the Home Rule conference – the Austrian government handed its infamous ultimatum to Serbia. It contained two particular items that would have led to the end of the Serbian state. Austria-Hungary had demanded that Serbia accept 'collaboration' inside the Serbian government to eradicate the Serbian nationalist movement and also claimed the right to dismiss all Serbian 'officers and functionaries' who were suspected of having connived in the assassination.[7] Serbia had two days to reply.

Although the severity of the demands contained in the ultimatum far exceeded anything that Europe had witnessed in modern times, they raised no concern in the Cabinet on the following day. During a discussion on the arcane intricacies of the religious affiliations of villages in Fermanagh and Tyrone a telegram was handed to the Foreign Secretary. As Sir Edward Grey read out the ultimatum to the assembled ministers, Churchill quickly recognised the danger that it embodied. The equation was simple enough – even if beyond the deductive powers of his fellow ministers. If Austria-Hungary attacked Serbia, Russia would have to support her, and if Russia became involved, her ally France would be called to arms. And, although Britain and France had no formal alliance, their mutual interests were deep and strong. War would be hard to avoid. Immediately, Churchill left the Cabinet room and returned to his office – just a few minutes' walk across Horse Guards Parade. He cancelled a conference to be held the next day and sat down at his desk to write out a list of twenty-seven actions to make the navy ready for war. Top of the list was 'First and Second Fleets: Leave and disposition'.[8] Churchill had taken the first step to ensure that if Armageddon came, Britain would be ready. No other minister – let alone the Prime Minister – had yet taken in the fact that war was now unavoidable.

In the case of Asquith, his failure was all the more serious since, in addition to being Prime Minister he was also Secretary of State for War, a post he had taken over in March when Seely had resigned over his involvement in the Curragh incident. Although war was daily becoming ever closer, Asquith had taken no steps to appoint a new War Minister.

Nor had he taken steps to open the famous War Book, which had been carefully prepared by Colonel Maurice Hankey, the Secretary of the Committee of Imperial Defence. Hankey, a soldier turned civil servant, was the brains behind the prosecution of the war. He sat in on every meeting of the War Cabinets and councils and was an unfailing source of wise advice to ministers. The War Book set out the defensive actions that Britain needed to take when war threatened. The actions ranged from mobilising signal centres to dealing with enemy ships in British harbours, and arrangements for cable censorship to the internment of aliens. This great machine was set in motion by two telegrams. The first, 'the warning telegram', put hundreds of offices and depots on alert. The second, 'the war telegram', triggered the despatch of thousands of further telegrams which were in offices around the country, already written with pre-addressed envelopes set out in order of priority. Even the necessary orders-in-council and royal proclamations were at hand for King George V to sign. The War Book was to remain closed until 29 July. But Churchill had no need of a war book to complete his own preparations.

On the day before news of the ultimatum had reached Britain, Callaghan had told the Admiralty that he was about to disperse the fleet. On hearing the ultimatum, he knew that his peaceful naval review had been a dress rehearsal for the real thing. Another signal was sent to London. It warned Churchill that if he took no action, dispersal of the fleet would be complete by 27 July. After that date the First Fleet would disband, with the Second Battle Squadron going to Berehaven in southwest Ireland and the Third Fleet to Lamlash on the Firth of Clyde in Scotland. The Second and Third Fleets, which were manned by reservists, would return to their peacetime state. This was a matter of the utmost significance. From the humblest citizen to the King, it was generally assumed that any war with Germany would begin with a decisive battle between the two great fleets. But in peacetime, Royal Navy ships in home waters controlled the seas from Gibraltar to Scapa Flow. Once dispersed it would take days – and an enormous cost in coal and oil – to reassemble the fleet. If Churchill were mistakenly to disperse the fleet he could, as he said later to Admiral John Jellicoe, 'lose the war in an afternoon'.

These events compelled Churchill to face a problem that he had ignored for far too long: the men who were to command the navy in war. He had already complained to Fisher in April 1912 regarding the lack of competent seamen amongst the vice and rear admirals. The effects of this could be seen in the upper echelons of the fleet, where there was a distinct lack of drive. In particular he had issues with his two top men.

First, there was Callaghan. Born in 1852, Admiral Sir George Astley Callaghan was nearing the end of his naval career after an adventurous life, including fighting with the Naval Brigade in the Boxer Rebellion of 1900. By 1914, he had been at sea as a fleet commander for eight years – long enough to wear down a much younger man. For three years as Commander-in-Chief of the home fleets, he had controlled the largest single naval force that any country had ever put to sea. The admiral had a fine reputation as a commander and was an able and considerate manager of men. But, Churchill still felt uneasy about the elderly sailor being in command of Britain's first line of defence in war.

Secondly, there was Admiral Prince Louis Alexander of Battenberg. Although German born in 1854, he had been naturalised as a young boy before joining the Royal Navy and had spent all his adult life in British ships and on Admiralty postings. In 1912, when Churchill chose him as Second Sea Lord, Fisher noted that Battenberg was 'quite excellent at details of organisation, which is what you require in the Second Sea Lord'.[9] Now that he was First Sea Lord his limitations had become all too obvious. Reserved and ill at ease with people, his diligence had failed to compensate for his lack of imagination. He was dull and remote – hardly a man in the Churchill mould – and there was also the difficulty of his German origins. Churchill did not hold that against him, but others did.

The First Lord knew that both men had to go but, for the moment, he took no action.

The following day, Saturday 25 July, all was relaxed in England. Ministers had travelled to their country retreats, from which no sound came other than the plop of tennis balls and the thwack of golf clubs. On the Continent, the headlong race to war continued unabated. Russia had requested Austria-Hungary to extend the time limit on its ultimatum to Serbia, but this was refused. Russia's response was to mobilise thirteen army corps to protect the frontier with Austria. Serbia, now in a desperate position, was also mobilised as the humiliating reply to Austria was handed over at 5.58 p.m. The world stood still while Austria decided for peace or for war.

Meanwhile, all Churchill could do, as he recalled after the war, was to wait. Three years of work had placed the navy in a state of total preparedness for the momentous war signal.

Certain in his preparations, Churchill and his private secretary, (Wilson) 'Eddie' Marsh, took the 1.00 p.m. train to Overstrand, near Cromer, to join his family for a weekend on the beach. The relaxed nature of the break was enhanced by the presence of his sister-in-law Gwendeline 'Goonie' Churchill (wife of John Churchill) and her children. The charming fishing village of Overstrand had been discovered by wealthy Victorians in the late nineteenth century. With vast sandy beaches and a railway station it had become a fashionable tourist destination and had been first brought to notice under the name Poppyland in a newspaper article of 1883 by the author Clement Scott. The Churchills, following the trend, had rented the dreary-looking but delightfully named Pear Tree Cottage, which was ideal as a retreat from the hustle of Whitehall but, on the eve of war, the lack of a telephone was a serious drawback. Fortunately, the financier and philanthropist Sir Edgar Speyer was a neighbour and allowed Churchill the use of his telephone and so helped to ensure the timely mobilisation of the British fleet. (Kitchener, too, was without a telephone at this critical moment in history. His grand house at Broome Park at Barham in Kent relied on a telephone in the local village.) This kindly act did not save Speyer from being hounded out of Britain for his alleged financial dealings with Germany.

On 26 July, when Churchill first telephoned Battenberg in London at 9.00 a.m. there was no news from Austria. He returned to the beach and there he played with his children as they dammed the small streams that ran down into the sea. The North Sea was calm and enticing in the heat of a blazing sun. But, somewhere beyond the horizon there waited a not to be underrated foe in a high stage of readiness.

At midday, he again telephoned Battenberg and on a crackly, barely audible line he heard the news that Austria had rejected the Serbian note. The two men were later to disagree on just what had been said. Churchill maintained that he had told the First Sea

Lord not to disperse the Fleet; Battenberg insisted that Churchill had not given him 'specific instructions to halt the dispersal' but had left the matter to his judgement. [10] Each knew, though, that Britain's command of the seas was about to be threatened.

Churchill returned to his sandcastles while the First Sea Lord went back to the Foreign Office to watch the stream of telegrams arriving from European capitals. The news worsened throughout the afternoon and, feeling extremely gloomy, he returned to the Admiralty. At 4.05 p.m. he telegraphed Callaghan and ordered him not to disperse the fleet. Although he was proud of his own action, Battenberg was most disparaging of the ministers who, even in a time of national crisis, had retired to the country at the weekend. Asquith's approach to the impending war had been to play golf in the country. The leader of the Tory Party, Bonar Law, was playing tennis at another country retreat.

By the evening, Churchill had returned to London, where he drafted a press statement to announce that the Fleet was not to disperse and that the shore-based reserves of the Second Fleet were to remain near their ships. He could rely on the German Ambassador to pass this news on to Emperor Wilhelm II (popularly known as 'Kaiser Bill' in Britain), who, he hoped, would now think twice before moving troops towards Belgium and France.

As Churchill and the First Sea Lord responded to the impending catastrophe, the relaxed Asquith maintained an idiosyncratic and semi-detached state. The international crisis, he told Venetia Stanley on the Sunday, 'is the most dangerous situation of the last 40 years' but he bizarrely consoled himself with the thought that it would have 'the good effect of throwing into the background the lurid pictures of "civil war" in Ulster'. Miss Stanley brought him to his senses by pointing out that welcoming a European war as a means of relief from Ulster was like 'cutting off one's head to get rid of a headache'. [11]

On 27 July, the Cabinet met in crisis mood. At no time before this day had they discussed the possibility of war, so members were astounded when Sir Edward Grey put forward reasons for supporting France. For him this was a dismal moment. Grey had been involved in foreign affairs since 1892, when Gladstone had made him Parliamentary Undersecretary. Until he was thirty years old, he had showed little political ambition, always preferring to fly-fish for trout on his beloved River Itchen. In 1905, despite his lack of ambition, he had been appointed Foreign Secretary. Since then, no man had done more to prevent a European war, never sparing himself in his attempts to cultivate the goodwill of both France and Germany. His tireless reading of telegrams and drafting despatches had ruined his eyesight, but he refused to abandon his honourable task. Yet his determination to leave the European countries guessing as to Britain's military intentions in a European war was much criticised. It was said that the failure of his policy in August 1914 gave him many a sleepless night in later years.

When the Cabinet heard their arch-Europeanist argue for a step that might well lead to war, there was universal revulsion. However, ministers soon shrugged off their first reactions and it was to take just one week for the significance of what Grey had said to be appreciated. Asquith shared the same delusions as his colleagues when he told Miss Stanley that there was no need to worry about war since 'we have no obligation … to France or Russia'.[12] Nevertheless, he received four letters of resignation.

Few would have predicted that just a week later this same divided Cabinet would plunge Britain into war.

While ministers closed their eyes to the coming conflict, Churchill's mind raced as he brooded over the challenges of war and he returned to Downing Street to warn Asquith of the unguarded ammunition and oil supplies located around the country. The Prime Minister readily agreed to troops being positioned at these sites and around coastal lights and guns. Churchill also concentrated his naval aeroplanes over the area of the Thames estuary as a precaution against Zeppelin attacks. Orders were sent to all naval commanders in home waters to be prepared to shadow enemy vessels.

On 28 July, the situation on the Continent worsened as Austria–Hungary declared war on Serbia and Russia. Churchill returned to the precarious disposition of his fleet, which he called his 'crown jewels'.[13] Anchored at Portland on the Channel coast, it was essential to send the fleet to a place of safety before German warships entered the English Channel and the North Sea. There was still time for the fleet to take the short east coast route to the war station of Scapa Flow in the Orkneys; any delay risked having to send it by the longer west coast route. After what Churchill had heard on the previous day, he dared not ask the Cabinet to authorise the move, so he privately consulted Asquith, who consented.

[Handwritten margin note: Serbia only. Aug 6 × Russia. A major error!]

At 5.00 p.m. a signal was sent from the Admiralty ordering Callaghan to move the First Fleet on the next day. He was to take his ships through the Strait of Dover at night with no lights showing. His destination was to be kept secret from all but his flag officers. (Only after the war did Churchill discover that, despite the secrecy surrounding this move, the German Naval Attaché in London was providing Berlin with an accurate account of these movements. He warned his masters that the Grand Fleet was on high alert and at its stations. He was even able to provide a list of the orders sent to the ships.)

Although the Cabinet still saw the war as avoidable, Churchill restlessly sought ways to maintain the momentum at the Admiralty. Knowing that in the event of war he would need every available ship, he ordered his staff to seize two warships under construction for the Turkish Navy in British shipyards. The matter was of the greatest urgency since one of them, the *Osman*, was ready to be handed over – the crew were billeted in a Turkish liner moored alongside. The two warships were taken and named as HMS *Agincourt* and HMS *Erin*. The action gave rise to much ill-feeling in Turkey, which may have helped to push the country into an alliance with Germany some weeks later.

At midnight, Churchill bared his soul to his wife, telling her of his confused mental state. He was perplexed as to how he could be so keen and in such high spirits as the world faced a calamitous war with the prospect of death and devastation on a scale never seen before. 'Is it not horrible to be built like that?' he asked.[14] More prosaically, he told her that during the day he had found time to admire the black swans on the lake in St James's Park with their new downy cygnet.

On 29 July at 7.00 a.m., before Britain had even considered going to war, and with a Cabinet hostile to the idea of supporting France, ships of the First Fleet quietly slipped their moorings at Portland. Churchill saw in his imagination the mass of 'castles of steel' speeding through the darkness and stretching for eighteen miles.[15] By dawn, the ships were safely in the North Sea, speeding away from the German Fleet. The move was reported in the newspapers the next day, emphasising that there had been no military mobilisation.

Churchill was congratulated from all sides. One of the first people to hear of the move was an excited Lord Fisher, who happened to be in Admiralty House on that morning. Churchill invited Fisher to his room and there he described all the details of the fleet movements to the evident delight and approval of the old admiral. A short while later, as Fisher was leaving the building he met Arthur Balfour, an ex-Prime Minister and leading Tory who was thrilled to hear the naval news.

All was well with the fleet. On 30 July, a signal from Scapa Flow confirmed its safe arrival. The German Ambassador did not approve, even though Grey reassured him that the fleet operations had no sinister purpose and it would not encroach upon German waters.

The final day of July proved to be the last quiet day that Churchill was to have until his dismissal in May of the following year. With detached incredulity he watched as the City of London plunged into chaos. The Stock Exchange was near to suspension, two more companies had collapsed the previous day and the bank rate had been raised from three to four per cent. Bullion to the value of £2 million had been withdrawn from vaults of the Bank of England in one day. The governor of the Bank had asked Asquith for permission to suspend gold payments – a desperate measure last taken one hundred years earlier. Churchill was fearful that it would soon be impossible to cash cheques. Aware of the impending meltdown of the national finances, Churchill took stock of his own financial position. He was horrified to find that he and his wife had spent £175 (£7,500 today) in the previous month. He declared to Clementine that economies had to be made in the household accounts. (Churchill was prone to fits of austerity with the household accounts, but these rarely lasted more than a week or two.)

By 1 August, Churchill was revelling in his duties. He was still the only minister to have come to terms with the near inevitability of war – naval mobilisation was now inescapable. In Cabinet that day, he argued that since 'the German Navy was mobilising ... we must do the same'.[16] The Cabinet was not convinced, contending that mobilisation only affected the older ships; there was no urgent need. That his request was refused is no surprise given that the meeting was dominated by a demand for an immediate statement that Britain would not go to war under any circumstances.

Churchill vigorously opposed this view. He was, Asquith told Miss Stanley, 'very bellicose' while 'Lloyd George – all for peace – is more sensible & statesmanlike, for keeping the position still open'.[17] Given Lloyd George's opposition to the Second Boer War of 1899-1902, his appeasing stance was no surprise to his fellows. Although he was to lead the country to victory four years later, in 1914 Lloyd George felt nothing but repugnance at the thought of war. Yet, in the end, he and Churchill were to prove to be the only two ministers who truly understood modern war and were there to the end.

In the evening, Churchill dined alone. Later, two Tory MPs arrived to play cards. The brilliant lawyer and virtuoso Commons debater Frederick Smith (known as F. E. Smith) was accompanied by the maverick Canadian investor, turned enigmatic Tory politician, William Maxwell 'Max' Aitken (later Lord Beaverbrook). It must have been quite some game involving as it did one man who was to be Prime Minister twice, another who was to be Lord Chancellor and a third who was to be a powerful press baron. All three were outsiders, rebellious risk-takers and unloved by their political parties. F. E. Smith was, and remained until his early death, one of Churchill's closest friends. Although they sat on opposite sides of the House, they were the joint founders in 1911 of Churchill's famous 'Other Club'. Operating under the greatest secrecy, this dining club still meets today. One of its rules specifies that 'Nothing in the rules or intercourse of the Club shall interfere with the rancour or asperity of party politics.'

As the game progressed, a red box was brought in. Inside was a single sheet of paper which read 'War declared by Germany on Russia'.[18] The party immediately broke up and Churchill hurried to Downing Street, where he found Grey, the Lord Chancellor (Richard Haldane) and the Secretary of State for India (Lord Crewe) in discussion. Once more Churchill demanded mobilisation, telling the Prime Minister that he would answer for his action at Cabinet the next day. Asquith, a man who always baulked at making a decision, said nothing, which Churchill took as assent. As he left, he also revealed to Grey that he had upstaged the Cabinet earlier in the day by informing the French Ambassador, Monsieur Paul Cambon, that the Royal Navy would not permit the German High Seas Fleet to enter the English Channel. That night Churchill told his wife 'It's all up.'[19]

Churchill's conviction that mobilisation should not be delayed was reinforced by fresh news from Germany. At Hamburg, British ships had been detained because of 'important naval manoeuvres' to be held the next day.[20] It was more than likely that this meant mobilisation. Time was running out for Churchill.

This news had reached the Admiralty from the Foreign Office at 1.45 p.m. Thirty minutes later the signal for mobilisation was sent over the telegraphs. Officers of the Third Fleet joined their ships, ready to receive shore-based crews; patrols were ordered to sea to watch for minelaying; hospital ships, colliers and oilers were sent to their stations. Twelve hours later, on 2 August at 1.25 a.m., the naval reserves were also mobilised and this was completed at 4.00 a.m. on 3 August. Fisher's great fleet based on his economical system of dedicated crews had gone smoothly into action. He was content that Churchill, whom he greatly admired, had been the man to carry through its first mobilisation.

Following Churchill's informal promise to Cambon that the British fleet would keep the Germans out of the Channel, Grey now confirmed this officially. Churchill copied Grey's note to his commanders, adding 'Be prepared to meet surprise attacks.'[21] Later, he sent another signal authorising his commanders in the Mediterranean to talk to their French counterparts. The situation, he told them, was 'very critical'.[22]

Earlier in the day, Churchill had met the French Naval Attaché to discuss co-operation in the Channel and they had agreed to distribute the secret signal books to be used by the two navies in war. Hour-by-hour the atmosphere became more and more warlike. Rear Admiral Rosslyn Wemyss spoke for many when he described how, at that moment, 'we still oscillated between hopes and fears'. He found it hard to believe that 'we were actually witnessing the commencement of a war'. The seriousness of the situation became even more obvious to him the following day when he said goodbye to his Swiss servant, Michael, at Paddington Station as he left for Switzerland to be mobilised.[23]

Until 3 August, the developing war on the Continent had had the appearance of a spectator sport for the British public but events took a serious turn when Germany declared war on France. Churchill's day began with a Privy Council meeting at Buckingham Palace, where the King signed various mobilisation orders. Having already secured communication between French and British naval commanders in the Mediterranean, Churchill now asked Asquith for the authority for full co-operation in the Channel, telling him that his professional staff had requested this. Asquith consented.

In Cabinet, Asquith reported the resignations of John Morley (Lord President of the Council) and John Burns (President of the Board of Trade). He had persuaded Sir John Simon (Attorney General) and Lord Beauchamp (First Commissioner for Works) to remain. Charles Hobhouse, the Postmaster General, noted in his diary that Asquith's eyes 'filled with tears' as he told his colleagues that such resignations were 'the first time in his 6 years of leadership'.[24] Hobhouse had first been elected to Parliament as a Liberal in 1892 and had entered the Cabinet as Chancellor of the Duchy of Lancaster in 1911, becoming Postmaster General in 1914. He was one of the few Cabinet ministers to have kept a diary while in office and his vivid, blunt and opinionated entries provide invaluable insights into the working of Asquith's Cabinet.

Apart from those who resigned, the Cabinet, which had been so anti-war only two days earlier, now fell in with Grey's belligerence. It is ironic that it was the mild, anti-war Grey and the squeamish Asquith who made the case for Britain to enter a war in which no power remotely threatened her or her interests. Neither was fitted in any way to run a war and both recoiled from its reality when it began. Oddly, the two men most able to run a war – Churchill and Lloyd George – had very little influence on the decision. Churchill was too belligerent to have any influence over his Cabinet colleagues while Lloyd George's well-known pacifist tendencies left him temporarily without authority in the Cabinet.

When the Cabinet broke up at 2.00 p.m., Grey, who was to make the speech of his life in the Commons just one hour later, dashed to the Foreign Office to check the telegrams and snatch some lunch. At 3.00 p.m. he entered the House to make his famous statement. He faced anxious and bewildered members, every seat was taken and the central gangway had been filled with chairs – something last seen in 1886 when Gladstone had made his first Home Rule speech.

Grey was always impressive at the despatch box. He was a tall imposing man, good-looking to a fault, with an athletic build and an arresting presence. His speech was long – he had a lot to tell members having spent years of his life trying to stave off this war – but it was uncompromising. At first, as he distanced Britain from the French position, it seemed that the conciliatory wing of the Cabinet was to have its way:

I can say this with the most absolute confidence – no Government and no country has less desire to be involved in war over a dispute with Austria and Servia[25] than the Government and the country of France. They are involved in it because of their obligation of honour under a definite alliance with Russia. Well, it is only fair to say to the House that that obligation of honour cannot apply in the same way to us. We are not parties to the Franco-Russian Alliance. We do not even know the terms of that Alliance.

Then Grey began a subtle twist in his argument as he talked of Britain's friendship with France: 'let every man look into his own heart, and his own feelings, and construe the extent of the obligation for himself.' He went on: 'The French coasts are absolutely undefended.' It gradually became clear that Grey would not allow the Germans to use the English Channel to attack France.

He then turned to Belgium and gave the House a discourse on its history. Grey argued that Britain could not evade her obligation under the Belgian Treaty of 1839 to defend that country's neutrality. When he closed, Andrew Bonar Law, the uninspiring businessman turned politician and Leader of the Opposition, rose to assure the House that the Conservatives would give their 'unhesitating support' to 'whatever steps' the Government felt needed to be taken.[26]

So it was to be war unless by some miracle Germany stepped back. When Churchill reflected on this moment after the war he appreciated its inevitability. As the German armies poured into Belgium, Germany had revealed what 'had really menaced us hour by hour in the last ten years'. If war had to come it 'was better that it should happen now' just when Germany 'had [put] herself so hopelessly in the wrong'.[27]

The Prime Minister listened as his Foreign Secretary made the case for war. Yet Asquith could still not come to terms with its reality. He mocked Churchill when writing to Venetia Stanley the following day. Churchill had, he told her, 'got on all his war-paint' and was 'longing for a sea-fight in the early hours of tomorrow morning'. He added 'The whole thing fills me with sadness.'[28] Asquith had stumbled into war and now shrank from the unavoidable necessity of sinking ships and killing men.

While his colleagues were still reeling from the calamitous news of war, Churchill's military mind raced ahead as he surveyed the new scenario. The first task of his navy was to immobilise the German fleet. How much easier that would be if the coasts of Norway, Holland and Belgium were in Allied hands. Under the cover of 'Urgent & Secret' he wrote to Grey to propose alliances with these powers.[29] It was an idea that Grey never pursued.

The last hours of peace now slipped away. The British ultimatum to Germany requiring that Belgium be kept neutral expired at 11.00 p.m. British time (midnight in Germany) on 4 August. The London streets had seen a frenzy of patriotic outpouring in the early evening, but as the fatal hour approached, the shouting and the singing died away. Then as the first chime of Big Ben rang out over the expectant city, the crowds burst into cheers. On and on they went for a full twenty minutes and, reported *The Times* newspaper: 'The National Anthem was then sung with an emotion and solemnity which manifested the gravity and sense of responsibility with which the people regard the great issues before them.'[30] Meanwhile, Churchill's war telegram ordering his ships to begin hostilities went out from Admiralty House to the waiting fleet. All that remained was for him to walk across Horse Guards Parade and report his action to the Prime Minister. Lloyd George was there when he arrived and later described, no doubt with some exaggeration, how

> Winston dashed into the room, radiant, his face bright, his manner keen, one word pouring out on another how he was going to send telegrams to the Mediterranean, the North Sea, and God knows where. You could see he was a really happy man.[31]

Distressed as he was at the prospect of war, Asquith drew comfort from the fact that there had been no more resignations. Churchill meanwhile was the man of the moment. There was an audience with King George V and a handsome tribute in *The Times*, on 4 August, to 'Mr. Churchill, whose grasp of the situation and whose efforts to meet it have been above all praise'.[32] From Walter Long, a leading Tory MP and frequent critic of the Admiralty, came congratulations to Churchill on his prompt mobilisation of the fleet. This tribute was particularly generous given that, for years, Walter Long and the retired Admiral Lord Charles Beresford had plotted to take over the posts of First Lord and First Sea Lord respectively.

Outside Westminster and Whitehall, the enormity of what had happened had yet to be appreciated. The *Daily Mail* relegated the war to page four while the *Manchester Guardian* noted that 'War and rumours of war seem to have made no diminution of the happy holiday crowds at Brighton.'[33] Readers of the *Daily Mirror* were more forcefully reminded that the war would reach out to touch all the people. Doctors were asked to present themselves to the War Office for service, motorcyclists were required for the army and men were called to enlist.

Meanwhile, over the weekend, printing presses had been furiously pounding away on a most secret operation. When the banks opened on 5 August, customers who asked for gold were handed ten shilling and one pound banknotes. Paper money, so feared by the British for so long, became a reality overnight and was accepted without a murmur. Gold was never again to be handed out over bank counters.

CHANGE OF COMMAND

While Churchill had been mobilising his fleet he had also been busy at work on another, rather distasteful task: the removal of Callaghan. He and the First Sea Lord had met on 1 August to discuss what to do about the ageing commander, who was due to leave his post two months later. They had agreed that, in the event of war, Jellicoe would become his second-in-command. Now they concluded that Callaghan should be removed on the outbreak of war because, Churchill said later, the admiral's health did not seem robust enough for the task ahead.

While Fisher had for years advanced Jellicoe's claim to high command, Jellicoe's only clear advantage over Callaghan was his age. He had a first class mind and had assiduously mastered the details required in all his posts. But his cool, detached and undemonstrative personality was matched by a nervous disposition and an absence of the aggressive streak that is essential in war. His reaction to his appointment was sufficiently bizarre as to raise doubts about his suitability for high command.

On 1 August, Churchill informed Jellicoe of his decision to give him command of the Grand Fleet. As his train sped north, Jellicoe pondered on the change. When he reached the end of the line at Wick in the north of Scotland at 10.00 p.m., he could contain himself no longer. He telegraphed his concern, saying the handover 'might easily be disastrous'. The next day Jellicoe once more telegraphed to Churchill and Battenberg, this time declaring '[I] am more than ever convinced of vital importance of making no change.' Churchill replied personally at 8.30 p.m., telling Jellicoe 'I can give you 48 hours after joining [;] you must be ready then.' Still Jellicoe would not accept an order when given. Back came another whingeing cry: 'Can only reply am certain step contemplated most dangerous beg it may not be carried out.' The next morning – 3 August – Jellicoe returned to his obstructive behaviour, telling the Admiralty that they courted disaster in making the change before he had had a chance to get to know the fleet. Before London could reply to this, Jellicoe sent in yet another telegram to say that the 'Fleet is imbued with feelings of extreme admiration and loyalty for Commander-in-Chief. This is very strong factor.' Battenberg brought this farce to an end by ignoring all the points made by Jellicoe and informing him that 'I am sending [Rear Admiral Sir Charles] Madden tonight to be at your side.' (Madden was, coincidentally, Jellicoe's brother-in-law.) Battenberg then despatched a telegram to Callaghan ordering him to transfer his command to Jellicoe.[34]

It was an extraordinary way to begin a war. No admiral since the Napoleonic wars had assumed as much responsibility, yet Jellicoe appeared to shy away from it in an alarming manner.

Churchill then had to settle with his wife over the episode. She wrote from Overstrand to say how upset she was over the way Callaghan had been treated. She felt that he would be deeply hurt by his abrupt removal and that offering him an honour would be no compensation. Her appeal succeeded and Callaghan took up a special service post at the Admiralty and was made principal aide-de-camp to the King. These were temporary appointments until he was able to take up the post of Commander-in-Chief at the Nore in December.

And so, with men and machines in place, Churchill was ready to face the German High Seas Fleet. But first he had to turn his mind to trouble in the Mediterranean.

CHAPTER 3

THE ELUSIVE FOE

He brought an element of youth, energy, vitality and confidence that was a tower
of strength to Asquith's Cabinet in those difficult early days. – Hankey[1]

THE SEARCH FOR THE *GOEBEN* AND *BRESLAU*

During the last week of peace Churchill had found himself in an awkward position
over the German battleship SMS *Goeben* and the light cruiser SMS *Breslau*, both then
in the Mediterranean. These powerful vessels were steaming in the same waters as the
Mediterranean Fleet. It was also the sea over which French troop transports would
pass from Algeria to France in the event of war. How tempting it was for Churchill to
order the sinking of the two warships! But this was impossible to do before war had
been declared.

The German ships were based at the Austro-Hungarian naval port of Pola on the
Adriatic. They were under the command of Rear Admiral Wilhelm Souchon, who
was to prove a formidable opponent to the British Commander-in-Chief in the
Mediterranean, Admiral Sir Archibald Berkeley Milne. Known as 'Arky-Barky', Milne
was a competent but unimaginative admiral who found himself thrust into a scenario
where bold initiative was desperately needed. But Souchon was of superior mettle.
Since his appointment in 1913, he had familiarised himself with every detail of the
Mediterranean: 'I made it my business not only to visit personally and appraise all
naval bases and sources of supply of possible interest, but also to become acquainted
with such leading men as I might be called upon to regard as opponents or as helpers
and allies, in the event of war.'[2] This detailed knowledge, combined with his calm
manner and capacity for hard work, gave the German the edge over the less energetic
Milne. Rear Admiral Souchon was eager for news that France and Germany were at
war so that he could attack the French transport ships. For Churchill this would have
been bad enough, but the possible escape of the two ships into the Atlantic Ocean was
a terrifying thought. They had to be taken.

Milne had a modest fleet in the Mediterranean. Under his command at Malta, he
had three fast modern battlecruisers – HMS *Inflexible*, HMS *Indefatigable* and HMS

Indomitable – supported by four armoured cruisers, four light cruisers and fourteen destroyers. But it was not the ships that he needed to worry about. It was Churchill. In the new age of wireless, the First Lord had no intention of leaving the hunt for the *Goeben* and the *Breslau* to his local commander. He intended to run the show himself.

Did Milne realise this when the first signal came from Churchill on 30 July? After warning Milne not to antagonise Italy, Spain and Greece, Churchill set out his instructions:

> Your first task should be to aid the French in the transportation of their African army by covering and if possible bringing to action individual fast German ships, particularly *Goeben* … You will be notified by telegraph when you may consult with the French Admiral. Except in combination with the French as part of a general battle, do not at this stage be brought to action by superior forces.[3]

Poor Milne, he was to help the French but not to talk to them. He could act with them in a 'general battle' but had not been told how that was defined. And he was not to take on 'superior forces', another vague phrase. For the time being he simply despatched the light cruiser HMS *Chatham* to patrol the south of the Strait of Messina.

On 31 July, the *Goeben* and *Breslau* had entered the port of Brindisi on the Adriatic coast of Italy to coal, but were turned away by the Italians. This was a surprise to Rear Admiral Souchon since Italy was a member of the Triple Alliance with Germany and Austria-Hungary. He continued south down the Italian coast to Messina in Sicily. Once more Souchon was refused coal so his men simply took coal from the bunkers

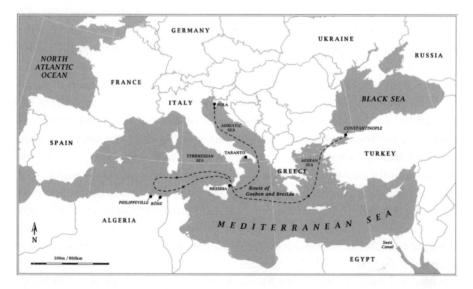

The escape of SMS *Goeben* and SMS *Breslau*.

of the other German ships in port. Meanwhile, Milne kept his forces together, ready to assist the French.

On 2 August, Churchill instructed Milne to shadow the *Goeben* with two battlecruisers and to keep a watch on the approaches to the Adriatic, but he himself was to remain at Malta. There was no way he could act on the first part of the message since he had no idea as to the location of the warship. All he could do was to despatch HMS *Indomitable* and HMS *Indefatigable* with five cruisers and eight destroyers under the command of Rear Admiral Ernest Troubridge to watch the entrance to the Adriatic. Troubridge, a descendant of a family of notable naval men, had had a modest career with steady promotion but nothing of distinction. The war plans that he had drawn up as Chief of the War Staff in 1912 had been thoroughly rejected by his colleagues and Churchill had eased him out to return to sea in early 1913. His appointment to the 2nd Light Cruiser Squadron in the Mediterranean was to bring an ignominious end to his sea-going career.

Milne was still at Malta when the *Goeben* and *Breslau* sailed at midnight on 2 August, exiting the Strait at its northern end. At ten minutes past midnight on 3 August, Milne received yet another signal from Churchill. There was now a change of emphasis in his orders as he informed Milne that '*Goeben* is your objective.'[4] He was to shadow the ship and be ready to act when war was declared.

Churchill now cast aside his concern for the French transport ships as his active mind imagined the destruction that the *Goeben* and *Breslau* could possibly wreak in the Atlantic. Later in the day, his opinion hardened around the idea that the two ships were heading for the open sea rather than the French ports in the western Mediterranean. Another signal to Milne was sent at 8.30 p.m. to order him to send two battlecruisers to Gibraltar in order to keep the *Goeben* in the Mediterranean. This item of Churchillian-style micro-management had not been necessary. Milne had already detached *Indomitable* and *Indefatigable* from Troubridge's squadron to search westward.

While these signals had been pouring in on Milne, Germany had declared war on France. This news reached Souchon at 6.00 p.m. He was now free to attack both French ships and French ports.

Increasingly concerned at the thought of the *Goeben* and *Breslau* destroying British ships on the high seas, Churchill urgently appealed to Asquith and Grey for authority to allow Milne to attack the German ships if they first attacked the French transports. Grey and the Prime Minister agreed to this action. But when the issue was raised a few hours later at Cabinet the answer was a firm 'No'. In his optimism Churchill had already authorised Milne to attack, so in the early afternoon he had to withdraw his signal. He covered his embarrassment by issuing a general signal to all ships, reminding them that the British ultimatum to Germany did not expire until midnight. In fact the true expiry time was 11.00 p.m., which was midnight in Germany. (Churchill was not the only politician to make this mistake. Several post-war memoirs repeat this error.)

Later in the day, Battenberg reminded Churchill that, since Italy was neutral, British ships would need to keep outside the six-mile limit around the Italian coast. Churchill agreed, fearing some minor clash if the limits were breached. He promptly telegraphed to Milne advising him that he was to respect this limit without fail. Milne's task suddenly became much more problematic, since he was forbidden to seek the *Goeben* in just those waters where Souchon could best conceal his ships – the Strait of Messina.

It was the French who located the vessels when the *Goeben* and the *Breslau* began to bombard Algerian ports on 4 August. In the early hours of that day, Souchon had received an urgent signal ordering him to go immediately to Constantinople. But as he was so near to his enemy he could not resist a token attack on the ports of Bona and Philippeville. The attack over, he turned his ships east and set course for Constantinople taking a northerly route through the Mediterranean.

Later that morning, steaming towards Gibraltar, Captain Francis Kennedy of HMS *Indomitable* was staggered to find himself passing the *Goeben* and *Breslau* sailing in the opposite direction. (It had been assumed that the German ships were bound for the Atlantic.) In his obituary, Kennedy was described as 'one of the most experienced of the Grand Fleet captains of the war' and 'a fine seaman and a zealous officer'. He had been mentioned in despatches after the bombardment of Alexandria in 1882, had received the General Africa Medal in 1895 and was mentioned in despatches again in 1897. The navy had few captains who had shown such dash and daring in recent years. But now Milne was to deprive him of this latest chance to show his valiant nature. (Kennedy's chance came later at Jutland, where his actions won him a CB for his 'great skill and gallantry'.) [5]

As the two German ships sailed past, Kennedy turned the *Indomitable* and the *Indefatigable* to pursue the enemy. There was joy in the Admiralty when Kennedy's news reached London. Churchill keenly replied with the instruction 'Very good. Hold her. War imminent.'[6] What no one in London knew at that moment was that a British merchant ship, the SS *Isle of Hastings*, had been seriously damaged in the German bombardment of Algeria. Had Churchill known, he would surely have rushed back across Horse Guards Parade to plead for permission to order an attack.

The next day, 5 August, the *Goeben* and *Breslau* arrived at Messina to coal. Britain was now officially at war with Germany so Milne's ships were free to attack. But, once more, Souchon's location was unknown since he had outrun Kennedy's ships during the night. By mid-afternoon, wireless signals revealed the location of the *Goeben* as somewhere in the Strait. Milne, of course, could not enter since the waters were all within the six-mile limit.

What happened next is hard to appreciate. On 6 August, Milne took his ships to the northern exit of the Strait, leaving only the light cruiser HMS *Gloucester* to patrol the southern exit. It had never occurred to Milne that the *Goeben* might exit that way, but she did. (The British had no idea that the destination was Constantinople.)

At least Captain Howard Kelly of HMS *Gloucester* was alert that day. As soon as he saw the *Goeben* emerge from the southern end of the Strait he began a pursuit. At first, the *Goeben* went south as though Gibraltar would be her destination. But then the ship unexpectedly altered course to the east. Kelly signalled the course change to Milne. Unknown to Souchon, he was now sailing towards Troubridge at the southern end of the Adriatic. It would surely be impossible for the *Goeben* to pass.

Troubridge set off in pursuit at eight minutes past midnight on 7 August, and it was at this point that Churchill's initial signal came back to confuse the proceedings. His instruction had forbidden Milne to attack superior forces, but what constituted 'superior forces'? Troubridge, unable to decide, asked his flag captain for his opinion. If we are generous to Troubridge, we could say that he heeded Captain Fawcett Wray's advice that *Goeben* represented a superior force. A less generous interpretation is that Troubridge readily allowed himself to be talked out of going into action. At 4.05 a.m., Troubridge signalled to Milne that he had given up the chase.

Kelly in HMS *Gloucester* was still shadowing the German ships. On 7 August at 1.35 p.m. he opened fire on the *Breslau* at long range. The *Goeben* halted and turned to investigate. Kelly did not have the firepower to engage the German ships, but did continue to shadow the enemy ships until he reached Cape Matapan at the southern end of Greece. Milne had forbidden him to go beyond this point, leaving the *Goeben* and the *Breslau* to proceed unhindered to Constantinople.

We can disregard Milne's last attempt to catch the *Goeben* since subsequent events did not involve Churchill. The two German ships reached Constantinople and remained there for the rest of the war. Kelly was highly commended for his shadowing operation – his ship was the only one to get within range of the enemy – and made a KCB. Troubridge was recalled to appear before a Court of Inquiry. The court refused to accept that *Goeben* was a superior force and described Troubridge's behaviour as 'deplorable and contrary to the tradition of the British Navy'.[7] The court martial which followed was more lenient, declaring that he was 'justified in regarding the enemy's force as superior to his own in daylight'. He was 'fully and honourably acquitted'.[8] But he never received another sea-going command.

The other casualty of the fiasco was Churchill, who had put himself in a difficult position by taking such a central role in the chase. All the key signals to Milne were his handiwork. In taking such an active part in the operation Churchill was fully within his powers as First Lord. He could direct the navy as he pleased. But in doing so he was departing from tradition both in the Admiralty and in every other government department: ministers set policy; professionals implemented it. It would have been legitimate for Churchill to have told Milne that his priority tasks were to help protect the French transports and to sink the *Goeben* – that was policy. But he could not restrain his urge to tell Milne how to carry out his task. Worse still, Churchill filled his first signal with vague phrases such as 'superior forces' and 'husband your force', all of which suggested to Milne he was to avoid action except in the most favourable circumstances.

There was a rather Churchillian-style postscript to the escape of the *Goeben* as his muddled signals continued. With the *Goeben* out of reach at Constantinople, Milne's next task was to make sure she stayed there, or was destroyed should she re-enter the Mediterranean. Once more Churchill wrote his own signal, and once more it led to confusion. He told Milne to set up a blockade of the Dardanelles, which puzzled the admiral. He telegraphed to ask whether Churchill really intended a blockade. Did he mean to deny entry to ships of all nations or just German vessels? As he pointed out, a formal blockade would need to be announced by the government. Churchill climbed down. He had not meant a blockade; all he had wanted Milne to do was to lie in wait for any German warships that attempted to come out. Churchill had still not learned that signals was best left to the professionals.

No one emerged well from the *Goeben* fiasco. The navy was shocked at Troubridge's refusal to pursue the German vessels; Churchill was downcast; and the failure of Milne and Troubridge brought the end to their sea-going careers. Milne was ordered to strike his flag and report to the Admiralty. Later the Admiralty backed their ineffective admiral with a fulsome statement of support, saying that his 'conduct and dispositions' had been 'the subject of careful examination' and 'their Lordships have approved the measures taken by him in all respects'.[9] Despite this, he was never employed again.

FIRST DAYS OF WAR

In order to recount the *Goeben* saga coherently we have moved deep into August. It is now time to return to the first full day of war and explore Churchill's other opening activities as a war leader.

For years, the navy had assumed that the first day of war would see a mighty battle between the British and German fleets. But when dawn broke on 5 August, there was no sign of the German High Seas Fleet. Lord Jellicoe, with no enemy to fight, lay at anchor in Scapa Flow. He had to content himself with a message from the King – an ex-naval man himself – which told him of his sovereign's confidence that he would 'renew the old glories of the Royal Navy' and provide 'the sure shield of Britain and her Empire in the hour of trial'.[10] Something that was rather difficult to do with an enemy that refused to fight.

Meanwhile, Churchill attended to the intricacies of war as he despatched a flotilla of ships to close the Strait of Dover, cut all the German undersea telegraph cables and kept the mouth of the Scheldt open so that supplies could reach Antwerp. Nor did he forget diplomacy as he sent his naval secretary Admiral Horace Hood to the German Embassy to offer the navy's assistance in the repatriation of its diplomatic staff.

The high profile that Churchill had maintained over the last few weeks had not gone unnoticed by the public. In Ulster, the brewer John Gretton observed that when the reservists embarked for England they enthusiastically cheered at the mention of

Churchill's name. He was now one of the four men who would dominate the direction of the war, along with Asquith, Kitchener and Lloyd George. His relationship with Asquith was complex as the two men had little in common. Asquith was intellectual, lethargic and had no military experience of any kind. Churchill was practical, energetic and with combat in his blood. Despite these differences the Churchills were frequent visitors at both Downing Street and The Wharf (Asquith's country retreat at Sutton Courtenay). The Prime Minister's hospitality also extended to 'Goonie' Churchill and Nellie Hozier, Clementine's sister. That Asquith kept such varied company is explained in part by his finely tuned capacity for ironic detachment. This allowed him to find both Clementine 'a thundering bore' and belittle Churchill's 'rampageous enthusiasm and loquacity', while still enjoying their company.[11]

There was also the close geography of Whitehall, which promoted intimacy. Admiralty House and Downing Street are at opposite ends of Horse Guards Parade, so Asquith and Churchill could drop in on each other with ease. In fact, when Asquith sat working in the Cabinet room he could see the Admiralty flag flying above Admiralty House with, below it, the lights of Churchill's room. But their formal work was done through the War Council, which held its first meeting in Downing Street on 5 August.

Asquith had not yet grappled with the question of how to run a war, so his regular Cabinet of twenty was enlarged that day by the addition of six generals plus Lord Kitchener. Two grave matters had to be decided: which forces to despatch abroad, and where to send them. Churchill's opinion was central to the first point since, once the army was abroad, the navy would be the sole defender of the homeland. Sir John French, who was to be Commander-in-Chief of the British Expeditionary Force (BEF), recorded in his diary on that day that Churchill described 'Home Defence [as] reasonably secure'.[12] After hearing these views, the Council took a cautious line and decided to hold back two army divisions against any invasion attempt.

While the Cabinet debated what to do with the army, the navy saw its first action in home waters when the scout cruiser HMS *Amphion* sank the German minelayer SMS *Königin Luise* on 5 August. It seemed a brilliant feat, especially if it were true, as reported, that the minelayer had sunk before placing her deadly payload.

Alas, she had not. As the *Amphion* made her triumphant return, she struck one of the *Königin Luise*'s mines. One hundred men died as the ship rapidly sank. Twenty or so Germans rescued from the minelayer also lost their lives as the bow section of the *Amphion* was blown off by the explosion.

It fell to a sorrowful Churchill to inform MPs of the loss. It was due, he said, to 'the indiscriminate scattering of contact mines about the seas'. This was 'new in warfare' and needed to be closely studied. But, ever conscious of the importance of sustaining morale, he added that the Admiralty was neither alarmed nor disconcerted by the loss. It was something to be expected in war. This was no mere bravado. As the war progressed and the country became accustomed to ever bleaker news, many a minister trembled at the enormity of it all. Not Churchill – for him, setbacks and losses only renewed his determination to win an undisputed victory. He was also beginning to develop the ability of using defeats as opportunities to boost morale. His frank and measured admission of the *Amphion* debacle won him praise from the *Manchester Guardian*.[13]

The *Amphion* episode reminded the government of the need to control sensitive information in wartime. Churchill announced that the Government was to set up a Press Bureau. They had been spurred to do this by the false information and rumours that were circulating only three days into the war. The Bureau was to supply 'a steady stream of trustworthy information' which the government expected would 'exclude the growth of irresponsible rumours'. In plain language, press censorship.[14]

Churchill's assured command of the naval war led *The Observer* newspaper to end its years of hostility towards him. The newspaper declared, on 9 August, that Churchill had shown over the last few weeks 'the qualities of a great executive minister' and his prompt mobilisation of the fleet, combined with his appointment of Jellicoe 'showed himself to be a statesman who well understands the nature of war'.[15]

※

In the first days of war, Churchill and Kitchener found themselves working closely together. The Field Marshal was the odd man out in the government's war machine as he had spent almost all of his working life abroad, notably in Egypt, the Sudan and South Africa. The last winter that he had spent in Europe was forty years earlier. At home he was not at home, having few friends and no social life. He compounded this isolation by his secretive methods, his inability to work through committees and his taciturn manner. In the club-like world of the Cabinet and Whitehall he was an outsider. Few warmed to him, although many admired his courage and achievements. But Kitchener and Churchill worked well together as they shared a capacity for labour and a strategic vision of the war. Both saw it as a long haul. Both abhorred the trenches and the simplistic approach of the strategy on the Western Front. And, crucially for our story, Kitchener had a high regard for Churchill's military judgement.

Their first major collaboration was over the troop transports for the BEF. While Churchill was boldly accepting the hazards of war, he was taken aback when he discovered the nervousness of the new Secretary of State. Kitchener had visited Churchill to talk about arrangements for transporting troops across the English Channel. The navy had long planned for this and was confident of its capacity to deny the Channel to the German Fleet. Major General Sir Charles Callwell, Director of Military Operations and Intelligence at the War Office, listened to Churchill's assurances that the navy could thwart any German naval attack. He was completely reassured, yet his superior officer was not. When Kitchener learnt that the risk of submarine attack could not be completely eliminated he ordered the immediate suspension of daylight crossings. Later, when Churchill emphasised that serious delays would result from night-only crossings, Kitchener relented. But Churchill was left astounded at Kitchener making such sweeping decisions without first consulting his staff.

If the Germans had decided to attack the transport ships, they would have found a formidable barrier of warships. At the northern end of the approach to the English Channel, cruiser squadrons and destroyer flotillas from Harwich patrolled night and day. Patrolling the Dover Strait were more destroyers, backed up by the submarines of Commander Roger Keyes. Should any vessel have penetrated these outer defences, it would have been intercepted by the eighteen battleships of the Channel Fleet. (Keyes, one of the boldest and finest naval commanders of the twentieth century, shared Churchill's view that war was meant to be waged. Outside the confines of our story he was to mastermind one of the greatest actions of the war: the blocking of Zeebrugge in 1918.)

Despite these formidable precautions, Churchill still thought it necessary to warn Jellicoe that the Germans might see the transport ships as an opportunity for raids on the east coast, or even an attempt to break through the Strait. His worries were ill-founded. While the German army daily proved its vigour and energy on land, her navy remained in port devoid of any enterprise. When the Royal Navy began to ferry the BEF to France, on 12 August, there was not a German ship in sight. Churchill was staggered to find that the enemy made not the least attempt to interfere with the transport of the soldiers. Fearing that the Germans were plotting some surprise attack, Churchill asked Jellicoe to bring his ships farther south as a precaution.

Before the war was a week old, Churchill was eager for some offensive initiative by the fleet. No action seemed possible as long as the German navy refused to put to sea but Churchill was determined to find some way to provoke the German fleet into leaving port. The first proposal that he explored was a plan to capture Ameland – one of the German Frisian Islands.

Churchill wanted to use the island as a flotilla base from which to observe the approaches to the Elbe. In a lengthy memorandum to Battenberg and Admiral Sir Frederick Sturdee, the Chief of the War Staff, he set out a detailed scheme for its capture. After two pages on ships to be used and bombardments to be made, Churchill launched into the uses to which his prize could be put. In his mind the island would swarm with destroyers, submarines, planes and seaplanes, all harassing the Germans. But he perhaps gave away his main motive for this wildly ambitious scheme when

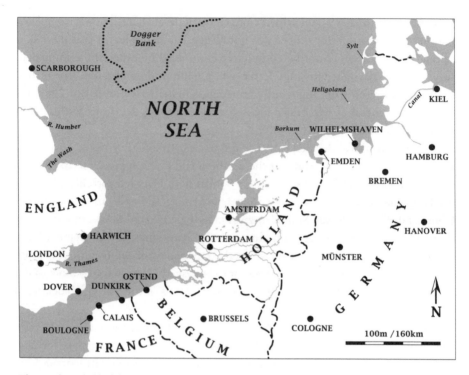

The southern half of the North Sea.

he added that a principal benefit would be 'to maintain in lively vigour the spirit of enterprise & attack'.[16]

There was no enthusiasm for the project from the professionals. Captain Herbert Richmond, Assistant Director of Operations, described the plan as 'futile' in his diary. He had not bothered to argue the point with Churchill since, he wrote, 'no words could check his vivid imagination'.[17] This negativity is not entirely surprising since Churchill never got on with Richmond – few people did. The captain indulged in ungenerous and acerbic criticism of practically everyone at Admiralty House. His diary is full of extreme opinions on his masters and their plans. It was typical of Richmond to be so dismissive of the Ameland plan that he would not even enter into discussions. He took a similar view three days later when Churchill asked him to plan a destroyer raid on Heligoland. 'It is not reconnaissance,' he wrote in his diary, 'for there is nothing for one to reconnoitre. It is not an attack, for the most it can do is to cut off some isolated detachments.' Richmond preferred that the Admiralty 'sit tight' and do nothing: 'we have the game in our own hands.'[18] Not surprisingly he left the Admiralty in May 1915.

One of Churchill's greatest weaknesses was his inability to imagine how others viewed his actions. This frailty landed him in trouble when he tried to do a favour for his cousin, Lord Wimborne. Ten years earlier, when Wimborne was still Ivor Guest, Churchill had persuaded the Liberal Party to find him a seat and he was duly elected MP for Cardiff. Now in the Lords he once more needed some patronage, which Churchill foolishly attempted to provide. He proposed to sack the Civil Lord to the Admiralty, George Lambert, and ease his cousin into the seat. It was an odd move since Wimborne was said to be unpopular and he had never shown any particular administrative or political talent. The conclusion of Professor George Boyce that Wimborne 'at least meant well' is enough to damn Churchill's judgement on this occasion.[19] The Lord Chancellor, Richard Haldane, who greatly admired Churchill, was shocked at his brazen attempt at nepotism. He pointed out that Lambert had no wish to go and to push him out would be a humiliation. In private Asquith told Miss Stanley that it 'would be cruel' to remove Lambert, even though he was 'not very competent'.[20]

In mid-August, Churchill put his mind to the navy's surplus reservists. He informed Battenberg that he intended to form these men into a Marine Brigade and two Naval Brigades. He asked that the resources to form these should be arranged within a week; the officers were to be appointed immediately. Churchill was not specific as to the role these men were to play, nor could he have foreseen the controversial use to which he was to put them only a few weeks later. The new brigades did not escape Richmond's vitriolic pen. 'I really believe Churchill is not sane,' he protested. 'What this force is to do, Heaven only knows. ... This is the beginning of a great war in which our whole future rests upon the proper use of the navy!! It's astounding.' He went on to criticise the amateurish nature of the brigades, their lack of training and their lack of discipline.[21]

Although Churchill had been in post for three years and revelled in disposing of the prodigious force at his command, he still sought succour in Fisher's vibrant company. More than a generation can pass without producing a man like the old admiral. Although short and stocky, he was a giant and a genius. Until his later years, those who met him invariably came under the spell of his personality and the force of his arguments. Women of all classes were attracted to him, entering into intimate correspondences and dancing with him into the small hours. His capacity for work was prodigious. His prolific pen poured out a seemingly unstoppable stream of lengthy, ebullient and forceful letters, littered with underlining and capitalisations. The key to his personality can be found in these letters: he always said exactly what he thought in vigorous, direct and often earthy language. His career in the navy had been marked by one glorious triumph after another, culminating in his massive naval reforms of 1904–09.

It is no wonder that the life and energy of this old admiral relieved Churchill's tedium at having to work with the colourless quartet of his sea lords. Battenberg was the sort of man whose presence went unnoticed. Even his biographer could find almost nothing to say about his time as First Sea Lord. He was 'frightfully pompous and heavy in hand', according to Admiral David Beatty who was in command of the First Battlecruiser Squadron, 'he rarely seems to have troubled himself to take any initiative.'[22] It is hard to imagine that a man who wrote *British Naval Medals* and *Men-of-War: Names, their Meaning and Origin* was a bundle of fun. In addition to Battenberg, there was the Second Sea Lord, Vice Admiral Sir Frederick Hamilton, who was said to be 'a rather lazy officer of no great distinction'.[23] His Third Sea Lord, Vice Admiral Sir Frederick Tudor, was no more than fairly competent. Lambert completed the group as Fourth Sea Lord. His appointment had been greeted with astonishment since he was an enthusiastic farmer and highly regarded for his agricultural expertise.

In the first few days of the war, Churchill called Fisher in to talk over his plans and dispositions. Although ill with pleurisy, and against his doctor's advice, Fisher travelled to London to be admitted into the high secrets of Admiralty House. Churchill's decisions, Fisher told his ex-assistant Commander Thomas Crease, were 'very fine decisions'. His appointment of Jellicoe, his premature mobilisation and his seizure of the Turkish warships had 'humbugged' the Germans. Their mutual admiration was without limits – a bond that Churchill would soon call on when others failed him.[24]

After nearly two weeks of war, events were beginning to tell on Britain's relations with Turkey. In particular, the seizure of the Turkish warships and the delivery of the *Goeben* to the Turkish Navy had done nothing to persuade Turkey to join the Allies or, as second best, to retain neutrality. It was vital that Turkey did not go over to the Germans since the country lay between the Balkans and Britain's oil supply in Persia. On 18 August, Grey wrote to Churchill to ask him to order Troubridge to avoid engagements with Turkish vessels.

Churchill duly telegraphed to Troubridge – who was still patrolling the mouth of the Dardanelles – to say that he was to avoid hostilities with Turkey while also preventing the *Goeben* and *Breslau* from entering the Mediterranean. All this was to be achieved without making any threats. What Troubridge made of these contradictory instructions is hard to tell.

While Churchill was prepared to avoid the unnecessary provocation of Turkey, he was not willing to lower his defences. On the same day that he asked Troubridge not to show hostile intentions, he also asked Battenberg whether, should Turkey prove to be antagonistic, it would be possible to remove the mines from the entrance to the Dardanelles.

SAFE TRANSPORT OF THE BEF

The Fifth Division of the BEF was successfully shipped to France on 19 August. Three days later Churchill felt able to tell Kitchener that he would be happy to see the sixth and last army division depart the English shore, leaving the navy and the Territorials to stand guard for the nation. His confidence both in the navy's capacity to deny the English Channel to the German High Seas Fleet and to repel any invasion attempt grew by the day.

The navy's success in transporting troops to Flanders was not matched by any military success in deployment. The very day after Churchill had proposed the departure of the

Sixth Division the Battle of Mons began and by the end of that day the BEF was in full retreat. On that same day, the French decided to abandon their attempt to defend the Belgian city of Namur. Churchill was working on his papers in bed at 7.00 a.m. the next day when Kitchener arrived. One look at Kitchener's face told him that the news was bad. The Field Marshal handed Churchill a telegram from Sir John French. Churchill read how the men of the BEF had been pushed back at Mons and, worse still, that Namur fortress had fallen after being under attack for only one day. No one on the Allied side had for one moment imagined that the Belgian forts would collapse so easily. Churchill quickly recognised that the rapid advance of the Germans now meant that the precious Channel ports were threatened and he foresaw Dunkirk, Calais and even Boulogne falling to the unstoppable enemy. There was little the navy could do to aid the faltering BEF and Belgian forces, but, at all costs, the army had to have safe and accessible ports. Churchill turned to Jellicoe and asked him to propose plans for a war in which the Germans held Calais and much of the French coast.

FIRST ACTIONS AT SEA

Churchill was anxious to see his fleet in action and to make some contribution to the land war. He consulted Grand Duke Nicholas, Commander-in-Chief of the Russian forces, on the utility of getting the British fleet into the Baltic. Would such a move be of help to the Russians, he asked the Grand Duke. Churchill explained that a prerequisite of this would be either the destruction of the German High Seas Fleet or the blockade of the Kiel Canal. (The canal gave German warships safe passage between the Baltic and the North Sea.) Although seeking the Duke's opinion, Churchill did not hesitate to set out his own as he dreamt of landing armies to attack the German flank or to smash their way through to Berlin. When Churchill told the Cabinet of his plan three days later, Hobhouse mocked it in his diary as '[a] Napoleonic plan' for 'a coup de theâtre' on the German coast.[25]

This Baltic proposal led to a clash with Grey. Churchill told Grey that he needed to go to France for discussions with his counterpart, the French Minister of Marine. He particularly wanted to discuss the idea of naval action in the Baltic. Churchill would take his Director of Naval Intelligence, Captain Henry Oliver, with him but would keep his visit secret. Asquith had given his permission for the trip and passports were on the way for Churchill, Oliver, the Duke of Marlborough (then the King's messenger) and 'Eddie' Marsh. Grey refused the request. His letter is lost, so what his objections were is not clear. Nevertheless, the request in itself demonstrates how much importance Churchill attached to the Baltic – a point we shall return to when the War Council opted for the Dardanelles operation in January 1915.

The most important 'behind the scenes' man in Churchill's political life was 'Eddie' Marsh. Over a period of thirty-two years he was Private Secretary to Churchill at the

Colonial Office, the Board of Trade, the Home Office, the Admiralty, the Duchy of Lancaster, the Ministry of Munitions, the War Office, the Colonial Office again, and the Treasury. It was an unlikely pairing; Marsh had a passion for the Georgian poets, not politics, and history remembers him as a patron of the arts rather than as a civil servant. On their first meeting in December 1905, Marsh did not take to the young politician, but he accepted Lady Lytton's advice that 'The first time you meet Winston you see all his faults and the rest of your life you spend in discovering his virtues' and agreed to dine with him. Marsh now found Churchill to be 'perfectly charming' although the thought of what he sought in a private secretary was 'simply terrifying'. Marsh was soon working for Churchill, who delighted in his newfound companion: 'Few people have been so lucky as me to find in the dull and grimy recesses of the Colonial Office a friend whom I shall cherish and hold to all my life,' Churchill told Marsh in 1908.[26]

The two men shared much more than office life. Before Churchill's marriage they used to play a game of 'Was this the face that launched a thousand ships?' As the ladies entered a ballroom or similar grand occasion, they would assess their beauty according to how many ships their faces would launch. A beauty might score 200 or 250. At the other extreme a face might have been worth just 'a sampan, or small gunboat'. But both Lady Diana Manners and Miss Clementine Hozier scored 1,000 ships.[27] (By a delightful coincidence, Manners and Hozier both married First Lords. Manners married Duff Cooper, who was First Lord in 1937-38.)

When the Cabinet met on 25 August – three days after the last of the five divisions had landed – it was to receive a dismal report from Kitchener. Less than two weeks after the first troop landings, the BEF had fallen back twelve miles, French troops were of doubtful capacity, and the British lacked horses, guns and ammunition. In a pessimistic mood, Kitchener began to talk of holding back the Sixth Division in case it was needed to rescue the French. As an expedient he talked of scouring the Empire for 'foreign garrisons, colonials, territorials, etc.'[28] Kitchener soon overcame his bleak mood and the Sixth Division left for France a week later.[29]

In this mood of panic, a stunned Cabinet showed no interest in Churchill's proposal for immediate conscription. Asquith asked why it was necessary to discuss it now, to which Churchill replied 'if not now we should never speak of it.' He predicted a rapid German victory, followed by political annexation. Whether Churchill was right or wrong to suggest immediate conscription he remained the only member that day to have made *any* suggestion for action in this moment of peril. Asquith's own contribution was shocking. It had been suggested that F. E. Smith should devise a system for MPs to explain the necessity of the war to the electorate. Asquith declared that only he and Grey had the eloquence needed for this but 'neither could spare the time for speeches.'[30]

The Cabinet's lack of decision was ended by the ever resourceful Maurice Hankey when he produced a plan to slow down the German advance. He suggested making a feint by landing troops at Ostend as if they were to advance in large numbers on the

German army's right flank. Kitchener accepted the suggestion and, having no forces of his own, called on Churchill's aid. He asked him to land a large body of marines at Ostend, parade them in a flamboyant manner, and then re-embark. Churchill agreed and put one of his War Staff, Sir George Aston, in charge.

The 3,000 men duly landed at Ostend on the morning of 27 August, impressing *The Times* correspondent with their 'splendid appearance' and keenness for 'a speedy fight'. When Churchill announced the landing in the Commons later that day, he was circumspect as to its purpose. It was 'for reasons which seem to be sufficient to the Government and to the military authorities'.[31] This brought cheers from the members, although Asquith was less exuberant in his daily letter to Miss Stanley. He ridiculed Churchill, who 'takes the whole adventure … very seriously'. Later he was a little more charitable, telling Stanley that 'Winston has been scoring some small but not unimportant points.'[32] He might have been more generous had he known how successful the feint had been. The operation had struck terror into the German army, which had estimated the landings to consist of 40,000 British soldiers and 80,000 Russians.

Churchill had more good news for the Commons when he announced the sinking of the German armed merchant cruiser *Kaiser Wilhelm der Grosse* off the West African coast. This brought even more enthusiastic cheers than his announcement of the Ostend landing.

It was not intended that the marines would be engaged in any significant fighting. But on the main battlefront the situation of the Allies became more serious by the day. The Allied Channel ports were under threat and, by 29 August, Sir John French was compelled to adopt St Nazaire on the Atlantic coast of France as a new supply base. Ostend ceased to be a priority as the massive task of moving bases commenced. French's masquerade of 'falling back' could no longer disguise the fact that the BEF was in ignominious retreat. On the night of August 30-31, the marines re-embarked and returned home.

The Ostend venture both raised the morale of the Belgians and demonstrated the capacity of the new Marine Brigade to respond swiftly to emergencies on land. Their use in the later Antwerp venture suggests that Ostend gave Churchill too much confidence in his brigades.

As the war moved into its fourth week Churchill grew increasingly certain that the much anticipated great naval battle was not far away. Confident of victory, he told his brother Jack that he would join him overseas after the 'decisive battle'.[33]

THE HELIGOLAND RAID

While the German armies were rapidly advancing into Belgium and France, Churchill was frustrated by his lack of opportunity to destroy the German High Seas Fleet. He was ready to consider any proposal to engage the enemy.

The first suggestion that reached him came on 23 August, from Captain Roger Keyes, who was in charge of the submarines in the North Sea. Keyes was a man who spoke Churchill's language. He was daring and dashing, and he detested the idea of a navy that avoided action. It has been said that in his 'indomitable spirit and eye for action there is also much to remind one of Nelson'.[34] Keyes had been despatching his submarines on regular patrols into the Heligoland Bight area off the mouth of the River Elbe, where they had noted that the Germans were sending out destroyers on a strict timetable. The night patrol left port at around 5.00 p.m. and returned at dawn. Moreover, the destroyers were escorted in and out of port by cruisers. Keyes was sure that British destroyers could take the cruisers by surprise. So fast would be the attack that the British could be out of the area before the large German ships could come out in support.

When Keyes arrived at the Admiralty to discuss his project, he found that the staff were far too busy to see him so he casually asked the Naval Secretary whether he could talk to Churchill. Within minutes, Churchill was bursting with enthusiasm for the venture. They met again with the planners the next day and the raid was quickly planned for an attack on 28 August. The plan was, said Churchill, 'simple and daring'.[35]

Keyes was to be joined by Commander Reginald Tyrwhitt, who commanded the destroyers at Harwich. Tyrwhitt was another outstanding officer, known for his ability, his leadership and his eagerness for the offensive. He was to take two of his flotillas to Heligoland together with nine submarines. Three of the submarines were positioned in the attack area, where it was hoped they would attract the attention of the German ships. The rest of the British ships were to take station at night on the east side of the

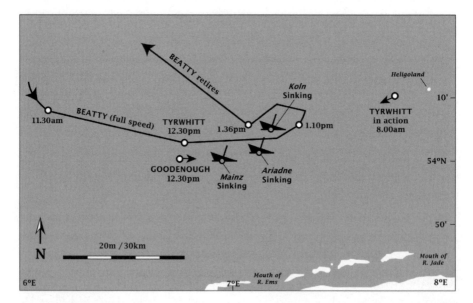

The Battle of Heligoland Bight.

proposed battle area. At dawn, they would sweep westwards, attacking what enemy ships they could and then return to port.

After discussion, Keyes and Tyrwhitt decided that it would be wise to have some backup in case of the arrival of the larger German ships. They asked for the support of the 1st Light Cruiser Squadron and that the Grand Fleet should come south. Sturdee refused both requests and Churchill saw no reason to override him.

Two days later, the Admiralty informed Jellicoe of the plan. Alarmed at the lack of proposed support he ordered Beatty and three of his battlecruisers to join the action. He also called on Admiral Sir William Goodenough's six light cruisers to act in support. Jellicoe's decision to ignore Sturdee's optimism was to save Churchill from what might have been a disastrous day for the Admiralty.

The Battle of Heligoland Bight was a naval battle of firsts when it took place on 28 August. It was the first Royal Navy battle in which its ships moved at high speed, fired at long range and worked in waters infested with submarines. No one at the Admiralty and no officer in the action had any experience on which to draw. It was also the first battle in the age of wireless, and it was the first battle with multiple command posts: it had been planned at Harwich, in London and at Scapa Flow. Unfortunately, planning was not the same thing as co-ordination.

So poor was the co-ordination that Tyrwhitt and Keyes never received the signal to tell them that Beatty and Goodenough were to take part. Jellicoe's signal to them had been left on a desk rather than handed on. These problems were aggravated by the poor relations between Jellicoe and the Admiralty. Jellicoe simply did not trust Sturdee to do a good job and once Sturdee had vetoed his request to send reinforcements, Jellicoe decided to bypass Admiralty House. Rather than risk another rebuff from a desk-bound admiral, Jellicoe did not tell London that Goodenough was to take part until he was safely at sea.

Unaware of the support plans, Tyrwhitt and Keyes had every reason to assume that any large ships found in the Bight would be German. No one else could possibly be there.

The operation had one other serious handicap. Keyes always liked to be in the midst of the action so he decided to join the conflict in his new flagship – HMS *Arethusa*. In principle this was a good idea, but the defects revealed during *Arethusa's* sea trials had not yet been resolved. The most serious of these was the repeated jamming of the 4-inch guns. Nor was it wise to go into battle with an inexperienced crew.

A blow-by-blow account of the action is hardly needed to illustrate the highs and lows of the first naval battle of the war. Tyrwhitt successfully located a group of German destroyers shortly after 7.00 a.m. and began his attack. Two were put out of action, but the exchange alerted the Germans to the presence of British ships. Soon enemy light cruisers were on their way to the scene. As Tyrwhitt chased further German destroyers he found the cruisers SMS *Stettin* and SMS *Frauenlob* blocking his course.

The arrival of the German cruisers so early in the action soon put the British ships in difficulties. Tyrwhitt, now aware of Beatty's presence, radioed for his urgent assistance. It took Beatty just over an hour to arrive on the scene where his powerful battlecruisers outgunned the German ships, sinking SMS *Mainz, Koln*, and *Ariadne* and damaging three more cruisers. After five hours of pursuit, turns, misidentifying enemy ships and other errors, more German ships were nearing the battleground. Beatty ordered the confused British ships to retreat.

No one will ever know how close Tyrwhitt and Keyes came to firing on Goodenough's and Beatty's ships. But had they done so, they could hardly have been blamed for what would have been an almighty Admiralty blunder.

Despite all the mistakes and confusion, the navy scored a superb victory having sunk three German light cruisers, severely damaged a fourth, and lightly damaged two others. The Germans had lost 712 men (including a rear admiral) and 336 prisoners had been taken. All the British ships returned home, although the *Arethusa* and three destroyers were badly damaged. Only 35 British men had been killed.

The real victory, though, was the effect that the battle had on the Kaiser. He was so shocked at the loss of his cruisers that he ordered his High Seas Fleet not to fight outside the Bight and not to fight against superior forces inside the Bight. This was not, though, the result that Churchill and Jellicoe wanted, as both were eager to deal a mortal blow to the High Seas Fleet. Jellicoe would have to wait until mid-1916 to have his opportunity at Jutland, but by then Churchill had long since left the Admiralty.

Churchill came out of the battle well with the press reporting 'a brilliantly successful engagement', which was 'evidence that the spirit of the old navy still inspires our seamen'.[36] From Haldane came his warm appreciation of the fleet's success. Churchill himself was so delighted at the result that, said Tyrwhitt, '[he] fairly slobbered over' him at the landing at Sheerness and offered him his choice of ship.[37] The reactions of the men involved were in line with their personalities. The vain Beatty was satisfied by the 'good work' of the fleet but was 'disgusted' that he had not 'received an expression of their appreciation from their Lordships'.[38] The adventurous Keyes on the other hand dismissed the action as a 'small affair'. He could not understand why so much fuss was being made of it, especially when he thought of 'what a complete success it might have been' had he been given the cruisers that he had requested.[39]

MAN OF THE MOMENT

Heligoland was a piece of good news that the country sorely needed. On land the BEF continued to struggle alongside a faltering French army, both reeling under the unstoppable advance of the Germans. There was, recalled Churchill, an 'impression of overwhelming disaster'. When newspaper correspondents (their movements not yet controlled by the army) ranged over the Belgian countryside, they met thousands of straggling troops, many too exhausted and dispirited to fight. Despite censorship, much of this reached the newspapers.

As the minister who had presided over Heligoland, Churchill's reputation was now higher than ever and he was requested to ghost-write an army communication designed to reassure the public about the land war. But even Churchill's pen could not rise to the occasion. He had not yet developed his 'blood, sweat and tears' approach so his communiqué rather ploddingly described the ebb and flow of battle. All he could do to raise the spirits of the home population was to downplay the importance of the losses. He told his readers:

> These losses, though heavy in so small a force, have in no wise affected the spirit of the troops. They do not amount to a third of the losses inflicted by the British force upon the enemy, and the sacrifice required of the army has not been out of proportion to its military achievements.[40]

This was written from the ease of the magnificent office of the First Lord in Admiralty House. When Churchill reached the Front in 1915, he soon dropped any attempt to see glory or comfort in the slaughter. For now, though, he accepted the conventional words used to sell as success what was clearly a disaster.

On the day that Churchill was basking in the press reports of triumph at Heligoland, a more painful matter arrived on his desk. Admiral Lord Charles Beresford had been the Admiralty's greatest scourge since his resignation from his post as Fourth Sea Lord twenty-six years earlier. His slurs, smears and denigrations had reached a peak in 1909 when his command of the Channel Fleet had been ended on account of his belligerent attitude towards his superiors. This had led to a Cabinet inquiry into naval affairs, which ran from April to July of that year. The report's innocuous conclusions gave no support to Beresford's wild accusations, but nor did they show any warm enthusiasm for the then First Sea Lord, Sir John Fisher. Fisher resigned and Beresford went off into the wilderness of backbench politics. Yet he never ceased to attack the Admiralty and its leaders at every turn. Now he had another First Sea Lord in his sights: Battenberg.

On 28 August, Beresford, in the full hearing of other members of the Carlton Club (essentially the home of the Tory Party), delivered a vicious racially motivated attack on the First Sea Lord. The members had been talking about German spies when Beresford declared that all Germans in Britain should be sent abroad. By 'all' he made clear that meant every single one, including the First Sea Lord. The remarks were heard by the Conservative MP Arthur Lee, (now renowned for his donating Chequers to the nation) who, 'sizzling with indignation', pleaded with Churchill to take all possible steps 'to frustrate his [Beresford's] campaign of slander'.[41] Later Churchill remonstrated with Beresford. Spreading such reports, he said, 'is a military offence' and he threatened 'serious' action unless Beresford offered 'an absolute retraction'. He reminded Beresford that 'Your name is still borne on the retired list of the navy.'[42] Beresford replied in a manner that he had used for years: denial. He simply stated that he had never denigrated or attacked Battenberg.

In fact there is abundant evidence in Beresford's letters that he regularly made similar remarks about Battenberg. In 1906, for example, he had asked the MP Carlyon Bellairs to table a parliamentary question to ask 'Whether it is a fact that during the time this German Prince was Director of Naval Intelligence, he employed German servants, who had charge of Dispatch Boxes, and took them from the Admiralty to the Prince's house, and from the Admiralty to the Prince's estate in Germany?'[43]

Churchill let the matter go. He was right to do so since, vile as Beresford's behaviour was, Churchill would not have had much political support for tackling Beresford's loathsome demeanour when a war was waiting to be fought. As is so often the case, the innocent party suffered. The Carlton Club committee 'strongly condemned' Lee for his informing on another member and he was pressed into resigning.[44]

The importance of Beresford's spiteful and cowardly denunciations palled in the light of the news on the last day of August. The Germans had occupied Amiens – the original base of the BEF. Every single foot of territory gained by the British army had been lost.

CHAPTER 4

EXIT FIRST SEA LORD

Asquith said to me that you were the equivalent of a large force in the field. –
Haldane to Churchill[1]

THE FIRST RECRUITING CAMPAIGN

At the beginning of September, there was an impromptu indication of Churchill's popularity when he was present at a war rally at the Guildhall in the City of London. Few venues were more redolent of British history than the Great Hall, famed for state trials, including that of Lady Jane Grey in 1553, and decorated with monuments to heroes such as Nelson and Wellington. The City of London was also Balfour's political constituency so he was expected to speak after Asquith's opening call to arms. But before Balfour could begin, the hall filled with loud cries of 'We want Churchill.' The demand was too great to refuse and Churchill delivered a brief speech on how the navy would buy the country time 'to create the powerful military force which this country must wield before the struggle is brought to its conclusion'.[2]

But such oddments of raising morale were too few and too erratic to answer the dire situation that existed in Great Britain during early September. The happy morning of the arrival of the BEF in France and its confident entry into battle had begun to fade with the retreat from Mons on 24 August. When the first cries of 'over by Christmas' had rung out in early August, 'over' had meant victory. Now, as Sir John French's army retreated, alongside that of the French, 'over' sounded perilously like defeat.

Churchill's immediate response was to call for more men but as yet there was no means of co-ordinating such demands. At the end of August, Lord Curzon approached him with a proposal that they should organise an all-party national recruitment campaign. Curzon, a leading Tory and an ex-Viceroy of India, has been described as 'one of the outstanding political intellects of his generation'.[3] His contemporaries were hard on him, not least because of his abrasive personality, but he was a wise and thoughtful man. It was typical of him that, even out of office, he strove to make a contribution to the war. The two men met in London to discuss how a recruitment campaign might be organised. That the issue of recruitment – a matter of immense importance to the government – had been left to a member of the opposition and the First Lord of the Admiralty seems odd, but that was typical of the *ad hoc* arrangements that prevailed in the early months of the war.

Churchill began to play his part in recruitment at a rally at the Royal Opera House on 12 September. The theatre was full as were two overflow meetings and some 10,000 people heard his call to arms. It was the first of his great war speeches so it deserves some extensive quotation. He began by referring to the struggle on the Continent. Anxious as the days had been, he told his audience that 'the situation tonight is better, far better, than a cold calculation of the forces available on both sides before the war should have led us to expect.' In fact, he said, 'The battle … gives us every reason to meet together tonight in good heart.' He reminded his listeners that 'We entered upon this war reluctantly … with a full realisation of the sufferings, losses, disappointments, vexations, and anxieties, and of the appalling and sustained exertions which would be entailed upon us by our action.' Referring to the navy's success in destroying German commerce raiders, Churchill proudly told his audience 'We have either blocked [them] in neutral harbours or blockaded [them] in their own harbours or hunted down the commerce destroyers of which we used to hear so much and from which we anticipated such serious loss and damage.' As to the troop transports, he continued, 'We are transporting easily … great numbers of soldiers across the seas … And we have searched the so-called German Ocean [the North Sea] without discovering the German flag.'

Rallying his audience, Churchill concluded: 'But let us not count on fortune and good luck. Let us assume at every point that things will go less well than we hope and wish. Let us make arrangements which will override that.' Rather than retaliations and reprisals, he added, 'Let us try to concentrate on the simple, obvious task of creating a military force so powerful that the war, even in default of any good fortune, can certainly be ended and brought to a satisfactory conclusion.'

From start to finish Churchill's words were interrupted by wild and enthusiastic cheering and, reported *The Times*, the audience showed a 'quiet confidence and patriotic determination'. His speech had not yet gained that natural flow and power that he would find two decades later. By then, no phrase as clumsy as 'can certainly be ended and brought to a satisfactory conclusion' would slip through into a Churchill speech.[4]

It had been agreed between the three main political parties that recruitment meetings should be all-party affairs. This had worked well at the Royal Opera House, where Churchill shared a platform with F.E. Smith for the Tories and William Crooks MP for the Labour Party. The next meeting was due to take place in Birmingham just two days later, but it was cancelled due to the ever intractable problem of Home Rule.

At the outbreak of the war, Irish Nationalists had offered to suspend their hostilities against the British government for the duration of the war. Asquith sought to cement their co-operation by putting the Home Rule Bill on the Statute Book, but suspending its operation until after the war. The Tories declared that this was a breach of an agreement not to enact any legislation which was not essential to the war effort.

Austen Chamberlain, the Tory MP who was billed to join Churchill at Birmingham, declared that he could not possibly speak alongside a representative of a government that had reneged on the promise not to revive the dispute over Home Rule. Churchill could not accept this viewpoint, maintaining that the proposed legislation was vital to the prosecution of the war. On receiving this reply, Chamberlain telegraphed the Mayor of Birmingham to say that neither he nor Churchill would be able to speak at the meeting as they both had pressing business in London.

Churchill was frequently asked to send messages of support to war rallies. A meeting at Acton, on 19 September, heard his call for 'nothing less than a million British soldiers in the line' as the only means to 'finish this war as it has got to be finished'. He told the Acton public that 'The cause is worthy of the effort, and the effort is well within our strength. Victory is certain, if we act and organise resolutely, and act and organise now. This is the time for sacrifice and daring. Prussian military tyranny must be broken forever.'[5]

Having lent his support to the one million men target, Churchill now promoted their recruitment. At Liverpool on 21 September, he told an audience of 12,000: 'I have not come to ask for your cheers. I have come here to ask you for a million men … the flower of our manhood, nothing but the best, every one a volunteer.' They were to be 'equipped with everything that science can invent or money can buy'. In buoyant mood Churchill confidently declared that 'There is no reserve of manhood or vitality on the side of our enemies which can prevent that million men from turning the scale in our favour.' As to Germany, they, he said, 'had preached a gospel of force … the crude brutal force of adding regiment to regiment, bureaucrat to bureaucrat to the tune of "Germany over all"'. He added, '"Blood and iron" is their motto. Let "soul and fire" be ours.'

Turning to the talk in the United States of America of peace negotiations, Churchill spurned such suggestions: 'Peace! Why we were only just beginning.' Yes, there would be 'Peace with the German people' someday, 'but peace with Prussian Militarism! No peace short of the grave with that vile tyranny.' He ended with another bold peroration in his emerging style as he told his audience:

The end may come sooner, the victory may come to us more easily; then let us rejoice, but let us not count on an easy solution. Let us make our resolutions calmly and soberly that in a reasonable time we shall compel our antagonists to come to our conclusion of this fight.[6]

It was, declared the *Manchester Guardian*, '[a] remarkable call to arms'.[7]

CHURCHILL'S DUNKIRK AIR BASE

Whereas war had found the navy fully ready to defend Britain against the might of the German High Seas Fleet, the army was in no state to fight a war or to take a role in home defence. Its six divisions – dubbed 'a mere visiting-card' by the eminent historian Sir Basil Liddell Hart[8] – were totally inadequate to take part in a major Continental war. Once despatched, they were soon entangled in battles beyond their strength. Also, the army had taken all of its aeroplanes to France, leaving Britain with no air defence. Churchill and the Royal Naval Air Service were left to fill the gap; his pre-war insistence on the navy having its own independent air service had proved providential.

Churchill realised that the navy's small air service could in no way provide defensive cover for the southeast of England, so he chose a bold alternative: to take his aeroplanes to France where they could destroy German aeroplanes and Zeppelins before they reached the Channel. In a letter to his Director of the Air Division, Churchill asserted that the best way to defend Britain was to use aeroplanes based in France to search out German aeroplanes and airships and destroy them on the ground. To facilitate this he planned to send up to forty machines plus several hundred men and a number of armoured cars to be positioned at Dunkirk. It was a masterful plan that squeezed the maximum possible effect from minimal resources. It was his work and his alone.

In reporting his air plans to the Cabinet on 1 September, Churchill graphically described an expected night raid by Zeppelins. According to Hobhouse, he assured ministers that 'in the last resort the officers in charge of aeroplanes will charge Zeppelins, but in view of their certain death have arranged to draw lots for the task.'[9]

No other minister could have responded as quickly as Churchill did to Kitchener's unloading the air-defence portfolio onto his desk. By 5 September, he had worked out a scheme, with machines, men and bases detailed. He set out a three-part strategy. First, was the need to send aeroplanes to France so that they were in place ready for the planned search and destroy operations. The bases were to be supplied with the latest telephone and radio equipment so that they could respond to intelligence from the army or from London. Additionally, all the London parks were to be provided with landing strips, well-marked in day and well-lit at night for the operating of the aeroplanes. (This part presumably referred to the air defence of London.) It was a perfect example of the speed with which Churchill could master a new brief – and in this case without relinquishing his old one.

Churchill found time to visit his new airbase at Dunkirk on 10 September. He also took the opportunity to inspect the port defences, which he concluded were not of a high order and would hold only for a day or two. On the other hand, he was attracted by the suitability of the anchorage for Majestic-class ships. (These were pre-dreadnought battleships built in the 1890s.)

THE CHURCHILL-FRENCH ALLIANCE

In early September, Churchill and Sir John French, Commander-in-Chief of the Expeditionary Force, found themselves working together as a result of Kitchener's all too limited people skills. The two men had met during the Boer War when, Churchill recalled, French had ignored him and had been very discourteous. The rift had been healed when they met at some cavalry manoeuvres in Wiltshire in 1908. Once Churchill became First Lord, French was a regular guest on HMS *Enchantress,* where the two men discussed the coming war with Germany. French admired Churchill's 'indomitable courage, tireless energy, marvellous perspicuity and quick virile brain-power'. He possessed 'a combative nature', which led him into 'political strife' and 'the sharpest controversy'. For these reasons, said French, 'perhaps only his intimate friends … know the real manly, generous kindliness of his disposition and his perfect loyalty'. French was equally admiring of Churchill's political achievements: 'His experience and knowledge of public affairs must be unrivalled; for, at an age when most men are undergoing the grinding drudgery which falls to the lot of nearly all successful statesmen, lawyers, soldiers or ecclesiastics, he was holding the highest offices in the Government; and not even his most inveterate enemies can say that he has failed to leave his mark for good on every department he has supervised.'[10]

French himself will ever remain an enigma. His detractors are many (and were many during the war); his cheerleaders are legion. Some found his warm, emotional and at times hot-headed nature inspiring while others thought him a hazard on the battlefield. Churchill was one of his greatest admirers and told Lieutenant Colonel Charles à Court Repington of *The Times* newspaper that 'French, in the sacred fire of leadership, was unsurpassed.'[11]

Following the retreat from Mons, French had informed Kitchener that he would have to take his forces out of line behind the Seine for ten days. His confused and often contradictory reports showed a man under strain and at the limit of his strength. At a midnight meeting of the Cabinet on 31 August, it was decided that Kitchener should visit French. The two men met the next day in the British Embassy at Paris. Kitchener arrived wearing his field marshal's uniform, which immediately put French on edge. When Kitchener announced that he wished to inspect the BEF, French became visibly angry and the War Secretary backed down. Difficult as the meeting was, Kitchener succeeded in persuading French to put his troops back in the line.

The clash between the two field marshals was observed by French's ADC, who happened to be yet another of Churchill's relatives: Captain Frederick Guest – a brother of Lord Wimborne. Alarmed at the hurtful way in which Kitchener had treated French, Guest wrote to Churchill to plead that French's difficult position should not be undermined by the War Office. He asked Churchill to make sure that there were no more similar incidents.

Churchill quickly wrote to French to sympathise, but also to offer practical advice. He recommended that French appoint a liaison officer to keep London informed of the military situation, stressing how willing he was to help and sustain French. Sensing French's feeling of abandonment, he emphasised that if French had any need of him he was only to ask and Churchill would come over. In fact, Churchill longed to be at the Front and he admitted how frustrated he was to be behind a desk in London rather than out on the battlefield. French's reply was fulsome. He was so grateful for Churchill's friendship and always looked forward to his letters. He hoped that Churchill would get Kitchener off his back – '[he] knows nothing about European warfare' – and begged him to 'stop this interference with field operatives'.[12] A few days later Churchill showed this letter in confidence to Asquith. Perhaps this was a confidence betrayed; perhaps he had a duty to ensure that Asquith appreciated the clumsy deficiencies of his Secretary of State.

Churchill's warm support for his friend did not go unrecognised. After the war, French wrote 'I cannot adequately express my sense of the valuable help which I received throughout the War from Winston Churchill's assistance and constant sympathy.' He rebutted 'the shameful attacks which his countrymen have so often made upon him' by people who did not have 'a full knowledge of all the facts'.[13] In return, Churchill called French 'a natural soldier'.[14]

THE RETURN OF CHURCHILL'S 1911 MEMORANDUM

Much disparaging material has been written about Churchill as a military man. But the two military men who worked most closely with him (Kitchener and French) had a very high regard for his abilities. Kitchener entrusted Churchill with the Antwerp expedition in October and on more than one occasion despatched him to France to resolve issues with Sir John French. As to French, he was for ever pleading with Churchill to visit him and greatly looked forward to their joint campaign to retake the Belgian coast.

For a short time, even Churchill's political colleagues marvelled at his perspicacity when he re-circulated a memorandum that he had written at the time of the Agadir crisis in 1911. On 1 July that year, the German gunboat SMS *Panther* had arrived in the Moroccan port of Agadir under the pretext of protecting German commercial interests. For weeks Europe was on the brink of war. Only when Germany backed down and signed the Treaty of Fez with the French was the crisis resolved. (The treaty made Morocco a French protectorate, so Germany had gained nothing by the venture.) In a paper that Churchill wrote at the time he described how, if war broke out, German armies would roll across the frontier and race into France and within twenty days would be approaching Paris. But then the flow would weaken and by the fortieth day the maximum extent of the German advance would be reached. As the re-circulated memorandum arrived on the desks of ministers and generals on the thirtieth day of the 1914 attack, all were taken aback at the accuracy of Churchill's forecast. Haldane, General Sir Ian Hamilton (in command of Home Defence), Balfour, Fisher and French variously described it as 'a triumph of prophecy!'; 'a masterly paper'; 'a wonderful forecast'; and 'astonishing and exhilarating!'[15] Asquith concluded that Churchill was 'the equivalent of a large force in the field'.[16] What General Sir Henry Wilson (Sub-Chief of the General Staff with the BEF) said we do not know, but when Churchill had first circulated the paper in 1911 he had described it in his diary as 'ridiculous and fantastic'.[17]

The accuracy of his 1911 predictions bolstered Churchill's confidence in his ability to win the war his way. In Cabinet, on 3 September, Churchill declared that he had the authority to capture or sink any vessel that appeared in the vicinity of the Dogger Bank, no matter its 'nationality or occupation, or cargo'. According to Hobhouse, no member of the Cabinet challenged him until he, Hobhouse, pointed out that this was tantamount to 'a declaration of war on the world'.[18]

It was the army, though, that consumed the attention of the Cabinet as it had been in retreat since 22 August. Finally, on 5 September, the British and French armies halted on the River Marne, so ending the first phase of the land war. The Allied armies had nothing to show for all their efforts in the first month of the war.

THE WAITING GAME

In early September, Churchill was ready to announce the formation of his Naval Brigades. Few innovations brought him as much criticism as did these forces. Although primarily composed of surplus naval reservists, they were also open to volunteers who wished to join the navy rather than enlist in the army. When the scheme was announced in early September, there was a promise that 'these men shall not be used for any expedition to the Continent until the naval situation is entirely favourable.' The news was welcomed by *The Times*, which described Churchill's action as 'altogether to be commended'.[19] The paper admired the 'characteristic energy' which had led him to 'take advantage of this patriotic feeling'.[20] There were to be eight naval battalions, each named after an admiral, and three marine battalions. Each brigade was to have an honorary colonel. Fisher selected the first brigade; retired Admiral of the Fleet Sir Arthur Wilson had the second, while the third went to Beresford. Within a week of the announcement, Churchill was able to inspect 2,000 men of the Naval Division at Crystal Palace.

With so little opportunity for action on the naval front, Churchill leapt at any chance to move men and machines into battle. When General Joseph Joffre, Commander-in-Chief of the French army, asked Kitchener to stage a diversion on the north coast of France, it was to the Admiralty that Kitchener turned. Churchill despatched the Marine Brigade, along with armoured cars and aeroplanes. To these Kitchener added the Queen's Own Oxfordshire Hussars in which, by coincidence, John Churchill was a major.

These forces landed at Dunkirk on the night of 19–20 September, where they were joined by Charles Samson of the Royal Naval Air Service. Later, additional armoured cars and fifty omnibuses were sent 'to give the force greater mobility'. The plan had been drawn up by Hankey, who hoped that this mass of men and machines would appear to the Germans to be 'the advanced guard of a considerable body of troops'.[21]

In mid-September, Kitchener despatched Churchill to France to discuss with French the need to move his base to the coast. The Duke of Westminster (serving with the Cheshire Yeomanry) accompanied Churchill on the visit. Before commencing their talks, French had arranged for Churchill and Westminster to see the whole British front. Churchill was thrilled as he watched British aeroplanes diving and swooping amongst the enemy shells overhead, while below the German artillery shelled Paissy village to destruction. Later Churchill and French discussed Kitchener's proposal to move the BEF from its base on the River Aisne and relocate it nearer to the sea, where communications with the navy would be easier. French readily agreed. After the war, French wrote that the visit did 'great good'. He was impressed by Churchill's 'characteristic energy and activity' as he 'visited and examined every part of the battlefield'. As a result Churchill was able 'to send reassuring information to his colleagues'.[22]

⟫●⟪

On his return from France, Churchill took a train to Scotland to pay a visit to the Grand Fleet. The group included Captain Keyes, who in a general conversation about naval affairs mentioned something called 'the live bait squadron'. When Churchill enquired what this was, he learnt to his horror that three slow, old and poorly armoured Bacchantes Cressy-class cruisers (HMS *Aboukir*, HMS *Cressy* and HMS *Hogue*) of the 7th Cruiser Squadron were regularly patrolling the Broad Fourteens in the North Sea. At times the ships would be steaming at no more than nine knots and, having never observed a periscope, had ceased zigzagging manoeuvres. In August, Keyes had warned the Admiralty of the grave risk that these ships were running, but no action had been taken.

The next day, Churchill ordered the immediate recall of this patrol: 'The Bacchantes ought not to continue on this beat,' he told the First Sea Lord.[23] Clearly these words were not emphatic enough, for Battenberg and his staff took no action beyond planning a redistribution of the ships in the North Sea. Ill-fortune would have it that on the very day after Churchill had written his memorandum, the weather worsened in the North Sea. The destroyers protecting the cruisers were ordered back to harbour. Now the cruisers were alone – three easy targets in line-ahead formation.

Three days later, at 6.20 a.m., HMS *Aboukir* was hit by a torpedo fired from the German submarine U-9. Thinking that his ship had hit a mine, Captain Drummond hoisted a signal to warn the other two ships of mines and to ask for assistance. Not long after, HMS *Hogue* was hit by two torpedoes and sank at 7.15 a.m. HMS *Cressy*, was then torpedoed and sank at 7.55 a.m. Keyes' worst prediction had come true. The bait had been well and truly taken. Some 1,400 officers and men had drowned; a high proportion of those were married since the ships were manned mainly by naval reservists. It was, said the official historian, 'a national loss to be lamented'.[24]

Although the loss of the vessels was entirely avoidable, it is still true to say that the navy had been fortunate up to that point. *The Times* newspaper took a realistic view when it warned readers, 'We must expect more occurrences of this character.'[25] The Cabinet were made of weaker metal. Asquith's own reaction was typical when he told Venetia Stanley that the news of the losses was 'the worst ... since the war began'.[26] Such a strong reaction to a naval disaster was to be typical throughout the war. After 60,000 casualties on the first day of the Somme in 1916, *The Times* was to report that 'the great offensive in the west has made a good beginning'.[27] Yet the loss of fewer than 2,000 men in the North Sea made experienced politicians tremble. Hankey later recalled that no other setback at this stage of the war 'caused such an atmosphere of depression'.[28] There was to be a similarly unbalanced reaction to the casualties at the Dardanelles: they caused much heart-searching, while the slaughter on the Western Front was calmly accepted.

The exaggerated response to the loss of the ships hit Churchill hard. The journalist Thomas Bowles published a libellous article in which he said that the deaths were the direct responsibility of Churchill; he went on to allege that the ships had been sunk because Churchill had refused to accept the views of his professional advisers to recall them. He further accused him of interfering with naval operations as a whole and countermanding his staff's orders. It was Admiralty policy never to comment on actions in a way that would reveal operational practice. Churchill had to remain silent while a torrent of abuse poured from the pens of ignorant and over-imaginative journalists. Meanwhile, an impassioned German press gleefully forecast Churchill's imminent retirement, along with the court martial of Jellicoe.

A subsequent enquiry squarely placed the blame on the Admiralty War Staff, since they had ordered the cruisers to remain on station and had withdrawn the destroyers. The First Sea Lord contested this outcome, but Churchill stood his ground. He was, though, disappointed that the Court of Inquiry had not held the captains of the ships partly responsible, given that they had not even taken the most elementary precautions against attack. It was perhaps with this in mind that Churchill issued a confidential order which emphasised the importance of preserving 'irreplaceable units with their crews' since their main role was 'fighting the enemy'.[29]

There was not much light relief for Churchill during the war, but he did enjoy an amusing incident when on a visit to the Grand Fleet in September. Throughout the war, the country was gripped with spy-mania and every German-born waiter was seen to be noting down conversations at table. Every stranger within a few miles of the coast was taken to be an enemy agent. No ship entered or left port without numerous detailed reports being sent to Germany. No vessel was sunk except as a result of German espionage. Despite the presence of these thousands of easily identified spies and their frenetic level of undisguised activity, actual arrests were few and far between.

It was Jellicoe who alerted Churchill to the apparent presence of a spy operating under the nose of the fleet, telling him that he had seen 'lights and searchlight beams' on the shore. Jellicoe had not reported the matter to the police – surely a lapse of security on the part of the Commander-in-Chief. Instead, he happily put the matter into the First Lord's hands. Assuming the role of self-appointed amateur sleuths, Churchill, his naval assistant Captain Henry Oliver and Keyes set off in search of adventure before their long journey back to London. Jellicoe had armed them with some ancient revolvers. On 17 September, after landing, the party drove off in the direction of the source of the light. At 10.30 p.m. they arrived at Lochrosque Castle, a large, isolated structure set in its own grounds at Achanalt. Uncharacteristically, Churchill remained outside the gate, while Keyes and Oliver went to the door. Their knock was answered by the butler, who let the party enter. The owner then appeared, who Oliver described as 'a Knight who had made a fortune in South Africa', but who was actually the ex-Liberal MP Sir Arthur Bignold, who was well-acquainted with Churchill. Of course he had a searchlight, he told them, which he used 'to look at the eyes of the deer and other animals at night'. Oliver and Keyes went up to the roof to see the offending 18-inch light. When they returned to the hall, there was Churchill, who had tired of waiting and had come in to see what was taking so long. The alleged spy immediately recognised the First Lord and offered a friendly greeting. Later the police removed the searchlight solving yet one more bogus spy story.[30] Both Oliver and Churchill left accounts of this escapade; neither reflected on the consequences that would have followed had the First Lord and his Chief of Staff been killed by alien bullets.

We can be sure that Churchill never told Asquith about his escapade, since there is no mention of the incident in his indiscreet letters to Venetia Stanley. In fact that night, when Asquith sat down to write, he rejoiced that Churchill had been absent from the House and that there was no news from French because gales had damaged the telegraph wires. That gave him time to look back over the year. He recalled the 'golden times' with Venetia at Alderley Old Hall (the Stanley seat in Cheshire) in January; their drives in March; her comforting letter over the Curragh incident; a 'heavenly time' at Whitsun, despite gun-running in Ireland. But then, of course, the war had come: 'Since then I have seen you exactly 7 times.'[31]

There was yet another visit to Sir John French in the last week of September. By now, Kitchener had overcome his suspicions of Churchill's Continental visits and looked forward to using his calming influence on the nervous and touchy French. Colonel J.E.B. Seely, then on French's staff, but who had been at school with Churchill when the latter was still 'a pudgy little ginger-haired boy', made the arrangements, ordering two Rolls-Royce motorcars to meet the Churchill party at Boulogne. Seely had well earned his sobriquet of 'Galloper Jack', being a man who found an adventure round every corner. He let loose his untramelled imagination when he warned Churchill of the dangers he would face on the road. Not only could driving at speed puncture the tyres on the rough French roads, but a fast car was likely to be shot at by French soldiers.

After avoiding these hazards, Churchill and French entered into detailed conversations for a joint naval-military operation in Belgium. Both men had the same idea of a coastal attack on the German right flank as a means of slowing down the enemy's advance. Possession of the Belgian ports was also at stake: 'We examined,' wrote French after the war, 'the possibility of a failure to effect a decisive turning movement, and agreed in thinking that, in the last resort, we might still be able, with the flank support of the Fleet, to snatch from the enemy's possession the Belgian coast-line as far, at any rate, as Zeebrugge.'[32]

There was no time to pursue this further. Churchill had only just returned to London when he was required to return to the Front – this time on a matter of the utmost urgency.

CHURCHILL'S ANTWERP TRIUMPH

By the end of September, the position of Antwerp was grim as the German armies approached ever nearer in their attempt to occupy the Belgian coastline. Although the threat was military, Churchill was determined that the navy would play its part in forestalling the imminent disaster of the city falling into German hands. He despatched Oliver with a demolition team to sabotage any merchant ships in the Scheldt and avoid any of the vessels being captured by German forces. The operation could not have gone more smoothly as Oliver and his men used explosives to quickly disable the engines of thirty-eight vessels. Their objective completed, Oliver and his men slipped away unnoticed. For the moment it appeared as if Churchill could do no more to stave off disaster. Grey informed the ambassadors at Bordeaux and Antwerp that there was little likelihood of British or French troops being able to reach Antwerp in time. The Allies were preparing to abandon the city.

Somehow ministers rallied themselves and agreed that they should make one more attempt to save Antwerp. There was only one resource that they could despatch immediately: Churchill. On 2 October, he was hurried onto a train with instructions to survey the position and to advise on what could be done.

The train had just pulled out of Charing Cross station when a telegram arrived in London from Sir Francis Villiers, Envoy Extraordinary in Belgium. The Belgian government and its army were about to abandon Antwerp. He thought the city could hold out for up to a week if they stayed but once they had gone, resistance would collapse.

On his arrival at Dover, Churchill was handed a note recalling him to London. He went straight to Kitchener's house, where he found Grey and his Private Secretary, William Tyrrell, in conference with Kitchener.

The ministers were numb with the shock of yet another defeat. It was Churchill who roused them and urged them not to abandon Antwerp. Once compelled to action they enthusiastically decided to despatch Churchill and his marines to 'try to infuse into their [the Belgians'] backbones the necessary quantity of starch'.[33]

On 3 October, at 12.45 a.m., a telegram was sent to Villiers informing him that a brigade of marines was being despatched. Despite Churchill's optimism, the meeting had no expectation that Antwerp could be kept from the Germans, but they urged Villiers to make 'one further struggle to hold out. Even a few days may make the difference.'[34] The wording of this telegram makes it abundantly clear that Antwerp was to be a delaying operation, not an attempt to defeat the German attack. Those who later severely criticised Churchill when Antwerp fell were ignorant of the limited purpose of the operation. As we shall see, that purpose was fully achieved, if with unfortunate side-effects.

Thirty minutes later, Grey telegraphed the Belgian government to ask that their King give Churchill an audience on his arrival. Lights also burned late in the Admiralty that night as a message went to Major General Paris, in command of the Naval Division, to tell him to provide five armoured cars to meet Churchill at Dunkirk.

Churchill reached the beleaguered city at 3.00 p.m. On being approached by the Burgomaster, Churchill, forgetting the limited purpose of the mission, pronounced 'You needn't worry. We're going to save the city.'[35] After meetings with the King and Colonel Alister Dallas from the War Office, Churchill met the Belgian Prime Minister, Monsieur de Broqueville, to agree a plan of action. As they talked, the outer forts were, one by one, being destroyed by the fearsome German artillery and attacks were just beginning on the inner forts. The Belgian army was exhausted and supplies of every kind were critically short; even the water had been cut off. At 6.53 p.m., Churchill was able to telegraph his agreement with de Broqueville to Kitchener. The Belgians, he informed the War Secretary, were now prepared to hold the line for ten days provided that the British mobilised a large force to come to their aid. If they did not receive a promise of such aid in the next three days they would give up their defence of Antwerp and retreat. Then the decision that was to be so disparaged for years afterwards was sent:

We will meanwhile help with local defence in all minor ways, such as guns, marines, naval brigades, etc.[36]

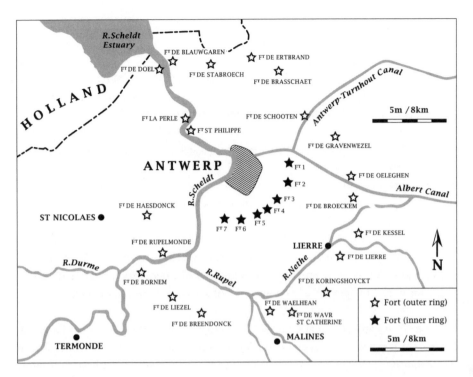

The siege of Antwerp.

It had been a monumental day, starting with a midnight meeting in London and ending with a hurried plan to reinforce a demoralised Belgian army with a few thousand marines and inexperienced men from the Naval Brigades. After all those dull days at his desk in Whitehall, Churchill was in his element at last.

On the following day, Churchill received a telegram from Kitchener detailing the forces that were to be sent. These included the 8,000 men from the Naval Brigades who were to leave later that day. In another two or three days' time, 18,000 men of the 7th Division would arrive with sixty-three guns, as would 4,000 men of the Cavalry Division with twelve guns. Another day or so later there would be 15,000 Territorials. In all, Kitchener intended to despatch 53,000 men to defend Antwerp. Again we see how a military operation that is often derided as a wild Churchillian-style stunt was seen by Kitchener as a critically important mission. It was, in any case, no better or worse than any of the endless disasters of the First World War.

By now Churchill was positively enjoying his command. He was seen tranquilly standing on the battlefield, wrapped in a large cloak, a yachting cap on his head and large cigar in his mouth. Shrapnel fell around him but 'he smiled, and looked satisfied.'[37] His head had been turned by the drama of battle.

Further good news reached Churchill when a message from the First Sea Lord confirmed that the Naval Brigades were to embark at 4.00 p.m. and would arrive at Dunkirk in the early evening.

Churchill was still hard at work at 11.50 p.m. that evening when he telegraphed for a long list of supplies, including guns, ammunition, duffle suits and field telephones. As if to justify this frenzied activity, he also received a letter from de Broqueville, underlining the Belgian government's commitment to the fight. Antwerp had to be defended 'at all costs' and he emphasised that their determination to fight to the death had never wavered for a moment.

It was with some incredulity that Asquith read a telegram that he found on his desk early on 5 October. His First Lord was proposing to resign:

> If it is thought by H.M. Government that I can be of service here, I am willing to resign my office and undertake command of relieving and defensive forces assigned in Antwerp … provided that I am given the necessary military rank and authority, and full powers of a commander of a detached force in the field.[38]

In the heat of battle, the real Churchill had burst through the ministerial façade. At heart he was a frustrated general and for the moment he was free to act as one. It was, Asquith told Venetia Stanley, 'a real bit of tragic-comedy'.[39] Without consulting his colleagues, Asquith telegraphed back to say that Churchill could not be spared from the Admiralty. Later he reported the incident to Cabinet, where the offer was greeted by fits of uncontrolled laughter. To one person, though, it did not seem such a mad idea. Kitchener offered to make Churchill a lieutenant general so that he could remain in command at Antwerp.

Fighting continued throughout that day. Churchill, Asquith told Venetia Stanley, '[had] succeeded in bucking up the Belges', who had '[given] up their panicky idea of retreating to Ostend'.[40] Alongside the battered Belgian troops Churchill now had his Marine Brigade, which was on the north side of the River Nethe at a point where, he told Kitchener, he expected the Germans to attempt a crossing. At 10.18 a.m., Churchill was able to report that the brigade was successfully holding the position and was adequately supported with artillery, but he expected an imminent German infantry attack.

In London, Kitchener was doing everything he could to support Churchill. He appointed General Rawlinson to take charge at Antwerp, where he was expected to arrive later that day. In a telegram to Churchill, Kitchener emphasised how vital it was for the Belgians to hold out; reinforcements would arrive by sea the next day.

At exactly the time that Kitchener had written, Churchill was sending another report to him. The expected infantry attack had transpired and, although the marines were holding their line, the Germans had crossed the Nethe in a few places. His upbeat talk of Belgian troops being sent to drive the Germans back could hardly disguise the fact that the Belgians were losing ground. Churchill worryingly added that he still had no information as to when the Naval Brigades would arrive. Nevertheless, in the early evening he was able to tell Kitchener that the German attack had been repulsed and the line of the Nethe was being held. Killed and wounded now amounted to some 150 men. There was also bad news from London. Rawlinson was only just leaving Dunkirk and the Naval Brigades were now not expected to arrive until 1.00 a.m. on 7 October. Time was pressing.

Later that evening, Churchill visited General Paris at his headquarters to put him in charge of the Naval Brigades once they arrived. The journey proved hazardous as Churchill's car came under fire on the Antwerp–Lierre road. As he got out of his car, a shell burst overhead and a man standing nearby fell to the ground dead. Conditions were not much more comfortable at Paris's headquarters in a cottage near the battlefield. As they sat round the table, deep in their discussions, the house was rocked and their voices regularly drowned by the thunderous roar of shells exploding outside.

On his return to the Belgian headquarters at midnight, Churchill received a report from Lieutenant General Victor Deguise, in charge of the city's defences. Deguise boldly declared that all was well in the sectors under his command. Encouraged by this, Churchill sat down at 1.00 a.m. on 6 October to write an optimistic report to Kitchener, informing him that the line of the Nethe was holding. As he went to bed at 2.00 a.m., Churchill was extremely satisfied with his work of the last few days. Tomorrow, he could hand over to Rawlinson and then return to the Admiralty.

During the night, the Belgians mounted a counterattack that failed badly. It was soon clear the optimism of the previous day had been misplaced. The German offensive was too powerful for the exhausted Belgians. The Marine Brigade was also struggling and it was into this rapidly deteriorating situation that Churchill placed his newly recruited and inexperienced Naval Brigades. They arrived by train, while the ammunition and supplies were carried in London omnibuses. The scene was witnessed by the American journalist E. Alexander Powell who saw the omnibuses 'placarded with advertisements for teas, tobaccos, whiskies, and current theatrical attractions and bearing the signs "Bank," "Holborn," "Piccadilly," "Shepherd's Bush," "Strand"'. Powell also watched as the men detrained at Vieux Dieu station and 'tramped down the tree-bordered, cobble-paved high road to the sound of *It's a long way to Tipperary*'. The men, he reported, 'were as clean-limbed, pleasant-faced, wholesome-looking a lot of young Englishmen as you would find anywhere' but 'they were not "first-class fighting men"'.[41] Their deployment was totally irresponsible as Churchill had seen the battlefield and knew that it was proving beyond the powers and endurance of well-trained men, yet he nonchalantly plunged his untrained brigades into the battle. In *The World Crisis,* he came as near as he ever got to admitting how mistaken he was:

It was one thing to put these partially trained and ill-equipped troops into a trench-line, and quite another to involve them in manoeuvres … Solidly dug in with rifles and plenty of ammunition, these ardent, determined men would not be easily dislodged. But they were not capable of manoeuvre.[42]

It was for these reasons that Churchill told Deguise that the men were to be held four miles behind the front trenches. This was much their position when, at 5.00 p.m., Rawlinson arrived to take over.

After reviewing the situation, Rawlinson optimistically wrote in his diary 'The Marines and Naval Brigades can hold this line for ever.'[43] All that remained for Churchill was to join the new commander in a Council of War at the Belgian Royal Palace and then to write his last despatch to Kitchener. It was 10.37 p.m. when he began this dismal task. The German attack had pushed the Marine Brigade back to a line between Contich and Vremde. Now the Germans were close enough to commence a bombardment of the city. When Churchill, Rawlinson and the Belgians reviewed the situation they quickly agreed that it was time to pull back to the line of the inner forts.

As to the controversial involvement of the Naval Brigades, it had all been for nothing. They had arrived too late to take part, Churchill told Kitchener. Such was his faith in the brigades that he still believed that had he had them a day earlier, the Nethe would have been held.

In London, Churchill's continued absence was giving rise to a growing list of complaints. Asquith was annoyed, since he had to deputise for him in his absence at the Admiralty: 'I have had to tell them to submit all decisions to me,' he pathetically complained to Miss Stanley. But, he added, 'He has done good service.'[44] Meanwhile, the King's Secretary, Lord Stamfordham, declared Churchill to 'be quite off his head!'[45]

Antwerp was doomed by the time Churchill departed for home. On 7 October, the Germans began their bombardment and on the night of 8 October, the Naval Brigades were evacuated. In Cabinet, Churchill put forward the case for persuading the neutral Dutch government to allow ships up the Scheldt to take both food and arms to Antwerp. His colleagues were not convinced but, at Grey's suggestion, agreed to send foodstuffs openly up the Scheldt, with arms hidden in the same ships. In his diary Hobhouse scorned this proposal which, he said, 'would bring down on us 250,000 Dutch, and the certain loss of Antwerp'.[46] On 8 October, Churchill heard of the decision to evacuate the city. Asquith described how 'Winston was furious (and I quite share his anger) at his General, who is in an almost impregnable entrenched position & ought to hold on even by his eye-brows, until either the situation becomes really desperate or succour is at hand.'[47] On 10 October, German troops entered Antwerp and the city surrendered.

The losses in action were small compared to most First World War operations: ten officers and 185 men killed or wounded. But these losses were nothing in comparison to the tragedy of the men left behind. The proximity of German troops and the state of the roads and railways hampered the return of the remaining men. Some 1,500 managed to escape to Holland, but were interned there for the duration of the war. In addition, some 1,000 men were taken prisoner by the Germans. It had been, as the official historian noted, a 'desperate expedient to meet a desperate situation'.[48]

The press was generally hostile in regard to the Antwerp venture. The *Morning Post* thought Churchill had no right to leave his office in London as it was his job to be in the 'Admiralty day and night'.[49] Inevitably, Bonar Law was highly critical. Antwerp, he told an unknown correspondent, was 'an utterly stupid business' and blamed Churchill since 'the Belgians had decided not to defend Antwerp, and Churchill persuaded them to do so.'[50] Clearly Law had no idea of the importance Kitchener, Asquith and French attached to the venture. Had he known that Kitchener had sent over 50,000 troops to the aid of Antwerp, he might have taken a more generous view of Churchill's part.

Frances Stevenson, Lloyd George's secretary and confidante, shared the same misapprehension. Writing in her diary she states that 'It seems that but for his promise of British help, Antwerp would have surrendered a week earlier.' She then went on to say 'C[51] is rather disgusted with Winston still about Antwerp, and thinks that the P.M. is too. Having taken untrained men over there, he left them in the lurch.'[52] Since Lloyd George must have had access to the full facts, it is clear that Stevenson had misunderstood the true position.

No one had been more supportive than Asquith of the need to hold Antwerp and of Churchill temporarily directing the operation. But when he discovered from his son 'Oc' (Arthur), who had been with the brigades, that the untrained men had been used, he was furious: 'nothing can excuse Winston' for such a 'wicked folly'. He had, he told Venetia Stanley, been 'assured that all the recruits were being left behind'.[53]

When, shortly afterwards, the government announced a delay in the opening of Parliament, Antwerp's detractors claimed that this was in order to 'avoid discussion on the policy pursued at Antwerp'. The *Manchester Guardian* wrote that there was no truth to this rumour and attributed the delay to the government not needing a vote of credit as soon as had been expected.[54] In fact, the votes of credit for the army and navy were not presented until 12 November.

The many critics of Churchill's part in Antwerp were happy to disregard the views of those close to the events. Hankey, French, Kitchener and Asquith were all agreed that Antwerp had made a decisive contribution to the war. Asquith concurred in Hankey's judgement that Antwerp 'has prevented the Germans from linking up their forces'. The week had 'not been thrown away', as some alleged. It might even have been of 'vital value'.[55] The King of the Belgians later described Antwerp and Gallipoli as 'the two strategical master-strokes of the war'.[56] A later opinion came from that great historian and critic of the Western Front, Liddell Hart, who wrote that 'this first and last effort in the west to make use of Britain's amphibious power applied a brake to the German advance down the coast which just stopped their second attempt to gain a decision in the west.'[57]

Grey, writing to Clementine Churchill, bubbled with enthusiasm as he told her how he felt 'a glow' when he sat next to the 'hero' Winston in Cabinet. 'I can't tell you how much I admire his courage & gallant spirit & genius for war.'[58] Lloyd George congratulated Churchill on his 'brilliant effort to rescue Antwerp'.[59] And, even though he was writing nearly fifty years later, it is impossible to ignore the judgement of so wise and informed a man as Hankey, who wrote:

> It cannot be denied that Churchill and Kitchener, under Asquith's wise guidance, displayed high qualities of decision, executive capacity and resource. ... Their decisions ... were preferable to inaction and produced useful results.[60]

Another voice that must have pleased Churchill was that of French, who wrote to congratulate him on his 'splendid work at Antwerp' and told him to ignore what the papers wrote about him.[61]

PROBLEMS, DISASTERS AND A PRECIOUS GIFT

While opinions raged over Antwerp, Churchill received one of the greatest bonuses of the war on 13 October – a bonus that could not be talked about. In August, the German light cruiser SMS *Magdeburg* had run aground off the coast of Estonia. Almost immediately two Imperial Russian Navy cruisers arrived and, after a short exchange of gunfire, captured the ship intact. Inside the vessel they found copies of the German naval codes used for wireless communication. Safely arrived in London, these code books were to yield priceless information on German operations and enable Churchill and his staff to, on many occasions, place ships to intercept unsuspecting raiders.

Later that month, the war moved into the next phase with the First Battle of Ypres, which began on 19 October. For the next four years, the war on the Western Front would be fought from trenches as the generals on both sides were content to throw men at machine guns. Just ten days later Churchill commissioned the first trench-spanning vehicles, which did not turn out to be a success. He was now less than three months away from initiating the development of bullet-proof vehicles – the future tank. Whether on land or sea his active brain could not stop offering up new ways to win the war.

⟿⟐⟐⟐⟵

In his letters to Venetia Stanley, Asquith showed no concern for national security as time and again he revealed secrets that, at least today, could bring down a Prime Minister. So when on 27 October, he told her that Churchill 'has suffered to-day a terrible calamity on the sea, which I dare not describe, lest by chance my letter should go wrong', it was obvious that something quite out of the ordinary had occurred.[62]

The news from Jellicoe that the battleship HMS *Audacious*, a King George V-class vessel, had struck a mine off the northern coast of Donegal and was feared to be sinking reached Churchill at 11.15 a.m. The ship was one of the latest super-dreadnoughts and for it to be lost in home waters so early in the war and without having seen any action was unthinkable. But the unthinkable had happened. Frantic efforts had been made to take the ship in tow but, at 8.45 p.m., the vessel sank. No lives were lost, but the damage to the reputation of the navy was considerable. Jellicoe appealed to the Admiralty to keep the sinking secret. It seemed a futile gesture since the steamship SS *Olympic*, returning from the United States, had arrived at the scene and its 1,000 or so passengers had witnessed the sinking. Churchill answered Jellicoe's appeal by suggesting that it would be almost impossible to suppress the news and he recommended that Jellicoe send a signal to the Admiralty stating that HMS *Audacious* had suffered damage that would take some weeks to repair.

When the Cabinet discussed the sinking the next day, the conversation quickly turned to the proposal to suppress the story. Churchill, McKenna, Kitchener and Hobhouse were in favour of suppression although Hobhouse pointed out it would be 'impossible to conceal it' because of the presence of the *Olympic*. Others opposed suppression, including Lloyd George, Grey and Haldane. In the end, the Cabinet accepted Asquith's recommendation to simply delay the announcement. And delay it they did. The sinking was finally announced in the press three days after the end of the war in November 1918. As *The Times* newspaper noted, the sinking had been 'kept secret at the urgent request of the Commander-in-Chief, Grand Fleet, and the Press loyally refrained from giving it any publicity'.[63] Abroad, though, the sinking was a front page story in newspapers as far away as the United States and Australia.

Given the role that Lloyd George was later to play in the war, his reaction was most surprising. The sinking led him to feel that the war was going to 'overwhelm him'. It was 'all so horrible' that he wanted to 'go away somewhere and get out of it all'.[64]

At the very time that Churchill was in Antwerp, a home-grown problem was waiting to demand his attention: the First Sea Lord. Fisher, who kept a very close eye on Churchill's management of his beloved Admiralty, told his friend Mrs Pamela McKenna (wife of Reginald McKenna, Home Secretary) on 3 October that Battenberg was 'played out'.[65] This had not escaped public attention and rumours abounded with regard to the First Sea Lord. According to some newspapers he had been arrested as a traitor and was now incarcerated in the Tower of London.

There was no truth to these rumours, but Churchill was aware that the public had lost faith in the navy. So bad was the situation in mid-October that he considered resignation. His friend Richard Haldane, an ex-War Minister, pleaded with him to stay and came up with the suggestion of bringing back Fisher while keeping Battenberg on as the Second Sea Lord.

Churchill seized the proffered lifeline and on the following day he told Asquith of the old admiral's possible return. That night, Asquith told Venetia Stanley that 'He has quite made up his mind that the time has come for a drastic change in his Board; our poor blue-eyed German will have to go.' He was to be replaced by Fisher as First Sea Lord, with Admiral Arthur Wilson also coming back in an advisory role. They were, Churchill told Asquith, 'well-plucked chickens', respectively seventy-three and seventy-two years old. After talking to Asquith, Churchill informed Battenberg of their decision and discussed how they should best handle the resignation correspondence.

Had there been any way to avoid the departure of Battenberg, Churchill would have gladly taken it, but he knew that the man had already been broken by a stream of newspaper articles. The most polite simply declared that no German 'whether naturalised or unnaturalised' should be allowed to hold a high post in war.[66] Other newspapers directly accused him of treachery. Protests from the likes of the retired Admiral of the Fleet, John Hay, were to no avail. He declared that the First Sea Lord had been the victim of 'slander' for which 'not a tittle of evidence had been forthcoming'.[67] Churchill was well aware of the chauvinist nature of the attacks, which he duly explained to King George V. The King would have been familiar with the rumours but he was staggered when Churchill proposed Fisher as his new First Sea Lord. Fisher had been an intimate friend of King Edward VII, who had tirelessly supported him in his battles with his enemies. But King George V had always been antagonistic towards Fisher and he had no intention of overseeing his return to power. What about Admiral Hedworth Meux[68] (Commander-in-Chief, Portsmouth) or Admiral Henry Jackson (a member of the War Staff)? asked the King. Churchill would have neither, at which point the King terminated the interview, saying that he would speak with Asquith.

On 28 October, Churchill received Battenberg's formal offer of resignation; in it he explained how he had 'lately been driven to the painful conclusion that at this juncture my birth and parentage have the effect of impairing in some respects my usefulness on the Board of Admiralty'.[69] In a private letter to Churchill, he wrote 'I beg of you to release me. I am on the verge of breaking down.'[70]

Stamfordham, Private Secretary to the King, had the difficult task of putting to Asquith the King's objections to Fisher. In a note that he made after the meeting, he described his valiant effort to make the King's case and to promote the other candidates. But Asquith, in an unusually decisive and forthright mood, rebutted them all. Meux? '[He] would surely not inspire the confidence of the navy'. Jackson? 'Able, but no personality'. Sturdee? Asquith brushed him aside too. Only Fisher would do – 'there was no one else suitable for the post'. Churchill, he told Stamfordham, would resign if he did not get Fisher.[71]

This interview tells us more about Asquith's confidence in Churchill than it does about his belief in Fisher. Despite all the wry, ironic and sometimes snide comments that Asquith had made about his First Lord in his letters to Venetia Stanley, he had a deep liking and a profound admiration for him. It is doubtful whether Churchill ever knew just how far Asquith had gone that day in his defence.

Churchill and Battenberg had agreed that the resignation correspondence should be published, so Churchill had to choose his words carefully when he alluded to the background events. In his public letter to the Prince, Churchill wrote: 'The anxieties and toils which rest upon the naval administration of our country are in themselves enough to try a man's spirit; and when to them are added the ineradicable [sic] difficulties of which you speak, I could not at this juncture in fairness ask you to support them.' In writing the letter, Churchill took the opportunity to acknowledge publicly the First Sea Lord's 'timely concentration of the Fleet' before the outbreak of war. He closed by expressing his 'deep indebtedness' to Battenberg and acknowledged 'the pain I feel at the severance of our three years' official association'.[72]

The change of First Sea Lord was announced in *The Times* newspaper on 30 October, when it printed the letters supplemented by an obituary-style review of Battenberg's career.

In peacetime, Churchill had luxuriated in his Admiralty appointment. He had had at his command the greatest navy in the world. Week in, week out he would board the Admiralty yacht, HMS *Enchantress*, to visit his fleets, port facilities and minor stations. Often he would take along other ministers and Members of Parliament. But now, in wartime, he found himself in command of a fleet that was at anchor behind anti-submarine nets in Scapa Flow while generals commanded armies on vast fronts on the Continent. He yearned for action. Whenever his brother Jack was abroad he expressed the hope that he would soon be free to join him. And just a few days of Antwerp were enough for Churchill to offer his resignation to Asquith. When he returned from Belgium, Churchill sought a private moment with the Prime Minister to reveal a deep secret. Asquith recalled 'he implored me not to take a conventional view of his future. Having, as he says, tasted blood these last few days, he is beginning, like a tiger, to raven for more.' What Churchill wanted was no less than a senior military command. 'His mouth,' Asquith continued, 'waters at the sight and thought of K.'s new armies.' Churchill rhetorically enquired whether 'these "glittering commands" [are] to be trusted to "dug-out trash" bred on obsolete tactics of twenty-five years ago, "mediocrities who have led a sheltered life mouldering in military routine"'.[73]

Most of this was simply 'essence of Churchill'. But a part was doubtless due to labouring with his dull and spiritless Admiralty Board. Would Fisher be able to breathe new life into his weary First Lord?

CHAPTER 5

THE DYNAMIC DUO

One felt at once the difference made by the substitution of Fisher for
poor L.B. – élan, dash, initiative, a new spirit. – Asquith[1]

FISHER TO THE RESCUE

'Isn't it fun being back?' wrote the seventy-three-year-old Fisher to his friend
Viscount Esher after working twenty-two hours on his first day in the Admiralty on
I November.[2] (Esher was a courtier and a self-appointed expert on military affairs.) But,
Fisher admitted to Esher that he could not manage on two hours' sleep, 'so I shall slow
down!' After this impossible first burst of energy the old admiral settled into a routine
of rising at 3.30 a.m. and going to bed at 9.30 p.m. Buoyed up by his new job, he told
Pamela McKenna that he was 'more fit and virile' than when he had left the Admiralty
in 1910.[3] The King's prediction that the job would kill him was clearly mistaken.

Despite his age, Fisher had lost none of his impressive physical presence. When he
sat in the privileged seat above the clock in the Commons in February 1915 to listen
to Churchill making a statement on the navy, the *Manchester Guardian* reporter noted
that he had 'the sea and the strength of the sea about him'. He had 'a strong weather-
worn face with its touch of superior scorn' and a thatch of 'unruly grey hair'. He
showed no 'sign of wear and tear' from his onerous labours.[4]

Although Fisher tired more easily than he had done when he was First Sea Lord in
1904-10, he was still a formidable worker. So too was Churchill and it was rumoured,
said the *Manchester Guardian*, that some people doubted 'whether Mr. Churchill ever
left his room'.[5] Fisher's habit of starting work before dawn combined with Churchill
often being in the office after midnight resulted in their running an almost twenty-
four-hour operation in Admiralty House.

Vice Admiral Beatty nicely expressed the navy's reaction to Fisher's return when he
told his wife, 'I think he is the best thing they could have done, but I wish he was ten
years younger.' He delighted that Fisher 'still has fine zeal, energy, and determination,
coupled with low cunning, which is eminently desirable just now'. He looked
forward to the Admiralty taking up 'a strong offensive policy' and hoped that Fisher

would 'rule the Admiralty and Winston with a heavy hand'.[6] *The Times*, too, seemed to expect a burst of action when it reminded its readers of a Fisher maxim he had declared at the Hague Conference in 1899:

> The essence of war is violence.
> Moderation in war is imbecility.
> Hit first, hit hard, and hit anywhere![7]

Churchill and Fisher had agreed from the outset never to take a decision without consulting one another. Major decisions were taken by the War Staff Group that now comprised Churchill, Fisher, Oliver, A.K. Wilson, Graham Greene[8] (Secretary to the Board) and Commander de Bartolomé (Naval Secretary). Despite these collective arrangements, Churchill gave Fisher a free hand in building up the fleet – materiel was Fisher's speciality. Within a week of taking office he had agreed a programme for 612 new ships and boats. On 3 November, orders began to pour out of the Admiralty with instructions that 'cheapness must be entirely subordinated to rapidity of construction'. He ordered that 'the technical departments must have a free hand to take whatever steps are necessary to secure this end without any paper work whatever'.[9] Churchill and Fisher foresaw a long war and so were in full accord on the importance of construction. They were, though, not necessarily in agreement with what the ships were to do. After the war, Fisher declared that 'Mr. Churchill was behind no one both in his enthusiasm for the Baltic project' (invading Germany via the Baltic coast) and that he, Fisher, had supported attacks on the Belgian coast in co-operation with the army.[10] But the records of the time show that Fisher was determined to raid the Baltic and Churchill was set on taking the island of Borkum off the German coast. Churchill went along with Fisher's ship building for the Baltic bombardment but intended to use the same ships at Borkum.

After the languorous atmosphere of the Battenberg era, Fisher breathed new life and vigour into the Admiralty. Just two days into the Fisher regime Asquith observed the air of 'élan, dash, initiative, a new spirit'.[11] His arrival proved providential since it happened to coincide with a naval disaster of the first order.

On 4 November at 1.29 a.m., a telegram arrived at Admiralty House from the British Consulate at Valparaiso in Chile. This reported that Rear Admiral Christopher Cradock's squadron had been in battle off the coast of Chile against the German East Asia Squadron commanded by Vice Admiral Maximilian von Spee. HMS *Monmouth* had been sunk and HMS *Good Hope* was on fire. Later, an explosion had been heard.

The news was greeted with incredulity at the Admiralty. Churchill had gone to great trouble to ensure that Cradock would not find himself outgunned by von Spee. What could have gone wrong?

Back in September, Churchill had reviewed the situation in the Pacific Ocean where von Spee's squadron then was, with two powerful armoured cruisers SMS *Scharnhorst* and SMS *Gneisenau*. These ships were a major threat to British merchant shipping in the Pacific Ocean. Unless stopped, they might enter the Atlantic and take the vital coaling station on the Falkland Islands. Churchill knew that he had to eliminate the German squadron but all he had at his disposal was the comparatively weak force under Cradock: the armoured cruisers HMS *Good Hope* and HMS *Monmouth*, and the light cruiser HMS *Glasgow*. To reinforce this small squadron he sent Cradock the slow but well-armed HMS *Canopus*, a pre-dreadnought battleship, in mid-September. The armoured cruiser HMS *Defence* was also on the way to Cradock from the Mediterranean. In sending the reinforcements Churchill gave the clearest possible order. Cradock was to

> Concentrate a squadron strong enough to meet the *Scharnhorst* and *Gneisenau*, making Falkland Islands your coaling base, and leaving sufficient force to deal with *Dresden* and *Karlsruhe*. …You should keep at least one County class and *Canopus* with your flagship until *Defence* joins.[12]

Three weeks later, Churchill warned Cradock that SMS *Scharnhorst* and SMS *Gneisenau* were working their way south towards Cape Horn. He once more ordered him to keep the *Canopus* with his squadron. All appeared to be well on 12 October, when Cradock signalled Churchill that he intended to concentrate at the Falkland Islands and keep his force together.

Even as late as 1 November, when Cradock's telegram dated 29 October reached the Admiralty, he stated that there was no reason for London to worry about his squadron. He told the Admiralty to forward mails for *Good Hope, Canopus, Monmouth, Glasgow* and *Otranto* (an armed merchant cruiser) to Valparaiso. This was the last message received from Cradock. Two days later, the Admiralty once more warned him to keep his forces concentrated. By then, Rear Admiral Cradock had gone down with his flagship HMS *Good Hope*.

It was not until 6 November that confirmation of the action at the Battle of Coronel reached London in a telegram from the captain of HMS *Glasgow*. This described how the *Good Hope, Monmouth* and *Glasgow* had met the *Scharnhorst, Gneisenau, Leipzig* and *Dresden*. The British ships were hopelessly outgunned. Both the *Good Hope* and *Monmouth* had been badly damaged early in the action. Both later sank, while the *Glasgow* and *Otranto* escaped into the darkness. It was this telegram that also confirmed Cradock had gone into action without HMS *Canopus*. He had sent the ship to the Falkland Islands.

Churchill feared the public reaction to such a naval humiliation. In an attempt to pre-empt the blame from falling on himself, he quickly let those in the inner circle know of his explicit orders to Cradock to keep the *Canopus* with his force. This ensured that Asquith's response was to absolve Churchill of any blame and declare that the disaster was 'all through sheer stupidity, for if the Admiral had followed his instructions he would never have met them with an inferior force'.[13]

Fearful of a hostile parliamentary question on the battle, Churchill drafted a reply in which he emphasised that the combination of the *Good Hope, Monmouth, Canopus, Glasgow* and *Otranto* had been of sufficient firepower to defeat von Spee, even though the ships were not fast enough to chase him. By the time Coronel came up for discussion in the House on 16 November, Churchill had discarded his proposed reply and simply refused to give any detail. The House could not 'form a true judgment upon this episode', he said, without knowing 'the dispositions of all the ships' and their orders. 'This is clearly impossible at present,' he concluded.[14]

<hr/>

While the news of Coronel was still on its way to London, Churchill was occupied with a curious occurrence. On 3 November, Vice Admiral Sackville Carden's ships (HMS *Indomitable* and HMS *Indefatigable*) opened fire on the Turkish forts at the entrance to the Dardanelles. Churchill had ordered this trial bombardment two days earlier, instructing Carden to fire at a range of 12–24,000 yards. After some ten minutes of firing, a fort at Sedd-el-Bahr was almost completely destroyed. Encouraged by this – and the surprising ease with which the Germans had destroyed the forts in Belgium during September – Churchill, Jackson and Oliver began to contemplate forcing the Dardanelles with the aid of the guns of old battleships. Much later, when the Dardanelles had proved harder to force than expected, Churchill's critics blamed him for this early bombardment. He had, they said, forewarned the Turks, who had then taken steps to strengthen their defences. In fact the Turks took not the slightest notice of the bombardment. As to Churchill, he soon put the Dardanelles out of his mind. By the time that Kitchener suggested an attack on the Dardanelles two months later, Churchill had dismissed the idea.

FISHER'S REVENGE

The Dardanelles were nothing compared to the importance of avenging Coronel. Had the Admiralty still been running at Battenberg's slow speed, Coronel might never have been answered. But now the task fell to the energetic Fisher and, on 4 November, he out-argued Churchill in the ferocity of the response that he proposed. Churchill had argued that they need do no more than send HMS *Defence* and HMS *Invincible* to reinforce Rear Admiral Stoddart's 5th Cruiser Squadron in the South Atlantic. Fisher had no intention of a defensive response. He was determined on nothing less than the annihilation of von Spee's squadron. For the first time in his life he had the chance to pursue his doctrine of 'moderation in war is imbecility'. That day, Stoddart was ordered to concentrate his forces and Jellicoe was ordered to release two of his finest battlecruisers (HMS *Invincible* and HMS *Inflexible*) which were 'urgently needed for foreign service'.[15] They were to be despatched immediately. Beatty was also ordered to release the battlecruiser HMS *Princess Royal*.

On 5 November, Churchill was left with the difficult job of explaining to the petulant Jellicoe why his fleet was being deprived of some of its finest ships. As he later wrote in *The World Crisis*, there may only have been five German warships in the South Atlantic, but it still required thirty British ships to search the oceans and bring von Spee to battle.

Meanwhile, the cunning Fisher neatly solved a personal problem by appointing Sturdee, his Chief of War Staff, to command the search and destroy operation. He had not liked Sturdee since he had sided with Beresford in 1907–09. In settling a score with his admiral, Fisher did him a favour. Ineffective in his war staff role, he was to achieve one of the few great naval victories of the war at the Falklands.

Churchill and Fisher now showed what the dynamic duo could do. Between them they fought off the complaints from Jellicoe, still smarting at the removal of his ships, which had been rushed to Devonport Dockyard for essential repairs and fitting out. Fisher was determined that they sail on 11 November, and they did, but with some dockyard workers still working on board. In the South Atlantic, Stoddart received further orders to concentrate his ships off the River Plate estuary and to protect his colliers from German attacks. There were also very particular orders for HMS *Canopus*, at anchor in the harbour at Port Stanley. Churchill, confident that von Spee would make for the Falkland Islands, ordered the *Canopus* to remain. It would take nearly a month for Sturdee to make the long passage south.

MARKING TIME

Although the opposition parties felt that patriotism forbade the asking of questions in the Commons on matters of strategy, dispositions and the progress of the war, the Tories still sought to make personal attacks on the renegade Churchill. In mid-November, Bonar Law asked why Churchill had run the Antwerp operation himself when 'surely [he] has plenty to do in his own Department'. Asquith responded with a most vigorous defence of his colleague. The operation, he said, 'was the responsibility not of any individual Minister, but of the Government as a whole' and Kitchener had been consulted throughout. As to the value of the enterprise, it had been 'a material and most useful factor in the conduct of this campaign'.[16] The Tories were determined to destroy Churchill before the war was out, but had yet to find a way to make their attacks strike home.

Another cross that Churchill had to bear was an endless stream of letters from Jellicoe about the weakness of his fleet and the vulnerability of his bases. In a letter of 12 November, Jellicoe presented a table comparing the strength of the British and German fleets. He considered the case of facing a German attack before the Channel Fleet could rendezvous with the Grand Fleet. In such a scenario, the 'worst feature is the lack of cruisers'. He went on to argue that 'the whole of the 3rd Battle Squadron [at Rosyth] should immediately rejoin my Flag.'[17]

Churchill replied, emphasising that there was a distinct risk of invasion given the deadlock on the Western Front. He expected the High Seas Fleet to come out 'with their whole force'. In such an event 'You will concern yourself exclusively with the destruction of the High Seas Fleet.'[18] Meanwhile the patrol flotillas farther south would move in on the raiding ships. Churchill was insistent that the 3rd Cruiser Squadron should remain at Rosyth.

Jellicoe was not happy with this response. Without advance warning, he argued, it would be impossible to stop a raid or an invasion force. He called for 'a radical change of ideas' and the 'abandonment' of current policy. 'The nation should be informed of the altered circumstances' and a large military force to forestall invasion should be created, he told Churchill.[19] Jellicoe had opened a vast rift between his strategy and that of Churchill and Fisher. The latter two men had total confidence in the navy's ability to deal a fatal blow to any invading force. Landings, they knew, could not be prevented, but the continuing support of beachheads was rendered unfeasible by the power of the Grand Fleet. It had been Churchill's faith in this policy that had enabled the War Council to send six divisions off to France. From now until the day he left the Admiralty, Churchill's determination for bold action would be accompanied by sniping comments from Scapa Flow.

Within a week of this acerbic correspondence, there were rumours of an imminent invasion. The concurrence of favourable tides and moon gave strength to the reports but the night of 20–21 November passed without incident. The failure of the Germans to take advantage of ideal conditions for invasion strengthened Fisher's faith in the navy's capacity to defend Britain's shores. However, it had been 'a splendid "dress rehearsal"', he told Churchill.[20] Despite this optimism, when the moon and tides were again favourable on 8 December, Fisher once more predicted a raid, but the Germans failed to seize the opportunity.

They are happy in the continent. British deluding themselves

THE SEARCH FOR THE OFFENSIVE

Churchill's enthusiasm for offensive action caused unexpected troubles when he planned a bombing raid on the Zeppelin sheds and the hydrogen factory at Friedrichshafen. The town lies on Lake Constance, the shores of which touch Germany, Austria and Switzerland. The proximity of the sheds to neutral Switzerland was to cause a diplomatic rumpus.

The raid took place on 21 November, when four Avro 504 aeroplanes of the RNAS took off from Belfort in France. One failed to become airborne, but the other three flew off towards the target where they dropped eleven 20lb, Hale bombs. One aeroplane was shot down during the raid and the remaining two safely returned.

Two days later, a protest was received from the Swiss government, accusing the pilots of having flown over neutral territory. Sir Edward Grey suggested to Churchill that Britain should apologise if the allegations were true. Churchill objected to this harmless suggestion since the pilots had been given clear instructions not to over-fly neutral territory. Two days later, Grey's intention to apologise brought a rebuttal from Churchill, who was convinced that the pilots had not crossed into Swiss territory. (He did not appear to entertain the possibility of an accidental infringement of territorial rights.)   *wonderful !*

But when a question was asked in the House on the following day, Churchill seemed to defend the right of pilots to fly over neutral territory. While denying that they had done so on this occasion, he argued that since there had been no agreement on flying over neutral territory at the 1910 Paris conference on international air law, no offence had been committed.

Two weeks after the raid there was still no resolution and the British Embassy in Switzerland, now convinced of the Swiss case, grew ever more impatient at London's prevarication. They reported the Swiss government as 'annoyed', while agitation in the press was growing.[21] From Churchill's point of view the incident ended when, faced with a demand from the embassy for closure, he simply scrawled on the document: 'I have sent an answer on other papers.'[22]

———⟫●⟪———

In the adjournment debate on 27 November, Churchill reviewed the progress of the naval war. He spoke about the success that the navy had achieved in limiting German attacks on merchant shipping. At the start of the war, the Admiralty had forecast five per cent losses in the first few months of war. The actual losses amounted to just under two per cent. As to German mining, he downplayed the damage that it could do to British shipping and was remarkably optimistic about measures to counteract the threat. On the subject of submarines, which had introduced 'entirely novel conditions into naval warfare', Churchill painted a ludicrously rosy picture. After emphasising the vital necessity to Britain of keeping sea lanes open he succinctly described the power of a submarine to sink a ship without it 'having a chance to strike a blow in self-defence'; he went on to ask the House to comfort itself by noting that 'our power in submarines is much greater than that of our enemies.' He rightly noted that Germany presented few attackable targets, but failed to draw the conclusion that the submarine was more of a threat to Britain than it was to Germany.

In his discussion of merchant shipping, Churchill happily noted that ninety-seven per cent of its pre-war strength was still sailing the seas. Of the German merchant fleet only some ten per cent was still operational. Although before the war the Germans had built up 'enormous supplies of all kinds of explosives and of all kinds of scientific apparatus directed to warlike purposes', the advantage that gave them would gradually pass. Britain's sea power would 'draw in ... from all over the world ... everything that is needed to procure the most abundant flow of munitions of war which can possibly be required'. Churchill was not alone in his optimistic forecast; members of his professional staff were equally dismissive of the submarine risk to merchant shipping. (The facts were misleading, since in the first few months of the war Germany had only around twenty-five submarines on patrol and the gross tonnage of shipping sunk was in the low tens of thousands. No one foresaw that these modest figures would rise to a fleet of some 160 submarines in late 1917 with shipping losses peaking at over 800,000 tons per month in early 1918.)

There then followed an optimistic comparison of naval losses on each side. Submarine losses were probably equal, but Germany had started with only half the number Britain had. 'Our [torpedo] boats have shown their enormous superiority in gun power,' with no losses, while Germany had lost about nine. Britain had lost more of the older-type cruisers but had maintained superiority in 'fast modern light cruisers'. At the start of the war, Britain had thirty-six to Germany's twenty-five. Of these, Germany had now lost about twenty-five per cent. Churchill was unable to reveal the number of dreadnoughts in service – it was important not to let Germany know how many new ships had been launched – but he assured the House that 'the relative strength of the Fleet is substantially greater now than it was at the outbreak of the War.' He did, though, reveal that from the start of the war to the end of 1915, Britain would launch fifteen large warships against three in Germany. 'All these ships are, of course, of the greatest power of any vessels that have ever been constructed in naval history,' adding 'it is no exaggeration to say that we could afford to lose a super-"Dreadnought" every month for twelve months without any loss occurring to the enemy and yet be in approximately as good a position of superiority as we were at the declaration of the War.'

Churchill ended by saying that he thought the House would welcome these 'few remarks of a general character' since 'despondent views are prejudicial to the public interest.' There was, he concluded, 'every reason for complete confidence in the power of the navy to give effect to the wishes and the purposes of the State and the Empire'.[23]

The poor attendance both for this speech and a similar one from Lloyd George disappointed Christopher Addison, Parliamentary Secretary to the Board of Education. He thought that 'In the years to come it will probably be found that these two speeches will rank as very important.'[24]

————————⊰⊙⊱————————

With a stalemate for Sir John French on the Western Front and Churchill frustrated by German attacks from the Belgian ports, the two men had a mutual interest in driving the German army from the coast. In late October, Churchill told French, 'We must have him off the Belgian coast.'[25]

Towards the end of November, Churchill expanded on his ideas for a joint operation to recover Ostend and Zeebrugge. He proposed that Sir John French advance along the sand dunes of the Belgian coast, while the navy would use up to 200 heavy guns to maintain a protective barrage inshore. Once French had taken the coastal strip, 'we could bring men in at Ostend or Zeebrugge to reinforce you,' he told French. He enthused: 'There is no limit to what could be done by the extreme left-handed push and swoop along the Dutch frontier.'[26] French responded with equal fervour and by the end of November the Cabinet had approved the operation.

Day-by-day the project grew in importance – it was, after all, the only offensive operation that the War Cabinet had under consideration. By 8 December, Churchill was able to tell French of Kitchener's strong support for French's participation; he was to send him the 27th Division. In turn, the Admiralty 'attach the greatest importance to the operation' and were 'making the necessary preparations on an extensive scale'.[27] There was one problem: General Joffre was opposed to the plan.

French and Churchill continued to fuel each other's passion for the operation. French declared himself to be as keen as ever to advance with the navy on his left flank, while Churchill looked forward to denying Zeebrugge to the German submarines. But Churchill was less keen on the requests from the army for general naval support for land operations along the coast. Towards the end of December he explained to French that all he could use for this type of work was ships which were too small to attack the shore-based artillery. He was eager to bring in his large ships for a big combined operation, but only if the prize was worth the risk. Meanwhile, French, still determined on the joint operation, had been scheming with the King of the Belgians in order to get round Joffre's objections. His plan was to mount a combined operation with the Belgians, which would give him a big enough force to advance along the coast.

And then it all fell apart. The modest, sensible, achievable plan of Churchill and French fell victim to the lack of a single planning and command structure for the war. While Churchill and French schemed on one operation, Joffre had another major offensive in mind and Kitchener, despite his support for the Belgian coast operation, was about to wreck the whole Allied operation. We shall leave his bolt-from-the-blue letter of 2 January 1915 to the next chapter. Suffice to say that, by early January, the Belgian coast had become the Dardanelles.

⸻►◄⸻

Unable to use his Grand Fleet in any offensive action, Churchill searched for more modest operations that could both damage Germany and advance the Allied cause. By early December, he was set on the capture of the island of Borkum, on the German coast. He first proposed his scheme at the War Council meeting, on 1 December, when he argued that

> ... the seizure and occupation of a suitable island might render possible the establishment of a flying base, by means of which the movements of the German fleet would be kept under constant observation. It would also enable us to keep large numbers of submarines and destroyers, including the older as well as the newer classes, constantly off the German ports. We could also drop bombs every few days. In these circumstances it would be very difficult for the Germans to prepare for invasion without our knowledge, or to escape from the North Sea ports. Invasion could then only come from the Baltic.[28]

Balfour thought it worth doing if it only required 20,000 men, but Kitchener had reservations about withdrawing soldiers from the Western Front for which 'we should require our best troops'. Fisher was in favour since 'The present defensive attitude of our fleet was bad for its morale, and did not really protect it from the attacks of submarines.'[29]

The next day, Churchill proposed an attack on another German island: Sylt. Balfour, after a discussion with Churchill on the project, began to have qualms. While he sympathised with the idea, Churchill, he told Hankey, could not see how monumentally difficult such an attack would be.

But Borkum was Churchill's passion, even though, as he told Fisher on 21 December, 'I cannot find anyone to make such a plan alive' – most naval officers thought the scheme to be totally insane. Despite this resistance Churchill insisted that 'The key to the naval situation is an overseas base, taken by force and held by force, from which our C [-class] submarines and heavily gunned destroyers can blockade the Bight night and day.'[30]

Early in the following year, when Asquith asked at the War Council what the navy could do to restrain German activities at Zeebrugge, Churchill replied that he 'attached greater importance to the seizure of an island off the German coast'. After describing his scheme, the Council approved it 'in principle' and subject to a feasibility study.[31]

FISHER'S GREATEST TRIUMPH

It is now time to rejoin Sturdee, who left Portsmouth on 11 November for the South Atlantic. Nearly a month later, on 7 December, his ships arrived in Port Stanley on the Falkland Islands where HMS *Canopus* was purposely grounded to guard the harbour against a German attack. Sturdee set about the urgent task of coaling, which was still in progress the next morning when smoke was seen on the horizon.

Vice Admiral von Spee was not aware of the mighty force that Fisher had delivered to one of the most isolated coaling stations in the British Empire. On 8 December, as his leading ships, SMS *Gneisenau* and SMS *Nürnberg*, approached Port Stanley they came under the fire from the massive 12-inch guns on HMS *Canopus*. It was not until some thirty minutes later that the *Gneisenau* was close enough to see the tripod masts of the British battlecruisers. The truth dawned on von Spee's commanders: the quiet isolated coaling station was guarded by the mighty guns of a battleship and lying alongside were some of the pride of Jellicoe's fleet. This was a force that could both outgun and outrun von Spee's squadron. The *Gneisenau* turned back to rejoin *Scharnhorst* and *Leipzig*. Sturdee ordered his ships to take up the pursuit.

With all the speed and precision that Fisher had always claimed for his battlecruisers, the ships began the systematic destruction of von Spee's flotilla. The flagship *Scharnhorst* sank at 4.17 p.m. with von Spee on board, and then the *Gneisenau* was scuttled at 6.00 p.m. The *Nürnberg* sank at 7.30 p.m., and the *Leipzig* sank at 9.05 p.m. The *Dresden* escaped, only to be scuttled after being attacked at the Juan Fernández Islands in March 1915.

The British losses were ten dead and nineteen wounded and the action saw the end of the German cruiser menace outside home waters. The Kaiser's big ships were now all contained in the North and Baltic Seas.

The Battle of the Falkland Islands was Fisher's greatest triumph. It was his plan and his ships combined with his determination to be merciless in war that avenged Coronel. It was, though, his swansong. The New Year was to bring a return to acrimony and discord, so hastening an end to the reign of the dynamic pair. Churchill, too, must be given credit since it was he who placed his faith in Fisher and gave him this chance of glory. And he had been correct about HMS *Canopus*.

Churchill was generous in his praise for Fisher: 'This was your show and your luck. ... Your flair was quite true. Let us have more victories together and confound all our foes abroad – and (don't forget) – at home.'[32] And Hankey – that shrewdest of judges of military matters – congratulated him on his 'triple triumph': 'A personal triumph. A triumph of correct strategical principle. A triumph for your type of ship.'[33]

THE EAST COAST RAIDS

On 14 December, Sir Arthur Wilson alerted Churchill to signs that German battlecruisers were about to venture out into the North Sea and after a brief discussion they decided that the uncertainty of the move did not justify alerting the Grand Fleet. This decision, Churchill explained after the event, was partly taken 'to save wear and tear of machinery' and was 'much regretted'.[34]

Jellicoe was ordered to send a sizeable force from Scapa Flow, led by Vice Admiral Beatty with his Battlecruiser Squadron, and supported by the 2nd Battle Squadron under Vice Admiral Sir George Warrender. To this force was added the 1st Light Cruiser Squadron under Commodore William Goodenough.

Churchill was in his bath on the morning of 16 December, when he first heard hard news of Germany's intent. He opened the bathroom door and an officer thrust a signal into his still dripping hand: Hartlepool was under bombardment from German battlecruisers. He dressed quickly and rushed to the War Room.

The residents of Hartlepool had been eating their breakfasts when shells began to fall on the town at around 8.00 a.m. According to local reports most residents of the town stayed indoors as the bombardment progressed. Three churches were hit, two of the town's gasometers were punctured and the lamp of the lighthouse was smashed. The local hospital escaped damage. When the German ships withdrew the town was left strewn with debris. Dead and injured lay amongst the ruined houses and workplaces. Some 100 people had been killed. Similar attacks took place the same day on Whitby and Scarborough. In total 105 people were killed and 525 injured.

Forewarned, the British had considerable forces patrolling off the Dogger Bank ready to intercept the German ships on their return to port. In their path lay four fast light cruisers of the 2nd Battle Squadron, four of Beatty's mighty battlecruisers plus two of Tyrwhitt's light cruisers and flotillas of destroyers. But, in the days before radar, fog and severe weather were enough to limit the British sightings of German ships to occasional glimpses of lone vessels. Despite desperate searching by Beatty's force, the German raiders slipped home. Only three ships on each side received minor damage.

Gloom hung over the Admiralty the next morning. Addison noted in his diary that 'Churchill was best left alone this morning, so sick with disappointment was he; and no wonder.'[35] Surprisingly, Fisher, usually so intolerant of failure, told Jellicoe 'not to be downhearted' and put his disappointment down to 'bad luck' and 'thick weather'.[36]

With no great victory to gloat over, Churchill fell back on public relations when he released his letter to the Mayor of Scarborough to the press. He had an easy target, given the cowardly and inhuman German raid, and he mocked the size of the force used to attack unarmed civilians, saying, 'Practically the whole fast cruiser strength of the German Navy ... has been risked for the passing pleasure of killing as many English people as possible.' He also rightly predicted the effect that the raids would have on public opinion when he told the Mayor that 'Whatever feats of arms the German Navy may hereafter perform, the stigma of the baby-killers will brand its officers and men while sailors sail the seas.'[37] Asquith was shocked by the tone of Churchill's letter. It was, he told Venetia Stanley, 'banal' and composed of 'cheapish rhetoric'.[38]

NURSING FRENCH AND UPSETTING KITCHENER

A few days later, on 17 December, Churchill wrote to Asquith to ask if he had any objection to his visiting French in order to discuss their proposed joint coastal operation. Asquith evaded the issue by telling Churchill that he ought not to go without Kitchener's approval. Churchill duly sent the War Minister a note explaining the purpose of his visit.

Instead of receiving a reply – civil or otherwise – from Kitchener, Churchill received another letter from Asquith. This recounted Kitchener's strong disapproval of Churchill's visit to French. The War Minister went so far as to claim that these visits were the cause of the friction between him and French. (It was absolutely true that there was friction between the two men but, as we have seen in Chapter 2, Churchill's visits were not the cause.) A furious Churchill wrote to Kitchener, complaining about his having talked to Asquith about the visits rather than to Churchill himself. Far from being reassured by this reply, Kitchener turned up the heat, writing to Churchill:

> I cannot of course object to your going over to discuss naval co-operation with Sir John French; but at the same [time] I think I ought to tell you frankly that your private arrangements with French as regards land forces is [sic] rapidly rendering my position and responsibility as S. of S. impossible.[39]

When writing to Venetia Stanley the following day, Asquith told her of 'a pretty abusive letter' that Churchill had sent Kitchener. Only a man as touchy as Kitchener could have taken Churchill's reasonable, if pained, letter to be abusive.[40] The correspondence continued, centring on Kitchener's denying that he had suggested that Churchill was the cause of difficulties between him and French.

That this quarrel became so serious can in part be blamed on Asquith, who should have supported Churchill more strongly in working closely with French. In fact, Asquith personally had no objection to these visits and in January happily sent Churchill off on behalf of the War Council to see French.

As this incident drew to a close, Asquith claimed that he had spoken in frank terms to Sir John French about Churchill's visits and found French to be 'substantially of the same opinion'.[41] Nothing in French's correspondence supports this. Indeed, French often pleaded with Churchill to visit him. It would seem that Asquith had heard what he wanted to hear and failed to pick up the value that French attached to Churchill's support.

On 23 December, whether by coincidence or not, Kitchener opened up another dispute with Churchill just as the quarrel about the visits to Sir John French came to an end. His target this time was Churchill's numerous land-based operations in France. In responding to Kitchener's objections to these forces, Churchill admitted to having five units at work. A Commander Astle Littlejohns was running three armoured trains; a Captain Geoffrey Howard had charge of some fifty-five omnibuses, which were being used to transport troops; then there were Churchill's RNAS aeroplanes, armoured cars and a 15-inch howitzer. Churchill put up a valiant defence of these units, listing the good work that they had done. He justified the buses on the grounds that they had transported some fifteen battalions of troops. The trains should stay, since French and Rawlinson had both made use of them. And so it went on, but Churchill had missed the point. Kitchener did not dispute the value of the units; he questioned their being under Churchill's command.

In reply, Kitchener emphasised that he considered land transport to be an army responsibility and added that 'the morale of the army in the field' was being damaged by Churchill's arrangements.[42] Wisely, Churchill gave way and simply asked Kitchener what he would like him to do with the naval forces then in France.

What happened next is not clear, but we find Kitchener still attacking Churchill over the armoured cars in February 1915. Since the second row arose from Churchill's offer to French of cars and men, it would seem that Churchill had not learnt his lesson. The truth of the matter was that Churchill longed to be a general and was wildly jealous of the land war, which was so much more glamorous than the limited activities of the Royal Navy.

THE YEAR'S END

Although Kitchener had forecast at the start of the war that it would last for at least three years, in late December Churchill now foresaw an early conclusion. So when Fisher proposed to lay a number of minefields around Heligoland, Churchill agreed, but decried 'scattering a few bouquets of mines' and 'building fast ships that will not be ready until it is all over' – an extraordinary turn-around from his strong support for Fisher's shipbuilding programme two months earlier. He then optimistically predicted that 'Long before they can be finished we shall have smashed up the German Navy in harbour with our monitors, or they will have fought their battle in blue water, or peace will have been signed.'[43] (Fisher was busy building these monitors – low freeboard, shallow draft ships that were basically floating gun-platforms. He saw them as key to waging a naval war in the Baltic; Churchill wanted them for attacks on the German coast.)

After five months of war, Kitchener, Churchill, Hankey and Asquith were all in despair over the stalemate in France. Churchill and Hankey both sought to define the war forward when they each chose to write an end-of-year review for Asquith.

Churchill's review was narrowly focused and after declaring that he thought neither side could expect to make progress on the Western Front, he set out the case for obtaining 'naval command of the Baltic'. There followed an outline as to how this could be done, beginning with 'the blocking of the Heligoland debouche'. Then he added 'the capture of a German island for an oversea base is the first indispensable step'. Borkum was his choice.

Turning to more general principles, Churchill set out the three phases of the naval war: 'First the clearance of the seas and the recall of foreign squadrons, that is nearly completed; second, the closing of the Elbe – that we now have to do; and third, the domination of the Baltic – that would be decisive.'[44]

This report shows clearly that, despite the trial bombardment of the Dardanelles in November, and despite Churchill's view that Gallipoli should be taken to protect Egypt, at the end of 1914 neither plan had any appeal to him. His own staff knew only too well that he was obsessed with Borkum and the Baltic. We shall see in the next chapter how Kitchener and the War Council pushed a reluctant Churchill towards the Dardanelles.

Hankey's preference was to drive Turkey out of the war by using three army corps to take Constantinople. By liberating the Dardanelles, the Allies would be free to send arms to Russia and to import wheat. The price of wheat in the west would fall, argued Hankey, and 350,000 tons of shipping would be freed from operations in the east.

Just as it is important to understand Churchill's thinking as the year ended, so we must understand Asquith's reaction. After noting that both Hankey and Churchill thought 'the existing deadlock in West and East is likely to continue' Asquith firmly placed himself in the same camp when he wrote in a letter to Venetia Stanley: 'When our New Armies are ready, as they will be soon, it seems folly to send them to positions where they are not wanted and where, in Winston's phrase, they will "chew barbed wire" or be wasted in futile attacks.'

Asquith showed no preference between Hankey's favoured action against Turkey and Churchill's desire to command the Baltic, but he clearly sympathised with their determination to avoid further slaughter in France and seek a quick end to the war. The weary Prime Minister concluded: 'I am profoundly dissatisfied with the immediate prospect – an enormous waste of life and money day after day with no appreciable progress.'[45]

By the end of the year, Churchill's style as First Lord of the Admiralty was well-established. Many officers in Admiralty House were appalled at the authority that he took upon himself. In a reflective moment after the war Churchill thought he had been too impetuous: 'I seem to have been too ready to undertake tasks which were hazardous or even forlorn.'[46] As examples he cited his taking over the air defence of London and his Antwerp operation. It was a rare moment of self-flagellation.

What truly upset the professionals was Churchill's capacity for wild schemes. Oliver recalled afternoon meetings in the First Lord's office where 'future possible and impossible operations' were discussed by Churchill, Fisher and Wilson. Under the impossible heading Oliver placed Borkum (Churchill), a Baltic landing (Fisher) and bombarding Heligoland (Wilson). He hated these projects, but he had no fear of their implementation since 'two of the three were always violently opposed to the plan of the third under discussion.'[47] As we have already seen, Richmond was so horrified at these proposals he ceased to comment on them.

More insidious was the way Churchill blurred the boundary between the political role of the First Lord and the professional role of the First Sea Lord. Within weeks of taking office Fisher noted that 'Winston has now monopolised all initiative in the Admiralty.' While he admired Churchill's capacity for work – 'absolutely amazing!' – he was concerned at the diminished role for the professional staff.[48] All these factors were to come to a head in May 1915, when the final clash between Fisher and Churchill took its dreadful toll.

For all his vigorous commitment to the Admiralty, Churchill was at heart a general. He was envious of his brother Jack and longed to free himself from his desk-bound job so that they could ride into battle together. His fierce courage and his total indifference to death that he had displayed on the North West Frontier and at Omdurman in his youth were undiminished. With the least excuse he would go over to France, both to discuss the war with the generals and to visit the Front. The sound of artillery thrilled him; the fire and smoke of weaponry were his adrenaline. His desire for military action distressed his wife, who pleaded with him to remain with the navy 'which will in the end decide the War'. She grieved at his gloom and dissatisfaction with his high post. 'It was wicked,' she told him, 'not to be swelling with pride at being 1st Lord of the Admiralty during the greatest War since the beginning of the World.'[49]

But the mere occupation of a high post was not enough for Churchill. He wanted action. On 31 December 1914, he was determined that it should take place at Borkum. But there was to be no Borkum adventure in 1915 or at any other time. Kitchener had other plans.

A shameful Cavalry charge after the dervishes had been

CHAPTER 6

THE DARDANELLES

The one brilliant idea of the war. – Asquith[1]

MANAGEMENT STYLE

By early January 1915, Churchill was widely seen as the most successful and hard-working Cabinet Minister. The British press began to take an interest in his salary. Before the days of global companies, most of the highest remunerated positions were in the upper echelons of the Establishment. The Archbishop of Canterbury was the highest paid at £15,000. But, puzzled the *Manchester Guardian*, there appeared to be 'a standardised salary' of £5,000 'at the top of the tree in England'. Asquith, Lloyd George and Kitchener were paid at this rate. So how was it that Churchill 'who seems to have as much to do as any of them' merited only £4,500? No answer came.[2]

The first two months of the Churchill-Fisher partnership had passed off without serious incident. Some indication of the simmering rivalry came in a letter that Churchill wrote on 4 January, which began 'We must be agreed on certain points.' Amongst the items that Churchill listed was Borkum: '[It] is key to all Northern possibilities' – something that Fisher never accepted.[3] Perhaps the most significant thing about this letter is that there was absolutely no mention of any Dardanelles project. As we shall soon see, despite what is said in so many published works, Churchill was not the instigator of the Dardanelles operation. On 4 January, his priorities lay in the North Sea.

The root of the friction that Churchill generated lay in his management style. Lloyd George's secretary Frances Stevenson noted in her diary that Fisher was complaining that Churchill 'overrules everyone at the Admiralty, even those who have far more experience than he'. She added, 'If he continues in his domineering course they fear there may be a catastrophe.' This forecast was to prove only too true.[4]

The day after Stevenson's diary note, Churchill once more demonstrated his prescriptive approach to running the Admiralty. Asquith had decided that it would be beneficial for Jellicoe to attend the War Council. Churchill sought every means he could find to block this decision. He filled an exceedingly long letter to Asquith with one persuasive excuse after another as to why Jellicoe should not be present. But, as Asquith noted, 'He is all for having French at these gatherings, but doesn't like his own man to be summoned & cross-examined.'[5]

Fisher could be difficult, too. He had always been prone to resigning and an opportunity to indulge this habit arose in early January over German air raids. He was insistent that the only way to stop the raids was to threaten to retaliate by shooting all the German prisoners in Britain. When Churchill demurred, Fisher sent in his resignation since 'the Admiralty under present arrangements will be responsible for the massacre coming suddenly upon and unprepared for by the Public.'[6] In reply, Churchill agreed to put his views to the Cabinet while brushing aside the resignation paragraph.

That minor quarrel was soon settled. But as the war entered a new phase, Churchill opened up what was to prove an unbridgeable gap between himself and Fisher. It was all over the Dardanelles campaign.

THE TRUE ORIGIN OF THE DARDANELLES CAMPAIGN

Popular mythology names Churchill as the originator of the Dardanelles campaign. In fact that honour goes to Kitchener. No longer able to repulse the onslaught of the German armies on his troops, Grand Duke Nicholas of Russia appealed to the British government for help at the end of 1914. He asked for 'a demonstration of some kind against the Turk'.[7] This message – delivered to the British Ambassador to Russia – reached Kitchener via Grey. The following day, 2 January 1915, Kitchener, without consulting any of his colleagues, promised the Grand Duke that 'steps will be taken to make a demonstration against the Turks.'[8] To make good his word he then wrote to Churchill, asking him whether there was any naval action that would deny Constantinople to the Turks. To remove any shadow of doubt as to his commitment to a new theatre of war, Kitchener then wrote to tell French, 'The feeling here is gaining ground, although it is essential to defend the line we now hold, troops over and above what is [sic] necessary for that service could be better employed elsewhere.'[9] And so, within twenty-four hours of receiving the Grand Duke's appeal, Kitchener had committed the British government to a new front in the Eastern Mediterranean.

On the following day, Churchill, at Kitchener's request, telegraphed Vice Admiral Sackville Carden, Commander of the British Squadron in the Mediterranean, to ask for his opinion. Churchill wrote: 'Do you consider the forcing of the Dardanelles by ships alone a practicable operation [?]' He added, 'Importance of results would justify severe loss.'[10] Quite coincidentally, Fisher, before knowing of Kitchener's move, had set out his own plan for attacking Turkey with 75,000 troops. He scorned 'a futile bombardment of the Dardanelles'.[11]

While Kitchener had settled on the Eastern Mediterranean as his new theatre of war, Churchill refused to relinquish his passion for an attack on the island of Borkum, for which he used the code name Sylt. (An odd choice since at one time Sylt was a proposed target.) On 3 January, he urged his staff to begin serious planning. In a note to Fisher, Wilson and Oliver, Churchill set out the resources needed and proposed two possible dates for the operation – 1 March and 15 April. He provided an outline plan of attack and emphasised that the island should be taken 'at all costs'.[12] This, Churchill declared, could be achieved three days after launching an attack. A week later he was struggling to persuade Jellicoe of the importance of Borkum as he saw the capture of the island as 'the first step in an aggressive warfare' which would 'beat him [the enemy] into all his ports'.[13]

Few officers thought the project practicable. Characteristically, Richmond's response as noted in his diary entry of 4 January was couched in the most extreme language, declaring that 'It is quite mad. The reasons for capturing it are NIL, the possibilities about the same. I have never read such an idiotic, amateur piece of work as this outline in my life.'[14] To counteract such views, Churchill set out his case in letters to Jellicoe and others. The possession of Borkum, he told Jellicoe, was essential to the army's operations, but Jellicoe was not convinced, basing his objections partly on the sheer impracticality of taking an island so near to Germany. He also feared the cost to the Grand Fleet of defending the island once captured. His preference was for more extensive mining and he recommended blocking the entrance to Zeebrugge – an action that was finally achieved on 23 April 1918. No doubt Churchill's commitment to Borkum was strengthened by the strong support which came from Keyes, who was confident that, once taken, the island could be held by small craft and submarines.[15]

A few days later at the War Council, Asquith asked what the navy could do to restrain German activities at Zeebrugge. Churchill replied that 'he attached greater importance to the seizure of an island off the German coast'. Churchill won the argument that day and the Council approved his scheme 'in principle' but subject to a feasibility study.[16] This was more than enough encouragement for Churchill to continue to advance his Borkum plan at every opportunity. While the rest of the War Council looked to the east, Churchill obsessed over Borkum. In early March, aware that six of Fisher's monitors were nearing completion, Churchill told Jellicoe that 'the attack on Borkum should take place on or about the 15th May.'[17]

THE BELGIAN COAST CAMPAIGN

Nor had Churchill and French discarded their Belgian coast project, but it was stalled on 4 January by a dispute between French and Kitchener. The former wanted a share of the latter's new armies. But Kitchener dreamed of his great forces being engaged in immense and decisive battles in new theatres and under independent commands.

He baulked at the notion of his men being used to fill the gaps in French's line – an action which Asquith said was 'repugnant in the highest degree to K'.[18] Certain that the dispute would be settled in his favour, French told Churchill that he was confident that Kitchener would let the two of them work together on their coastal advance. For the moment all he could do was to beg a visit from Churchill. But both men knew that they had little support for their project; Kitchener had no time for it and Joffre was totally opposed. Consequently, the Churchill-French negotiations took place in the utmost secrecy. French reminded Churchill not to tell a soul, and to burn his letters – a command that Churchill fortunately chose to ignore.

Meanwhile, Fisher was determined on his own plan to land 100,000 men on the Baltic coast. This led him to support any argument that would undermine competing operations. In an attempt to steer Churchill away from both Borkum and the Belgian coast operation, Fisher wrote to him to warn of the competing demands on resources. He reminded the First Lord that (taking into account inevitable losses) there were not enough ships to simultaneously attack Borkum, run an operation off the Belgian coast and land an army on the Baltic coast in order to take the Kiel Canal. Only Borkum had been approved by the War Council, but Fisher was happy to bolster his case with his own wild and fanciful schemes.

French's formal request for an additional 50,000 men for a move on Ostend and Zeebrugge was put to the War Council on 7 January. It was discussed in the context of the total commitments being made by the army. In his summary of the discussion, Asquith concluded that the troops could not be made available to French 'without dislocating the organisation not only of the existing Territorial Force, but also of the future armies'. Churchill challenged this decision, saying that French's plan to clear the Germans off the coast was of great importance to the Admiralty. If Kitchener could not supply the troops then 'the Admiralty would have to do their best to deal with Zeebrugge themselves'.[19] Pressing his argument, he reminded the Council of the serious threat to troop transports caused by the German occupation of the Belgian coast. The Council was unmoved and agreed that French had to concur with Joffre's plan for a new offensive. Belgium would have to wait.

After the meeting, Churchill wrote at length and in sympathy to French on 8 January to tell him how the discussion had gone. Kitchener had put French's case very fairly but 'he adduced a great mass of evidence showing the probability of a renewed German assault upon the Anglo-French lines'. Churchill urged French to attend the next War Council, when there would be further discussion of the role of the new armies. Referring to one secret paper that he had already sent to French, Churchill now sent him some more notes. Knowing French's sensitive nature, he concluded by telling him that 'we are on the stage of history'.[20] French replied the next day to say how determined he was not to let go of the coastal operation. In reply, Churchill reasserted his own commitment to the project and rightly predicted that Joffre's alternative – Ypres – would prove 'a bleak and dreary role for the Br army'.

On the other hand, 'The coast … offers not only the prospect of a definite success, but relief from a grave danger that threatens our sea-communications, etc.'[21]

French took Churchill's advice and attended the War Council on 13 January. Given that his full plan for a coastal assault was, at best, on hold, the discussion centred on a naval attack on Zeebrugge. Fisher opposed this since 'the navy had only a limited number of battleships to lose'. As to Churchill, he offered only a perfunctory defence of the plan, concluding that 'The possession of Zeebrugge by the Germans would not kill our naval supremacy.'[22] His commitment to Borkum far exceeded his allegiance to either the Dardanelles or Zeebrugge operations. On the other hand, Kitchener and Grey were supportive enough of Zeebrugge for it to remain on the table for a decision in February.

French refused to give up the full coastal attack and returned to France and began to refine his plans, based on just one additional corps of British troops. He had made an agreement with Joffre, which allowed him to also make use of Belgian troops. On 23 January, French asked Churchill if he could supply a few 15-inch naval guns. These Churchill provided a few days later. Effectively, though, the Dardanelles were to take priority from now on.

THE WAR COUNCIL AND THE DARDANELLES

Having examined the competing campaigns that were on the table in January, we can now return to the one that found favour and became reality.

On 5 January, Carden had replied to Churchill's request for an assessment of the bombardment proposals. He wrote: 'I do not consider the Dardanelles can be rushed,' but 'they might be forced by extended operations by a large number of ships.'[23] Meanwhile, Jackson had written his own appreciation of the project in which he forecast considerable damage to ships and warned Churchill of the risk of a force finding its line of retreat blocked. But Jackson did not go so far as to advise against it, nor did he assess the value of a successful outcome. These two opinions were enough to keep the plan in play.

In reply Churchill told Carden on 6 January that 'Your view is agreed with by high authorities here' and asked him for more details on how the operation could be carried out.[24] Authors such as Nicholas Black make much of the fact that Churchill used the phrase 'high authorities' in a manner which would have given Carden the impression that one such authority was Jackson.[25] Whether this was a deliberate attempt at deceit or not is debatable, although the point is somewhat academic since, at this time, Churchill had no enthusiasm for the Dardanelles proposal. (This may explain why he did not bother to consult the junior sea lords about the enterprise.) It was left to Kitchener to bring the topic up at the War Council on 8 January, when he made a forceful plea for action in the Dardanelles, calling it 'the most suitable objective' for a new theatre of the war. 'If successful,' he told the Council, 'it would re-establish communication with Russia; settle the Near Eastern question; draw in Greece and, perhaps, Bulgaria and Roumania; and release wheat and shipping now locked up in the Black Sea.' Churchill was not impressed and agreed to do no more than 'study' the operation, insisting that it was much more important to pursue 'the possibility of an action in Northern Europe'. In particular, he pressed both the need to draw Holland into the war and the value of an assault on Zeebrugge to reduce submarine attacks.[26]

Carden's proposed plan arrived at the Admiralty early on the morning of 12 January; in it he assertively set out four tasks for his fleet, beginning with the destruction of the defences at the mouth of the Dardanelles. He then proposed to clear all the Turkish defences up to and including Kepez Point battery No. 8, then attack the

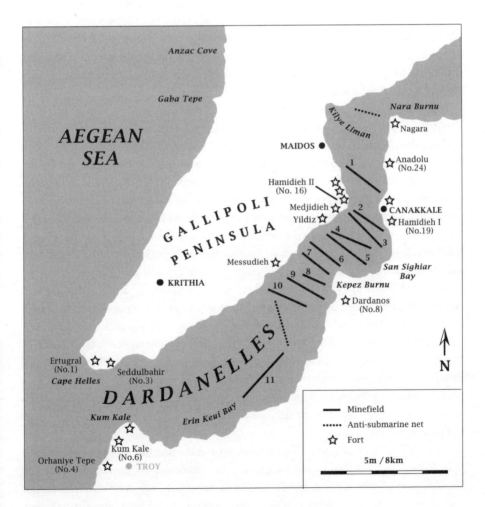

The forts and minefields at the Dardanelles.

Narrows and, finally, move on to the Sea of Marmara. He forecast that he could achieve this in a month, with a heavy expenditure of ammunition.[27]

At the War Council meeting on 13 January, Churchill reported on Carden's telegram. 'The sense of Carden's reply' he told the Council, 'was that it was impossible to rush the Dardanelles.' However, Carden thought that he could 'demolish the forts one by one'. On Carden's advice, Churchill said that the task would require 'Three modern warships, carrying the heaviest guns ... for reducing some of the more modern works'. Lloyd George liked the plan and Kitchener said it was 'worth trying'. He added 'We could leave off the bombardment if it did not prove effective' – words that were to haunt the Council for months to come. When Asquith summed up at the end of the meeting, he committed the Council to 'a naval expedition in February to bombard and take the Gallipoli peninsula, with Constantinople as its objective'.[28] No one asked how ships could take a peninsula or, even more to the point, a vast city. Hankey later recalled the atmosphere of this pivotal meeting. Despite Churchill's low-key presentation the Council was electrified as it forgot 'the dreary vista of a "slogging match" on the Western Front' and switched its attention 'to brighter prospects, as they seemed, in the Mediterranean'.[29]

Following the War Council decision, Churchill told Carden that his plan had been 'approved in principle'. Rear Admiral John de Robeck was likely to be his second-in-command and Carden was to have the new HMS *Queen Elizabeth* armed with 15-inch guns, which he had requested as his flagship. 'The sooner we can begin the better' concluded Churchill.[30] By 17 January, Kitchener had made plans for the 29th Division to sail to Lemnos (the proposed base for the expedition) and he had made provision to send other forces to Egypt as a convenient holding place. Thus, even before Churchill had shown any real enthusiasm for the Dardanelles venture, Kitchener was pouring in military resources. He clearly had not taken seriously Carden's claim to be able to take the Dardanelles by ships alone and was making his own contingency plans.

Despite Churchill's lack of enthusiasm for the project, he and Carden pressed ahead with arrangements for the attack. There was to be a two-week refit for HMS *Indefatigable* at Malta, while the French navy was asked to provide minesweepers. Anticipating success in the Dardanelles, Churchill requested the Grand Duke of Russia to have troops ready to exploit the expected breakthrough. More ominously, though, Fisher began to show signs of his determined resistance to the venture. In a private letter to Jellicoe, he deplored the use of vessels in the Mediterranean which were 'all urgently required at the decisive theatre at home!' He had no choice, he said, but to resign.[31]

Churchill's lack of faith in the Dardanelles project led him to propose a contingency plan in the event of failure. He suggested to Kitchener on 20 January, that the Turkish port of Alexandretta should be seized simultaneously with the Dardanelles bombardment. If the latter succeeded, Alexandretta would be a bonus. If it failed, the Dardanelles operation could be represented as a feint to disguise the taking of

Alexandretta. Fisher meanwhile agitated for the return of the destroyer depot ship HMS *Blenheim* from the Mediterranean to Jellicoe. His behaviour contrasted sharply with the stream of telegrams from Carden containing request upon request for ships and equipment.

While Fisher sought allies in his battle to halt the Dardanelles operation, Churchill acted to increase his own hold on the project. Although he welcomed the small French naval presence at the Dardanelles he was determined that the Royal Navy should run the operation. Dreading the thought of an attempted French takeover he forbade Carden to leave for Malta until Rear Admiral de Robeck had arrived to temporarily relieve him. In fact, Churchill had acted just in time to rebuff a French demand that they should control all naval operations in the Mediterranean. On 23 January, he appealed to Grey for support against the French, which was readily given.

By the third week of January, a frustrated and anxious Fisher sought out Maurice Hankey. In his distress he told Hankey how he had fought against Churchill's ship dispositions for the campaign, but in vain: 'he out-argues me.'[32] Hankey, perturbed by what he had heard, went to see Asquith who, in turn, recounted the tale to Venetia Stanley in his daily letter. With typical nonchalance Asquith saw no reason to act on hearing that his First Lord paid no attention to the professional advice of the First Sea Lord.

On 25 January, Fisher turned once more to Hankey, this time to ask for his help in drafting a paper for the War Council on his concerns over the use of the navy to attack coastal fortifications – a clear attack on both Churchill's Belgian coast and Dardanelles plans. Bombardment should only be used, he argued, when it was necessary to maintain supremacy at sea. Fisher asked that this note be circulated to the War Council but Asquith refused his request. However, a copy was seen by Churchill. In response, Churchill drew up his own paper for the War Council but he too was refused circulation. Neither party having won the point, Churchill contented himself by writing a private letter to Fisher in which he naively declared that 'There is no difference in principle between us.'[33]

With only two days to go to the next War Council, Fisher was at breaking point. He had appealed to Churchill, Hankey and Asquith but not one of them had taken his concerns seriously. He made one last attempt by means of an implied resignation. The War Council was due to meet on 28 January at 11.00 a.m. Early that day, Fisher handed Hankey a letter to pass on to Asquith in which he declared that he would not attend the Council since 'I am not in accord with the First Lord.'[34] This brought a swift response from Asquith who, through Churchill, told Fisher that his 'presence at the War Council [was] indispensable'.[35] In good head-masterly manner, Asquith commanded the quarrelling pair to see him at 11.00 a.m. The War Council would have to wait.

What precisely was said when the three men met is not known, but it was enough to get Fisher to the Council, which started at 11.20 a.m. and was to be the first of three meetings that day. At this first meeting Churchill reported on the enthusiastic reply that he had received from the Grand Duke to his plans for the Dardanelles. Still by no means strongly committed to the project, Churchill reminded his colleagues that the operation 'involved some risks'. Before the members could offer their views, a dismayed Fisher interjected to say that he had been told that the Dardanelles would not be discussed that day. If Asquith had previously given Fisher that assurance, he now departed from it. The matter, said Asquith, 'could not well be left in abeyance'.[36]

What happened next is of great significance in understanding the corporate nature of the Dardanelles campaign. It was Churchill who warned of the risks that day, but no one sought to discuss them. Instead, Kitchener 'considered the naval attack to be vitally important'. Its accomplishment 'would be equivalent to a successful campaign fought with the new armies'. Balfour declared that 'It was difficult to imagine a more helpful operation.' And Grey pronounced that 'the Turks would be paralysed with fear when they heard that the forts were being destroyed one by one.'[37] Asquith, elsewhere, declared the operation to be 'the one brilliant idea of the war'.[38] This discussion thoroughly debunks the statement of the Dardanelles Commission that Kitchener was not responsible for adopting the action. It was his enthusiasm and his phrases such as 'vitally important' and 'equivalent to a successful campaign fought with the new armies' that carried the day. Within four months, when the naval attack had failed, all the blame for a project that had received such universal and enthusiastic support would be solidly placed on Churchill – the one person who had warned of the risks.

On that same morning, Churchill also reported to the Council that the Admiralty was building monitors to attack Borkum (his dream scheme) and new light cruisers for the Baltic (Fisher's plan for instant German capitulation). No voices were raised against these plans. When the Council met for the third time that day, at 6.30 p.m., Churchill formally reported that the Admiralty had decided 'to make a naval attack on the Dardanelles'.[39]

THE BATTLE OF DOGGER BANK

The First World War was remarkable for the infrequency of naval battles. The last to take place under Churchill's administration was the Battle of Dogger Bank on 24 January. A German squadron under Admiral Franz von Hipper in command of the 1st Scouting Group set out with seven warships and eighteen destroyers to attack British fishing vessels at Dogger Bank. Unknown to von Hipper, Room 40 had decoded the German naval signals. When his group arrived at the rendezvous he found himself confronted by Vice Admiral Beatty's force of twelve warships and thirty-five destroyers, compelling von Hipper to turn for home. The British force gave chase and in the ensuing action, sank the heavy cruiser SMS *Blücher* and seriously damaged the battlecruiser SMS *Seydlitz*. On the British side, HMS *Lion* suffered serious damage and one destroyer was put out of action. The result was considered a great victory, which it was in the sense that, once again, the Royal Navy had beaten off ships of the German High Seas Fleet. But, Churchill was deeply disappointed at the sinking of only one ship. He noted also that they 'fled so fast' – something that was to be a habit when the two fleets met.[40] Indeed, so appalled were the Germans by the outcome that they abandoned their attempt to use warships against the Grand Fleet and turned to submarine attacks on merchant vessels.

There would have been a greater victory, but for an error on Fisher's part, which he readily admitted the next day. He had sent Beatty to a rendezvous point in front of von Hipper's forces. He realised afterwards that he should have directed Beatty to position his ships behind those of von Hipper, cutting off their escape route. Churchill never criticised Fisher on this point.

TAKING STOCK

On 4 February, Germany announced a submarine blockade of Great Britain, declaring any ship approaching British shores to be a potential target. In theory, this should have led to a massive increase in ships being sunk by submarines, but the effect in the remaining months of the Churchill–Fisher administration was small. In May, the number of ships sunk remained at the 100,000 tons a month level.

The only other significant event to interrupt the first phase of the Dardanelles campaign was Churchill's address to the Commons on the work of the Royal Navy in the first six months of the war. On 15 February, he praised the House for having made such generous provision for the navy over the previous five years: 'On the declaration of war we were able to count upon a Fleet of sufficient superiority for all our needs, with a good margin for safety in vital matters, fully mobilised, placed in its war stations, supplied and equipped with every requirement down to the smallest detail that could be foreseen.' When the test of mobilisation for war came, 'we were able to man, as I told the House we should be able, every ship in the navy fit to send to sea.' (This comment was aimed at Admiral Lord Charles Beresford who for years had declared that the navy was undermanned.) The navy, Churchill asserted, had now almost cleared the seas of German ships, the Battle of the Falklands having seen the end of the first phase of the naval war. He proudly told the House that 'Only two small German cruisers and two armed merchantmen remain at large of all their formidable preparations for the attack on our trade routes.'

Some of Churchill's remarks showed how easy the war at sea had been so far. The great German submarine campaign was as yet a horror unimagined, so Churchill was able to report that of '4,465 arrivals ... and 3,600 sailings ... only nineteen vessels have been sunk by the enemy, and only four of these vessels have been sunk by above-water craft.' As to the blockade of Germany, which was then limited to essential war materials, Churchill could declare it to have been a major success in restricting German imports of materials such as copper and manganese. As to food – so far excluded from blockade – Churchill warned that soon it too might have to be treated as contraband of war since Germany 'has, as a matter of deliberate policy, placed herself outside all international obligations'.[41] (This was a reference to Germany treating the North Sea as a war zone.)

FORTS UNDER FIRE

By the end of the first week of February, Carden was able to report that his preparations were going well and that he expected to begin his attack on the forts on 15 February. At the War Council on 9 February – a meeting dominated by a discussion of Serbia – Churchill had just a few minutes to report on the Mediterranean operations. All was in hand for 15 February. At this point Kitchener intervened to remind Churchill that 'if the navy required the assistance of land forces at a later stage, that assistance would be forthcoming.'[42] Once more the War Secretary had demonstrated his strong support for what is often portrayed as a wild Churchillian-style adventure.

Later that day, Churchill received a message from Carden to say that he had delayed his start date to 19 February because of a lack of minesweepers. Churchill showed no concern but Asquith was upset since, as he wrote to Venetia Stanley, the operation 'is all important as a preliminary to our demarche in the Balkans'.[43]

Although Kitchener had made plans to put a large body of troops on standby in the Mediterranean, there had been no discussion as to how they would be used. But on 13 February, after talking to Hankey – 'whose views are always worth hearing' – Asquith came round to his opinion that 'the naval operations … should be supported by landing a fairly strong military force.'[44] This appears to be the conversation that resulted in an informal meeting of the War Council on 16 February, of which no minutes were kept, although Hankey did record its conclusions. He noted that 'this meeting commenced as an informal conference between one or two Ministers, others subsequently being called in.' Given that the four conclusions of the 'meeting' all concerned sending troops to the Dardanelles it is likely that the discussions arose from Asquith seeking the opinions of others on the issue – perhaps even chivvying Kitchener over the delay. As a result it was agreed to send the 29th Division to Lemnos as soon as possible and to despatch troops from Egypt. Asquith had dramatically consolidated his personal commitment to the Dardanelles.[45]

The following day, Churchill made his own effort towards providing the landing force when he inspected a Naval Brigade at Blandford in Dorset. The heavy rain poured down in torrents as the men – amongst whom was the handsome and brilliant poet Rupert Brooke – put on 'an extemporised performance, plunging through rivers & morasses'. As Brooke emerged from under a muddy motorcar, he glimpsed what he took to be two gambolling children 'shrilling & pointing'. Closer inspection revealed them to be 'Eddie' Marsh and Clementine Churchill. This was a rare moment of humour before the sad misadventure of the Dardanelles.[46]

Then matters began to unravel. At the War Council meeting on 19 February, Kitchener announced that he was holding back the 29th Division because of 'the recent Russian set-back in East Prussia'. The Russians had suffered a massive defeat at the Second Battle of the Masurian Lakes where they repelled the German advance but lost over 150,000 men. Kitchener feared an imminent German defeat of Russia, which would allow the Germans 'to bring back great masses of troops very rapidly to France'. Although Churchill put up a strong case for the despatch of the division, Kitchener stuck to his view that the 'two divisions on the spot' were sufficient for the moment. The Council accepted this opinion and agreed to send the Australian and New Zealand troops stationed in Egypt to Lemnos. If events proved that the 29th Division was required, it would be sent.[47] Kitchener made out the orders for these troop movements the following day.

Churchill had asked Carden for daily reports on operations and eagerly awaited news of the first day's action on 19 February. Asquith, too, was very anxious on the following morning when he had heard nothing from Churchill.

When Carden's first report came it was quite low key. The bombardment had begun at 8.00 a.m. with attacks on forts 1, 3, 4, and 6. His remark of 'frequent hits on 1 and 4 but difficult to estimate damage' was to be the theme of the campaign.[48] The forts and guns, high up and well-concealed, were virtually impossible to observe. It was an inconclusive day.

Operations were held up by bad weather until 25 February, when there was a sudden improvement. By 8.30 p.m., Carden was able to report the destruction of forts 1, 3, 4 and 6 and that he was ready to begin minesweeping operations. Churchill replied: 'Good! We are following your operations with great interest, and full confidence reposed in your resolution and judgement.'[49] The favourable weather continued on 26 February, when the huge guns of HMS *Queen Elizabeth* were turned on forts 1, 3, 4 and 6. Carden reported all four forts as 'reduced' by the end of the day.[50] (The attack on forts that Carden had previously reported as having been destroyed showed the flexibility of his vocabulary. He would use terms such as 'destroyed', 'reduced' and 'guns destroyed' to the point where it was difficult to assess what had really been achieved.) However, to an eager audience in London, the day's action sounded like progress, but it had come at a cost. HMS *Agamemnon* was holed above the water line and three men had been killed and five severely injured.

On the following day, the minesweepers entered the Strait for the first time and after sweeping for four miles no mines had been found. Meanwhile, the warships shelled fort number 8, with no clear result. There was also further shelling of forts 1, 3, 4 and 6. This time, Carden claimed, they had been totally destroyed. During the day, a new hazard was revealed in the form of hidden guns, which, Carden reported, had caused 'considerable annoyance and small material damage'.[51] Both Asquith and

Churchill made much of these meagre results. According to the former, 'the sweeping of the minefields in the Dardanelles seems to be going well.'[52] Writing to the Grand Duke of Russia, Churchill was equally enthusiastic, saying 'the progress of an attack on Dlles is encouraging & good.' He advised the Duke to ready his fleet at Sebastopol. Privately, Churchill had some reservations since he took the precaution of depositing a signed note in the files to 'record my opinion that the military force provided … is not large enough for the work it may have to do.'[53] This was the first sign that he thought it necessary to take steps to distance him from an impending failure.

That same day – 26 February – the War Council met again and, very surprisingly, Churchill did not report on progress at the Dardanelles, nor did any Council member make enquiries. As before, Churchill spent a lot of effort in making the case for despatching the 29th Division, while Kitchener demurred. The Council made tentative attempts to support Churchill's point of view, but no one wished to openly challenge the War Secretary.

Optimism was again in the air on 28 February, despite Carden reporting that his work had been 'much impeded' by gales.[54] Asquith was happy, though. For months he had received nothing but bad news from the Western Front. Now he could tell Venetia Stanley that the Dardanelles news 'makes excellent reading', particularly when compared to 'the daily bulletin from the trenches'.[55] In high spirits, Churchill drew up a plan for getting through to Constantinople and sent Grey his proposed armistice terms for Turkey. Only 'total surrender' would do, he told the Foreign Secretary.[56]

On 1 March, bad weather again halted operations but Churchill had a smile on his face at the news that the Greek Prime Minister, Eleftherios Venizelos, was sending three divisions of troops to Gallipoli. Hankey joined the festive mood by writing a paper on 'after the Dardanelles'. The next day, forts 8 and 9 were the focus of attack, using just three warships. The famous naval historian of this period, Arthur Marder, has remarked how 'utterly lacking in vigour and determination' was Carden's bombardment. He used few of his ships and attained results which 'were partial and desultory'.[57] It was on this day that Churchill told the Cabinet that troops were to be used at the Dardanelles. According to Hobhouse, Churchill made these remarks 'with the air of imparting a great secret', whereas the servants in Brooks's were already gossiping about the move.[58] Hardly had Churchill digested the news of the Greek offer before his hopes were destroyed by the further news that the Russians would not allow Greek soldiers on the peninsula. Violet Asquith, who saw much of Churchill in these days, recalled that 'For Winston these were cruel hours to live through.'[59]

On 4 March, matters brightened a little. Churchill had been pressing Carden to tell him how many more days of bombardment it would take to reach the Sea of Marmara. Carden replied: fourteen days. Churchill burst into activity as he wrote to Kitchener to urge that '40,000 British troops … be available for land operations on Turkish soil' by 20 March.[60] He then instructed Carden how, on entering the Sea of Marmara, he was 'to destroy the Turco-Germany Fleet' and then 'to cut, by fire or landing parties … the Scutari-Ismid railway line'. Those trivial tasks out of the way, he was to attack the Bosphorus forts and advance on Constantinople.[61]

From 5 to 9 March, Carden's efforts were no more than half-hearted. He had nothing of substance to report for 6 March, and the following day was equally lacking in results. HMS *Queen Elizabeth* had been hit three times, but without suffering any damage. The minesweepers were being attacked by enemy howitzers positioned on the heights and could operate only at night. The seaplanes, Carden told Churchill, were 'unable to locate enemy from a safe height' and it was proving impossible to 'render a fort innocuous' without landing men to go in and destroy the guns.[62] It was a dismal report, but consistent with the slow progress of Carden's fleet. There was another poor day on 7 March. Fort number 8 was silenced by four French ships, while HMS *Agamemnon* and HMS *Lord Nelson* dealt with forts 13 and 19, putting both out of action. The ships suffered minor damage, the *Lord Nelson* being holed below the waterline. Minimal results were achieved on 8 March after attacking fort 13 with no observable results. Meanwhile, the ships came under heavy attack from the hidden howitzers and the seaplanes were unable to fly because of poor visibility. With such slow progress it is surprising to find Churchill congratulating Carden on his work which, in a fit of exaggeration, he declared was 'producing profound political effects throughout Europe'.[63] On 9 March, as bad visibility once more prevented Carden's naval guns from firing, Churchill continued to spread reassuring accounts of progress and told Jellicoe that the operation was 'prospering'.[64] To the Cabinet, he reported 'steady progress'.[65] Both reports were irresponsibly optimistic.

When the War Council met on 10 March, Russia and Constantinople were the main items discussed. In a surreal mood, as if the desperate war on the Western Front were no more than a mirage, the Council discussed peace terms, Germany's post-war possessions and the Russian claim to Constantinople. Kitchener had set the mood by telling the Council that 'the Russians were making good progress in the Caucasus' and he now felt it safe to despatch the 29th Division to the Mediterranean.

Only a short while before the meeting, Churchill had been agitating for the rapid arrival of troops to claim the spoils of victory; he now seemed to have a more realistic appreciation of the pace of the Dardanelles operation. After reporting that once again bad weather had interrupted the bombardment, he mentioned that Carden anticipated a further two weeks of operations before he was through the Strait. 'There was no hurry,' he added.[66]

Behind the scenes, Churchill began to show some anxiety with regard to progress. On the same day as the War Council meeting, he reminded Carden that he was still waiting for his appreciation of the Dardanelles. Carden was also pressed to destroy the forts at Chanak and reminded that success merited losing men and ships. In the midst of this correspondence, Carden's belated appreciation arrived. Rooted in the reality of three weeks of agonisingly slow progress, Carden declared that he could not reduce the forts without an 'expenditure of ammunition beyond all proportion to that available'. Paramount amongst the problems was the concealed howitzers: their 'plunging fire is very destructive'. He had insufficient air reconnaissance and the minefields were proving difficult to clear. He concluded 'Our experience shows that gunfire alone will not render forts innocuous.'[67]

On 11 March, as if spurred by the unrealistic air of optimism that surrounded the Dardanelles bombardment, Jackson wrote to Oliver with a new appreciation of the situation. He urged caution, warning against any attempt to 'rush over upswept minefields'. This would only result in unacceptable losses.[68]

Churchill was in no mood for caution. Writing to Carden, he reminded him that his original instructions had urged 'caution and deliberate methods'. These methods had not delivered; now Churchill advised Carden 'to overwhelm the forts at the Narrows at decisive range by the fire of the largest number of the guns great and small' when weather conditions permitted.[69] On another tack, Churchill urged the immediate despatch of General Sir Ian Hamilton, who had recently been appointed Commander of the Mediterranean Expeditionary Force. He declared to Asquith that enough time had been wasted already. (By a remarkable coincidence, John Churchill was to be Hamilton's Naval Liaison Officer.)

In response to Churchill's declarations, Kitchener warned against haste. In fact, Kitchener wished Hamilton to remain in Britain for two weeks for consultations. But Hamilton was keen to go and Churchill was, recalled Hamilton, equally eager to see him sail. According to Hankey, Churchill had urged Hamilton to dash out and drive his way through, using the troops already in the Eastern Mediterranean (there were large numbers in Egypt). Kitchener seems to have become aware of this and wrote to Churchill to warn him that there should be no significant attack until the 29th Division was at Gallipoli. In the end, Churchill and Hamilton had their way and, on 13 March at 5.00 p.m., Hamilton boarded a special train, arranged by Churchill, which took him to Dover to embark on the scout-class cruiser, HMS *Foresight*. Having had charge of the transport operations, Churchill had taken the opportunity to fill every spare corner of the vessel with aeroplanes for delivery to Carden.

For Churchill, the date 13 March marked a turning point in the campaign as he began to see how ill-suited Carden was to command the operation. It was Carden's report for that day's operations that caught his attention: 'Heavy fire last night impeded sweeping operations. No casualties incurred.'[70] This brought a swift response from Churchill who complained 'I do not understand why minesweeping should be interfered with by fire which causes no casualties.' He told Carden that 'Two or three hundred casualties would be a moderate price to pay for sweeping up as far as the Narrows.' Next, he revealed to Carden that the Turkish forts were short of ammunition. He could not tell Carden how he knew this as the information had come from the code breakers in Room 40. Nevertheless, this precious information gave Churchill the confidence to tell Carden that 'the operations should now be pressed forward methodically and resolutely by night and day … The enemy is harassed and anxious now.'[71]

Captain William Hall, Director of Naval Intelligence, left an astounding account of what happened when his staff decoded the German signal from Constantinople on 13 March. It read: 'Every conceivable effort is being made to arrange for the supply of ammunition.' Hall rushed into Churchill's office, where Fisher grabbed the message, 'read it aloud and waved it over his head' shouting, 'By God, I'll go through tomorrow!' Churchill then snatched the telegram and beamed 'That means they've come to the end of their ammunition.' Fisher mused, 'We shall probably lose six ships, but I'm going through.' The two excited men sat down and began to draft the orders. It was then that Hall revealed a secret so well-kept that even Churchill had not been told: for the last few weeks Hall had been negotiating with the Turks to buy them out of the war. It was all being done on his initiative and he had reached the point of settling for a sum of £3-4 million. Fisher and Churchill were horrified. Peace? Just when they had Turkey at their mercy? Fisher exclaimed 'Four millions? No, no. I'm telling you I'm going through tomorrow.' Hall was ordered to terminate his negotiations and Turkey was to remain in the war until 30 October 1918.[72]

On the night of 13-14 March, Carden made his last determined attack on the minefields inside the Strait. Although some cables and mines were destroyed, the night was a disaster. His minesweepers were, in reality, specially adapted trawlers manned by men with minimal training. As these slow vessels motored forward against the strong current in the Strait, they were illuminated by Turkish searchlights and fired on by concealed light guns. For little or no result, four trawlers and a picket boat were put out of action. In addition, twenty-three sailors had been killed and forty-three wounded. Carden concluded that 'efficient sweeping by night is impossible.' 'Fleet sweepers' (i.e. manned by naval personnel) were urgently needed.[73]

The combination of Churchill's telegram and a disastrous night's operations pushed Carden to declare that 'military operations on a large scale should be commenced immediately.' As to pressing ahead to the Narrows, Carden warned of great losses: 'submit that further ships be held in readiness … and ammunition be despatched as soon as possible'.[74] Churchill's faith in Carden was rapidly failing but before he could decide the best way forward events took the decision out of his hands.

Carden had planned to recommence operations on 17 March. During the morning of 16 March, Carden had sent Churchill various telegrams detailing progress and plans. Then, later in the day, came his staggering revelation that he had been ordered on the sick list by his own Medical Officer. Ostensibly, Carden was suffering from a digestive complaint, but there have always been suspicions that he had simply broken down under the strain of a command for which he was not suited.

Carden had never been Churchill's choice. When the Mediterranean command was changed in September 1914, the obvious man for the job was Rear Admiral Arthur Limpus, who had been Naval Adviser to the Turkish government in 1912-14. He had a deep knowledge of the Mediterranean and the Turks but it was felt to be politically provocative to face the Turks with the very man who had taught them how to run their navy. And so the key Mediterranean post had gone to Carden. Elderly, lacking recent sea experience, and looking forward to retirement, he was simply not up to the task. The decision to pass over Limpus was to be a major factor in the navy's failings in the Mediterranean. For the sake of diplomatic protocol, the one admiral who could have beaten the Turks was cast aside without a thought to the consequences.

In place of Carden, Churchill immediately appointed de Robeck, with Wemyss as his second-in-command, on 17 March. Churchill presumed that de Robeck was in agreement adding, 'Do not hesitate to say if you think otherwise' and if he was in accord he was to commence operations 'without delay'.[75]

By coincidence, the very day that de Robeck received his orders, Hamilton stepped on board HMS *Queen Elizabeth* for his first briefing. There he met de Robeck – 'a fine looking man with great charm of manner' – as well as the key British and French officers involved with the Dardanelles.

What Hamilton wrote in his diary at the end of the day is most revealing as to the difficulties they all faced. De Robeck, fresh and confident, had declared that he 'would prefer to force a passage on his own, and is sure he can do so'. He had no intention of calling on the army unless he felt it to be absolutely necessary. This suited Hamilton, who had arrived with vague instructions from Kitchener. (When he showed these to the group, Keyes remarked 'Is that all?') In the circumstances Hamilton described himself as 'a waiting man and that it was the Admiral's innings for so long as he could keep his wicket up'. By the time the briefing was over and Hamilton had seen the nature of the terrain and the extent of the dug-in Turkish soldiers, he was only too ready, he wrote, 'to accept K.'s order not to be in too great a hurry to bring the army to the Front. I devoutly hope,' he added, 'that the navy will pull us out the chestnuts from the fire.'[76]

Full of confidence, de Robeck launched his attack on the Narrows on 18 March at 10.45 a.m. The bombardment was led by HMSs *Queen Elizabeth, Inflexible, Agamemnon* and *Lord Nelson* together with four French vessels. By 1.25 p.m., the guns of ten battleships had silenced the forts which had been returning fire. Then at 3.15 p.m., as a change round of ships began, the French pre-dreadnought battleship *Bouvet* struck a mine and, belching out black smoke, suddenly capsized. Some 600 men were drowned before assistance could reach the ship. The forts commenced firing again, and at 4.09 p.m., HMS *Inflexible* struck a mine and was forced to withdraw. Less than thirty minutes later, HMS *Irresistible* also hit a mine and had to be abandoned. Just after 6.00 p.m., HMS *Orion* suffered the same fate and quickly sank. The French battleship *Gaulois* was badly damaged by shellfire and had to be beached on the Rabbit Islands. By the time de Robeck's force limped out of the Dardanelles, three battleships had sunk and three other large ships had been put out of action. All the serious damage had been due to mines. The 'by ships alone' plan was dead.[77]

After twenty-seven days of bombardment the naval attack on the Dardanelles came to an end. From 24 March onwards Churchill was to be a spectator as the battle became the Gallipoli campaign under the direction of Kitchener and Hamilton.

When the War Council met on 19 March, Churchill read out telegrams from de Robeck that recounted the disasters of the previous day. Pertinently, Lloyd George asked 'whether any success had been achieved to counterbalance the losses'. Churchill could offer him no comfort on that front. Kitchener also had bad news to impart, although none of his listeners understood the importance of what he had to tell. After noting that Lemnos had proved unusable as a base for the Gallipoli landings he added that the troopships which had just arrived there had not been loaded in battle order. Before the men could be sent into action the ships and men would have to go to Egypt, where the ships would be unloaded, only to be reloaded in battle order. This monumental War Office blunder was to cause a three-week delay in Hamilton's operations. Kitchener showed no great concern and reiterated his conviction that 'the Dardanelles must be forced' and, if needed, 'large military operations' would be undertaken.[78]

With that one sentence, the Dardanelles operation slipped from Churchill's grasp. The baton passed to the generals.

CHAPTER 7

FISHER WAVERS

There should be a very strong assurance of success in the Dardanelles project to justify the risks we run by this depletion of our strength in the decisive theatre of the war. – Fisher[1]

CARNAGE AT NEUVE CHAPELLE

As the Dardanelles operation faltered in mid-March problems continued on the Western Front. Sir John French had launched a new offensive at Neuve Chapelle and although he achieved a small gain of territory, including Neuve Chapelle, with some 11,000 casualties from a force of 40,000 men the price had been high. Kitchener had backed the Dardanelles campaign in search of an alternative to disasters such as this, but French cared not to see it that way. In his memoirs he talked up the battle as best he could, writing:

> Early in March a small reserve of ammunition had been accumulated, and the Battle of Neuve Chapelle was fought and won. Had proper steps been taken to increase the supply when my first strong appeals were sent in during September 1914, the offensive operation commenced so successfully at Neuve Chapelle might have been much further developed, and, indeed, possibly have led to great and important results. But the battle had to be broken off after three days' fighting because we were brought to a standstill through want of ammunition.[2]

The words 'small reserve of ammunition' was his code for what was to become the shell crisis in May 1915. Widely cited as the cause of Asquith's fall from power in that month, here we will present evidence that it was Fisher, the Dardanelles and Venetia Stanley that brought Asquith down, not a shortage of shells.

DIVISIONS OVER THE DARDANELLES

With the land attack now delayed, the War Council had left de Robeck free to continue his bombardments 'if he thought fit'.[3] Long after midnight, Churchill was still at his desk as he attempted to hearten his faltering admiral. He cabled his regret at the losses of 18 March and, oddly, congratulated de Robeck on the 'seamanlike skill and prudence' with which the ships had been handled. He urged the admiral not to suspend operations, nor to let the Turks repair the forts. The *Queen*[4] and HMS *Implacable* were already on the way to the Dardanelles. Churchill had that night also despatched HMS *London* and HMS *Prince of Wales* in their wake. There were, he told de Robeck, 'ample supplies' of 15-inch ammunition for HMS *Queen Elizabeth*.[5] On 21 March, all this was put in perspective by a cable from de Robeck when he told Churchill that 'organising a strong military mine sweeping force' had to be his first priority. De Robeck was in a cautious mood.[6]

But all was not calm confidence at Admiralty House. Fisher, ever nervous about reducing the fleets in home waters, had been assessing the British and French contributions at the Dardanelles. He was staggered to discover that, of the twenty-eight destroyers and torpedo boats on station, only six were French. 'It's ridiculous what little the French do!' he told Churchill on 20 March.[7] His greatest concern, though, was that the Dardanelles would drain the manpower of the home fleets. Churchill told him not to worry since the crews of the so recently lost ships could be used to man the new monitors that were about to be shipped to the Mediterranean.

On 22 March, Asquith surveyed the progress of an operation in which he had invested so much confidence. He noted that Churchill was 'fairly pleased' and Kitchener 'not dissatisfied' with progress.[8] As if to hurry on de Robeck, Churchill sent him more aeroplanes and passed on to him the news that Turkey had no submarines. There were, though, worrying rumours that Germany was sending arms and submarines to Turkey.

Hamilton, meanwhile, was pondering the difficulties of landing his troops under fire. The landing craft available to him offered no protection, but he had heard of some new lighters with 'bullet-proof bulwarks'. He was sure, he wrote in his diary, that Churchill would send him some. But how could he get a message through without it falling into Fisher's hands? 'He is obsessed by the other old plan and grudges us every rope's end or ha'porth of tar that finds its way out here.'[9]

Churchill never made a decision to end the naval campaign at the Dardanelles. De Robeck made the decision for him. On 23 March, the admiral suddenly declared that 'it will be necessary to take and occupy the Gallipoli Peninsula' before it would be safe to send large ships through to the Sea of Marmara and Constantinople.[10] Churchill's blandishments on de Robeck's seamanship had been for nothing. The admiral was not to be moved. In London, opinion was fully behind Churchill in his desire that de Robeck press the attack. Writing to Venetia Stanley, Asquith told her, 'I agree with Winston & K. that the navy ought to make another big push.'[11]

Unusually for Churchill, his response to de Robeck's refusal to force his attack was both muted and confused. In a cable of 24 March, Churchill told the admiral that 'It may be necessary to accept the check of the 18th as decisive.' If this was the case, 'you should not fail to say so.' But Churchill then went on to set out the case for attacking now – a case that was political rather than military. After (rather unnecessarily) warning de Robeck of the risks of attacking he added 'You must not underrate the supreme moral effect of a British fleet with sufficient fuel and ammunition entering the Sea of Marmara … Besides this, there is the political effect of the arrival of the Fleet before Constantinople.' In taking this line, Churchill was following War Council policy. Their hope was that a resounding victory at the Dardanelles would lure Italy, Greece and Bulgaria into the war on the Allied side. Having pressed the case for attack, Churchill asked de Robeck: 'What has happened since the 21st to make you alter your intention of renewing the attack as soon as the weather is favourable?' He closed by telling the admiral that 'this telegram is not an executive order.'[12] Nor did de Robeck take it as such. His understandable hesitation, the military delays and the atrocious weather would restrict action to sporadic bombardments in the two months that remained of Churchill's reign at Admiralty House.

Much as Churchill wished to see decisive action at the Dardanelles, three months of work on the project had not deflected him from his true priority: Borkum. In a new paper of 24 March, he once more pressed the case for the capture of the island 'as soon as the weather is favourable after May 15th'. He set out the forces to be used and a plan for a three-day attack. Possession of Borkum, he argued, would threaten the German coastline and so force the Germans to move troops to protect it against an Allied attack.

By March 25, the naval situation in the Dardanelles was more confused than ever. Asquith was bemoaning the fact that Churchill had not ordered de Robeck to attack, while de Robeck himself had changed his mind, telling Churchill that 'the resumption of a vigorous offensive is proposed as soon as the weather permits.'[13] Meanwhile, Hamilton, who was seeing more and more of de Robeck, had arrived at the conclusion that the admiral was 'the man for the job'.[14] No doubt his opinion was influenced by his concern about the military operation, which had been so badly prepared before his appointment. John Churchill's latest letter to his brother underlined the chaos created by the War Office as his ship approached Alexandria. Lemnos, he told Churchill, was of no use since it was without water and there were no landing stages suitable for disembarking horses.

While the War Council wrestled with high policy a small drama played out in the background. The journalist Harold Massingham had come to see Asquith in mid-

March to warn him of a plot in which Churchill was seeking to have Grey replaced by Balfour as Foreign Secretary. Recounting this to Venetia Stanley, Asquith remarked 'There is no doubt that Winston is at the moment a complete victim to B.'s charm.' When Asquith asked Lloyd George as to the credibility of the rumour, Lloyd George said 'he believed it was substantially true'. No evidence has ever surfaced to support this tale. Nevertheless, Lloyd George found Asquith in tears when he met him on 30 March.[15] It is easy to see how it might have been thought true. For all his great qualities, Grey was not suited to war, being over-cautious and slow to act. Time and again he rebuffed Churchill's attempts to use foreign policy to support naval practice. Doubtless Churchill saw in Balfour – one of the best friends the navy ever had – a more sympathetic mind.

True or not, the story led Asquith to regret 'that Winston has not a better sense of proportion' and mistakenly predicted that 'I do not think he will ever get to the top in English politics.'[16]

━━━➤●◄━━━

While the War Council kept faith with the Dardanelles, Fisher became ever more anxious about the resources being sent to the Mediterranean. On 26 March, he complained to Jellicoe that 'Against our will we are FORCED to send destroyers and submarines to the Dardanelles. We can't help ourselves!'[17] Then, at 3.00 a.m. on the following day he grumbled to Churchill about sending ships to the Dardanelles that were needed in the North Sea. He was incensed at HMS *Inflexible* and HMS *Queen Elizabeth* being taken away from what he saw as the key naval battleground of the war. Fisher was now slowly detaching himself from the enterprise – a move that was to have catastrophic consequences for him, Churchill, and the government.

On 28 March, Fisher began a new line of attack. A German invasion of Holland was widely expected following the seizure by Germany of five Dutch warships. This was one more reason for getting back the 'sixteen destroyers there that are very badly wanted indeed at home'.[18]

On the last day of March, Asquith called together Kitchener, Churchill and Hankey for what he called 'a small conclave'. Given what they discussed, the meeting was effectively a War Council, although it was never recorded as such. The only account available is Asquith's letter to Venetia Stanley. They had met, he told her, 'to go over carefully & quickly the situation, actual & prospective, at the Dardanelles'. Their conclusion was that, although there were risks and it would be 'an expensive operation', it would be 'right to go through with it'. Asquith then revealed just how much he was investing in the Dardanelles. 'So much,' he wrote, depended on 'whether the coin turns up Heads or Tails at the Dardanelles'. But, if things went well, and if Italy, Greece, Bulgaria and Romania joined the Allies, 'the war ought to be over in 3 months'.[19]

By the end of March, nothing had changed since de Robeck had abandoned his bombardment thirteen days earlier. Even if he had intended any serious bombardment, it would have been ruled out by the bad weather. All that Churchill could do was to temporise with an Admiralty press statement that said, rather meaninglessly, that 'nothing has happened which justifies the belief that the cost of [the] undertaking will exceed what has always been expected.'[20] Hamilton was praying that Churchill would persuade de Robeck to keep 'knocking the Forts to pieces' while his army organised itself. He hoped that the 'rough handling from Q.E. & Co.' would lead to a Turkish collapse:'nothing would suit me so well.' He imagined that his army could land directly on the Bosphorus:'The nearer to the heart I can strike my first blow, the more telling it will be.'[21]

Fisher, on the other hand, was far from happy. In an impassioned letter to Churchill, he declared 'we have now descended to the bare minimum of superiority in Home Waters, and that to despatch any more fighting ships of any kind to the Dardanelles operations would be to court serious losses at home.'[22]

While hoping for a naval breakthrough, Hamilton continued with his preparations. He had been despatched from London without the benefit of any staff work and so had to fend for himself. Matters were not helped by Kitchener's idea of the sort of assistance that generals might need in modern wars. Recalling how his troops had fought their way across the Sudan in the 1890s, attacking the enemy while they were camped in their night-time enclosures (zaribas) made up of grubbed-up thorn bushes, he warned Hamilton to beware of 'night attacks and barbed wire entanglements'. He was not to worry about the barbed wire though, since the 'zaribas were successfully crossed in the Sudan by means of the native angerib bed'. He went on to explain that 'Men carrying angeribs are placed immediately behind the hand grenade and attacking lines, and directly the fire of the defence is dominated, they rush forward and place the angerib on the entanglement.'[23] Sadly, although Hamilton's diary refers to this cable, he made no comment on the relevance of Sudan operations to the hell of Gallipoli.

At the same time that Hamilton was savouring Kitchener's hoary advice, Fisher was reaching breaking point. As long as he stayed in post, he was an implicit supporter of a campaign which he thought put the defence of home waters at risk. But, as he told Jellicoe on 4 April, 'no good purpose would be served by my resigning' since 'my opinions are known.'[24]

When an informal War Council met on 6 April, the only item on the agenda was the Dardanelles. The whole meeting was recorded in thirteen lines of text. Kitchener read out some of Hamilton's telegrams and then declared that he had not yet received a full plan of attack, while Churchill read out the now outdated report from de Robeck of the events of 18 March. Hankey then forecast that any landing would be difficult given the howitzers positioned on the peninsula. Churchill demurred, considering a landing to be a straightforward affair. And that was it. No military staff appreciations, no questions put to the absent military advisers. No meeting of the War Council more aptly supported the view of Edwin Montagu, Chancellor of the Duchy of Lancaster, that 'you do not get discussions in the War Council differing materially from those in the cabinet.' The Council should, he added, 'be used by its political members to get a frank opinion of the military experts; but … that is not done.'[25]

The oddity of the War Council structure is supported by the fact that the very next day Churchill reported something to the Cabinet which ought to have been said at the Council. He told Cabinet members that 'the Grimsby trawlers, who are mine sweeping, did not object to the risk of being blown up by mines, but declined entirely to face shellfire, and have had to be withdrawn.'[26] Given the urgent requirement of clearing mines in the Dardanelles, the withdrawal of these vessels was hardly a trivial matter.

Ever hopeful of finding an argument that would undermine the Dardanelles campaign, Fisher had the idea of halting operations while the delicate negotiations to lure Italy into the war were in progress. He feared that an Allied defeat at such a time might scupper the talks. Churchill would have none of it and in reply emphasised the need to take risks in war. Quoting Nelson he told Fisher: 'We are defeated at sea because our Admirals have learned – where I know not – that war can be made without running risks.'[27]

Another problem loomed on Churchill's horizon that same day when the sea lords wrote to Fisher detailing their concerns about the strength of the Grand Fleet. Was it being put in jeopardy, they asked, and they also voiced their concerns in regard to the ten battleships 'lost, or more or less demobilised' by the Dardanelles. While the navy was adding seven new battleships to the fleet, Germany had added six, they said – figures that Churchill later contested in *The World Crisis*. But the crux of the letter was a veiled attack on Churchill, with the sea lords declaring that the First Sea Lord must have 'the final voice' otherwise 'policy becomes one of compromises'. Since everyone at the Admiralty knew that Churchill reserved to himself 'the final voice', the letter was no more than a criticism of his methods. So sharply did the letter follow Fisher's own views it might as well have come from his pen.[28]

In an uncharacteristically diplomatic reply, Fisher made no reference to the issue of who had, or should have, the last word. Instead, he acknowledged that the Dardanelles operation was 'political' but disingenuously said 'I consented to this undertaking … subject to strict limitation of the Naval Forces to be employed.' He added 'our supremacy is secure in Home Waters.'[29] Given that Fisher had told so many people about his objections to the campaign and its effect on home waters it is hard not to assume that the sea lords had already heard all of his arguments. If so, whatever did they make of his insipid reply?

Acquiescent as Fisher may have been when writing to the sea lords, he was back on the attack a few days later when he asked Churchill to limit the use that de Robeck made of HMS *Lord Nelson* and HMS *Agamemnon*. Brushing aside this attempt 'to harass the Admiral', Churchill went to the heart of the issue:

Seriously, my friend, are you not a little unfair in trying to spite this operation by side winds and small points when you have accepted it in principle? It is hard on me that you should keep on like this – every day something fresh: and it is not worthy of you or the great business we have in hand together.[30]

A swift riposte came from Fisher: 'Never in my whole life have I ever before so sacrificed my convictions as I have done to please you! THAT'S A FACT!'[31]

If unappreciated at home, Churchill was able to bask in the warm praise which reached him from the Dardanelles via his brother on 11 April. John Churchill told him how pleased Keyes and de Robeck were 'at their treatment by the Admiralty' after the events of 18 March. They had 'fully expected to be superseded'. Keyes, who had been 'rather against you' had now 'become an ardent admirer'.[32]

The time for military action was approaching and on 12 April, de Robeck gave Hamilton a tour of the coastline in HMS *Queen Elizabeth*. Although the weather continued stormy, the general noted in a letter to Kitchener that 'with reasonable luck we shall get ashore without great loss.'[33] In his diary he lamented: 'What a ticklish affair the great landing is going to be!'[34]

⋙●⋘

The past was reawakened on 15 April, when a ten-page letter from Lord Charles Beresford arrived on Asquith's desk. Beresford had been a sworn enemy of Fisher and Asquith since his time as Commander-in-Chief of the Channel Fleet in 1907-09. He had added Churchill to his list of adversaries in 1911. When Asquith passed the letter to the Admiralty for advice on how to reply, both Fisher and Churchill saw red. Fisher described the letter as 'drivel'[35] while Churchill added that it was the work of an 'old clown'. Asquith sent a polite reply before filing the letter.

That Asquith had no time for the trivia of letters from retired admirals is not surprising given the strains of the war. Only the following day there was a disastrous Cabinet at which Kitchener attacked Lloyd George over his disclosure of some munitions figures and declared that he was resigning. Lloyd George and Churchill then began to be 'aggressive and tactless', while Grey and McKenna pitched into the argument. 'So I thought of you,' Asquith told Venetia Stanley, '[and] succeeded in getting us back into more or less smooth water.'[36] In a second letter later the same day he added 'Not for years ... have I been more disillusioned ... and depressed.'[37]

A few days after the Cabinet row, Churchill wrote to his brother who was awaiting the Gallipoli landing. Still showing great faith in his ships, Churchill told his brother that he hoped that the navy would spare the army as far as possible. The important thing was to have a strong fleet in the Sea of Marmara and this was possible since the Turks were short of ammunition. The essential thing was to accept losses and press on. For Churchill the taking of Turkey was a prize worthy of great sacrifice. That evening, when Hankey dined with Churchill and his wife, he found 'Churchill extraordinarily optimistic about Dardanelles operation'.[38]

———◆———

On 23 April at 4.46 p.m., the twenty-seven-year-old poet Rupert Brooke died on a French hospital ship in the Mediterranean. He, who had penned the lines 'Now, God be thanked who has matched us with His hour', had so longed for war. He had enlisted in Churchill's Naval Brigade and had taken part in the Antwerp expedition before sailing, in February, for Gallipoli. But, on the very day that had been set for the landings, an infected mosquito bite brought an end to his brilliant life. He was one of the poets whom 'Eddie' Marsh championed and it was through Marsh that Churchill had come to a deep admiration for the young bard. Not surprisingly, he was one of the first to write a letter of sympathy to Brooke's mother. He told her, in words that so many would have shared, 'I have never known or heard of anyone like him – his genius and his beauty, his wisdom, honour, gentleness and humour made him such a man as has seldom lived.'[39] Violet Asquith, who worshipped Brooke, thanked Churchill for his tribute. John Churchill's attendance at Brooke's funeral on the island of Skyros fittingly highlighted the extraordinary impact that this eloquent poet had had on his brother. He described in a letter to Winston how, at midnight, the officers 'carried the coffin about two miles up a beautiful gully' to bury him 'at a spot he had admired a few days previously'.[40] Never unable to find time for his friends, Churchill interrupted his great responsibilities to write a moving tribute to Brooke which appeared in *The Times* of 26 April. Hamilton also found time to record his sadness in his diary. It was tragic, he wrote, that 'the firstborn in intellect must die'.[41]

UNITED OVER GALLIPOLI

As if to emphasise the urgency of achieving a success at Gallipoli, the Second Battle of Ypres began on 22 April. A month later, there were another 70,000 Allied casualties. At Gallipoli, there had been a pause of more than a month between the end of the naval bombardments and Hamilton's initial landing. This should have begun on 23 April, but was delayed by a rough sea and was rescheduled for 25 April. As Fisher said to Jellicoe 'To-day begins ... a most momentous operation and the very biggest "gamble" that any government ever acceded to!'[42] Meanwhile that day, at St Julien in France, a fresh brigade went into the line and by the end of the day 2,400 men lay dead. Another 4,000 men were lost the next day. General Smith-Dorrien was in favour of withdrawal but the Chief of the Imperial General Staff thought the situation to be acceptable.

With Brooke interred in the stony soil of Skyros, his comrades boarded transport ships and set out for Gallipoli. On 26 April at 3.30 a.m., the landings began, and by the end of the day 29,000 men were ashore but had suffered heavy casualties in the process. The landings finally halted any prospect of the coastal bombardment being resumed. The Gallipoli campaign had begun.

Although the land attack was a solely military action, Churchill still felt the need to offer advice and spur on the commanders. The troops had barely made landfall before he was writing to Kitchener to warn him not to stint in the provision of men. Hamilton, he told Kitchener, was too loyal to ask for reinforcements, but Churchill advised sending another 20,000 soldiers.

By 27 April, Hamilton was brooding over the high casualties and the lack of progress on land. He was desperate for the navy to use 'man-killing H.E. shell', but this ammunition had not been loaded in the magazines of the warships. Protocol demanded that any request from him to the Admiralty went through 'routine channels', but he knew that 'officialdom at the Admiralty is none too keen on our show' and they would dump his request 'into the waste-paper basket'. He concluded 'As for me, I am helpless. I cannot write to Winston.'[43] It would take another war for the British to learn how to run combined operations. Meanwhile, Churchill's genius for getting things done was denied to the hapless Hamilton.

For the next week or so Churchill and Fisher faded into the background. De Robeck kept up his bombardments of the Turkish lines (but not the coastal forts) and he and Hamilton each sent a stream of daily cables reporting setbacks and progress. In London, readers drew their own conclusions. The pessimists, such as Fisher, decided that 'the Dardanelles news is not very good'[44] whereas optimists, such as Asquith, declared it to be 'quite good'.[45] The ultra-optimists, led by Churchill, enthused that 'The most heroic deeds have been accomplished in the last few days.' He foresaw, he told the journalist and diarist George Riddell, 'one of the great campaigns of history'.[46]

TROUBLE ON THE HOME FRONT

Around the time of the Gallipoli landings the first signs of serious trouble for Fisher and Churchill began to emerge. It began on 23 April, with an article in the *Morning Post* newspaper which had a fearless reputation for being forthright in its comment, as both the editor H.A. Gwynne and proprietor Lady Bathurst held the most extreme views. In a vicious attack on Churchill, Gwynne declared that there was 'no place for a civilian minister who usurps the functions of his Board, takes the wheel out of the sailor's hand, and launches ships upon a naval operation'. He continued: 'We have seen, at Antwerp, in the case of Cradock's squadron, and in this disaster of the Dardanelles, how a nation is punished which persists in allowing politicians to conduct naval operations.'[47] It was the usual mixture of half-truths and no truth at all. Churchill could not reply, but the article would have been read by people in high places, particularly those in the Tory Party who were soon to find Churchill's future in their hands.

Churchill and Fisher's enemies in the Commons took up the cry on 3 May, when Beresford and F.G. Kellaway, a Liberal MP, joined in Churchill-baiting. It was Beresford who set the tone when he asked to know 'whether the ships, munitions of war, and officers and men of both Services' in the Dardanelles were to the detriment of the campaign in Flanders.[48] Asquith naturally refused to answer a question involving current operations. Kellaway then asked whether Fisher had been consulted over the naval attack on the Dardanelles and whether he advised against the action. These questions almost certainly arose from Fisher's loquacity, but Churchill evaded them with ease stating that Fisher had been consulted, and that he had not advised against the campaign. Both statements were true since, despite all that Fisher had said against the Dardanelles, he had not yet formally opposed the operation in the one place that counted: the War Council.

In late April, Italy had been encouraged to enter the war by the promise of huge areas of land at the end of hostilities, mostly to be taken from Austria-Hungary. In early May, Churchill broke off Admiralty business for a trip to Paris to assist in planning the details of Italy's involvement. Bizarrely, he travelled under the name of Spencer, yet installed himself at the all too public Ritz Hotel. Sir Francis Bertie, British Ambassador in Paris, resented Churchill's presence, writing in his diary 'Winston Churchill is here, there and everywhere: he is due here tomorrow: I suppose that from here he will go to see French – and why not Joffre also?'[49]

Churchill did not help the situation by sending a message to the embassy to say that he had not time to call in person. Having snubbed the ambassador, he proceeded to arrange a large luncheon for naval people, followed by a dinner with the French Minister of Marine, Monsieur Jean Augagneur. Bertie was less than impressed as he heard Churchill praise the minister and concluded 'they probably thought themselves better Naval strategists than their Naval advisers.' But what most upset the ambassador was hearing Churchill talk about allowing the Russians to have Constantinople. In his diary, Bertie took fright at the implications of this: 'She will be quite unattackable by us: if one wishes to remain on good terms with a dangerous man, one does not give him a sword and rest satisfied with the scabbard.' Bertie clearly did not appreciate that the War Council was already committed in principle to this policy.[50]

On 9 May, shortly after Churchill's return from Paris, the *East Anglian Daily Times* carried a story that referred to the differences of opinion between Fisher and Churchill noting that these 'will be fastened upon by the enemy, and will give comfort to him'.[51] Coming so soon after the intervention of Beresford and Kellaway in the House, it was an ominous sign. Unfortunately for Churchill, circumstances had forced him to aggravate the situation. During the negotiations in Paris, Italy was offered the additional inducement of more British warships, four battleships and four light cruisers, to be stationed in the Adriatic. Churchill knew there was no way he could requisition these ships from Jellicoe's fleet – that would cause a split with Fisher – so they would have to come from de Robeck's force. Yet, at the same time, Churchill was eager to pressure de Robeck into further attacks on the forts.

Over the three days 9 to 11 May, Fisher's grumbling discontent came to a head and triggered the cataclysm that was to come in the last two weeks of the month. It all began on 9 May, with a cable from de Robeck in which he informed Churchill that 'the army is checked … This threatens a state of affairs similar to that in Northern France' and that he was unwilling to stand by and do nothing. Also, he regretted that 'The navy has not been able to give the army as great assistance as was anticipated' and asked whether the time had come for another attempt to force the Dardanelles.[52] Churchill drafted a reply, which he took to Fisher for his approval. The draft telegram has not survived, but Fisher's long and angry riposte has. According to Fisher the cable suggested that the board supported 'further operations against the forts' without any reference to the army's progress.[53] Fisher scribbled his objections to taking such action and the telegram was not sent. His letter objecting to the telegram had been no ordinary letter; he had drafted it with the assistance of Hankey. It was clear that he no longer felt able to prevail alone over Churchill. He was seeking allies, but he had left it too late.

In reply, Churchill was conciliatory but firm. He reassured Fisher 'You will never receive from me any proposition to "rush" the Dardanelles, and I agree with the views you express so forcibly on the subject.' Churchill admitted that 'we are now in a very difficult position' but there was no going back. Then, in a blast of Churchillian defiance, he implored Fisher to stand by him:

> We are now committed to one of the greatest amphibious enterprises of history. You are absolutely committed. Comradeship, resource, firmness, patience all in the highest degree will be needed to carry the matter through to victory.

He concluded: 'I beg you to lend your whole aid and goodwill; & ultimately then success is certain.'[54]

On 11 May, Fisher reinforced his position by asking Hankey to go and see Asquith. He was to tell him that he, Fisher, would resign if any attempt were made to force the Dardanelles. In his diary, Hankey described how Asquith called it 'a very foolish message' but promised that 'separate naval action would not be taken without F's concurrence.'[55] It was not a good sign. Fisher had clearly neither been reassured by Churchill's promises, nor swayed by his appeal for steadfastness.

A rough sort of peace was patched up the next day when Churchill offered some concessions to Fisher, using as an excuse the arrival of German submarines in the Eastern Mediterranean. There would be a 'lull' in operations and HMS *Queen Elizabeth* would be sent home.[56]

Fisher made no move other than to write to Asquith telling him how wrong he had been not to resign on 28 January, when he refused to attend the War Council. Since then he had remained 'a most unwilling beholder (and indeed participator) of the gradual draining of our naval resources from the decisive theatre of war'. To emphasise his objections, he enclosed a copy of the memorandum he had given Churchill on the previous day.[57] Later in the day, Asquith heard (presumably from Hankey) that the two men had come to 'an arrangement'.[58]

And then fate played its hand with an event that Asquith had for so long feared. A letter from Venetia Stanley told him that she was to marry Edwin Montagu. His reply on 12 May was brief: 'As you well know, this breaks my heart. I couldn't bear to come and see you. I only pray to God to bless you – and help me.'[59] Asquith had written 560 letters to Miss Stanley since 1912 – a total of 300,000 words. Only seven days earlier, he had told her that 'loving you I had won the supreme prize of my life.'[60] It was only five days since they had taken their last drive together.[61] He had been obsessed to distraction by Miss Stanley and suddenly it was all gone. The consequences of this blow should not be underestimated. Asquith was in no state to face the political crisis that was just three days away.

On 13 May, Churchill, too, was oblivious to the coming catastrophe as he planned a new phase for the Dardanelles. He noted that 'although there is good reason to hope that a speedy determination will be reached' it was still necessary to plan for a three-month operation. He thought that the Dardanelles fighting would 'develop into a great siege'. To this end, he requested siege artillery, 'landing stages of a semi-permanent character … with cranes, lines of railway'. There were to be masses of 'indicator nets' for submarine protection, and battleships were to be fitted with 'steel trellis work'. It is not clear whether this note was ever circulated; certainly it never reached the point of action.[62]

Also on that same day, Fisher issued his last order as First Sea Lord, commanding de Robeck to 'on no account take decisive action without our permission'.[63]

Kitchener, on the other hand, stepped up the pressure in a press briefing when he said that the Dardanelles operation 'was of the greatest importance from a political and military point of view'. He claimed that its 'effect upon the Balkan States and South Europe has been remarkable'. The losses were to be regretted 'but they were unavoidable incidents of a necessary campaign'.[64]

Within twenty-four hours, Fisher was once more at breaking point. Thanking Asquith for his letter of 12 May, Fisher told him that 'within four hours of the pact being concluded' Churchill had discussed with Kitchener the possibility of resuming the naval attack. In his last warning to Asquith, Fisher wrote 'I honestly feel I cannot remain where I am much longer … I feel my time is short!'[65]

FISHER'S RESIGNATION

All the tension that had built up since the army had landed on Gallipoli poured out at the War Council held on 14 May. The meeting was, said Churchill, 'sulphurous'.[66] It was chaired by Asquith as usual, but he was not himself. Later that day, he was to tell Venetia Stanley that 'This is too terrible … no hell could be so bad.'[67] He was in no condition to lead a meeting of such critical importance to the future of his government.

Kitchener opened the proceedings with a review of the gloomy military situation. Russia was in a wretched state and 'anxious to have a speedy decision in the Dardanelles'; the British attacks in Flanders had 'entirely failed'. Now, he declared, the defence of Britain was under threat and he admitted that he had 'bled white' the second-line Territorial divisions to reinforce Flanders. In consequence, he urged the Admiralty 'to take such steps as are possible to ensure this country against a German force landing'.

It was then Churchill's turn to report on the Dardanelles. Kitchener was a natural pessimist, so he was an easy act to follow. Hankey noted in his diary that '[Churchill's] stout attitude did something to hearten his colleagues'.[68] He explained how the Admiralty now accepted that 'the Dardanelles had become a military rather than a naval operation.' In the light of this, and because it was suspected that German submarines were now in the area, it had been decided to withdraw HMS *Queen Elizabeth*. Monitors were to be sent as a replacement. Kitchener had known of this in advance and had a prepared statement, which he read out. In it he attacked the Admiralty for having deceived him as to the potential of the *Queen Elizabeth*, while at the same time opposing the withdrawal of the vessel. This news would go down badly in the Near East, he said.

When Asquith asked Fisher for his opinion on HMS *Queen Elizabeth* he said it was 'vitally essential' that the ship rejoined the Grand Fleet. The minutes then record that Fisher 'reminded the War Council that he had been no party to the Dardanelles operations'. In fact, he had never told the Council of his opposition and all his objections had been expressed in private to Churchill and Asquith. There then followed a long, but inconclusive, discussion as to whether to continue the campaign or withdraw. Rather than reach a conclusion they decided to ask Hamilton what he required 'to ensure success at the Dardanelles'.[69]

Fisher's declaration opened a rift between him and the First Lord. As soon as he left the meeting Churchill wrote to Asquith saying 'I must ask you to take note of Fisher's statement today that "he was against the Dardanelles and had been all along," or words to that effect.' He pointed out that Fisher had 'agreed in writing to every executive telegram on which the operations have been conducted'. Sensing trouble ahead, Churchill declared that 'I cannot undertake to be paralysed by the veto of a friend who, whatever the result, will certainly say, "I was always against the Dardanelles."'[70]

That evening, Churchill drafted some proposals for reinforcements in the Mediterranean and then went to Fisher's room to discuss the plans. According to Churchill, the 'conversation was quite friendly' and Fisher 'did not object to any of the particular measures proposed'. Fisher then went home, while Churchill worked late into the night. Around midnight, the Italian Naval Attaché arrived with a request that naval reinforcements due at Taranto on 18 May should be provided by 16 May. Since Churchill saw the change as trivial, he wrote out an order which he left for Fisher to see the next day. When Commander Thomas Crease, Fisher's Naval Assistant, saw the memorandum he told James Masterton-Smith, Churchill's Private Secretary, that he was sure 'Lord Fisher would resign immediately'.[71]

When Fisher arrived at Admiralty House early on 15 May, he found a note from Churchill and four draft telegrams. There was nothing particularly new in these, but Fisher's exasperation had passed the point of calm reasoning. In anger he sat down to write his resignation letter – and this time he meant it.

He told Churchill that 'After further anxious reflection, I have come to the regretted conclusion I am unable to remain any longer as your colleague … I find it increasingly difficult to adjust myself to the increasingly daily requirements of the Dardanelles to meet your views. As you truly said yesterday, I am in the position of continually vetoing your proposals.' He concluded by saying 'I am off to Scotland at once, so as to avoid all questionings.'[72]

Fisher then left the Admiralty and went to see Lloyd George. In a brief conversation, he informed him of his resignation 'on the ground that he could not countenance what was going on in the Dardanelles'.[73] Fisher walked out on to the London streets and disappeared.

CHAPTER 8

THE REVENGE OF THE TORIES

Of course he's made mistakes but tell me who hasn't during
the war. – Tyrwhitt[1]

SITUATIONS VACANT

On the night before Fisher resigned, Asquith had gone up to the bedroom of his daughter Violet and placed a note on her pillow: 'Don't go from me now – I need you.'[2] Violet was about to leave for Alexandria to nurse her injured brother 'Oc'. That night, he also wrote to Venetia Stanley telling her 'No hell could be so bad.'[3] In the space of a week, Asquith was losing the two women on whom he had most depended during the war and it was in this broken state that he was to face the first great crisis of his political career.

It had been Fisher's habit to write an overnight letter to Churchill before he left his office at around 6.00 p.m. When Churchill awoke on Saturday 15 May, he was somewhat surprised to find no letter. His first meeting was at the Foreign Office, and it was only as he returned across Horse Guards Parade that he had the first inkling that something was wrong. Rushing towards him, with an anxious look on his face, was his secretary, Masterton-Smith, who informed him that 'Fisher has resigned, and I think he means it this time.'[4] Churchill was used to Fisher's resignation letters, so this latest effort did not perturb him. But once inside the Admiralty building he quickly discovered that Fisher had vanished. His home was closed and rumours abounded that he was on his way to Scotland.

Asquith missed all the early morning drama by indulging in one of his minor passions – weddings – when he attended the marriage of Geoffrey Howard, Vice-Chamberlain of the Household. Violet Asquith recorded in her diary how on her father's return to Downing Street he received 'a most astonishing piece of news'. Immediately a search operation was put in place. Masterton-Smith, certain that Fisher was going abroad, sent 'a troop of beagles' to scour the Continental railway stations. Lloyd George set off in a second direction and Maurice Bonham-Carter, Asquith's Principal Private Secretary, in a third. Meanwhile, a furious Asquith family delayed their departure to their weekend retreat at The Wharf. Some hours later Fisher was found, Violet Asquith recalled, 'carried in one of the receiver's mouths & dropped bloodshot & panting at the door of the Cabinet room!'. There Asquith ordered Fisher in the King's name to return to his duties.[5] Asquith, like Churchill, had seen enough of Fisher's resignations to consider the matter closed. The family set off for Berkshire in their motorcars.[6]

Later that Saturday morning, Churchill sat down to write a plea to Fisher for him to return. He appealed to him to do 'what is best for the country and for the brave men who are fighting' and reminded him that 'In every way I have tried to work in the closest sympathy with you.' He could not see where the breach might lie: 'If I did I might cure it.' Then in an emotional ending he reminded Fisher how 'In order to bring you back to the Admiralty I took my political life in my hands with the King and the Prime Minister.' Were Fisher to go now, he would 'let loose upon me the spite and malice of those who are your enemies even more than they are mine'.[7]

Fisher remained unyielding. Writing to Churchill on 16 May, he called his letter 'most persuasive' but refused to meet him, being determined to go. 'I know I am doing right.' The central issue was the Dardanelles: 'You are bent on forcing the Dardanelles and nothing will turn you from it. Nothing … You will remain and I shall go.'[8]

Churchill was now faced with a grave problem: he had no First Sea Lord. In peacetime this would have been unfortunate; in war it was potentially catastrophic, as the events of the next day were to underline. He turned to another tried and tested veteran: Sir Arthur Wilson. He was, after all, one year younger than Fisher. Thus, while the leading politicians were away in the country and the newspapers unaware of the unfolding drama, Churchill acquired his third First Sea Lord of the war.

With a new First Sea Lord appointed, a confident Churchill motored down to The Wharf on Saturday afternoon to enjoy what remained of the weekend with the Asquith family. He recalled 'I told him [Asquith] that Lord Fisher's resignation was final, and that my office was at his disposal if he required to make a change.' Asquith quickly dismissed this offer, only pausing to ask whether Churchill could put together a new board. That matter settled, it appeared that Fisher's resignation might prove to be a mere ripple. In fact it was to be the swelling of the first wave of a tsunami. Oblivious to the impending disaster, the family repaired to the dining room where Churchill recalled, 'we had a pleasant evening.'[9]

While Churchill had been busily installing a new First Sea Lord, Asquith had had second thoughts about Fisher. On the Sunday, he asked Reginald McKenna (an ex-First Lord) to write to Fisher and inform him that his resignation was 'void'.[10] The next day, all these elaborate evolutions in Berkshire were to be shattered by one brief letter from Bonar Law in London.

On the Monday, Fisher, working on the principle that it was better to bring down the government than to destroy the Admiralty, addressed an envelope to Law, enclosing nothing more than a newspaper report of his departure for Scotland. No one could mistake Fisher's distinctive and vigorous handwriting on the envelope and Law immediately saw the significance of this enigmatic message. In no time at all, Law was in Lloyd George's office, where he expressed his concern at 'the grave nature of the political questions raised'.[11] Lloyd George's sharp political antennae correctly read this as a demand for a coalition. He hurried over to Asquith and boldly told him that a Cabinet reconstruction was unavoidable.

With Asquith drowning in his personal misery, Bonar Law seized the moment. At last, his party could take its revenge on Churchill; all that was required was to demand a coalition and insist on his exclusion. Law's letter to Asquith concealed more than it revealed, being confined to his party's concern over Fisher's resignation and the vague assertion that 'things cannot go on as they are.' He added, 'some change in the constitution of the Government seems to us inevitable.'[12] The Prime Minister, still in despair over the loss of Venetia Stanley, distraught at Violet's impending departure, and shattered by Fisher's resignation, had no willpower to resist. For seven years, he had led his party and dominated the House but the war had taxed him beyond his limits. The antics of the attractive Venetia Stanley and the ageing Admiral 'Jacky' Fisher had tipped him over the edge. That morning, in the words of the historian A.J.P. Taylor, 'the last Liberal government in British history [was] killed, within a quarter of an hour.'[13]

The oddest aspect of the fall of Asquith's Cabinet, was that Asquith, Law and Balfour were united in their determination to keep Fisher as First Sea Lord. It had never occurred to Asquith that Fisher could not be persuaded to return; Balfour had told Churchill that the resignation 'would greatly disturb his Unionist friends';[14] and Law had told Esher that his party 'felt bound not to allow Fisher's resignation'.[15] But by the end of Monday morning, Fisher had faded from the scene. Greater issues were at stake.

The double pain of what now faced Asquith — asking his ministers to resign and living without Venetia Stanley — was beyond his physical and mental resources. For three days, according to his wife Margot, Asquith 'was constantly in tears'.[16] He had brought down his own government without even consulting his colleagues. His letter to them on 17 May was accompanied by a note which recorded his reasons for his actions. More designed for posterity than for the Cabinet, Asquith's note justified his move on the grounds of Fisher's resignation and 'the plausible parliamentary case in regard to the alleged deficiency of high-explosive shells'.[17] It is doubtful that any of his ministers noticed this passing remark. It was so unimportant that he did not discuss it with his colleagues until two days later. It appears to have been an excuse that he added for posterity so as to make his destruction of the Liberal government more justifiable. As we shall see in 1916 (Chapter 11), Asquith attributed the coalition solely to the disputes between Fisher and Churchill.

Later in the day, Asquith was in the Cabinet room assembling lists of names as he discarded old and loyal friends to make way for the Tories, whom he deeply detested. Violet witnessed his distress when she found him there 'with a heavy look of unhappiness I have rarely seen on his face before'. Unknowingly, in recording her conversation with her father, she underlined the irrelevance of the shell crisis at this moment:

'Father is it a Coalition?' – 'I'm afraid so.' … 'All this butchery I've got to do.' *Must* poor Haldane go?' 'Yes – one must harden one's heart about it all.' 'Was there *no* other way out?' 'No – we cldn't have had a public brawl between W. & Fisher at this moment – with Italy on the brink of coming in.'

If Asquith had really felt that the shell crisis justified a coalition even before a debate in the House, he would surely have mentioned it to Violet.

Later, despite it being only Monday, Asquith told Violet 'this has been the unhappiest week of my life.'[18]

At the same time as asking his ministers to put their portfolios at his disposition, Asquith asked Fisher to 'neither say nor do anything for a day or two'.[19] He clearly intended that Fisher should remain as First Sea Lord. And so he might have done had the admiral taken Asquith's advice and kept in the background.

At this stage, Asquith had no idea that the sea lords were determined on Fisher not returning. They asked Hall to convey this message to the Prime Minister. Hall at first agreed, but then had second thoughts, and instead passed the message on to the Lord Chief Justice. This unprecedented demand was soon overtaken by events – indeed, it is not clear that it ever came to the attention of Asquith.

Churchill had not yet realised that his own post might be under threat and was busy planning his new board. That Monday, he presented the board to Asquith who commented 'No, this will not do. I have decided to form a national Government by a coalition with the Unionists, and a very large reconstruction will be required.' Asquith went on to tell Churchill that Kitchener was to leave the War Office (he did not) and then added 'What are we to do for you?'[20] In this way Churchill realised he was not to return to the Admiralty. The conversation continued for a while as Asquith offered Churchill the Colonial Office or a command in France. Before any conclusion could be reached, Churchill received a telephone call of the utmost urgency and departed. Writing in 1928, Asquith referred to this account of Churchill's and did not contradict it, so it can be assumed that this is broadly what happened.

Churchill had no intention of leaving Asquith to make his own Cabinet. In a letter written after his interview, he advised Asquith that Lloyd George was not suitable for the War Office and bizarrely suggested Balfour. Lloyd George could manage the Treasury and Munitions at the same time. If there were to be a change at the Admiralty, he was only prepared to accept a military department but he rather hoped to stay at the Admiralty to finish his work.

In 1915, government was still largely carried on behind closed doors, so the public were unaware of the mighty events that were unfolding. On the following day, Tuesday 18 May, the *Bristol Evening News* noted that there had been 'considerable activity in Downing Street' on the previous day, but had no explanation to offer.[21] Other newspapers carried an agency rumour 'that Lord Fisher had resigned or was considering resignation'.[22] The *Evening Standard* was closer to the truth when it reported that 'sensational changes may be looked for at the Admiralty'.[23]

When Churchill had been called away from his conversation with Asquith it was for a full-scale alert at sea. The decoders from Room 40 informed him that the German High Seas Fleet had left port. Was this '*der Tag*', the day that Fisher and Churchill had so longed for and the day when the British Grand Fleet would have the chance to annihilate the German fleet? Such a victory would surely guarantee Churchill remaining in his post.

At 3.55 p.m., the signal ordering the Grand Fleet to sea was sent. Submarines were despatched to positions off the Dutch coast. The auxiliary patrols at Dogger Bank were recalled. The bases of Rosyth, Nore and Dover were ordered to have all their submarines ready for action by 3.30 a.m. At 8.10 p.m., Churchill sent his last signal to Jellicoe: 'It is not impossible that to-morrow may be *The Day*. All good fortune to you.'[24]

Then the long wait began. Wilson slept at Admiralty House and Churchill remained there instead of returning to the Commons. At daylight, Churchill went to the War Room to find that the German fleet was off the Dutch coast, while Jellicoe's fleet was still steaming southwards from Scapa Flow. If the German fleet could be enticed westwards Jellicoe still had a chance of arriving in time to block its return course to Germany. But at 7.00 a.m. the German fleet was reported sailing southeast and appeared to be returning home. It had never intended to give battle, having come out solely to protect minelaying operations. Churchill's last hope of remaining at the Admiralty vanished.

COALITION

'Max' Aitken was intent on preventing Churchill's departure. In his book, *Politicians and the War* he recounted how he 'pressed Bonar Law very strongly to retain Churchill at the Admiralty'. But Law told him 'it was useless to argue' since 'the Tory party had definitely made up its mind not to have him there.'[25]

In the hectic atmosphere of the last twenty-four hours, Asquith had not formally confirmed his coalition offer to Law which had been made on 18 May. This he now did, stating 'I need not enter the reasons (sufficiently obvious)' thus neatly sidestepping exactly what those reasons were.[26] Law accepted the offer on the following day.

Churchill now opened negotiations as to his own future and had said that if he were to be offered the Colonies he would accept it, though reluctantly. A War Office appointment would suggest that he had failed at the Admiralty, he argued, so he once more pressed his case for remaining. He suggested that Asquith could arrange this if he sent Balfour to the War Office. His letter is persuasive testimony to Churchill's egocentricity as he clearly expected the whole reshuffle to revolve around his remaining at the Admiralty.

On the Wednesday, *The Times* newspaper carried an article which reported that 'the protracted co-operation of Mr Churchill and Lord Fisher at the Admiralty appears to have become impossible' It noted that Fisher was still absent from the Admiralty and that 'Mr Churchill is said to be packing up.'[27] Wilson, now aware that Churchill was not to return, promptly wrote to Asquith to withdraw his acceptance of the post of First Sea Lord. He had only taken the post because, in his view, 'to undertake the office of First Sea Lord under Mr. Churchill' was 'the best means of maintaining continuity of policy'.[28]

Churchill proposed to take his fight to the Commons in the form of a personal statement. On 19 May, unwisely, he showed his draft to Lloyd George who told him that its 'effects upon foreign politics would be disastrous'. (This was a reference to the on-going negotiations to draw Italy into the war.) Churchill retorted 'You forget my reputation is at stake. I am wounded.'[29] He went on: 'You don't care what becomes of me. You don't care whether I am trampled under foot by enemies. You don't care for my personal reputation.' To this Lloyd George replied 'No, I don't care for my own at the present moment. The only thing that I care about now is that we win this war.'[30] It would be two years before these two great masters of the war reconciled their differences and saw Britain through the last year of the conflict.

Asquith, not yet ready to announce the details of his coalition, had taken steps to quell the rumours that had been building in the press. He told the Commons that 'steps are in contemplation which involve the reconstruction of the Government on a broader, personal and political basis.' It would be 'for the purposes of the War alone'. As to offices, all he could say was that he would remain as Prime Minister and Grey would continue as Foreign Secretary; there was to be 'absolutely no change' in policy. Law followed him in a similar high-minded manner saying 'we shall leave out of our minds absolutely all considerations, political or otherwise.'[31] In his heart, though, Law knew that he was already determined on a highly political act: to throw out one of the few ministers who understood war in a mean act of revenge for events of more than a decade ago. It was to prove an uneasy coalition as long as Asquith remained Prime Minister – he detested the Tories and gave them none of the strategic war posts other than Balfour at the Admiralty. This cunningly helped to negate the effect of the Tories entering 'his' government. As a well-known supporter of Liberal naval policy Balfour could be relied on to maintain the status quo.

Such narrow and petty behaviour was only to be expected from a man like Bonar Law. Sir Arthur Lee, sometime military attaché to the embassy in Washington and an ex-Civil Lord of the Admiralty, decried Bonar Law's 'complete ignorance' of defence matters. He was 'hopeless' in war and, worse, said Lee, he was 'playing politics' in order to force a coalition. Lee went so far as to claim that Law wanted to ban anyone engaged in war work from ministerial office.[32] Events were to bear out Lee's view. Bonar Law brought nothing to the councils of war.

Violet Asquith saw Churchill immediately after the Commons announcement. 'He took me into his room and sat down on a chair – silent, despairing – as I have never seen him. He did not even abuse Fisher, but simply said, "I'm finished."' When Violet tried to buck him up, he replied: 'No – I'm done. What I want above all things is to take some active part in beating the Germans. But I can't – It's been taken from me. I'd go to the Front at once – but these soldiers are so stuffy – they wouldn't like my being given anything of a command. No – I'm finished.'[33]

By the following day, Churchill was attributing his fall to the 'political intrigue' of Lloyd George. Riddell, recording the scene in his diary, described Churchill as 'this broken man … pacing up and down in his room' as he raged against Lloyd George. He had encouraged Fisher to resign so that he, Lloyd George, could take over the War Office. Asquith, too, had let him down, he told Riddell. He had been 'disgracefully weak – supinely weak'. Churchill added 'His weakness will be the death of him.'[34]

In Churchill's low state it was time for friends and family to rally round. His wife wrote a pleading letter to Asquith asking 'Why do you part with Winston? Unless indeed you have lost confidence in his work and ability?' She argued that any moves for change were merely those 'fostered by the press'. The only place where Churchill's move would be welcome was Germany. She rightly predicted that the government's war operations would be weakened by Churchill's absence. In private, Asquith brushed the letter aside, calling it 'the letter of a maniac'.[35]

Few men could match Churchill's capacity to fight lost causes. In a flurry of correspondence on 21 May, he hit out in every direction he could think of in an attempt to retain his post at the Admiralty. First he tried Bonar Law and sought to persuade him that his differences with Fisher over the Dardanelles 'ought to be settled by people who know the facts'.[36] Since Bonar Law and his aides had no access to the facts, Churchill argued for a Cabinet committee to review the whole Dardanelles operation. In reply, Bonar Law pointed out there could be no Cabinet committee since there was no Cabinet. Although he promised to consult his friends, he warned Churchill that 'what I said to you last night is inevitable'.[37]

Next Churchill contacted Asquith, pleading that 'at this critical moment' the Dardanelles operation should not be handed to a new person, who would not be familiar with the details. This was followed by a second letter in which Churchill now humbled himself to the point of begging 'any office – the lowest if you like'.[38] Asquith quickly replied to warn Churchill that 'it is settled that you are not to remain at the Admiralty', but did not tell him that this was Bonar Law's condition, not his own.[39] Churchill capitulated.

Amongst the reactions from those who had heard the rumours of Churchill's departure were three from men very close to his heart. His brother wrote from the Dardanelles to tell him that the news had fallen 'like a bomb among us'.[40] From the Western Front, Sir John French wrote to reassure Churchill that 'You know you are always welcome here.'[41] Hamilton, in his diary, described the rumour of Churchill's fall as 'an awful blow to us out here'. It was 'a sign that Providence had some grudge against the Dardanelles'. He went on to bemoan the 'tragedy' of his 'nerve and military vision' being 'side-tracked'. Recalling Churchill's 'brilliant effort of unaided genius' at Antwerp he declared that 'Any comfort our people may enjoy from being out of cannon shot of the Germans – they owe it to the imagination, bluff and persuasiveness of Winston.'[42] Nothing so well illustrates the tragedy of Churchill's position than the contrast between the opinion of the ignorant Bonar Law and that of the informed Hamilton. Churchill's political future as a war minister was in the hands of politicians who had never set foot on a battlefield nor looked down the sights of a gun. Indeed, the coalition itself was put together by two weak men with no military experience between them: Asquith and Bonar Law.

By 23 May, Churchill had accepted that he would go to the Duchy of Lancaster with a seat at the War Council. Only not being in office at all could have been a greater humiliation. His cousin the Duke of Marlborough appreciated the bleakness of Churchill's situation, writing 'I gather you have been flung a bone on which there is little meat.'[43] But tragic as his own position was, his party had suffered an even greater blow. Riddell, observing what was happening at the Commons, noted that 'the Liberal Party looks as if it were dead.'[44] Hobhouse (who had lost his Cabinet post) declared in his diary: 'The disintegration of the Liberal Party is complete. We shall not return to power for some years.'[45] Indeed, even now (2013) the party has still not formed a government in its own right.

There was one success, though, for Asquith: Italy declared war on Austria-Hungary on 23 May. For weeks his ministers and military men had been implored from all sides to avoid discord and avert risks in order that this prize should fall to him.

It was not until ten days after Fisher's resignation that the full coalition Cabinet was revealed to the public. There was little to reassure the country that Asquith was taking the war any more seriously than in earlier days. Only one appointment strengthened his team: Lloyd George was to establish a Ministry of Munitions. (And, incidentally, become the first politician to be appointed with the title of 'Minister of' in British history.) Balfour went to the Admiralty, where Lady Wemyss visited him the following day. She lamented the replacement of 'Winston, keen, young, full of energy and love of power' by 'A.J.B. [Balfour] so weary, reluctantly obliged to shoulder a heavy burden'.[46] Bonar Law was appointed to the (in wartime) near moribund Colonial Office. It was a reconstruction that could not last.

Churchill tried to depart with his head held high, telling Riddell that 'I leave the nation a navy in a state of perfect efficiency.' But he felt betrayed by both Lloyd George ('he has treated me disgracefully') and by the 'treacherous devil' Fisher.[47]

———◦◦◦———

In the midst of the tumult that was overtaking him, Churchill sought solace in a short visit to Cambridge. There he observed 'the elm-clumps greatly standing' and wandered through 'the mayfields all golden showing'. In a letter to Violet Asquith, he described how he had lost 'the two things I cared for supremely': Rupert Brooke and 'doing my bit'. 'Now Rupert is gone, and the day after tomorrow my bit will have eluded me.'[48]

CHAPTER 9

BYSTANDER

I have watched all these weary months folly, sloth and indecision ruining large
conceptions. – Churchill[1]

CHURCHILL AS FIRST LORD

Churchill described his bringing back Fisher to the Admiralty as 'one of the most
hazardous steps I have ever had to take in my official duty.'[2] The combination of one
man who was too old to take risks and another who was too young to see them was
bound not to last. Nor was it likely that two men whose principal management style
involved talking others into submission would work harmoniously together.

There was no problem between them over materiel – Churchill wanted a large
number of ships but took little interest in how they were built. But when it came to
how they were used, he was never short of vigorous opinions. For the first time in his
life, Fisher found himself giving way to a more powerful personality than his own.

Before Fisher rejoined the Admiralty, Churchill had enjoyed three months as the
undisputed master of Admiralty House at war. We have seen how he issued orders
to Milne in the Mediterranean and involved himself in the details of the Battle of
Heligoland. Battenberg, the First Sea Lord, raised no objections to allowing this most
unconventional practice to become the norm. Fisher more or less went along with
these methods until January 1915, when Churchill applied them to the Dardanelles
campaign. The disagreement between the two men reached a peak when Fisher told
Asquith that he had been against the Dardanelles from the start. Churchill's response
was to tell Asquith that he refused to accept Fisher's veto over the campaign. In
attacking Churchill, Fisher failed to recognise that the whole War Council was united
in its passion for the campaign. He was the one man out of line. Essentially, his attacks
on Churchill's methods were simply attacks on War Council policy. Had the two men
been of one mind, Fisher would no doubt have accepted the situation.

Not that Fisher was the only sea lord to query Churchill's interfering style of
management. A few days after the old admiral had left the Admiralty, the sea lords
complained that 'the conduct of the war' had been 'largely taken out of the hands

of the First Sea Lord'.[3] In his defence, Churchill pointed out that 'the First Lord had the power not only of veto but of initiation'. Surprisingly, Churchill said he had been willing to consult the sea lords but first Battenberg and then Fisher had resisted the move. This seems a weak excuse given Churchill's powerful personality. A more likely explanation for his not consulting more widely is that Churchill preferred to rule his own office. After all, he told Violet Asquith that 'I took him [Fisher] because I knew he was old & weak & that I shld be able to keep things in my own hands.'[4] He could have said the same about Battenberg. Basically, it suited Churchill to have First Sea Lords who bowed to his powerful and insistent arguments. But we have it on the authority of Graham Greene, the Admiralty Secretary, that Churchill never went so far as to act beyond his powers; 'no order of any importance was issued without the approval, or concurrence, of both the First Lord and the First Sea Lord'.[5]

The complaint from the sea lords blurred the distinction between consulting and deciding. There is abundant evidence that Churchill plagued his advisers with questions and requests for information. Rear Admiral Archibald Moore, who was Third Sea Lord 1912-14, told Churchill in 1915 that 'no one was in a better position than I to know how thoroughly you went into the minutest detail of any controversial matter, hearing all the pros and cons and taking opinions'.[6]

After these attacks on Churchill, we also need to consider what substance there was to those of his actions that caused so much outrage. The charges add up to very little. Before the Dardanelles, there were three main actions that brought criticism on Churchill: Antwerp, Coronel and the Bacchantes. In each case, there is little to criticise in Churchill's conduct. As to Antwerp, he was sent there by the War Council and was fully supported in all his actions. Kitchener poured in troops to defend the city and he even offered Churchill a high army rank to fulfil the task. In the case of Coronel, it was Cradock's failure to comply with Churchill's repeated order to keep HMS *Canopus* with him that led to the disaster. The allegations against him over the Bacchantes were even more absurd. Far from Churchill being to blame, he was the only person at the Admiralty who saw the danger and took steps to avert it.

The last operational charge against Churchill that we need to examine is his handling of the Dardanelles campaign. The attack on Churchill in the *Morning Post*, published in April, was typical of the accusations levelled against him:

Who is responsible for this costly blunder – costly whether the present operation succeeds or fails? We assert that the First Lord of the Admiralty acted against the opinion of his experts. We assert further that he led the Cabinet to believe he had behind him the opinion of Lord Fisher, whereas Lord Fisher's opinion was that the operation to have a chance of success must be conducted jointly by the army and the navy.

The truth is that Winston Churchill is a danger to the country.[7]

There was much to criticise in this bungled operation that promised such great rewards, but little of that criticism attaches to Churchill. We have only to reiterate some key points already made to exonerate him from any central responsibility for the disaster: it was Kitchener who asked for the attack; it was Carden who said he could demolish the forts without military help; at all stages in the naval operation Kitchener and Asquith were its greatest enthusiasts; Churchill was the only War Council member to warn of the risks. And, when it was clear that troops were needed, he urged speedy action, while Kitchener dithered.

None of these facts penetrated the minds of Churchill's critics at the time and the further they were removed from access to those facts, the more fanciful their stories became. For example, Bertie, the British Ambassador in Paris, started a rumour in early April that Churchill was planning the bombardment of Heligoland and Cuxhaven as well as the Dardanelles.

Churchill's one mistake was to trust the operation to Carden, whom he knew to be inadequate. Carden had no drive and pursued the bombardment at a snail's pace, allowing Turkish forces time to build up their defences. Despite this, the operation almost succeeded. At the point when Fisher resigned, the Turks were down to their last few rounds of ammunition and a determined attack by de Robeck would have broken through, but no one supported Churchill in his desire to put pressure on the admiral.

We should also remember that Asquith, who was effectively the overall director of the operation, called it the one brilliant idea of the war.[8] The future Prime Minister Clement Attlee, who served at Gallipoli, later called it 'an immortal gamble that did not come off' which was 'the one strategic idea of the war'.[9] Perhaps the final word should go to a man on the spot: Keyes. 'I think Winston Churchill's name will always be honoured in history for his great strategic effort.'[10]

Our assessment of Churchill's wartime performance at the Admiralty can best be concluded by the words of two men who both knew him intimately and were acknowledged military experts: Richard Haldane (ex-Secretary of State for War) and Maurice Hankey. Haldane wrote to sympathise with the 'ingratitude' that Churchill had received and rightly predicted (if a little prematurely) that 'Your time will come and soon.'[11] Hankey, in turn, wrote to thank Churchill on behalf of the Committee of Imperial Defence for his prompt mobilisation at the start of the war.

At the end we are left with a paradox. Few ministers had served Asquith better in the early months of the war. The navy had lived up to all that Fisher and Churchill had claimed for it before the war: it had driven the German warships from the seas; contained German ships with a long-distance blockade; and safely transported men, machines and goods day in, day out across the Channel. The army meanwhile had been a disaster. Kitchener had wasted six fine divisions by throwing them at an overwhelming German force. He had spurned the Territorials that were there to use and then put his faith in new armies of his own creation. Yet, when it came to forming a coalition, it was Churchill who departed. And with it, as the scapegoat, he carried on his back all the errors and vacillations of the War Council.

⸺❖⸺

As Churchill moved into his new post he tried to console himself with the thought that, although he had been in Cabinet for ten years, he was still the youngest member. Insignificant as his new post was, as Chancellor of the Duchy of Lancaster he was at least a Cabinet minister. His duties were minor, including the appointment of magistrates. A former office holder, Lord Shuttleworth, reassured him that he had an 'interesting' job with 'useful work'.[12] If such work existed, it escaped Churchill's notice. When 'Eddie' Marsh wrote to the poet Denis Browne at the Dardanelles he called the Duchy 'a farce so far as work is concerned'. He and Churchill had spent the last two days on a speech Churchill was to deliver in Dundee. He continued: 'He puts a very good face on it … but oh dear oh dear, it is a dreadful blow.'[13] But when the gloom lifted a little, Churchill was able to mock the dismal range of his responsibilities by telling Seely that he was mobilising 'a strong flotilla of magistrates' for the following year.[14]

As far as Churchill was concerned, the office was to be turned into a bunker from which he would venture forth to prod and provoke his fellow ministers into vigorous activity. Previous holders of the office had accepted the pitiful accommodation and minimal staffing, but after only a few weeks in post Churchill was demanding something more fitting to a member of the Cabinet and War Council. He asked Montagu at the Treasury to provide three rooms, permission to retain Edward Marsh and the services of a messenger. Churchill was about to go on the offensive.

Money was a worry, though, since Churchill's salary at the Duchy was £2,000 a year – a large reduction on the First Lord's salary of £4,500. On 12 June, he was rescued from penury by a decision to pool ministerial salaries during the war. This move gave him a salary of £4,360 a year, which was a negligible reduction from his days at the Admiralty.

A NEW LIFE

In losing his job, Churchill and his family had also lost their accommodation at Admiralty House. Balfour generously offered to let them stay on while they looked for somewhere to live but Clementine Churchill rejected this offer as 'charity'. As a temporary measure, they moved into 21 Arlington Street and then at the end of June they joined Jack and 'Goonie' Churchill at 41 Cromwell Road, where the two families remained until early 1918. It was quite a squeeze since between them they had six young children.

Just after Churchill had left the Admiralty, he and his wife rented Hoe Farm at Hascombe near Godalming as a weekend retreat. Built mostly in the sixteenth and seventeenth centuries, it had been extended by Sir Edwin Lutyens in 1890 when he was still in his Arts and Crafts phase. Churchill delighted in country living surrounded by a beautiful garden and with expansive views over the verdant countryside. He told Jack that they lived 'vy simply', which in Churchill's case included 'hot baths, cold champagne, new peas & old brandy'.[15]

It was at Hoe Farm that Churchill took up painting. His inspiration came from watching 'Goonie' at work with her watercolours in the garden. Taking over her materials he tried his hand, but soon found the medium very difficult to master, but when he tried painting in oils he was immediately captivated. His daughter Mary Churchill described how 'Clementine was so thrilled that Winston had found a distraction from his worries that she rushed to Godalming and bought every variety of oil paints available.' But neither of them was aware of the need for turpentine, so his first efforts were unsuccessful. Clementine Churchill called in the painter John Lavery, who lived nearby. Her appeal must have been expressed in desperate terms since, according to her daughter, Lavery 'leapt into a hired car and drove immediately to Hoe Farm'.[16] Churchill later described what happened as Lavery took control:

> '"Painting!" But what are you hesitating about? Let me have a brush – the big one.' Splash into the turpentine, wallop into the blue and white, frantic flourish on the palette – clean no longer – and then several large, fierce strokes and flashes of blue on the absolutely cowering canvas. Anyone could see that it could not hit back. … The spell was broken. The sickly inhibitions rolled away.[17]

And so painting in oils became Churchill's great solace during the darkest hours of his long life.

However, Churchill could not avoid brooding on recent events as he took to re-reading Fisher's letters. Although the breach with Fisher was 'among the most painful things in my life' he was still able to recall, he told Fisher, 'the vanished pleasures of his comradeship and society'.[18]

The other big change in Churchill's life was the move to coalition government. The new Cabinet met on 26 May, creating a novel situation. Until that day, it had always been the custom for new ministers to submit themselves for re-election in their constituencies before taking office. The 'extraordinary' circumstances of the day led the Home Secretary to propose the suspension of this rule for the duration of the war.[19] (The suspension was temporary. Despite two further Acts in July and

December 1916, Churchill still had to stand for re-election in 1917 when he became Minister of Munitions.)

The coalition Cabinet, Churchill said in *The World Crisis*, had been entered into 'under duress' and not because it gave any hope of waging war more effectively. Indeed, it was a strange coalition, formed out of the opposition's discontent with the way the war had been run. In marched (or rather shuffled) Law, Lansdowne, Curzon and Long, only to immediately adopt the very policies that they had earlier derided.

By mid-June, Churchill was able to report to Jack on the 'education' of the new ministers. Having opposed the Dardanelles campaign from its inception they were now convinced 'of the wisdom of the enterprise in strategy and politics'. But his claim that it had been 'a hard battle' appears dubious, given that their conversion seems to have taken place in less than a month of office.[20]

Later in the year, Churchill was much more critical of the newcomers as they settled too comfortably into power. 'The Tories are so glad to be in office again,' he told Riddell, 'that they are like sucking doves. They have lost all their sting. There is no effective opposition and no effective criticism. The House of Commons is muzzled.'[21] It was a gap that Curzon, Lloyd George and Churchill were soon to fill with vigour.

THE STRUGGLE FOR INFLUENCE

For three months from June to August, Churchill sought to drive the war forwards in the Dardanelles Committee (the new name for the War Council), in the Cabinet, and through his public speaking. The renaming of the War Council was most curious. On 18 March, the Dardanelles operation finished. On April 25, the Gallipoli campaign opened. So, if a change of name were needed, surely the committee should have been called the Gallipoli Committee. One result of this was to blur the question of responsibilities. The new members had no responsibility for the Dardanelles, but were fully responsible for the coming tragedy of Gallipoli. On the other hand, Churchill shared responsibility for the bombardments, but had no responsibility at all for Gallipoli. In *The World Crisis*, Churchill complacently recorded that he had been allowed to continue to sit on the left-hand side of Kitchener. Perhaps this symbolism meant something to him but the truth was that he was without influence. He spoke and wrote at length, but no one attached any importance to his opinions.

One of Churchill's first efforts in his new role was a paper of 1 June, entitled 'A note on the general situation' in which he considered the prospects for effective action on the Western Front and at Gallipoli. This lengthy paper essentially declared his strong opposition to frontal assaults in France and his preference for operations in the Mediterranean. In France, he argued, neither the Germans nor the Allies had the strength to break the other's lines, so it was futile to launch offensives at that time. In the North Sea, the navy's wide margin of superiority prevented any serious

German initiatives. But Gallipoli was another matter. There, 'The position ... is at once hopeful and dangerous. The longer it lasts the more dangerous it will become.' Urgent reinforcements were needed.[22]

There was nothing new in this paper and Kitchener would probably have backed every word it contained. Yet it elicited only one response: Sir Ian Hamilton declared it to be 'a masterly document'.[23]

On 5 June, Churchill was relaxed and ebullient when he addressed his Dundee constituents. After briefly referring to his work at the Admiralty, which he said could be judged in due course from the archives of the Admiralty, he gave his audience a rousing and upbeat speech. *The Times* newspaper called it 'a call for optimism and action'. And it was action which, Churchill said, the public expected to see from the new government. Referring to conscription (although avoiding the actual word) Churchill said that he did not believe that compulsion would be necessary. (This a reversal of his view in August 1914.) He talked of the growing strength of the navy: 'Between now and the end of the year, the British Navy will receive reinforcements which would be incredible if they were not actual facts.' Speaking of Gallipoli he warned his audience that 'you must expect [naval] losses' and 'military operations will also be costly'. But the prize to be gained justified the costs: 'The army of Sir Ian Hamilton, the Fleet of Admiral de Robeck are separated by only a few miles from victory ... I am speaking of victory in the sense of a brilliant and formidable fact, shaping the destinies of nations and shortening the duration of the war.'

The press did not escape his criticism. 'No other nation now at war would allow the newspapers such a licence.' There was, he said, 'irresponsible' and 'malicious carping'. A good deal of his speech was devoted to praising those who were running the war, and defending the old government. There was special praise for 'a great friend of mine' – Haldane. 'I deeply regret that he has ceased to fill the great office which he adorned. No more sincere patriot has served the Crown'; it was his work that 'enabled our army to be so swiftly brought to the field of action'. This was a courageous stand on Churchill's part since Haldane was being widely labelled a traitor on the grounds that he appreciated German culture and philosophy.

Apart from his stand in defence of Haldane, Churchill's speech was good rousing material and optimistic to a fault. Whether deep down he felt so optimistic is another matter.

As Churchill was speaking in Dundee, Lavery's new portrait of him was being unveiled in London. The portrait, remarked *The Times* on 7 June, 'managed to make us believe in his [Lavery's] statesman. You feel, the moment that you look at the picture, that someone remarkable is represented.'[24]

Within days of telling his constituents that he saw no need for 'compulsion' Churchill was busy drafting a bill to introduce 'war service'. Since his Bill would have empowered the government 'to direct any person to perform any duty necessary for the prosecution of the war' it is hard to see this as anything other than compulsion.[25]

The draft bill of 9 June led to nothing, but it was the first indication of Churchill distancing himself from mainstream Liberal thinking on the war.

Having called for action in his speech at Dundee, Churchill endeavoured to stimulate some movement at Gallipoli. The initial landings had produced no useful results and Gallipoli, he wrote on 11 June, now resembled the Western Front as lines of Turks faced lines of Allied soldiers. It was all too clear that further frontal assaults of the Turkish positions would yield no useful results. Against this background, Churchill's fertile mind came up with a plan to cut off the Turks from behind their lines and so starve them off the peninsula. His argument was simple: all their supplies came from Constantinople. An army placed across the Bulair Isthmus would cut the Turkish forces off from their source of supply. This, he argued, would starve their army into submission.

When the Dardanelles Committee discussed his proposal the next day, a telegram had already arrived from Hamilton to say that he had previously rejected the idea of landing troops on the Bulair Isthmus. In the meeting, Kitchener objected to the scheme both on grounds of the difficulties of landing on that coast and because an army on the peninsula would be exposed to fire from two sides. The proposal was not rejected outright and Hamilton was asked for more information on the Turkish supply routes. This outcome, though, hardly justified Churchill's claim in a letter to Seely that he was still 'able to influence events'.[26]

On 12 June, just as Churchill was settling into his role at the Duchy of Lancaster, Lieutenant General Sir Pitcairn Campbell, in charge of Southern Command, wrote to offer Churchill the command of 2/1st Oxfordshire Hussars. Churchill was not tempted to take up the offer.

When the Dardanelles Committee met again on 17 June, members were as eager as ever to press on in Gallipoli but a principal concern was the lack of transport ships and escorts to move reinforcements. Typically, it was Churchill who had the one constructive idea, which was to enlist the help of the French navy. But he had little faith in the energy of his colleagues and, after the meeting, wrote in secret to Masterton-Smith at the Admiralty, with his suggestions for expediting the troop transports.

Churchill's apparent lack of success over Gallipoli did not stop him from writing yet another appreciation paper on 18 June, this time on the general military situation. He returned to the paper that Hankey had written on 1 January 1915, which had pressed the need to develop means of crossing open ground under fire. After the war, Churchill described the lack of progress on this front as 'remarkable'.[27] Except that it was not remarkable. Who other than Churchill or Hankey would have had the drive and initiative? It would certainly not be Kitchener or Balfour. As for Asquith, while flinching at the slaughter on the Western Front, he never pushed anyone to look for other ways of making war. In his paper, Churchill repeated his opposition to further attacks on the Western Front, while continuing to place his faith in Gallipoli. He shared with Hankey the view that re-equipping Russia was of the highest priority. To do this, Hankey wrote a few days later, the Dardanelles had to be forced, 'cost what it may'[28]

There was a limit, though, even to Churchill's capacity for self-deception. The Dardanelles Committee of 25 June discussed the issues but did not reach a single conclusion. In the meeting, Churchill remained uncharacteristically quiet as he was slowly becoming aware of his lack of influence.

Despite his declining power to influence the war, Churchill remained very close to Kitchener in his assessment of events. When Kitchener wrote his own military appreciation the day after the dismal Dardanelles Committee meeting, he reinforced all the points that Churchill had been making in recent weeks. The Western Front had been just one reversal after another; nothing more than 'active defence' was feasible, said Kitchener. The two great hopes were Russia, with its enormous population, and Gallipoli. Echoing Churchill, he underlined his commitment to the east, saying that success at Gallipoli was imperative to winning the war. History does not record what the Tory members of the Committee thought as they heard the great Kitchener underlining all the points made by the renegade Churchill.

The month of June closed with Churchill writing yet another paper, this time to propose the setting up of an Air Department. No doubt he looked forward to being in charge, but at least he was fulfilling his commitment to action. The suggestion was not pursued by Asquith.

For a month Churchill had comported himself like a minister of the Crown, writing papers, attending meetings and putting forward ideas. For a man who had suffered such a humiliating defeat in May, it was a fine performance. Yet he had achieved nothing. True, he may have helped in converting the Tories to Gallipoli, but the Dardanelles Committee had not taken one single decision that made any difference during the month. How long could he continue just to go through the motions of governing?

—————⟫•⟪—————

An incident at this time brought out Churchill's capacity for pettiness. Balfour, as the new First Lord, had asked Fisher to chair an Admiralty Board of Invention and Research. This was to co-ordinate the use of science in the navy. Churchill attacked the appointment in a furious letter to Asquith. It was Fisher's fault that he, Churchill, had humiliatingly been removed from the Admiralty. Although he never sent this letter, he separately made his objections clear to Balfour who was shocked by Churchill's language. He had had no idea that Churchill was so upset. Nor could he understand Churchill's antagonism towards Fisher, a man whose 'great gifts' were once more being used by the nation.[29] Any reasonable person would have let the matter drop, but that was not in Churchill's nature. He turned his attack on Balfour for appointing a man who had walked out of his office during wartime. According to Fisher, Balfour pronounced that 'he didn't see what concern it was of Winston's'.[30]

In mid-July, Churchill decided on a more vigorous approach in his attempt to force action at Gallipoli. In yet one more lengthy paper, he protested against the many delays at Gallipoli and their impact on events. He reminded his readers that the original military attack on 25 March had been delayed by the belated despatch of troops, which had allowed the Turks to simply reinforce their positions. Now events were being repeated. The impending attack, which could have taken place at the end of June, was being delayed by an indecisive government. All the while the Germans were moving ever closer to the isthmus as they advanced from the north. He summarised his forceful attack on the government's inaction by noting that the story of Gallipoli had been one delay after another. But, rather contradicting himself, Churchill concluded there was still time to regain the offensive. What was needed was urgent action to bring Bulgaria into the war on the Allied side and to send the Third (new) army to Gallipoli immediately.

Just after writing this paper, Churchill called on his insurance broker William Bernau, to make a rather special request. He wanted cover for nothing less than a private civilian visit to Gallipoli and that no one was to be told. His purpose was to carry out a review of the situation with the intention of presenting a report to the Cabinet. Churchill undertook to take no part in military operations and not to hazard his safety. Although he expected to be away for three to four weeks, he asked for cover for two months since he might visit the battlefields of France on his way home.

Despite Churchill's pretence that no one was to know of his visit, there was no way that he could go without Asquith's permission. In fact, by the time that he consulted Asquith he had already obtained Balfour's blessing and persuaded Kitchener to agree the wording of a telegram to Hamilton. Asquith accepted the visit with alacrity. All seemed settled.

By 17 July, Churchill's visit had become common knowledge. Keyes heard the news with horror, telling his wife 'it is all wrong'. He had visions of Churchill acting the 'Generalissimo' and trying to upstage de Robeck: 'I am afraid I shall have my work cut out to keep the peace between de R. and W.C.'[31] Thus began the complications. Although Kitchener welcomed the visit he still thought it sensible to take the precaution of sending Lieutenant Colonel Maurice Hankey to accompany Churchill. Hankey was most upset, recording in his diary that he would be in a 'very awkward position' since he would be 'intended as a check on Churchill'.[32]

Churchill continued with his preparations by drawing up a letter to his wife, for her to open in the event of his death. In a summary of his assets he listed his securities, which he thought would be enough to pay off his debts to his brother Jack. There was a life insurance policy which would provide her with £300 per year. Then he turned to his literary archive and his biography. He appointed Clementine as his literary executor and concluded by saying 'Death is only an incident.'[33]

Two days after Churchill had seen his broker the complications worsened. Even his dear and loyal friend General Sir Ian Hamilton had reservations, as he had hoped that his forces could be left in peace without visitors for a while. Meanwhile, Churchill had already begun work on expanding his mission, telling Asquith that if there were a victory at Gallipoli while he was away, he would be on the spot ready to rush to 'Sofia or Athens' in order to seize any political benefits.

And then the Tories made their move. After representations from Curzon and others, Asquith reluctantly wrote on 19 July to cancel Churchill's participation in the visit. Hankey was to go alone. It was one more example of Asquith's pitiable inability to support Churchill. Curzon's own explanation tells all. He and his colleagues had objected to the very principle of a minister visiting war areas on behalf of other ministers. It was a stupid objection, effectively saying that no Cabinet could ever ask one of its members to collect information and report back to the full body. By pressing this argument, Curzon and his colleagues were admitting that it was better to remain ill-informed than be well-informed by Churchill. Kitchener was most disappointed since he had seen the Gallipoli visit as a good means of getting Churchill out of the way.

⟶►◉◄⟵

At last on 6 August 1915, the long-delayed offensive was launched at Gallipoli. The night before the attack, Hamilton had written to Churchill to thank him for his unstinting support – Churchill had been (and perhaps still was) Hamilton's strongest champion. No wonder that Hamilton closed his letter with the line 'Now is the moment I would have loved you to be here.'[34] (This and the many similar appeals from French to Churchill are a testament to the surprising impact that Churchill had on generals.)

The main assault took place at Suvla Bay where fresh divisions, commanded by Lieutenant General Sir Frederick Stopford, made a landing. There was also a diversionary attack at Helles and a thrust northwards from Anzac Cove. If all had gone well, the forces from Suvla Bay and Anzac troops would have linked up and swept forward across the peninsula.

Nothing was achieved. Stopford's divisions made a promising start with a highly successful landing, with all the advantages of surprise. But he delayed his advance, allowing the Turks to strengthen their positions in front of his troops. Both of the other actions were characterised by the delay and indecision which seemed to have been endemic in Gallipoli generals. It was not long before Hamilton was once more bogged down on every front and asking yet again for reinforcements.

Churchill's reaction to the news was to urge Asquith to send troops from Egypt where, he estimated, there were 75,000 men. There was also a need to 'rush' more ammunition by train across Europe. Showing a sense of drive and urgency that seemed to be sadly lacking elsewhere, he added: 'We are so near a great victory that nothing humanly possible should be neglected to secure it.'[35]

On 11 August, not long after the assault on Gallipoli had failed, Curzon, Lloyd George and Churchill made a strong plea in Cabinet for conscription. It was the beginning of a long fight between those who believed that the war could be won with a volunteer army and those who saw no hope without compulsion. Churchill was now firmly on the side of compulsion.

A committee was set up to consider the issue. Churchill wrote a lengthy paper asking the committee to decide on the numbers of men needed and to determine the size of army required for 1916. It was an unusual paper, since it was mostly devoted to the methodology by which such figures could be established, rather than to making any strong case for their collection. Churchill did, though, conclude that such a survey would provide the data to estimate the forces needed to take the offensive in the following year. At the committee on 18 August, both Lloyd George and Churchill vigorously made the case for compulsion, but they were opposed by members such as Grey, whose political philosophy could never encompass the idea of the compulsory mobilisation of a population; for him such a notion was 'madness'.[36] After twelve meetings the members were no nearer agreement and the committee was disbanded.

Since de Robeck had abandoned the bombardment of the forts on 18 March, the navy had done little other than provide transport facilities at the Dardanelles. Now, five months later, on 21 August, Churchill suggested a return to the offensive. In a lengthy letter addressed to Asquith and Balfour, he reminded them that de Robeck had only abandoned the offensive in March because the army had favoured a joint operation. At the time de Robeck had been keen to continue. (And, although Churchill did not mention him, so had been Keyes.) Comparing losses, Churchill noted that the army had suffered 100,000 casualties at Gallipoli to absolutely no effect, yet no one was concerned. What a contrast, he argued, to the fuss over the navy's negligible losses in March.

There was now a new and stronger argument for putting ships into the Sea of Marmara. There they could block supplies to the Turkish troops on the peninsula and since the land route was not able to supply the Turkish front, the naval blockade could starve them into submission. There followed much more about the detailed methods that Churchill proposed for reaching and holding Marmara. When the issue came before the Dardanelles Committee, Balfour gave no support. It was Churchill's last attempt to put the naval case. Doubtless he had exacerbated his failure by acting alone. Had he been able to agree a joint paper with Balfour, the Committee might have accepted their recommendations.

There was just one act left open to Churchill in his efforts to progress the slow-moving Gallipoli campaign: show his support for Hamilton. The failure of Hamilton's offensive in August was rapidly undermining faith in him, both in the Mediterranean and in London. At the Dardanelles Committee on 27 August, the questioning of some of the Tory members was dangerously hostile. Law asked if Hamilton 'was going to continue his course of sacrificing men without a chance of success'. Later he asked if Hamilton 'was to continue attacking when such action was obviously hopeless'.

(Law could have asked the same questions about the Western Front, but he did not.) Both Law and Carson argued that Hamilton should be ordered to assume a defensive position. Kitchener protested strongly against issuing such a restrictive order to a general. Churchill, too, thought that the Committee should allow the commander on the spot to take his own decisions. (Yet Kitchener had told French to adopt a defensive stance on the Western Front.) But the tenor of the meeting was that of a faltering confidence in Hamilton; a widening breach between Kitchener and Churchill on the one hand, and the Tory members on the other.[37]

DEFEAT AND WITHDRAWAL

The end of August 1915 marked the point at which Churchill began seriously to face the truth about his position. For all the drive, vigour and imagination that he had poured into his papers, letters and committee work, he had made precious little impact. He was surrounded by men who were lost. They had no idea what to do beyond wait-and-see on the Western Front and they were rapidly running out of conviction over Gallipoli. They had also lost faith in Kitchener, yet could see no way of deposing him.

It was no place for a man like Churchill. He could not yet see that his only salvation lay in making the move from faux-counsellor to true opposition. The route was to lie through France, a fact that he was slowly coming to appreciate.

It was Curzon who helped Churchill to take the first step, almost in an aside. He had written in early September to thank Churchill for some documents about Gallipoli. Then he launched into an attack on Asquith's methods of governing as he could not see how a Cabinet of twenty-two could be made to work properly. Was there any way, he asked Churchill, of questioning the system without it reflecting on Asquith? But it was clear what he had in mind: a very small war staff to work full time on the war without other departmental responsibilities. While Churchill would have fully shared these views, it is hard to understand why Curzon thought Churchill – then without influence – could have helped bring about these changes.

A few days later, Curzon and Churchill dined with Lloyd George. Frances Stevenson, recounting what Lloyd George had told her afterwards, recorded 'they had a most important talk. The Tories are going to approach the P.M. & say they cannot proceed any longer under the present state of things. They will demand conscription and the removal of K.'[38]

⋙●⋘

Unable to influence events, Churchill embroiled himself in what Addison at the Ministry of Munitions called 'a rather unpleasant incident'. He recorded it in his diary even though it was 'scarcely worth reporting' because it showed how, at times, Churchill 'lets himself in for trouble'.

A Lieutenant Sutton, of the Trench Warfare Department, alerted Churchill when he told him that 'nothing had been done' about an order, placed on 27 August, for Stokes trench mortars. Churchill, through Marsh, wrote to Lloyd George who, in turn, asked Addison to investigate. The latter reported that the order had been fulfilled. Churchill refused to accept this answer and wrote a four-page letter demanding to see a report on the action taken. A furious Addison went to see Lloyd George and told him he would not send the report to Churchill unless he was ordered. Churchill arrived in person and, said Addison, 'being fairly warmed, I fell upon him.' He showed Churchill the part of the report that confirmed twenty of the guns, which Churchill alleged had not been ordered, had already been sent to France. Another thirty were to be delivered that week. Rather than back down, Churchill then alleged that the two men involved in placing the order 'had been dismissed … because they had been talking to him'. The ever patient Addison showed Churchill the correspondence to confirm that Sutton had been given two weeks' sick leave and the other man, a Captain Rose, had just obtained Kitchener's permission to remain in the Ministry for a further month. Addison's diary entry closed with the comment that 'L.G. roared with delight at Winston's discomfiture.'[39] It was Churchill at his worst. But Churchill was nothing if not brazen – two weeks later he was again in Addison's office complaining once more about deliveries of Stokes trench mortars to Gallipoli.[40]

———◆———

An event then took place that was to profoundly change how Churchill viewed the war on the Western Front. On 25 September, Lieutenant General Douglas Haig in command of 1 Corps took six divisions into battle at Loos and when the fighting was finally abandoned in October the British had suffered 50,000 casualties. The battle had two consequences for Churchill. Firstly, it was to bring about the removal of French and his return to England. As one of Churchill's most ardent supporters, the loss of French was to profoundly affect Churchill's period of service in France. Secondly, Loos was yet further evidence that frontal attacks in Flanders were futile. Churchill told Lloyd George: 'the same effort and expenditure which had given us the village of Loos would have given us Constantinople.'[41] More importantly the shocking losses of yet another futile frontal assault re-ignited Churchill's determination to replace men with machines in battle.

But Churchill's position was weakening by the day. In early October, the newspaper proprietor Harold Harmsworth was circulating rumours of Churchill's imminent downfall. According to Freddie Guest MP, the government was about to fall and intended to put the blame for Gallipoli on Churchill. He recommended that Churchill leave the government in the next few days. Somehow, Guest worked out that in this way Churchill would be able to return to power as Prime Minister in the not too distant future. Little of this should be taken at face value but the bizarre nature of Guest's advice underlines the level of mutual hostility and suspicion in Asquith's Cabinet.

Guest had chosen a bad moment to recommend that Churchill flee since the very next day, 11 October, the evacuation of Gallipoli was forcefully pressed for by several members of the Dardanelles Committee. Although the minutes record that Churchill said he favoured evacuation if there were not enough forces to capture the peninsula, this gives a false impression of his position. He remained adamantly behind the venture provided there were enough troops. But Carson and Lloyd George viewed sending troops to help embattled Serbia as a far higher priority. Grey, meanwhile, wanted a straightforward evacuation. Kitchener was horror-struck at the discussion as such a move, he said, 'would be the most disastrous event in the history of the Empire'. He frightened off his colleagues by forecasting losses of up to 25,000 men in an evacuation. (The evacuation was eventually carried out without a man being lost.) It was left to Asquith to declare there would be no evacuation.

The pro-withdrawal group was now in the ascendancy and at the next meeting of the Dardanelles Committee, on 14 October, Curzon demanded Hamilton's recall. Asquith concurred, but Churchill put up a strong if bizarre defence of his friend. True, 'he had failed to retain confidence' but he had faced 'appalling difficulties' and had 'attempt[ed] what was demanded of him'. His failure had been 'partly due to inexperienced officers'.[42] But it was Kitchener who had the final say. Hamilton was to be recalled and General Sir Charles Monro was to be sent as his replacement. Asquith said he would rather have sent Kitchener, a view seconded by Churchill. Part of his argument was the weakness of Monro, whose promotions had been due more to the increases in the size of the army than to his military ability.

Towards the end of October, Asquith announced the end of the Dardanelles Committee and its replacement by a small War Council. Roy Jenkins recounts in his biography of Asquith the pressures that had built up on him in the preceding days. His troubles had begun with a sleepless night on 19 October, followed by a day in bed and a call to his doctor. Margot Asquith declared him to be 'absolutely done' and his doctor diagnosed 'overwork, hot rooms and no sort of exercise'. Asquith then slept for thirty-six hours. In this period he received Curzon's resignation from the Cabinet and various critical letters from three senior Tories: Walter Long, Lord Selborne and Lord Robert Cecil. Too ill to attend the Cabinet meeting, it was left to Lord Crewe (by now Lord President of the Council) to preside and afterwards to report to the King that they had unanimously agreed that a smaller council was needed.[43]

Of course, part of the drive for a smaller council was the desire of many ministers to force Kitchener out of the War Office. To this end, a faction of the Dardanelles Committee met after the Cabinet meeting to discuss what to do next. Balfour declared that he would not serve on the new committee unless there was a change at the War Office. In reporting this to Asquith, Churchill then set out his own demands. He told Asquith that he would leave the government if Kitchener remained at the War Office. It was a threat that the Prime Minister could safely ignore.

At the end of the month, Asquith formally advised his colleagues that he was setting up a small council of three to five ministers to run the war. Ministers had to wait until 11 November to hear who was in and who was out. When the list was announced, the favoured five were to be Asquith, Balfour, Lloyd George, Bonar Law and McKenna. None had ever served in the army or the navy. The two military brains – Kitchener and Churchill – had been unceremoniously dumped.

When Riddell met Churchill a few days later he found him gloomy. 'Things are looking very bad,' Churchill told him, adding that he was 'tired of his present mode of life, and would not stand it much longer'.[44]

All that was left for Churchill was resignation. His letter to Asquith on 11 November was diplomatically generous, in sharp contrast to what Churchill was soon to say in private. He accepted the problems that Asquith had in selecting the members of his council and agreed with the principle of the small decision-making group. But he realised there was now no role for him so he asked Asquith to submit his resignation from the Duchy to the King. He, in turn, would offer his services as a soldier to the War Office. He could not help adding: 'Time will vindicate my administration of the Admiralty.'[45] Interestingly, when his friend Archie Sinclair resigned from the Scottish Office, Churchill advised against his action, saying that any office was better than none at all. He did not follow this advice himself.

In reply, Asquith said he regretted Churchill's decision to resign. Despite all the friction between the two men we can assume that Asquith was most reluctant to see Churchill depart. There was no one who could replace his energy, imagination and courage.

CHAPTER 10

IN SEARCH OF A BATTALION

And now the country which has been attacking him unjustly … is repaying him by letting him leave the Government for France. – *Manchester Guardian*[1]

RESIGNATION

The news of Churchill's departure from government was received with shock and incredulity by many. Vice Admiral Sir Charles Coke echoed the feelings of many when he told Churchill that he did not think the country could manage without him. The *Manchester Guardian* stated that Churchill had 'the best strategic eye of the Government' and 'His absence from the counsels of the Government is a great national loss.'[2] Violet Asquith was sure that her father would miss his advice and his drive. For once the praise was non-partisan. Inveterate Tories, such as Walter Long, went out of their way to praise Churchill's achievements. He had, said Long, 'rendered incalculable service to the country at the beginning of the war' and 'had been animated from the beginning by a real desire to serve his country'.[3]

There were also many in the navy who were distressed at Churchill's departure from the war councils. For Masterton-Smith he was simply the best First Lord.

But there was mocking praise from the German press. They read Churchill's departure, following so closely on Sir Edward Carson's resignation in October, as an indication that Asquith's government was crumbling. One newspaper noted that 'Carson has withdrawn … Kitchener has gone travelling … while Churchill is not willing to go on playing now that the first violin has been taken from him.' It then asked 'Who will be next?'[4] German soldiers even went so far as to taunt their French opponents by tossing mocking messages into the French trenches saying that 'Churchill had resigned so that he will not be blamed for the defeat of his country.'[5]

But of more importance was the public debate, which began with Churchill's resignation statement in the Commons on 15 November. Hardly had Churchill stood up to speak when the first cheers erupted from the Commons benches and within minutes he had the House laughing. From that moment on he had members hanging on his every word as he defended his time at the Admiralty. Little did Asquith know that, in starving the Commons of war information for fifteen months, he had guaranteed Churchill a famished audience, ready to gratefully accept any morsels that he tossed to them.

He opened his speech by describing the events surrounding the battles of Coronel and the Falklands. He saw no reason why the story could not now be told since 'more than a year has passed' and 'the seas have been swept clear of the enemy's flag'. He insisted that all his dispositions had been in writing 'and my right hon. friend [Balfour] has my full authority to publish or quote any minute of mine'. He urged that all the telegrams should be handed to a man such as the naval historian Sir Julian Corbett to write the full story: 'it would be shown that the Admiralty dispositions were sound.'

Next, Churchill turned to the Bacchantes debacle. Cheers followed as he declared: 'The charge has been made publicly and repeatedly that I overruled the naval authorities in keeping these cruisers out against their advice. That charge is not true.' Once more he said that he had no objection to the full papers being published. 'Let it be fully understood that I am not the cause of any withholding of papers from publication.'

Inevitably, he now had to deal with the torrent of abuse that had been heaped on him over Antwerp. Not that the task was particularly difficult since the facts spoke for themselves. All the vile and libellous stories that had been spread about his role had come from those who had no access to any of the documents. And so the House discovered for the first time that it was not Churchill who instigated the Antwerp intervention: 'It originated with Lord Kitchener and the French Government.' In the context of an ill-informed House, this was a staggering revelation. A project that carried (so many members thought) the hallmark of the reckless Churchill, now turned out to be the brainchild of their great hero, Kitchener. They heard how Kitchener had despatched Churchill to Antwerp, carrying his plan to send a relieving army. The offer of an intervention had been accepted by both the Belgian and French governments, he told the House.

Churchill freely admitted that the operations had begun too late, but stunned the House by revealing that he had warned Asquith on 6 September of 'the dangerous situation which was developing at Antwerp'. As to his own role, Churchill said that once in Antwerp, 'I was told to do everything possible to maintain the defence' until the relieving army arrived. He was cheered as he added, 'This I did without regard to the consequences in any direction.'

Turning to what had been achieved, Churchill said 'I think it is a great mistake to regard Lord Kitchener's effort to relieve Antwerp … as an event which led only to misfortune.' He concluded 'I believe that military history will hold that the consequences conduced extremely to the advantage of the Allies in the west.'

Finally, Churchill turned to the Dardanelles. Knowing that the central charge against him was the failure to consult his advisers, he revealed to the House that both Carden and Jackson had said that the Dardanelles could be forced by naval power alone. He described how Carden had given this opinion at the start of the year and how he had produced a purely naval plan on 11 January. As to Fisher's role, 'He never expressed any opinion against this specific operation at all, at this stage.' In case all this appeared too much like evading accountability, Churchill added 'I state all these points not in order to shield myself from responsibility, but to show the House that the business of the Admiralty has been properly conducted.' After emphasising the close involvement of his staff ('day by day I held staff meetings at the Admiralty') Churchill refuted the central charge: 'I will not have it said that this was a civilian plan foisted by a political amateur upon reluctant officers and experts.' He was also careful to demonstrate how fully both Carden and de Robeck had been committed to the venture.

The speech was a parliamentary triumph, marred only by comments about Fisher that were both unnecessary and counter-productive.

As soon as Churchill sat down, Asquith rose to congratulate him on a 'very moving speech'. Churchill, he said, 'had dealt with a very delicate situation not only with ability and eloquence, but also with loyalty and discretion'. While Asquith declared that there were passages he would have preferred omitted, he left the House in no doubt as to his admiration for the speech. And for the man, too: 'I desire to say to him and of him, that, having been associated with him for 10 years in close and daily intimacy, in positions of great responsibilities, and in situations varied and of extreme difficulty and delicacy, I have always found him a wise counsellor, a brilliant colleague, and a faithful friend.'[6]

Later that day, the man who had so vilified Churchill and forced him out of the Admiralty rose to speak and few could have anticipated the generous tribute that came from Bonar Law. He first admitted his past reservations, saying 'I entered the Cabinet, to put it mildly, with no prejudice in favour of the right hon. Gentleman.' But after sitting in Cabinet with him for five months, he had concluded that 'in my judgement, in mental power and vital force he is one of the foremost men in our country.'[7] The Observer newspaper astutely noted that Law's speech was 'the best comment' on Churchill's statement since it came from 'a quarter not suspect of undue partiality'.[8]

As he was about to leave the Commons, Churchill met Violet Asquith. She later recalled that 'the after-glow of his speech shone in his eyes' as 'the moment of triumph blotted out past and future.'[9]

The press followed the Commons in its appreciation of the speech. The Times declared it to be 'an undoubted Parliamentary triumph', which had been 'punctuated by cheers from all parts of the House' and terminated with an ovation. It had been a skilful composition, 'admirably calculated to achieve its object'. As to the detailed content, the paper declared 'the country ... should have been told everything he said yesterday many months ago.' Churchill's speech had explained a lot, as it exposed to the public gaze 'with painful clearness the great gulf between the War Office and the

Admiralty'. It was obvious to the newspaper that the main failure at the Dardanelles had been a military one because 'it was undertaken in driblets at long intervals'.[10]

The *Manchester Guardian* chose to focus on the irony of the warm reception that Churchill's speech had received from those very people who had 'been attacking him unjustly'. Now they were 'repaying him by letting him leave the Government for France'.[11]

There was one particular note of reticence. Fisher was stung by Churchill's comments on his failure to support his chief over the Dardanelles, but he declined to enter into public dispute. In a brief statement in the Lords he merely said 'I leave my record in the hands of my countrymen.' It was, he told his peers, 'unfitting to make personal explanations affecting national interests when my country is in the midst of a great War.'[12]

While Churchill could content himself with his declamatory speech and the Commons could enjoy the restoration of its right to know what ministers were doing, *The Times* pondered a more serious matter. Succinctly, it noted, 'Another strong man has left the Cabinet.' The resignation, it added, showed that the Cabinet had a 'tendency to shed its elements of strength instead of shedding its elements of weakness'.[13] These were wise words. Asquith's ability to hold on to his Cabinet depended more and more on the able men departing. Another of the strong men in the Cabinet was also known to be at odds with Asquith over conscription. Curzon told Churchill that he was on the edge of resigning. In pushing (intentionally or not) Churchill out of power, Asquith had fatally weakened his own position and this gave Churchill, Curzon and Carson an excuse to form a faction outside the Cabinet – a faction that Lloyd George willingly supported.

The ineptitude of Asquith's management of his strong men appeared obvious on the other side of the Atlantic, where Shane Leslie (a first cousin of Churchill) reported to Lady Randolph Churchill that the government was seen to have failed in everything that it had attempted and was now stupidly sending one of its ablest members to face mortal danger in the trenches.

⸺⸻▶◀⸻⸺

As soon as the echoes of Churchill's speech faded away, speculation as to his military posting began. Bonar Law, in his tribute to Churchill, had hoped that 'the Commander-in-Chief will find some means of utilising his great ability'.[14] But the *Manchester Guardian* doubted that Churchill would accept a 'soft job' since 'he desires to go to the front in the ordinary, arduous, dangerous way.'[15] All this was marred only by some critical questions in the House as to whether Churchill was qualified to command an infantry brigade.

Captain Henry Oliver, the Director of Naval Intelligence, in fact spoke for the majority of Churchill's admirers when he questioned the wisdom of his going to the

Front. He was needed at home in Parliament, where he could still have great influence. Others were more concerned that he made the right choice of posting. The former Liberal MP, Captain Kincaid-Smith, warned him to avoid the cavalry since he would be bored stiff. (Presumably because there was no role for the cavalry in this war.) Perhaps the most constructive suggestion came from Commander Carlyon Bellairs, MP for Maidstone. He proposed that Churchill be appointed 'Eye-witness on the Western Front'.[16] Had this proposal been accepted, Churchill would no doubt have produced some pungent reports on the inane activities of the French and British armies.

All this discussion was brought to an end when Churchill left for the Front before any offer of preferential employment had been made. 'Max' Aitken was one of the last people outside the family to see him at that time:

> The night[17] before his departure for the front I went to see him in his house in the Cromwell Road. The whole household was upside down while the soldier-statesman was buckling on his sword. Downstairs, Mr. 'Eddie' Marsh, his faithful secretary, was in tears … Upstairs, Lady Randolph was in a state of despair at the idea of her brilliant son being relegated to the trenches. Mrs Churchill seemed to be the only person who remained calm, collected and efficient.[18]

The meal was a disaster according to Violet Asquith since Margot Asquith dominated the occasion by haranguing Churchill over the 'evils' of a coalition.[19]

In the midst of the chaos, Churchill had found time to take care of Marsh. He immediately found himself on Asquith's staff to oversee Civil List pensions; with such light duties it would seem that Asquith simply wanted to keep him available for when Churchill returned to politics.

On the morning of 18 November, Major Winston Spencer-Churchill arrived at Charing Cross station to board a troop train for Dover. Apart from the presence of a throng of journalists, his departure, reported the *Manchester Guardian*, was like that 'of any other officer hurrying away at the end of his leave'. In his new uniform he 'was not very easy to recognise' and the 'returning soldiers and their friends' failed to spot the ex-Cabinet minister. Not that Churchill had adopted a particularly modest demeanour, being seen 'striding along … his head thrust out', while saluting all and sundry. At his side, his sword rattled at he pushed his way down the platform and boarded his reserved carriage. Avoiding the temptation to make a speech, Churchill told the press that 'I am joining my regiment just as any other officer does, for work.'[20]

But an event of two days earlier emphasised how far Churchill was from being 'any other officer'. He had attended a meeting in the Commons to receive the John Lavery portrait, commissioned by the officers of the Armoured Car Squadrons. The vehicles, said Lieutenant Commander Wedgwood, 'had proved invaluable' as they had been used in France, South Africa, East Africa, West Africa and Gallipoli. In accepting the portrait, Churchill noted that 'the course of the war in the West had not been such as to give proper scope to engines of that character.'[21] The armoured cars had been designed for large and fast-moving manoeuvres. Surely there was some irony in Churchill receiving this honour just as he was departing for the static war of the trenches.

WITH THE GUARDS

Once in France, Churchill went straight to French's headquarters in a chateau at St Omer, where he found his colleague to be as friendly as ever. French promptly offered him a brigade. After the hostile questions in the House about Churchill's fitness to command a humble battalion, he turned the offer down. As he told his wife, he felt he needed to learn about trench warfare before seeking promotion and he thought that the Guards would be the best place for him. French readily agreed to a temporary posting. Meanwhile, Churchill was able to enjoy life in the chateau, which had all the conveniences of a luxury hotel.

On Churchill's second day in France, Field Marshal Sir John French took time off his arduous duties to write to the wife of a certain major. He told Clementine that her husband was getting on well and that he was keeping a special eye on him – French was well aware that he had under his protection one of the few men who absolutely had to be returned intact to England.

On 19 November, Churchill met Major General Lord Cavan who was in command of the Guards Division. Churchill told Cavan that he was honoured to serve with the Guards, to which the Major General reciprocated by saying how pleased they were to have him with them. In an attempt to reassure his anxious wife, Churchill told Clementine that his posting was well away from danger since there were only some fifteen casualties each day on that front. Despite the war he was enjoying the peaceful atmosphere.

Now away from the cauldron of Westminster, Churchill was able to reflect on the months since his departure from the Admiralty. He told his brother how frustrated he had been at the Duchy, where he had been powerless to spur his colleagues into life. Writing to his wife, he grieved at having nothing to show for those months without power or influence.

The day after these despondent thoughts, Churchill joined the Grenadier Guards in the trenches near Neuve Chapelle. Raymond Asquith, the son of the Prime Minister, was serving nearby and had just missed meeting him at the battalion HQ. In his low mood, Churchill would have been pleased to hear that Raymond wrote in his diary 'He is a really splendid fellow and comes out of the war better than anyone, I think.'[22]

The battalion's diary noted that the trenches were in a very poor condition with water underfoot and the sides falling in. At home, although most concerned for her son's safety, his mother accepted his hazardous plunge into the front line, realising that there was no way in which he would have stayed fifty miles from the Front.

Admiration at home and the backing of French were not enough to ensure a warm welcome in the trenches. One soldier wrote 'He has hit about as hard as can be met with in the service, and they are going to put him through it good and proper.'[23] This unwelcoming attitude did not escape Churchill's notice. The officers, he told his wife, had been frosty and unfriendly. The colonel of the battalion was brutally honest when he told Churchill that they had neither asked for him to be sent to them nor agreed to have him.

On his second day in the trenches, Churchill wrote the first of many letters home from the Western Front in which he did all he could to play down the risks that had to be faced. There was little military action and the only injuries sustained were from stray bullets. While his life was tough, he felt in fine form, although there was always the problem of cold feet. His mind, though, was on his career and he was determined to learn all he could from the colonel, a man he held in high regard. He promised not to rush off as long as the regiment stayed at the Front. Bodily needs also had to be considered and he closed his letter with a long list of requisites, including a periscope and a warm sleeping bag.

Two days later, Churchill and the battalion had completed their forty-eight-hour duty in the trenches and were now billeted in support some 1,000 yards behind the front line. Even so he had chosen to spend an additional night in the trenches, which had given him a chance to learn more about trench warfare. He reassured his wife in a letter of 23 November that this was just as safe as being at headquarters.

Life was easy enough for Churchill to pay a visit on horseback to Raymond Asquith, who was stationed six miles away. As they enjoyed a cup of tea, Churchill found the Prime Minister's son to be very soldierly and matured by his military command. As to his own military standing, Churchill revelled in the fact that, as a major, the men and junior officers had to salute him. Food was never far from his mind and after just four days at the Front he was appealing to his wife to send him weekly supplies of small luxuries.

Despite a decade of sedentary office life, Churchill's body responded well to the harsh conditions of the trenches. He declared himself to be capable of coping with the physical demands of trench warfare and assured his mother that he felt like a young man once more. But neither his wife nor his mother were reassured and they both sent him letters begging him not to attempt too much too quickly.

Having so far underlined the harmless nature of his section of the Front, Churchill felt emboldened to recount a less comforting story. He was sitting in a dugout having a meal when a telegram arrived from the Corps Commander ordering him to go to a certain point on the main road that afternoon, where a motorcar would collect him. He told Clementine 'I thought it a rather strong order to bring me out of the trenches by daylight – a 3 mile walk across sopping fields on which stray bullets are always falling.' But since the order implied something of importance, Churchill felt he had no option but to obey. Just as he set off, the Germans began to target the area and, at one point, a number of shells fell close behind him. When he reached the main road there was no motorcar. After a while an officer arrived to say that the vehicle 'had been driven off by shells'. But no matter since the general had only wanted to chat with Churchill about routine matters. All he could do was turn back and retrace his steps through the mud.[24]

Fuming with anger at the thoughtless general who had put him to so much trouble and exposed him to needless danger, Churchill arrived back at the trenches. There he discovered that the general had possibly saved his life. The dugout from which he had been called away had been hit by a shell. One orderly had been killed and all of Churchill's clothes and equipment had disappeared under a thick layer of mud and rubble.

Once he had his own battalion, Churchill was to be accused of being too light on punishments. An incident during his time with the Guards illustrates his sympathetic treatment of men. He had found a young sentry sleeping at his post; knowing that reporting the boy might result in his execution, Churchill gave him a terrifying lecture and walked on. His own compassionate treatment of men did not stop him admiring the battalion's refusal to countenance or overlook even the smallest infringement of the regulations or slackness in routine duties.

After a week at the Front, Churchill's mind drifted back to politics and he saw himself returning to the Commons when the war was over. Meanwhile, he urged his wife to cultivate the newspaper editors James Garvin (*The Observer*), C.P. Scott (*Manchester Guardian*) and Viscount Rothermere (*Sunday Pictorial*) who were all good friends with great influence. She was also to cultivate the senior members of the government lest they should forget him.

On the last day of November, Churchill celebrated his forty-first birthday in the reserve billet. The next day the battalion was pulled out of the front line for eight days. It was even possible, he told Clementine, that they would not return.

Edward Grigg, a journalist who was later to serve under Churchill in the Second World War, was with the Guards at this time and left a sympathetic account of their time together. In a letter to his mother, he told her how they had endured the cold, wet winter weather and trenches knee-deep in water and filth. They had survived in a dugout no more than thirty inches high, where they slept on the bare earth, and worked and ate doubled up under the low roof. But Churchill was enjoying himself and was in good spirits.

Churchill was now ordered to GHQ to await a posting. His immediate future depended critically on whether his friend and mentor French was sent home or not. He was aware of how his own advancement depended on French staying. Lord Cavan had advised a battalion as a start and since he had given the impression that promotion would follow at some stage, Churchill was inclined to accept this advice.

While Churchill was settling into life in the Guards, Kitchener was at Gallipoli. Following Hamilton's recall in October, General Monro had submitted his review of the situation to the War Council in which he recommended evacuation, much to Kitchener's irritation. Unable to decide between the views of the two generals, the War Council then sent out Kitchener who, after little more than a week at Gallipoli, advised the evacuation of Suvla Bay and Anzac Cove but the retention of Helles. However, the War Council was not convinced and decided on total evacuation. The campaign had been neither more nor less successful than the years of pointless attacks on the Western Front, although it had been far more economical in lives lost and resources destroyed. As Brigadier-General Aspinall-Oglander wrote after the war, 'the Western Front [was] a gamble with pounds for a possible gain of pence', whereas in the east 'pence were to be wagered in the none too sanguine hope of winning pounds'.[25]

By early December, Churchill had heard of Kitchener's return from Gallipoli. He fumed as he told Clementine of his anger at Kitchener's three purposeless weeks and his recommendation to evacuate Gallipoli while sending more troops to Salonika. He also raged against the two failing campaigns, which he considered had been criminally mismanaged.

While he was in the trenches Churchill was kept informed by Curzon as to the discussions about the evacuation of Gallipoli. When he passed Curzon's latest letters on to Clementine he advised her to lock them away and, if asked, to deny all knowledge of them. Both Curzon and Churchill were edging their way into opposition, with the evacuation being one more reason for distancing themselves from Asquith's administration.

On 8 December, when he heard of the decision to evacuate Gallipoli, Churchill vented his anger in a letter to Garvin. He felt betrayed by a man whom he had seen as a friend and hero. He wrongly predicted that Asquith and Kitchener would shortly go, leaving the field open to Lloyd George. In fact Asquith was to hang on for another year. Four days later, Churchill asked his wife to reassure Curzon that his letters were safe and to ask him to keep writing. As he brooded on these events, Churchill's attitude hardened and he began to think of returning early in 1916 in order to precipitate the demise of Asquith and Kitchener.

LIMBO

A few weeks of the trenches, combined with the disaster at Loos, were enough to convince Churchill that frontal attacks by unprotected infantry were no way to fight a war. Confined to the Brigade HQ, Churchill sat down on 3 December to write what was his most important contribution to the land war. *Variants of the Offensive* firmly placed his thinking years ahead of the professional generals. There had to be an alternative to ordering men to advance into machine-gun fire. While he accepted that armour was incompatible with mobility, he thought that some kind of shield, either for individuals or carried by several men, could be devised. Or there might be a shield which could be pushed along on caterpillar tracks.

Then followed a discussion of assault machines on caterpillar tracks, of which seventy were already in production. He saw these advancing across rough terrain, surmounting breastworks and rolling over trenches as their machine guns and flamethrowers kept up a lethal barrage. His machines would smash through the enemy line as they crushed the barbed wire and tore through the defences. And because they would be so close to the trenches they would be immune from shell fire. He drove home his message by describing how these vehicles would resemble a reaping machine that worked in the peaceful fields of England.

Installed in GHQ, Churchill now fell into a period of limbo while his future was being decided. Although he was only a major, Asquith, French and Haig were all to be drawn into one of the great issues of the war: should Major Churchill be allowed to command a brigade?

Clementine Churchill was strongly against his taking a brigade as she thought it would look better if her husband first served in a battalion and so avoided any suggestion that his promotion had come through favouritism. For her, the departure of French would be welcome since he was too keen on Churchill being prematurely promoted. But French urged him to take a brigade. Captain Edward Spiers, then a liaison officer with the French Army, also recommended that Churchill take a brigade. In Downing Street, too, opinion was hardening around a brigade. This, Clementine told her husband, was only because they felt guilty for the way he had been hounded out of office.

And then, suddenly, everything seemed to be resolved. On 10 December, Churchill told his wife that he was to command the 56th Brigade in the 19th Division. He had asked for Spiers to be appointed as his Brigade Major and Archie Sinclair as his Staff Captain. (Sinclair became one of Churchill's closest friends. He was present at the last dinner that Churchill gave at 10 Downing Street on 4 April 1955.) He knew there would be malicious comments over his appointment, but he told his wife that they should just ignore them. But since the appointment was not effective immediately, he decided to stay with the Guards until he went to the brigade. Nevertheless, his wife was to order him his new uniform. There was also the good news that French was to arrange for Spiers to join Churchill, although this would take a while to organise.

Buoyed up by his new status Churchill went off to visit Lieutenant General Henry Wilson, Chief Liaison Officer with the French Army who, somewhat belatedly, advised Churchill not to take a brigade since it would be resented in many quarters. The advice fell on deaf ears since, Churchill maintained, Asquith had now offered him a division.

Although she knew that there was much criticism in London at Churchill's preferment, Clementine Churchill could not hide her delight, saying that she was 'thrilled'.[26] But in the Commons, Major Sir Charles Hunter asked whether Churchill had been promised an infantry brigade and he also wanted to know if he had ever been in command of a battalion, and for how long 'he had served at the front as an infantry officer'. Mr Harold 'Jack' Tennant,[27] Undersecretary of State for War, replied that the government had no knowledge of the offer and that Churchill had never commanded an infantry battalion. There were further hostile questions about the appointment, ending with a Mr Cecil asking 'Is the right hon. gentleman aware that if this appointment were made it would be thought by many persons inside this House and outside to be a grave scandal?'[28]

Inevitably, Asquith took fright. When French had first told him that Churchill was to have a brigade he had welcomed the news. On 18 December, he wrote a curt note to French to say that he was concerned about potential disapproval of the promotion; it was not to take place. Churchill, recalling that Asquith had offered him a brigade, raged about the decision in a letter to his wife. He neatly pinned down Asquith's abiding weakness: his habit of abandoning friends and colleagues whenever he himself came under fire. He almost certainly said worse things, since he also told Clementine to burn the two letters that he had sent to her the previous day. They have never been found.

But it was not only Asquith who was blocking the appointment. In December, Haig learnt that he was to replace Sir John French as Commander-in-Chief. Before Haig had taken command, the Military Secretary, Brigadier-General Lowther, came to discuss the Churchill problem. When Haig heard of French's intention to give Churchill a brigade he said that was 'impossible until W. had shown that he could bear responsibility in action as C.O. of a Battalion'.[29] Churchill accepted the decision, telling Marsh that 'I have fallen back reposefully [sic] into the arms of Fate.'[30] At dinner with Spiers the next day, he appeared resigned to them all dying in the next offensive.

On 18 December, Haig met French at St Omer. French wanted to discuss what he called 'a delicate personal matter': he wanted Churchill to have a battalion. Haig readily agreed. Whether by coincidence or through French's stage management, he had hardly walked out of the room when Churchill called on Haig and learnt the good news.[31] Two days later, when French had tidied up various administrative matters before his return to England, he chose to spend his last moments in France with Churchill. Churchill told his wife of his profound sadness at the departure of French.

Churchill now had to wait for a battalion. He had moved into 'Max' Aitken's house at St Omer where he idled away his time. He found this curious after so many years of the frenetic pace of a government minister's life. With his mind temporarily off military affairs, Churchill wrote to Lloyd George urging him to keep up their correspondence and to maintain the pressure on Asquith: 'Don't miss your opportunity. The time has come,' he concluded.[32] It was just one more channel that he wished to keep open in readiness for his return to political life.

On 27 December, after a short Christmas home leave, Churchill returned to France with his future still undecided. The sea passage in a destroyer was rough and he had been violently seasick. Matters were made worse when the rough sea kept the vessel outside Dunkirk harbour and he was only able to disembark when the ship grounded on a mud bank.

With no battalion vacancies in sight, Churchill set off on a vigorous round of visiting. The day after landing he lunched with Lieutenant Colonel Bridges, Head of the British Military Mission, Belgian Field Army, and then visited Neuve Chapelle with Bridges's Chief of Staff. In the evening he dined with Spiers who found him in an excited mood over an imminent political crisis arising from conscription. He thought the Cabinet impasse would deliver the government into the hands of Lloyd George, Carson, Curzon and himself. Lloyd George or Bonar Law would be Prime Minister, while he would go to the Admiralty or Munitions.

The next day he and Spiers went to the French lines where, in contrast to the Guards' peaceful sector, the least movement visible to the enemy was met by sniper fire. This rush of activity was rounded off by dinner with the corps and a discussion of the possibilities for offensive action. At table Churchill expounded the ideas in his *Variants of the Offensive*. He told his wife that the officers were in agreement with him.

On 30 December, Churchill returned to 33 Corps HQ and once again indulged in the luxury of a good bathroom before slipping into bed to write a long letter to Clementine before dinner. As he enjoyed the comfort of the headquarters safely behind the lines, his thoughts turned to the style of living at 41 Cromwell Road. He advised his wife and sister-in-law not to deny themselves unnecessarily and that they were to live and eat well. They were also to make sure that they had enough servants and Clementine should retain her maid. If they were careful with their entertainment they should be able to live on £140 a month – a twenty per cent reduction on their pre-war budget.

At home, Clementine was thinking ahead as she watched the quarrels in the War Council over conscription. She suspected that Asquith, playing a long game, was going to succeed in bringing in conscription without suffering any resignations. The Prime Minister was not finished yet and she advised her husband to keep his options open. (That is, he was not to side prematurely with Lloyd George to push Asquith out.) Indeed, she felt that there was not much to choose between the two men, who had both treated her husband badly. Despite her repugnance for the two leaders, she promised Churchill that she would visit Downing Street and keep open the lines of communication.

On 2 January and still with nothing to do, Churchill set out to visit the 9th Division. As usual, he wanted to inspect the front line, which he did in the company of a Lieutenant Colonel White who observed that Churchill was fascinated by all that he saw, but was rather alarmed when he showed himself above the parapet. At dinner that evening, Churchill probed the officers about the battalion that he was likely to command. The unit had fought at Loos with great courage in the previous autumn but had suffered dreadful losses. Observing that it would take a fortnight to get it into shape, he decided to accept the posting. In a letter about the visit, Churchill forecast that his battalion would be settled on 4 January. Since it was a Scottish battalion, he asked Clementine to send him a one-volume edition of Burns, from which he intended to recite quotations to his men.

Finally, all was settled. On 4 January 1916, Churchill became a colonel of the 6th Battalion Royal Scots Fusiliers and he was to take over at noon the following day. Almost all of the regular officers had been killed and those who remained were young and inexperienced. Getting the battalion into good shape would be a tough assignment, but Churchill relished the thought that at last he was to do something useful.

6TH BATTALION ROYAL SCOTS FUSILIERS

There was disbelief in the battalion when news spread of Churchill's appointment. Captain Andrew Gibb thought he was being fooled and joked that he had heard a rumour that 'Curzon had been appointed Transport Officer'. He added, in his memoir of this period, that hilarity quickly turned to 'a mutinous spirit' when they realised the rumour was true.[33] The coming of such a legendary figure aroused great interest in the local people. When Churchill arrived at the 'more than usually dirty farm' that was battalion HQ, there was a great deal of saluting and deferential bowing. The well-informed ladies of the house quickly grasped the situation and in loud whispers exclaimed '"Monsieur le Ministre!" "Monsieur le Colonel!" "Ah, c'est lui?!" This display of 'international colour,' said Gibb, 'produced a most happy effect'.[34]

There was no elation in Churchill's first letter sent after he had joined the battalion in the reserve billet. Although he was absorbed in the finer points of command and strongly desired to make a success of his battalion, he felt low. He became aware of the limited sphere in which he was now working. Also, he was beginning to realise just how weak his officers were. Betraying his own class background, he more or less wrote them off because they were Scottish and middle class. Matters were made worse by him watching Seely travelling to London to vote in the Conscription Bill debate. All he could think of was the fact the he, Churchill, would not be there to influence the outcome. He rightly predicted that the debate would fail to support conscription. Only his own return, he told Clementine, would force the changes that were needed in the running of the war. Meanwhile, he felt deeply the absence of French. For all his glorifying of trench life and his repeated denials of any wish to return home, the truth was that Churchill yearned for his old life. His despondency was heightened by his conviction that he had no chance of returning to power before the end of the war. Nothing, though, could stop him scrutinising The Times for political news, even though it disturbed him. None of this did him any good, since the more he brooded the more he felt left out of the world of power and politics. In his isolation, he drew some slight comfort as he anticipated how guilty Asquith would feel if he were killed while serving in his humble role at the Front.

It was impossible for Churchill not to dominate any scenario and the effects of his presence were immediate. Even the cats had disappeared from the orderly room the next morning. His next enemy was lice. On discovering the presence of the vermin he announced to his four company commanders that 'War is declared, gentlemen, on lice.' Although the officers were bewildered at the long lecture on the history of lice in warfare that followed, it served its purpose. Within no time, all lice had been eradicated from the battalion.[35]

But there was work to be done and on the morning of 7 January, Churchill took his battalion out on parade and drilled them. He wanted to 'make them feel a corporate identity' and to feel 'my personal control'. His intention was sound but his method proved hilarious. As a cavalry man, Churchill assumed that his officers paraded on horseback. Unaware that some had never even ridden a horse, and impervious to the fact that the battalion's horses were of dubious origin, the parade went ahead. The untrained horses and the inexperienced officers then received a stream of cavalry commands, which meant nothing to infantry officers. Gibb described the result:

> The companies lurched forward, the subalterns swore, the horses rammed the companies from behind and before, the commands ground out unceasingly, as one or other fence of the enclosure was encountered … the whole matter was a mêlée of blasphemous humanity and outraged horseflesh.[36]

Even if his commands on the parade ground proved ineffective, Churchill still proudly told his wife that, as a colonel, his word was law. Small as that sphere was, Churchill was determined to extract some sense of power.

Soon after Churchill had joined his battalion, the government announced on 8 January its intention to pass a Military Service Act. The Derby scheme of the previous autumn had failed to improve recruiting. This programme had enabled men to record their willingness to serve without having to sign up. Those married men who attested in this way were guaranteed that they would not be called up before the supply of single men had been exhausted. Not enough men came forward, forcing Asquith to acknowledge public opinion and accept the inevitability of conscription. His new Act imposed compulsory military service on men aged eighteen to forty-one. Its proponents believed that such an Act would identify the 'slackers', whom they estimated at 650,000, and increase recruitment. In fact the Act, brought into effect on 27 April, was a total failure since, instead of 650,000 'slackers' joining the ranks, nearly 750,000 men came forward to claim exemptions. As a result enlistments plummeted by over fifty per cent to 40,000 men a month.

But from Churchill's viewpoint, the most significant factor was that Asquith had succeeded in passing the Act at the cost of only one ministerial resignation –

that of Sir John Simon, the Home Secretary. As Clementine Churchill had rightly predicted, Asquith was not finished and any hope that Churchill might have had that conscription would bring about his fall was now gone.

In the battalion matters were a little brighter as Churchill became engrossed in his work. He found, he told his wife on 8 January, that he was 'gaining control & confidence' and was now more favourably inclined to his officers, who were 'so keen, plucky & intelligent'.[37] However, his attention to his duties did not deflect him from the delicacies of keeping up appearances at home. He duly asked Clementine to order some printed notepaper with the regiment's field address. A few days later, far away in the Eastern Mediterranean the last men of the Gallipoli expeditionary force were safely embarked in the ships of the Royal Navy on 13 January 1916. The Gallipoli campaign had reached an ignominious end.

Military service in the First World War forced many middle-class men into close contact with working people of modest standing. Churchill was no exception. After a week with his battalion he began to see another side to his non-commissioned officers. Those humble men who had served him at home – 'grocers, fitters, miners' – had suddenly become non-commissioned officers and were learning the arts of war.[38]

Slowly trench routine was taking over. Churchill's life, he told Clementine, was now filled with such practical matters as inspecting equipment and making sure that gas masks were in good order. His previous low mood had passed as he found himself enjoying the work and the days no longer dragged.

It was more than typical of Churchill that he should arrange a sports day for his men in mid-January. He declared the races and acts of prowess – which he was sure the men had never experienced before – to have been a great success.

On 18 January, Churchill went to Hazebrouck to hear a lecture on the Battle of Loos, and he was prompted once more to think about his *Variants of the Offensive* paper. As he listened to Colonel Arthur 'Tom' Holland[39] all he heard was the usual tale of war at that time: heroism of the highest order combined with a doomed strategy and ineffective tactics. When Holland asked afterwards what lessons could be drawn, Churchill pithily replied 'Don't do it again.'[40] But they did – over and over again. Churchill's view that there must be an alternative way of fighting found few sympathetic listeners at this stage in the war.

On his return from Hazebrouck, Churchill was reminded of the real reason that he was in France: the Dardanelles. He knew that there was no future for him in wartime politics until he could clear his name as the scapegoat for all the War Council's failures. So the news that Rothermere thought Churchill's reputation had been unharmed by Gallipoli was most welcome. He urged Clementine to keep in touch with Rothermere and Bonar Law: 'It is fatal to let the threads drop.'[41]

CHAPTER 11

IN SEARCH OF A ROLE

You are deluded if you think that by remaining here & doing nothing, I shall recover my influence on affairs. – Churchill to his wife[1]

SETTLING IN

On 22 January, all of Churchill's dedicated effort to turn his battalion into a front-line force became a reality when Lieutenant General Charles Fergusson, the Corps Commander, came to inspect his troops. The general marvelled at the change and immediately became most friendly towards Churchill. There came an invitation to ride with him, to take tea and accept his profuse apologies for having been given such a weak battalion. Fergusson, falling under the Churchill spell, offered him a better battalion. Having revelled in the challenge of turning his disheartened soldiers into a formidable force, Churchill declined the offer, telling Fergusson that he felt he was of more use with his battalion. The next day, Churchill confided to his wife that he thought Fergusson was ready to help him gain promotion quite soon.

As he waited to go into the front line, Churchill wrote to Lloyd George on 25 January asking him to visit. He warned him that Asquith's position was still solid even though the Tories had every intention of forming their own government. As to the war, it was gloom on every front.

Churchill's advance headquarters was located at Laurence Farm, a few hundred yards from the front line. Around a mile to the rear, the battalion headquarters had been installed in a hospice run by nuns and farther to the rear was the small Belgian village of Ploegsteert. Despite being in a war zone, two nuns remained in residence and the hospice chapel continued to hold services. The presence of a piano and the homely cooking of the nuns, recalled Captain Gibb of D Company, left little reason for any complaints. Among other reminders of peacetime were two pigs that rooted around in the many shell craters.

The men – most were survivors of the Battle of Loos – were pleased at the prospect of being in such a quiet part of the line. It was the best section that the men had ever seen. Anticipating a stay of two to three months, Churchill found the trenches to be dry and he thought they could make themselves comfortable. There seemed to be little danger from shelling, even though his headquarters was within range of German artillery. So content was Churchill that he began to look forward to spring when the surrounding countryside would burst into flower.

On 25 January, Churchill led his battalion towards the trenches. Churchill was impressed as his men marched along in their newly issued steel helmets across the ground frozen solid and white with frost. Already, he was looking forward to returning to the comfort of a proper bed and good food in six days' time. Yet none of these minor details stopped him thinking about the larger aspects of war. A recent meeting with Seely (in command of the Canadian cavalry brigade) led him to remark on the obsolescence of the cavalry in modern warfare. Thus did an ex-cavalry man show more common sense than the entire British high command, which retained the cavalry up to the end of the war.

On 27 January, the battalion finally moved into the trenches. Churchill was now at war. As usual this move was made in the early hours of the morning with all lights extinguished. Every effort had been made to muffle the sound of hundreds of men on the march.

That day Churchill made the first of his trench rounds – his routine was three rounds in twenty-four hours, one of which would be at night. He probed and inspected to seek out every weak point in the defences as his brain filled with grand plans for repairs and improvements. At the end of the day when darkness fell, fires could at last be lit and hot meals prepared.

Although an experienced soldier, trenches, mud and standing water were all new to Churchill. None of this stopped him issuing copious guidance to his officers. They were to keep a spare pair of clean boots to wear at night. Alcohol was to be used 'in moderation' – a restraint he did not apply to himself – and they were to avoid 'a great parade of bottles in yr dugouts'. In typical Churchillian style, he urged his officers to 'live well' and 'teach your men to laugh'. He concluded 'war is a game that is played with a smile.'[2]

In recounting this to his wife, Churchill set a bold example of living well as he placed orders for quantities of pies, meats and other delicacies. He also told her about the telephones that linked him to his companies, the brigadier and also the guns, which enabled him to call up an artillery attack more or less on demand.

For all the doubts and even derision that was heaped on Churchill behind his back when he joined the battalion, his rapport with his officers and men proved exceptional. In Gibb's view, Churchill 'achieved a remarkable measure of success in dealing with the rank and file'. He was 'ideally sympathetic'. Knowing how lonely and terrifying sentry duty could be in the trenches, Churchill would go down into the front line and explain to the men how to select the best positions both for shelter and line of view. He also went to great lengths to ensure men did not sleep on sentry duty, so saving them from inevitable punishment. When it came to the treatment of wounded men he was painstakingly attentive and, said Gibb, 'utterly impervious to all feelings of aversion from the unpleasant sights of war'.[3]

Even the most menial tasks were of interest and concern to Churchill. 'He was always in the closest touch,' continued Gibb, 'with every piece of work that was going on.' His attention may, at times, have been 'extravagant' but 'his kindliness and the humour never failed to flash out.'[4]

Churchill did not like to see good men held back. While GHQ deprecated promotions within battalions, Churchill believed in promoting men on merit. He was, recalled Gibb, tireless in his pressing of cases for promotion both by 'long distance bombardment by means of the usual paper ammunition' and through personal visits to headquarters. There he 'met stout resistance' but 'did achieve results'.[5]

CHURCHILL'S COMFORTS

Few battalion commanders took as great a care of their own comfort as did Churchill. He had provided himself with all manner of clothing and in wet weather his approach could be easily distinguished as he strode around dressed head-to-foot in waterproofs and wearing a light-blue French helmet on his head. At the end of the day he could relax in his bathtub – 'a breach of custom and of war etiquette' – which was gladly overlooked by his fellow officers as he encouraged them to share his luxury.[6]

Churchill's mess had a reputation all its own. 'Nobody who was entertained there ever forgot it,' recalled Gibb.[7] This may well partly explain the extraordinary number of visitors that he received. Some, such as Curzon and F.E. Smith, were simply part of keeping in touch, but there were also some Canadian generals (including the strangely named 'Foghorn' Macdonald), Seely (who sang and played the piano 'very nicely'), General Tudor and airmen from the coast, who came to pay homage to their old chief.[8] There was also an endless stream of brigade and divisional visitors. At one dinner party, Gibb counted the Divisional General, the Brigadier General on the General Staff of the Corps, two 'very distinguished' airmen and the Divisional General's ADC.[9] Churchill did not limit his guest list to the famous and influential. 'Every poor stray who blew past' was enticed in, said Gibb, and, 'if he left without a large cigar lighting up his mollified countenance that was because he was a non-smoker.'[10] Those in cantankerous mood were treated to copious quantities of peach or apricot brandy.

A VISITOR'S ARREST

The next three months were to see Churchill employ his extraordinary powers of application and concentration to his new role of battalion commander, while at the same time keeping abreast of the political situation at home. The first indication that

Field Marshal Lord Kitchener, scourge of Boers and Arabs; but he lost his way in the morass of the War Office and Whitehall.

A confident and youthful Churchill as First Lord in 1912.

Churchill's 'crown jewels': the fleet at the Naval Review, July 1914.

Herbert Asquith, accomplished peacetime Liberal Prime Minister but political casualty of war.

The young Churchill hauls the ageing Fisher on board in October 1914.

Admiral John Jellicoe, master of technical detail, who rose to eminence at Scapa Flow and fell to earth at Admiralty House.

Bonar Law, who engineered Churchill's downfall in 1915 and realised his mistake in 1917.

Lloyd George, the giant of the war. He risked all in 1917 to bring Churchill back to power.

'Machines not men': a Mark 1 British tank in September 1914.

Women working alongside men in the munitions factories.

he was to be no ordinary battalion commander occurred when F.E. Smith arrived on 30 January. He had been due to visit in December when he had been keen to discuss the political situation at home with Churchill. At the same time, he intended to cajole Haig over Churchill's case for promotion. In the light of what happened this was to be a forsaken pledge. Never can there have been a more bizarre visit to a colonel in the field than this disastrous foray by F.E. Smith.

The cause of the debacle lay back in 1914-15 when Major F.E. Smith had served in France as a Staff Officer with the Indian Corps. As one of Britain's most celebrated lawyers he had attempted to promote the reform of the antiquated court martial procedures. Such suggestions from a junior officer made him unpopular at GHQ. Now visiting France in his new role as Attorney General, the time was ripe for retribution. Somebody, somewhere in GHQ was about to play a very nasty trick on His Majesty's leading man of the law.

All was well on 27 January, when Mrs Churchill told her husband that Smith was about to depart for France, bearing with him a 'type-writer ... cigars, brandy & periscope'.[11] (The typewriter, which cost 11 guineas, was to enable Churchill to issue smartly typed orders rather than 'a scribble in pencil'.[12])

On 28 January, the party – Lloyd George, Bonar Law and F.E. Smith – crossed the English Channel. Leaving Lloyd George and Law in St Omer, Smith set off for Ploegsteert. It was Smith's misfortune to be a man with a high disregard for petty details and so he had given no thought to the consequences of his travelling in uniform. In France, a uniformed soldier at the Front required a pass and Smith had no pass. An officer at St Omer spotted this irregularity and telegraphed to Ploegsteert to request them to supply Smith with a pass, but the telegram never reached its destination. It was intercepted and then amended to request the recipient to arrange the arrest of Smith. A person at GHQ had not forgotten the Major F.E. Smith who dared to tamper with military law.

Despite the amended telegram, Smith reached Ploegsteert and dined with Churchill and some of his officers on 30 January. The diners, unaware that anything might be untoward, enjoyed a fine meal and finished with a copious amount of brandy. Churchill held up well but Smith retired in a poor state.

On 31 January at 4.00 a.m., Churchill and Smith were awakened by the loud knock of the Provost Marshal who was bearing an arrest warrant for the Attorney General. Neither man was in a position to forestall this 'Gilbertian' scenario. So one of the most important men in the government was driven away to St Omer, where he was locked up in the Hôtel du Commerce with two armed sentries guarding his door.

When Smith woke the next morning, he attempted to leave the room but the sentries told him they would shoot if he did. Later, he was taken to see the Adjutant General, Sir Nevil Macready. Smith used all his oratorical skills as a leading barrister to attempt to facilitate his release, but Macready was unimpressed. 'If you are a civilian,' he said, 'why are you in uniform? If you are a soldier, why don't you obey regulations?'[13]

Churchill, Law and Lloyd George were due to meet Haig at Hazebrouck later that morning. When Churchill found that Smith was still detained he ordered a car to drive him immediately to Hazebrouck. By now the Adjutant General had apologised to Smith and released him. Naturally, Smith was furious at his treatment, although he had no idea that it was all a practical joke at his expense.

The incident would have closed there had Law and Lloyd George not taken an interest. When they and Churchill met Haig later in the day, Bonar Law swore that Smith would have to leave the Cabinet if it all became public and he, Law, would also have to resign. Haig showed more restraint and simply invited Smith to lunch. Once Haig had pacified the agitated politicians he agreed to 'keep the story as quiet as possible'. Smith was apparently satisfied but, thought Haig, 'seemed most afraid of the ridicule of his friends'. Writing in his diary later that day, Haig noted 'I was only too glad to be rid of the lot and be free to get on with my work.'[14]

That was not quite the end of the story since Macready, who we can assume was not a party to the altered telegram, was most embarrassed by the incident and apologised profusely when he next met Churchill in early February. His only regret was that Churchill had not asked him to help arrange Smith's visit. Doubtlessly, senior officers viewed Churchill's visitors as a most irregular business but carefully avoided upsetting such a powerful politician. Indeed, these four men saw themselves as the government-in-waiting, ready to rush in when Asquith was pushed off the stage. The solidarity of this group was demonstrated by Lloyd George and Law both telling Haig that 'there wd be no difficulty at home' if Churchill were to be given a brigade.[15]

——>•<——

On 3 February, the realities of war returned at the end of a convivial dinner. Churchill and his officers were drinking coffee and port when there was a thunderous bang as a shell hit the bedroom shared by Churchill and Sinclair. The dining room was wrecked with all the furniture and crockery shattered and the bedroom was in much the same state. Gibb recalled Churchill's reaction:

> … there was an outburst of the most feverish eagerness on the part of the Battalion Headquarters to sandbag themselves and make such accidents less probable for the future. The wretched Ramsay [OC D Company] was summoned and was forced to devise shelters and scarps and counterscarps and dugouts and half-moons and ravelins.

All this required 'huge working parties' which had to fulfil their tasks in 'ludicrously inadequate time'.[16] Ten days later, the battalion HQ had two new dugouts, each with a steel roof.

A BRIGADE COMMAND

With only a few days' experience at the Front, Churchill unexpectedly found himself an acting-brigadier. The brigadier had been sent home sick at the end of January and since that time substitute officers had been in charge. On 6 February, Churchill was ordered to take command. As he told his wife 'I am now in command of 5 battalions & 4,000 yards of front.'

Despite his elevated command, Churchill still found time for politics as he entertained Curzon and gave his visitor a full tour of the front-line trenches and the now 'shattered' farm. There was also welcome news from Masterton-Smith on the progress of what everyone saw as Churchill's tanks. When demonstrated to Balfour they had 'performed miracles'.[17](In February 1915, Churchill had set up the Landships Committee to develop the tank.)

There was more controversial news from home the next day, when Clementine Churchill told her husband of the call by *The Observer* newspaper for Fisher and Churchill to return. Exactly one month later this appeal was to have devastating consequences for Churchill.

The brigadier did not return as expected on 7 February, so Churchill remained in charge, but he told his wife: 'It is not a very satisfactory arrangement, as of course I am only a caretaker and cannot attempt to take a grip of the whole machine. ... I wait from hour to hour.'

It was not, though, the power of a brigadier that Churchill sought. He yearned for some vast action that would shorten the war. Once more Loos came to mind and he wrote to his wife: 'My dear what mistakes they made at Loos. You simply cannot believe them possible.' What was needed was mechanisation: 'This war is one of mechanics & brains [;] & mere sacrifice of brave & devoted infantry is no substitute & never will be.' And then, uncannily echoing the language that Fisher was using at home, he added: 'By God I wd make them skip if I had power even for a month.'[18] After less than two weeks at the Front, Churchill's yearning for power was overwhelming him. Almost every day would see him writing a letter lamenting the lack of action at home and his own incapacity to press the war forward.

On 10 February, a colonel senior to Churchill arrived to take command of the brigade. Churchill did not regret relinquishing his command since, as a stand-in, he could only follow the established routines. There was little to be cheerful about. Although his men had been stood-down for two days, eight had been killed. His battalion, which usually had a nominal strength of 1,000, had been reduced to 680 men. On the home front, he saw no hope of his getting the Air Ministry and from Flanders he told his wife that Haig showed no signs of being about to offer him promotion.

STILL DOWN ON THE FARM

At Laurence Farm, Churchill could not keep his mind away from the new session of Parliament and the debate on the naval estimates on 7 March. He endlessly deliberated as to whether he should attend. On 11 February, he decided against returning, feeling that the time was not right, although he continued to change his mind almost daily.

February the 14th brought no respite from daily duties and dangers of trench life. Churchill had inspected the lines at 6.00 a.m. and narrowly missed 'a vy sulky bullet' which hit his own doorstep. There had been shelling while he entertained General Tudor to lunch and they had all had to take shelter – no doubt Churchill welcomed this chance to demonstrate his new defences. Churchill had appointed Major Hearn, an acquaintance, to supervise the strengthening of his trenches. At the end of this varied day, as he relaxed in an old wicker chair 'by the glowing coals of a brazier in the light of an acetyline lamp', Churchill felt he had 'earned [his] 25 shillings'.[19]

For the next two weeks until his leave in early March, Churchill's days were filled with the boredom of a waiting and watching existence. Despite more shelling, he made tours of inspection with Sinclair, including night patrols to visit the listening posts.

On 16 February, the farm was once again a target at breakfast time. One wall in the dining room was penetrated, there were several shrapnel holes in the bedroom walls and the signals office was completely wrecked. Grabbing their half-eaten breakfasts the officers retreated to a dugout. With two of his officers wounded, Churchill had to accept that the German artillery had located the farm and had every intention of bombarding it again. Indeed, there was a widespread belief in the battalion that the Germans knew Churchill was there and were determined to kill him. Churchill, said Gibb, 'would have none of this'.[20]

Further shelling on the following day left Churchill unperturbed. He wrote to his wife that he was in good health and the busy days soon passed. He was enjoying being away from the strain of the long hours of ministerial life. Even the food was good, and the air was fresh.

There was to be no respite from German shelling and, on 20 February, Churchill's shared bedroom was hit for a third time. Later, Sinclair and Churchill had a very animated argument as to what to do; Churchill favoured more sandbags while Sinclair opted for sleeping with the family in the cellar. Before a decision could be made either way another shell landed and exploded in the cellar.

The following day, German forces launched their massive attack on Verdun, starting the largest and most deadly battle of the war, which continued until 18 December, with the loss of over one million men. Meanwhile, one of the very few men who had the imagination to find an alternative to the deadly exchanges on the Western Front languished in a shell-shattered farm house at Ploegsteert.

With his leave approaching, Churchill wrote to his wife on 22 February to ask her to draw up a programme of activities. He wanted her to arrange dinners at home, with his mother and with colleagues. He also wanted time to paint with Lavery. But, there was not a word about the forthcoming debate or his other political plans.

Before he left for home, Churchill organised one final round of hectic entertaining. On 26 February, the Corps Commander, the Divisional Commander, the Brigadier, General Tudor and Lieutenant General Bridges attended a function at Laurence Farm. Whatever the military thought of Churchill when he first arrived in France, he now seemed to be the man to be seen with.

A VISIT TO THE COMMONS

After a delay, when leave was halted because of snow, Churchill boarded a destroyer on 2 March to begin his leave. It was to prove one of the most controversial periods of his life.

Despite Churchill's plans to fill his leave with painting, socialising and entertainment, temptation overcame him as he poured heart and soul into his preparations for a speech in the naval estimates debate.

Fisher had played a major role in this reversal. He had been lobbying both Asquith and members of the opposition for months over the lethargic state of the Admiralty. By early February 1916, he was ready to tell Bonar Law 'I propose at an early date to take a drastic step to make the Country acquainted with my views.'[21] He was also busily running a campaign of 'Get Fisher in! … Get Balfour out!' while deprecating his own Inventions Department role as 'keeping a chemist's shop in Cockspur Street'.[22] In his determination to return to the Admiralty, Fisher had arranged for the renowned doctor Sir Bertrand Dawson to examine him and testify to his remarkable constitution. By 19 February, he was presenting himself as a saviour to Garvin, saying 'We are at the very blackest period of the War.' He urged Garvin to call for the fall of the government but added 'for God's sake don't mention Fisher!'[23]

It was into this fevered atmosphere that Churchill stepped in early March. His absence from British politics had left his political acuity blunted. Overwhelmed by Fisher's contagious enthusiasm, he embraced his old friend with abandoned pleasure. Within days they had effected their reconciliation. Fisher told C.P. Scott that Churchill was 'the inevitable Prime Minister' and, until he was so installed he should 'remain in England [and] take the lead of an independent Opposition'.[24] In forming this alliance, Churchill had fatally misread the political mood. Fisher was yesterday's man; all his credit was long spent.

When he met Scott on the day before his big speech, Churchill discussed the conundrum of his future. He had no money – indeed, he had had to borrow money to support his wife and children while serving in the army. Even so, he told Scott that '[he] would sweep a crossing in Berkeley Square if it would help to win the war'.[25] His wife, though, wanted him to accept the brigade that was about to be offered.

The real purpose of meeting Scott and Fisher had been to read them his draft speech. Churchill declared himself satisfied with his text. 'If it were the last he was to deliver he would be content to stand by it.'[26] Fisher's own enthusiasm for the speech was boundless, written as usual in a jumble of underlining, capitalisations and exclamation marks. The speech was 'magnificent' and 'will have (justly) an immense effect on your popularity'. Churchill was to recognise that 'the Government are strong as THERE IS NO OPPOSITION LEADER!' and he should 'Get up every night and batter the box from the Opposition Bench!' More crucially Fisher asserted that 'To win the war and with no other heartfelt feeling do we two coalesce! We can do it! Come on!'[27]

Unable to resist Fisher's insistent blandishments, Churchill laced his speech with his ill-judged call for the return of Fisher. Neither Scott nor Clementine Churchill made any comment on the references to Fisher. His friends and advisers having failed in their primary duty – to warn – sent him naked into the lions' den.

That evening the Churchills dined with the Asquiths and given what happened the next day, we can be certain that Fisher was not mentioned.

On 7 March, Balfour opened the debate with a protracted but vague review of the state of the navy and its development since the start of the war. His speech ('long and dull' according to Scott[28]) was full of generous praise for the earlier work of Churchill and Fisher while asserting the competence of his own board. Unable to release precise figures in wartime, Balfour assured the House that the navy had 'enormously expanded since the outbreak of hostilities' and the personnel had 'broadly speaking doubled'. Over one million tons of warships had been added to the fleet. There was a vigorous defence of the enlarged Air Service while admitting that progress had been slow on aeroplanes because there was insufficient labour to build assembly and storage sheds. Although Balfour claimed that 'the very fact that we are pressing on building' showed that the board were not complacent, the speech was complacent from beginning to end. His hope that 'nothing I have said … will approach anything in the nature of over-confidence' was forlorn.[29]

As members expected, Churchill rose to reply. The House was, he said, indebted to Balfour for his 'calm, broad survey' and for his 'courtesy and consideration' towards the work of earlier boards. Yet he felt obliged 'to strike a jarring note' which would be 'in some respects of warning'.

His central concern was the speed and adequacy of new shipbuilding. He noted that Balfour had at no point assured the House 'that the dates to which Lord Fisher and I were working would be substantially and with inconsiderable exceptions maintained'. Information which he had received from various sources left him with 'impressions of a less completely satisfactory and reassuring kind'. (Both Fisher and Jellicoe were greatly concerned at the lack of drive in the Admiralty's shipbuilding programme and had no doubt made sure that Churchill was well briefed.)

According to Churchill, Balfour, who admitted he had no knowledge of German shipbuilding since the start of the war, was underestimating the German threat. 'Can we conceive that the German Government … would be content to allow that navy to lie impotent and derided in the Kiel Canal?' He continued: 'We are bound to assume that Germany has completed every vessel begun before the war.' He further noted that at this point in the war not only had both sides completed vessels laid down before the war but they were now completing ships begun since the war started. 'For this reason we cannot afford to allow any delay to creep into the execution of our programme.'

Then there were new developments – something Balfour had not even mentioned. Perceptively, Churchill warned that Germany would develop new types of submarine which would challenge the navy's current technologies. 'You must be ready with your new devices before the enemy is ready with his,' he warned.

Had Churchill stopped there the House and the press would have cheered him to the rafters. But he did not.

'But I have not spoken to-day without intending to lead up to a conclusion.' He recalled how in late 1914, when Battenberg had resigned, he had turned to Fisher as the only man 'who possessed the power, insight, and energy' to do the job. After references to his breach with Fisher in 1915, Churchill continued 'We cannot afford to deprive ourselves or the navy of the strongest and most vigorous forces available.' There was in the Admiralty 'a lack of driving force and mental energy … which must be rectified'. And then he dropped the bombshell: 'I urge the First Lord of the Admiralty without delay to fortify himself, to vitalise and animate the Board of Admiralty by recalling Lord Fisher to his post as First Sea Lord.' Although this remark was met with loud cheers, in those few words Churchill had lost all the authority that his speech had earlier possessed.[30]

There was one truly enthusiastic champion of the speech: Fisher. He was delighted and foresaw Churchill's imminent return to power. More typical was the reaction of *The Times* newspaper, which regretted 'for many reasons that Lord Fisher's name should have been raised'. It would only 'provoke a personal controversy'. Nevertheless, the newspaper still congratulated Churchill on his clear views on 'the vague popular anxiety which has lately been prevalent about our general naval position'.[31] A similar supportive view was expressed by the *National Review*. 'The labour issue,' the newspaper said, '[had] been allowed to drift on from month to month, like everything else under the Wait and See dispensation.'[32] Others focused their regret on the manner in which Churchill had thrown away his chance to influence shipbuilding policy. Addison at the Ministry of Munitions considered Churchill's remarks on shipbuilding to be 'well-founded',[33] while Hankey noted in his diary that the outcome was not likely to help his career. Margot Asquith, never given to understatement, declared to Balfour that Churchill had sunk to 'the lowest sense of political honour'.[34] What finally put an end to any influence that Churchill might have had was the reaction of Asquith. In private, he described the speech as 'a piece of the grossest effrontery'.[35]

Scott, who exchanged opinions with ministers on an almost daily basis, was so concerned at Churchill's ill judged speech that he went to see Asquith the following day. In a long defence of Churchill, he assured Asquith that there had been 'no spirit of hostility to the Ministry'. Asquith had sat stony-faced while Scott offered his apology for Churchill's speech. Then he rose from his chair and broke out into a torrent of abuse about Churchill as he paced up and down the room. 'Did I know that only 3 [8] months ago when Fisher was appointed as head of the Inventions Department both Churchill and his wife had been furious and had denounced it as an outrage, so much so that Mrs Churchill had almost cut him and his wife would not speak to him.' When they were together, Fisher and Churchill 'did nothing but quarrel' and Fisher was always resigning. Had he not gone, there would have been no ministerial crisis and no coalition. 'He deserved to be shot.'[36]

Apart from Asquith yet once more asserting that the shell crisis had had nothing to do with his forming a coalition, this was an extraordinary performance from a man not given to anger. But he was given to fostering resentments. Fisher and Churchill had caused his downfall in May 1915 and Asquith wanted nothing to do with either of them. (To Asquith, the Department of Inventions was a mere backwater.) Despite the depths of his animosity towards Churchill as a minister, Asquith remained on polite enough terms to promise that he would do nothing to oppose Churchill's return to politics.

Fisher seemed unaware of the damage that Churchill had done to himself and continued to press him to act as the official opposition. With an army debate coming up in the Commons, Fisher urged Churchill to attend and 'brand the Government with the massacre of our troops and the utter ineptitude of the conduct of the war'. Churchill was the only man who could call for Kitchener to go.[37]

AT THE FRONT

Churchill's request for an extension to his leave to allow him to attend the army debate was turned down. On 12 March, he returned to his military duties in France. Still hopeful that he would be permitted more leave, he wrote to his constituency chairman to tell him that he would be back very shortly.

One week in London had been enough to undermine Churchill's commitment to soldiering. While on leave he had asked Asquith for permission to resign his commission. On arrival in France, he telegraphed to cancel that request, yet he had also left a resignation letter with his wife to release on his instruction. For the rest of his time in France, Churchill would hourly swing between a determination to return to politics and a fear that it was too soon. On leave he had been, he told his wife, 'vy weak & foolish & mentally infirm'. He had been torn apart by 'dual obligations, both honourable, both weighty'. Even so, in reality he had taken the decision to return

– 'my true war station is in the H. of C.' All that was left was to decide the day.[38] Clementine Churchill's instinct was for her husband to stay in France; now was not the right moment to return.

To complicate matters, within a few days of Churchill's return to France the brigadier was shipped home. There was now a new motive to stay. Meanwhile the army debate, on 14 March, only served to remind Churchill that he had not been able to participate: 'How different I cd have made it!' he told Clementine on 17 March.[39]

Once at the Front, Churchill fell into trench routine. There was the usual shelling, leaving five men injured, and a Sunday concert by the divisional band. He was looking forward to dinner with Tudor while reflecting over the retiring brigadier's rebuke for his leniency in punishments.

There may well have been some substance to this accusation. Gibb, in his memoir, wrote that Churchill's attitude to discipline was his 'only serious criticism' of him. He gave as an example the many occasions on which tired, bored or despairing men refused to immediately obey the orders of a corporal. Regimental practice treated this as a serious offence, which was dealt with promptly. But Churchill preferred to give a man 'a chance to depart from his insubordinate attitude'. Gibb acknowledged that this might be 'strict justice' but he did not approve: 'We permanently differed on this matter.'[40]

The day had put Churchill in thoughtful mood. As he and Sinclair strode towards the land held by the neighbouring battalion they had walked over abandoned battlefields, littered with sad reminders of past defeats: shell craters, abandoned trenches and the temporary graves of fallen soldiers. The lives lost there, the pain that remained and the resources spent had bought nothing. Churchill wondered if he could help to end this more quickly if he was in the House of Commons.

On the same day, there was the welcome news that an old acquaintance – Lieutenant General Frederick Trotter – had been appointed Brigade Commander. While Churchill was content to see the matter settled, he nevertheless noted that 'the appointment clearly shows that I have no prospects.'[41]

Although Churchill told his wife that 'I do not mind a bit' when Trotter was appointed, his actions belied his words. Just three days later, he wrote a heart-searching letter to Clementine in which he reviewed his situation with a new intensity. While claiming that he was yet undecided, all his arguments pointed towards an imminent return. He had done enough to justify resuming politics: 'Five months at the front' were enough to earn him an honourable discharge to the Commons. Then there was the fact that 'I have a recognised position in British politics ... enabling me to command the attention ... of my fellow countrymen.' The situation was 'critical & grave'. He concluded: 'I cannot exclude myself from these discussions or divest myself of responsibilities concerning them.'[42]

These were the words of a man who had made up his mind. All thoughts of military glory at the Front, all doubts about his friends' importunate calls to return, were gone.

Mentally, Churchill had left the trenches and in less than a month, he would have bodily departed.

For the next three weeks, Churchill was bombarded with letters urging him to return or pressing him to stay. Those against return included Clementine and Carson as both felt that the moment was not right. As Carson stated, Churchill needed to show there was some imperative reason for his return. Clementine felt that her husband needed a reason such as his regiment coming out of the line. To leave for no external reason was 'such an awful risk to take'. In any case, she optimistically added, 'the war is (D.V.[43]) ¾ over'.[44] Carson and Clementine were supported by the reservations of Churchill's constituency chairman, who felt that a premature return would lead to accusations of opportunism.

One of the most insistent voices in favour of return was that of Scott, who thought that the opposition in the House desperately needed leadership that only Churchill could provide. Garvin shared Scott's earnest desire for Churchill's return, but he was to ease his way in and not appear in the Commons until a month after leaving the army. He should not push himself forward but wait for others to call upon him. But the Liberal MP and industrialist Sir Arthur Markham urged Churchill to return to the Commons where he could do far more good than he could at the Front.

These conflicting pressures took their toll on Churchill. At the end of March, he reached a low point, telling his wife that 'I think I wd not mind stopping living vy much.' He found himself 'devoured by egoism' and unable to decide on any action.[45] He also faced that most deadly enemy of his: boredom. He was jaded by sitting hour-after-hour in his dugout with nothing to do but read and write.

But brooding soon gave way to action. Longing for some political crisis at home that would justify his recall, Churchill put in place means of emergency communication on 7 April. At the merest hint of an approaching crisis his wife was to contact Masterton-Smith, who would radio a message to Dunkirk, from where it could be sent by telegram to him at the Front. His great fear was that the Tories would break with Asquith while he was too far away to profit from the consequences. More hopefully, Lloyd George and Bonar Law would seize the moment and form a new administration. He looked forward to being given the Ministry of Munitions as 'the easiest opening for me'.[46]

THE SECRET SESSION

Churchill expected the break-up to come over conscription, which Asquith was resisting by every possible means. It was widely thought that he would never give way. The best means to remove him was to force through a Compulsion Bill. Churchill urged Carson – the leading figure in the compulsion movement – to ensure the recall of all military Tory MPs for the debate. He was sure that Sir Frederick Cawley MP[47] would do the same for the Liberals. To add to the feverish atmosphere in Westminster,

Churchill also urged Lloyd George to resign if there was no commitment to compulsion. On another course, he wrote to C.P. Scott to urge him to use the columns of the *Manchester Guardian* to sweep away the inept Asquith.

Churchill's now inevitable decision followed two days later. In a letter to Asquith, Churchill requested him 'to take the necessary steps to give effect to my wishes'.[48] He had decided to return to the Commons as soon as the formalities permitted.

As Churchill prepared to go back to the trenches, on 15 April, he turned his thoughts to the war as a whole. There was, he told his wife, no prospect of victory in the coming year. All preparations must focus on the summer of 1917. For now the force on the Western Front should concentrate on improving its armies and the stockpiling of arms. Offensive action in the Mediterranean must end, although Turkey should be destroyed. But where were the brains to do all this?

Churchill, having heard that there was to be a secret session in the Commons, applied for leave and returned to London on 19 April. Major General Furse of the 9th Scottish Division had granted Churchill's leave with alacrity. Any attempt by a man with Churchill's skills to propel the government into action was welcome as he had no faith in the Cabinet's capacity to win the war. He urged Churchill to persuade Lloyd George to leave the Cabinet. Furse, not in any way a politician, showed considerable foresight in correctly identifying Churchill and Lloyd George as the two men who would turn the war around. The army's concern regarding Asquith's government was further demonstrated two days later when Haig extended Churchill's leave to two weeks. Major Ivo Vesey, on Haig's staff, hinted at the reason: that the army thought Churchill could do more for them in London than he could in a dugout.

On 25 April, when Churchill appeared in the Commons for the debate, many of the more senior members on both sides of the House would have already heard the rumours of his imminent return to politics. This added extra excitement to an already charged occasion.

The session was to be held in secret, which simply meant that newspaper reporters and other 'strangers' had to leave the chamber and the usual verbatim report in Hansard would not be published. There was, though, an official – that is government – account of the proceedings in the newspapers the next day.

The House was packed by the time Churchill arrived and he was unable to find a seat. Parliamentary questions were taken as usual and then Asquith turned to address the Speaker and said, 'Sir, I have to call your attention to the fact that strangers are present' – the traditional statement to announce a secret session. After the question to eject them was put for a second time, only one lone voice cried 'No!' Peers, public and reporters filed out. The House then received a report from an earlier secret session of the Lords. (Their Lordships had been even more thorough than the Commons, having searched the vaults of the House before commencing their debate.)

Asquith then reviewed the recruitment situation since the beginning of the war. Referring to the recent attempts to boost recruitment, he noted that these 'had fallen short of requirements'. He then set out the government's proposals which had the stamp of Asquith all over them. Compulsion was appalling to him so the proposals merely altered the existing regulations and imposed the threat of full compulsion if these methods did not recruit 200,000 attested men.[49]

The usual politicians spoke in the following debate, including Carson, Law and Churchill. There is no record of what they said but it is safe to assume that Carson and Churchill vigorously condemned the half-measures proposed and called for full conscription.

The whole business of a secret session had been an elaborate Asquith smokescreen to conceal from the public the raging disagreements between the parties in the Commons. As events turned out he need not have bothered. On 29 April, the British garrison at Kut in Mesopotamia surrendered and this event was to unite the parties in a demand for conscription. (The deaths of hundreds of thousands on the Western Front were acceptable, but the surrender of a major general and over 13,000 men was a national humiliation.) Asquith withdrew his compromise scheme and a new Military Service Act was passed in May, which extended conscription to all men up to the age of forty-one. Only Ireland was excluded. The result was a mixed blessing for Churchill. He had the conscription that he and Carson had fought for for so long, yet Asquith had survived its introduction.

Churchill had only just returned to France when the break-up of his battalion was announced. The command had not been replacing troop losses for some time and, all along the Front, the size of each battalion was daily becoming smaller. Amalgamation was needed. Since this would leave Churchill without a command, it was the perfect excuse he needed for his return home.

His battalion's last day in the trenches was 2 May. The German artillery fired a final thirty shells, four of which struck the farm. For their last evening, Churchill once more organised a grand dinner, this time in a restaurant opposite the railway station at Béthune. Replete with good food and fine brandy, Churchill regaled his guests in a great flow of garrulity which astonished the other diners and even the young ladies who ran the establishment. The following day there were farewells in the orderly room. Every man, said Gibb, felt his leaving as 'a real personal loss'. 'No more popular soldier ever commanded troops.' Gibb, who had shared his fellow officers' feelings of mutinous disdain when he first heard of Churchill's appointment, now concluded that 'I think he could have been a very great soldier.' He was 'beyond question a very great man'.[50]

Six days later, Churchill returned to civilian life. He was fortunate that he had chosen this moment since, just two months later, the Front would turn once more into killing fields when the Battle of the Somme began on 1 July. He might well not have survived that reckless sacrifice of so much of the British army.

In contemplative moments, he must have reflected that no one who had called for his return had any position of influence in government. He would have a long struggle to regain influence and power.

CHAPTER 12

PUBLISH AND BE SAVED

What fools they are. They could get more out of me now in two years of war
than in a hundred afterwards. – Churchill[1]

ON THE DEFENSIVE

After six months in exile at the Front, Churchill had returned to exile on the
backbenches. But he was to be no ordinary backbencher. The authority that he had
derived from his high ministerial office at the start of the war and his newly acquired
knowledge of the Western Front raised him to the rank of unofficial leader of the
opposition. He was, he told reporters, not seeking office. Churchill knew only too
well that office depended on clearing his name of the Gallipoli disaster. Nevertheless,
C.P. Scott noticed that he was 'in great spirits and full of plans'.[2] Fisher, too, was in
optimistic mood when he welcomed Churchill home, saying 'at last this accursed year
has now come to an end'. He hoped for 'better luck' for the two of them.[3]

Within a few days of returning home, Churchill was making his first intervention
in the Commons during a debate on the Military Service Bill. Once more Ireland was
the issue. It was only nine days since the Irish rebellion in Dublin had been crushed.
With the deaths and injuries of some 500 British soldiers on his mind, Asquith feared
the consequences of extending the Act to Ireland. Churchill, speaking from the
opposition benches, did not agree, saying that there was an urgent need for more men
from Ireland. Conscription would be possible if 'mutual concessions' were offered,
including 'a really national policy for Ireland' so that country could 'share in the
prosecution of the general War'.[4] It was a typical Churchill intervention, being both
positive and creative when others said that nothing could be done. He was similarly
inventive over a proposal to let go of all service men who had reached the age of
forty-one. Their experience was too valuable to the war effort, Churchill said. Instead
they should be kept on 'as instructors at home'.[5]

In mid-1916, there was a good deal of discontent over the vague arrangements for
developing airpower during the war. In response to these concerns, the government

proposed the setting up of an Air Board under Lord Curzon. When Churchill enquired as to its powers, he found them limited to making recommendations to the Admiralty and the War Office. Suspicious of this proposal, Churchill asked 'Will the Board have executive power?' Harold Tennant, the Undersecretary of State for War, replied with a masterpiece of bureaucratic avoidance. 'The Board,' he said, 'shall organise a complete system for the interchange of ideas on air problems between the two services.' Churchill retorted that the proposed board was 'a mere attempt to parry the demand for an Air Ministry'. It would do nothing, he said, to overcome 'the lack of any commanding initiative and design and overriding authority in affairs of the air'.[6]

By the end of March, Churchill's role as unofficial leader of the opposition was more or less officially recognised. On 25 March, the Speaker of the Commons called on him to reply to Asquith's request for a further £300 million for the war. (This was on top of the £2,382 million already spent.) Churchill noted that it was the first time in his life that he had followed Asquith in a debate, but he promised that he was not going to 'resist or oppose' the financial request. What followed was a *tour de force* as Churchill forensically examined the government's use of manpower. He first, though, reminded the House that it was foolish to expect the war to 'turn decisively and suddenly in our favour at the present time'. The two opposing belligerents were 'far too evenly matched'. He added, perceptively identifying an issue that would never be resolved under Asquith's leadership, that the Germans had the advantage of unity of command.

Next, Churchill drew on his knowledge of the reality of the Western Front: 'The first thing that strikes a visitor to our Armies in France or in Flanders … is the very large number of officers and men in the prime of their military manhood who never, or only very rarely, go under the fire of the enemy.' Although, he continued, 'all our soldiers, all our officers, are brave and honest men':

> … the fact remains that the trench population lives almost continuously under the fire of the enemy. It returns again and again, after being wounded twice and sometimes three times, to the front and to the trenches, and it is continually subject, without respite, to the hardest of tests that men have ever been called upon to bear, while all the time the non-trench population scarcely suffers at all, and has good food and good wages, higher wages in a great many cases than are drawn by the men under fire every day, and their share of the decorations and rewards is so disproportionate that it has passed into a byword.

War, he told the Commons, is won by the 'killing, fighting, suffering part' of the army. This led him to take up an issue that he would pursue with vigour for the rest of the year: 'the disparity between rifle strength and rations strength'. One cause of the worsened ratio of rifle strength to rations strength was, Churchill argued, the army's habit of running battalions at below strength. Every battalion required around 250 men for 'transport, signalling, and orderly services, and as stretcher bearers, clerks, servants, cooks, musicians, road wardens, and brigade and divisional employees'. This number was the same whether the battalion was at or below strength. Once a battalion had this core of men every new man added was '[a] pure gain to the rifle strength'.

Next, Churchill turned his analytical eye on servants in the army. He estimated that the army's 200,000 officers were being supported by 200,000 servants and 50,000 grooms: 'That is an army in itself.'

Nor did Churchill overlook that monumental waste of manpower in the First World War – the cavalry, which had spent years 'behind the lines in France and Flanders' to no effect at all.

Churchill still had not exhausted his attack on the inefficient use of manpower. He described how indiscriminate recruiting had filled depots, training schools, camps and hospitals with 'men who have never been and will never be fit to put in the field'. They would be much better employed in the factories at home, he argued.

While some of Churchill's figures would be disputed later, his speech nevertheless was an extraordinary demonstration of his power to analyse and to think deeply and creatively. By the end of the debate, it was clear that he was now the leading critic of the government's conduct of the war. No one else could match his combination of authority, experience and mastery of technical detail.[7]

In the following week, Tennant had the difficult task of responding to Churchill. He envied Churchill, he said, because he had the time 'to prepare his very carefully thought-out speeches'. Harold Tennant had tirelessly spent thirty-four of the last fifty-two days defending the estimates in the House. Even so he poured out a stream of statistics and a mass of argument to justify the government in rejecting Churchill's case. But he did not convince the MP Major General Sir Ivor Herbert. The speech, Herbert said, had been 'powerful, well-argued, well-informed' and he moved a motion to reduce Lord Kitchener's salary by £100.

Concerned as Churchill was about the inefficient use of manpower, he was even more preoccupied by the inefficient use of himself. On 1 June, when James Dalziel, MP for Kirkcaldy Burghs, called for the Dardanelles papers to be published, Churchill leapt to support him. Disingenuously, he suggested that it was in ministers' own interests to publish so that it could not be thought they were laying the blame 'upon the military or naval commanders at the scene of action'. He received a surprisingly positive response from Bonar Law, who declared that the papers would be presented 'as soon as possible … nothing shall be withheld which is not against public interests.'[8]

However encouraging Law's statement had been, Churchill was not going to ease off. Later that day, he wrote to Asquith to offer his and Hankey's assistance in selecting the papers to be published. In particular, Churchill was anxious to see in print those minutes which showed how hard he had pressed for the immediate despatch of the 29th Division, plus all the decisions of the Council and the names of those who attended. He well knew that publication would prove both how enthusiastic Asquith, Grey and Kitchener had been about the Dardanelles and just how corporate the operation had been. Or, to put it more succinctly, as Churchill did when in conversation with C.P. Scott, 'the Dardanelles papers would put various eminent persons – Jackson, Kitchener, Balfour all "up to the neck" in the business.'[9]

Arthur Balfour began the move to block publication. On the day after Law had assured the House that the papers would be published, Balfour laid his objections before Hankey. In his diary, Hankey recorded 'We agreed that I should ask the PM to withdraw the promise ... nothing more foolish than to do this during the progress of a great war.'[10] When Hankey told Churchill what he had done, Churchill 'became quite furious' and declared 'Whenever I open my mouth in Parliament someone shouts out that I am the man who let us in for the Dardanelles mistake ... My usefulness in Parliament is entirely ruined.'[11]

An interesting footnote on Hankey's involvement can be found in Major General Callwell's war memoirs, where he recalled looking at the papers when publication was first discussed. He concluded:

> There could be no question that, no matter how drastic might be the cutting-down process, the Admiralty, the War Office and the Government would come badly out of the business. Furthermore, any publication of papers must make known to the world that Lord Kitchener's judgement in connection with this particular phase of the war had been somewhat at fault.[12]

A comment which, coming from the Director of Military Operations himself, vindicates Churchill's view that publication would have damaged a good many careers.

Few men in politics have been more duplicitous than Balfour. He was a master of being all things to all men, who moved behind the scenes and rarely left a trace of his passing. So it is no surprise that, on the day that he was secretly sabotaging Churchill's attempt to have the Dardanelles papers published, Balfour asked for Churchill's aid over a very public matter.

Just three days earlier, on 31 May, the great fleets had engaged at the Battle of Jutland. The result was a British victory as the German High Seas Fleet, commanded by Admiral von Scheer, fled the scene barely forty-five minutes after encountering the British Grand Fleet under Admiral Jellicoe. But the Admiralty communiqué had led the newspapers to report the battle as an apparent defeat: 'Great Naval Battle. Heavy Losses' ran the headline in *The Times* newspaper. It was a public relations fiasco for Balfour, who now turned to Churchill to redeem the situation.

Opinions differ as to Balfour's motive. Riddell, in his diary, suggested it was 'a skilful device ... to draw the teeth of his chief potential critic'.[13] Whatever the reason, Churchill agreed to draft a new press statement, which he thought would be put out in the name of the Admiralty. His approach was to concentrate on a comparison of the losses and the effect of these losses on Britain's margin of superiority. This margin, he concluded, was 'in no way impaired'. Meanwhile, he assured British newspaper readers, 'the despatch of troops to the continent should continue with the utmost freedom.' The result was a disaster all-round since the Admiralty was widely criticised for having asked Churchill to write the statement and Churchill was vilified for being the author. Indeed, the outcome for Balfour was so bad that C.P. Scott wondered if Churchill had taken on the task 'with Machiavellian astuteness ... to discredit the Admiralty'.[14] Balfour's own defence of the incident appeared in *The Times* on 8 June: 'Let it be remembered that Mr. Churchill was thoroughly acquainted with the position of the Fleet. He had been two-and-a-half years First Lord of the Admiralty.' Given Churchill's well-known criticisms of naval and military policy, no one would have accused him of being 'unduly biased in favour of the Administration'. So, wrote Balfour, 'I cannot imagine a better authority for dealing with the neutral Press on the subject.'[15]

On the day that Churchill found that he had lost Hankey's support over the Dardanelles papers, another incident happened in the cold and often stormy seas off Scotland. When the news reached London, Churchill was with Hankey. The phone rang and Hankey answered. Churchill could tell from Hankey's demeanour that something calamitous had happened, but Hankey made no mention. Later, Churchill was with Sir Ian Hamilton to discuss which Dardanelles papers they wished to see published. 'Suddenly,' said Hamilton 'we heard someone in the street crying out Kitchener's name. We jumped up and Winston threw the window open.' There below was a newspaper vendor shouting 'Kitchener drowned! No survivors!' On hearing this, Churchill remarked to Hamilton 'Fortunate was he in the moment of his death!' Hamilton later commented on the macabre coincidence that Kitchener 'should have vanished at the very moment Winston and I were making out an unanswerable case against him'.[16]

On the day after Kitchener's death, C.P. Scott visited Churchill and found him in a meeting with Hankey, pressing him to include various papers in the extracts that Asquith had promised to publish. After Hankey had departed, Scott was surprised as Churchill switched from the serious issue of clearing his name to the 'frivolous' matter of his paintings.[17] As he showed Hankey one painting after another, Churchill's face beamed with pleasure at his own achievements. What Scott perhaps did not realise was how essential painting was to Churchill when his 'black dog'[18] overcame him.

By mid-June, the first moves were being made towards Churchill returning to office when Lord Reading, the Lord Chief Justice, suggested that he might take Lloyd George's old post at Munitions. When Reading discussed this with Lloyd George, the latter thought it was too early for Churchill to come back. Although Churchill did not know of these conversations, it is significant that, a few days later, he told

C.P. Scott that 'he was a little sore that George never said a word in his defence.'[19] At this stage of the war, Lloyd George was too busy securing his own interests to take up the case of a man whom Asquith had resolutely decided to ignore. A week later, now aware of the discussions, Churchill told his brother Jack that the press was extremely hostile towards him and he was pinning his faith on their changing their minds once the Dardanelles papers were published.

It was around this time that Churchill began to link his own defence of his role in the Dardanelles with that of Fisher. He urged Fisher to go to the offices of the Committee for Imperial Defence and read the minutes. Meanwhile, Churchill decided to confront Asquith once more over the question of publication. It was not a subtle letter as he reminded the Prime Minister of how strongly he, along with other ministers, had supported the naval attack. He reminded Asquith that the War Council minutes recorded his, Churchill's, warning in February that the operation would fail without sufficient troops. It was important for him that these facts were made public. Only a man as self-centred as Churchill could have failed to see that his letter underlined exactly why Asquith, Grey, Kitchener and Balfour might not favour publication. As long as the papers were hidden from view, Churchill was the scapegoat. Publication would tell another story. Four days later, Asquith told the Commons that 'a considerable period must elapse before these Papers are likely to be ready.'[20]

Five days later, on 1 July, the Battle of the Somme commenced. By sunset, some 60,000 British soldiers had been killed or wounded. (Such figures did not appear in the newspapers, where 'progress' and 'successes' was the order of the day.) As to Churchill, he was not deceived, telling Riddell that 'he thought the progress very disappointing'.[21] Churchill had been ousted for an offensive in the Mediterranean which had cost the lives of 700 men. The architects of the Somme went on to accumulate over 600,000 casualties before moving on to further 'glorious' campaigns.

On the following day, Churchill was at Cherkley Court, the country home of 'Max' Aitken. There he spent five hours talking with Lloyd George, mostly about his great desire to get back into the Cabinet. On this occasion, Lloyd George seems to have supported his moving to Munitions, but this was opposed by Asquith. When Riddell pointed out 'Winston's mind is concentrated on the war', Lloyd George retorted 'Yes, but it is more concentrated on Winston.'[22] In fact, Churchill had little else to think about as he had no job and no immediate prospects. His main task that day was a landscape painting that he was working on when Riddell arrived: 'A poor devil without a job must do something to occupy his mind,' he said. Riddell concluded that he was 'in a very unhappy, disgruntled state of mind'.[23]

On 13 July, Dalziel asked in the Commons as to when the Dardanelles papers were to be published, but Law's reply was evasive and he asked members to await the Prime Minister's announcement in the following week. It was not the outcome that Churchill had battled so long to gain. Asquith told the Commons that it was the unanimous opinion of 'the military and diplomatic advisers of the Government' that the papers could not be published 'without omissions so numerous' as to be 'misleading'. Had Kitchener been consulted about publication, Churchill asked. Asquith attempted to avoid answering but after three attempts Churchill pressed him to admit that Kitchener had been in favour of publication.[24]

Later, when Asquith announced the setting up of a committee 'to inquire into the conduct of the Dardanelles operations', Churchill said in the House that he was 'quite content' although he would have preferred publication.[25] But the next day, Riddell judged Churchill to be 'very depressed' and recorded him as saying 'my life is finished. I only care about the war and I am banished from the scene of action.'[26]

Nevertheless, Churchill was still capable of rising to an occasion when needed. Having written himself off in the morning at his meeting with Riddell, in the afternoon he stood in for Lloyd George at a fund-raising matinee for an Anglo-Russian hospital. In a powerful speech, he praised 'the stubborn and skilful defence made by the Russian Armies … against an attack superior in numbers and overwhelmingly superior in artillery and munitions' in 1915. And, at the time of Verdun, 'General Brusiloff shattered the Austrian armies, rescued the fair province of Bukowina, and changed, in a single stroke, the whole aspect and fortunes of the world-wide war.'[27]

Four months after his forensic attack on the government in the supply debate of March, Churchill was back in the Commons, on 24 July, with a similar attack during a supply debate for a further £450 million of funding. As in the March debate, he criticised Asquith for his failure to provide any kind of survey of the war when 'asking for this immense sum of money'. He had looked forward to hearing, he said, 'some reference to events like the naval battle, or the brilliant tactics of General Brusiloff, or the sustained and magnificent defence made by our Allies at Verdun'. Next, he harangued the Prime Minister for still retaining the War Office – a post he had taken up on the death of Kitchener: 'When the office became vacant it ought to have been filled within forty-eight hours in the interests of the War. It ought not to have been left vacant, with only such time as the right hon. Gentleman could spare from his already most severe labours.' (Asquith's role here is a puzzle. *The Times* newspaper of 7 July announced the appointment of Lloyd George as Secretary of State for War, yet Asquith was still doing the work on 26 July.)

Having dealt with the intricacies of administration Churchill then returned to his criticisms of the government's handling of manpower:

What is being done to secure, as far as possible, that all fit men shall take their turns, especially men between twenty and thirty years of age, in the trenches in the fighting units? What has been done to provide, as far as possible, substitutes for young, fit, military males who are at present engaged in non-combatant services far from the front? What has been done to afford relief to war-worn soldiers, and particularly to wounded men, who are sent back time after time to the trenches which others have never visited at all?

He did not apologise for troubling the House with the detail, since 'we are fighting for our lives.' Then he lamented the low number of medals awarded during the war, which was not commensurate with 'the extraordinary frequency with which acts of gallantry and good service are performed, and the terrible losses both of life and limb with which the fighting is attended'. He thought the number of medals should be 'three or four times' more. Next, he worked his way through the need for light railways at the Front, better field telephones, more steel helmets, more heavy guns, more ammunition and more use of naval guns not required for ships.

In reply, Lloyd George – who had been in office for only three weeks – opted for the easy answer and declared himself 'infinitely grateful' to Churchill, while stating that 'it will take a very long time to master even some of the elements of the problems which he has suggested for my consideration.'[28]

The appointment of Lloyd George had resulted in a bizarre disagreement between Northcliffe and Churchill. It all began on the morning of 7 July, when Churchill called on Lloyd George. As he entered the building he met Northcliffe, who suggested that Churchill had called in order to lay claim to Lloyd George's Treasury post. So offended was Churchill that he returned a statuette of Napoleon Northcliffe had given to him as a gift. In reply, Northcliffe protested that he had not meant Churchill to take the remark to heart. A mutual exchange of apologies smoothed the matter over and the statuette was returned to Churchill.

It was around this time that rumours began to circulate that Asquith's precarious finances (he had no income other than his salary) might cause him to leave office for a more remunerative appointment, such as Lord Chancellor. Churchill savoured the prospect of his indecisive ex-colleague's departure. Asquith was the core of all his problems: dismissing him from the Cabinet in May 1915, vetoing his brigadier appointment in December 1915, and refusing him office since his return from France.

While he waited for the inquiry into one military fiasco to begin work, Churchill drew attention to yet another that was in progress: the Battle of the Somme. In a memorandum which he persuaded F.E. Smith to submit on his behalf to the Cabinet, Churchill attacked the futile campaign which, after one month, had still not met the first day's objectives. There was nothing to show for all the lives lost and it was a battle that was rapidly destroying the British army as 'division after division' was used up. He urged that the offensive be abandoned, but found no supporters in the Cabinet.[29]

This memorandum was an important turning point in Churchill's war. When at the Front he had written his *Variants of the Offensive* paper, in which he identified ways of attacking without exposing men to machine-gun fire. Now he went one step further and actually recommended calling off offensives where the cost in men could not justify the results. No one wished to hear this message and Haig, confident in his methods, sent in his own reply to the Cabinet. In his journal Haig wrote of the enemy: 'The maintenance of a steady offensive pressure will result eventually in his complete overthrow.'[30]

Why Churchill thought it worthwhile to submit a memorandum to the Cabinet is hard to evaluate. He knew that he faced both the hostility of Tory ministers and the determination of Asquith to risk nothing in supporting him. In any case, he thought Asquith's position was increasingly precarious – 'there are vy hostile forces at work in the Cabinet' – and he anticipated an imminent collapse.[31]

Indeed, Churchill had no idea as to just how hostile the Tories were towards him. Lord Derby found him so 'distasteful' that he contemplated founding a new political party after the war, the principal merit of which would be that 'Winston could not possibly be in it'. As for the present, Derby told Lloyd George, 'Our Party will not work with him and as far as I am concerned personally nothing would induce me to support any Government of which he is a member.'[32] Oblivious to this antipathy towards him, Churchill told Fisher that he was 'hopeful of his own prospects' and was looking forward to office under Lloyd George.[33]

Isolation, though, gave Churchill the chance to stand back and the freedom to think outside the boundaries of the party. In an adjournment debate on 22 August, Churchill delivered a speech worthy of a statesman. He made no attempt to score party political points or attack individuals, but simply reviewed where the country was after nearly two years of war. He declared that the fighting of the previous six months had failed to produce 'any sensible change in the general strategic alignment of the Armies' and warned the Commons not to expect a 'speedy peace'. It was time, he said, to stop fighting war by means of 'makeshifts' and that victory would only come when the nation was organised as 'one vast, all-embracing industry':

Everything in the State ought now to be devised and regulated with a view to the development and maintenance of our war power at the absolute maximum for an indefinite period. If you want to shorten the War, do this. If you want to discourage the enemy, let them see that you are doing it. If you want to cheer our own people, let them feel that you are doing it.

Turning to food prices, he declared that the rapid rise was due to the government's failure to regulate the supply system. 'It is necessary,' he said, 'to abandon our dearly cherished, go-as-you-please, old-fashioned methods.' He underlined the need for shared restraint – even for shared suffering – in a passage that anticipated his great speeches of the Second World War:

It is not that the people of this country will not stand privation. They will endure any suffering and any privation to win the War, but they will not stand privations side by side with enormous profits made by private persons, and they will not stand them unless they believe and feel that everything humanly possible is being done to relieve them to the utmost.

He urged the government to regulate shipping, control profits and ensure that 'food is brought into the market at a reasonable and a moderate price to all classes'.[34] (This appears to be the first time that food rationing for the civilian population was suggested in the Commons. Asquith was still recommending 'the voluntary avoidance of superfluous consumption' in October.[35])

For all Churchill's critical appraisal in private of the futile incompetence of the land war, he was quite prepared to offer the public wildly optimistic interpretations of the military situation. In early September, at a rally in Chelmsford, he told an audience that 'Night and day, week in, week out, without rest or pause, the great new British Army is storming and thundering on the German lines with a courage never excelled in history.' At sea matters were not too bad even if the naval blockade was taking 'longer than we expected'. As for the war in the air, 'we have reason to be satisfied and proud … [about] the superiority which our airmen have obtained over the enemy.'[36]

Churchill had taken a continuing interest in the development of the tank ever since he had set up the Landships Committee in February 1915. When a small number of the new machines were trialled on the Somme in early September, the results were varied. The trials proved the potential of the tank as an attacking weapon, but too few had been deployed and those few had not been fully developed. In a letter to Archie Sinclair, Churchill bemoaned this premature use of his brainchild.

THE DARDANELLES COMMISSION

On 28 September, the Dardanelles Commission began taking evidence for the first part of its work – the naval operations up to the landing of troops – with Churchill as the first witness. In his forthright opening speech, Churchill clearly showed the line he intended to follow. His defence was based on three key assertions. Firstly, that the operation was undertaken at the initiative of the War Office – it was Kitchener who was the channel for the Russian request for aid. Secondly, that the plans were based on the assessment of the admiral on the spot and had been approved by his professional staff in London. And thirdly, that it had been a corporate operation with all key decisions approved by the War Council. Additionally, Churchill sought to put Fisher's objections into perspective by pointing out that the admiral had never objected to the operation itself, but only to its implications for the margin of safety in the North Sea. Neatly and properly, Churchill asserted that the Dardanelles operation had been a War Council project, with the operational aspects delegated to the Admiralty.

When Churchill took the Commission through the details of how the operation had been planned and executed, the Commission showed a particular interest in how the naval plan was developed and approved. Churchill's telegram to Carden, in which he stated that the latter's plan had been approved by 'high authorities', came in for close scrutiny. The Commission was a little surprised that Fisher was not included under that term.[37] In response, Churchill laid great emphasis on the validity of Carden's plan – it was the most important telegram sent by an admiral 'who had been for weeks sitting off the Dardanelles, who had been presumably turning over the thing in his mind again and again … who produces a plan, and a detailed plan and a novel plan'. It made 'a great impression on everyone who saw it', he said.[38]

Churchill knew that his trump card was the evidence that he had not acted alone, so when the Commission continued to press him over the 'high authorities' Churchill reminded the Commission that he had tabled the full text of the telegram at the War Council meeting on 13 January. 'I am entitled,' he emphasised, 'to draw your attention to the members who were present, a very numerous gathering. The decision of the War Council was unanimous.'[39]

Later in the day, Churchill offered an additional line of defence based on his view of risk being the essence in war. 'All war is hazard,' he told the Commission, but an operation could be justified if it had 'full authority … a reasonable prospect of success … greater interests were not compromised … all possible care and forethought were exercised in its preparation' and it was executed with 'vigour and determination'.[40] This was a shrewd move. In any discussion, the person who first suggests criteria is the one who sets the tone for debate. He felt certain that his conduct met these criteria and so absolved him of any faults of procedure or judgement.

When Churchill turned to the military aspect of the Dardanelles, he stressed that he 'never swerved in the slightest degree' from his view that the naval plan as approved should be implemented and that as many troops as possible should be gathered in the Eastern Mediterranean before the bombardment.[41] He told the Commission that, in his view, there was nothing 'in France, or on the Russian front' at the time to justify not putting up to ten divisions into the Eastern Mediterranean in February 1915.[42]

A short while later, Churchill came to what he regarded as one of the most important pieces of evidence in his defence. Referring to the War Council meeting of 26 February, when he had pressed for the deployment of the 29th Division, he drew the Commission's attention to his having told the Council: 'If a disaster occurred in Turkey owing to insufficiency of troops, he must disclaim all responsibility.'[43] He went on to describe how he had met Kitchener in the presence of Asquith and asked him 'whether it was understood that he took full responsibility for any military operations that might arise in the Near East'. Kitchener confirmed that he did.[44] The rest of Churchill's evidence that day consisted of a detailed account (including reading out all the telegrams) of the naval actions up to abandonment of the bombardment, and then the military aspects up to Fisher's resignation on 14 May.

On 4 October, Churchill was again before the Commission to continue his evidence, which consisted mostly of a detailed account of the naval operations. One interesting point arose when he was challenged about using the phrase 'heavy losses' in his telegram to Carden dated 3 January. Was it not a leading question, he was asked. Churchill accepted that it could be so construed. But, when he was asked whether he agreed that 'when you ask naval officers to undertake a difficult and dangerous service they are always reluctant to say they cannot do it', Churchill retorted 'I have not found that so at all.'[45] He was indeed correct. Files at the Admiralty were overflowing with the many Churchill projects that his naval colleagues had deemed too dangerous to carry out – Sylt and Borkum being examples. What is more, Carden clearly produced a plan he believed in.

One of the more difficult moments for Churchill came when the Commissioners turned their attention to Fisher's memorandum, written on 25 January, in which he argued against wearing out ships while the German High Seas Fleet remained in harbour. It was suggested to Churchill that 'Lord Fisher's memorandum was of such importance that all the War Council should have had it before them.' Churchill demurred, saying the memorandum showed only 'a strong disinclination to undertake this operation' but did not attack its practicability.[46]

While Churchill was struggling to clear his name through his evidence to the Commission, a vicious attack on him appeared in the *Daily Mail* of 10 October. He was said to have had 'just intelligence enough to know that Antwerp and Constantinople were places of importance' but had been 'mad enough to embark on adventures in both places with forces and methods that were insanely disproportionate to the enterprises'.[47] He complained to Cromer that the rules of procedure for the Commission prevented him from defending himself against such attacks since he was not allowed to cross-examine witnesses. It is hard to see how cross-examination would have helped since the sessions were held in secret, and would have had no impact on the opinions of the *Daily Mail* or any other newspaper.

Churchill was the sole witness to be given the privilege of questioning (but not cross-examining) other witnesses. On 24 October, his first target was Admiral Wilson. But before he began, the chairman gave Churchill a sharp warning to limit himself to relevant questions. He was not to bring in Antwerp or Coronel (on both of which he had submitted documents) nor was he to talk about the margin of safety in the North Sea since, at this stage, the Commission was looking solely at the initiation of the Dardanelles campaign.

Admiral Wilson was questioned mainly on certain technical aspects of the bombardment, including the role of the naval guns and the Turks' ammunition supply, but for Churchill the critical issue was the Admiral's own role. He successfully established before the Commission that this highly esteemed Admiral of the Fleet, who had attended all the War Council meetings, had never advised against any aspect of the operation. Another witness, Graham Greene, Secretary to the Board, provided crucial evidence to support Churchill's assertion that he fully involved and consulted Admiralty staff. Greene's evidence demonstrated that Churchill had called ten board meetings during the first ten months of the war – the same rate as before the war – and that 'the method of direction of the Admiralty' under the Balfour regime was no different to that under Churchill. This evidence dealt a fatal blow to the endless rumours as to Churchill running the Admiralty in an authoritarian manner. Greene also corrected a misunderstanding on the role of the board. He explained that since 1869, the board had ceased to discuss 'war orders or executive orders to the fleet'. Churchill's failure to bring such orders to the board had a most respectable pedigree.[48]

Churchill then turned Greene's mind to the role of the Admiralty War Group in relation to the initiation and conduct of the operation. 'Did it [the operation] receive the same regular treatment and exhaustive discussion as other operations of war?' Answer: 'Oh, yes.' Had there been 'many discussions about the possibility of ships bombarding the forts'? Answer: 'Yes.' There were then questions as to why the Director of Naval Ordnance had not attended the meetings. Greene explained that he was 'a supply officer' and it had never been the custom to include such officers in operational planning meetings.[49]

<hr />

Isolated and under interrogation as Churchill was, there were still a few rare moments when he could be of use. Edwin Montagu, who had taken over the Ministry of Munitions from Lloyd George, had heard Churchill expounding his thoughts about 'ribs not stopping bullets' and his ideas on machines to replace men.[50] This was just the stimulus that Munitions needed. On 31 October, he told Churchill that the problem was that all the army wanted was an endless supply of men, guns and ammunition. They never stopped to think that there might be some other way to defeat the enemy. As a step towards this he invited Churchill to give a talk to some of the senior members of his department. In reply, Churchill agreed but made it clear that the group should be chosen carefully since he would be revealing proposals for weaponry of a highly secret nature. Interestingly, less than a year later, Churchill would once more be talking to the same group, but as their minister.

ASQUITH'S FALL

As the year neared its end, the discontent amongst Tory members with Asquith's administration was reaching new levels. On 18 November, their frustration, suppressed in public up to now, burst into the open during a debate on the obscure topic of the disposal of enemy property in Nigeria. The Colonial Office had proposed to allow bids for the property from neutral states, but many Tory MPs felt that only 'natural-born British subjects or companies wholly British' should be allowed to purchase the items.[51] When the vote came, sixty-five Tories voted against the government while seventy-one sided with it. Asquith had come within four votes of defeat. Churchill had voted with the Tory rebels. His rupture with his old master was now complete, although his vote was no more than symbolic since Asquith's own days were now numbered.

That weekend an informal group met at 'Max' Aitken's house, where they took the opportunity to discuss how to take advantage of the Prime Minister's weakened position. On the Saturday evening, F.E. Smith and Churchill – normally the closest of friends – engaged in a furious argument in which Smith attacked Lloyd George and defended the government, while Churchill attacked the government and defended Lloyd George. For once, Churchill's political antennae were pointing in the right direction.

The next morning, Churchill went to see Lloyd George at Walton Heath. Before he left, Aitken took him to one side and urged him not to give the impression that the Tories were hostile to Lloyd George. On returning to Aitken's house later in the day, Churchill began to argue with Bonar Law who was seemingly unwilling to recognise the growing political crisis. The more Law refused to budge, the fiercer became Churchill's attack on the government. When Law could take no more, he burst out: 'Very well, if that's what the critics of the Government think of it – we will have a General Election.' Aitken, the recorder of these events, noted that Churchill thought that 'Bonar Law's proposal to hold a General Election in the middle of a war was the most terribly immoral thing he had ever heard of'. Aitken himself thought that the true source of Churchill's anger was the fear that he would lose his seat in an election.[52]

The issue of the government's failure to take charge of food production and distribution was raised again in the Commons on 16 November. Churchill rejected the explanation that the Compulsory Service Act was responsible for food shortages, stating that 'indiscriminate recruiting' had caused the problem by taking away skilled workers. John Dillon (a leading Irish Nationalist MP) had argued against touching 'the food of the people' as such action was not democratic, he declared. As far as Churchill was concerned, the food supply was not only being 'touched' but was being 'trampled upon' and only government action could redeem the position. Referring to cases where producers were pouring milk down drains or feeding it to pigs, he said 'Has it really taken twenty-seven months of Armageddon, twenty-seven months of this terrible conflict, to convince the right hon. Gentleman that action to prevent proceedings of that kind is justified by the circumstances of the day?' He called for 'ration tickets for everything that matters' and prices fixed so that 'the poorest people in this country' could afford 'a certain modicum of food sufficient to keep up physical war-making efficiency'. He foresaw 'something very like universal service' for all aspects of life during the war.[53]

Perceptive speeches in the House were not enough to satisfy Churchill. He told C.P. Scott on 20 November that even when he did speak he was reported only in the *Manchester Guardian*. In the House, 'no one troubled to come in' when he spoke whereas in the past 'his rising was the signal for the House to fill'. He was, he said, 'the best abused man in the country'. 'What fools they are. They could get more out of me now in two years of war than in a hundred afterwards.'[54] Meanwhile, 'he preferred to find his public in the press. Then at least every word he wished to say was printed, and it took him no longer to write an article for the *Sunday Pictorial* for which he got £250 than to prepare a speech which was not reported.'[55]

At the end of November, Churchill reached his forty-second birthday. He had little to celebrate, other than a remarkably distinguished career for such a young man. As to the future, he felt it lay in Lloyd George becoming Prime Minister, but he was to experience a bitter disappointment.

The next day, Lloyd George wrote to Asquith with his proposals for a new War Committee made up of the First Lord of the Admiralty, the Secretary of State for War and a minister without portfolio. One of the three would chair the meetings. That the committee excluded Asquith can only have been a calculated insult to provoke the events that followed. When Asquith rejected this proposal, Lloyd George resigned. On 5 December, Asquith also resigned and the King sent for Bonar Law to ask him to form a government. When Bonar Law found that Asquith would not serve under him he abandoned his attempt and the King then called on Lloyd George. By 7 December, he was the Prime Minister of a three-party coalition with a Cabinet of fifteen Unionists, twelve Liberals and two Labour members. There were no startling new appointments (other than Lloyd George himself). His War Cabinet was to be Curzon, Law, Arthur Henderson (Labour MP) and Lord Milner. The change was, wrote the historian A.J.P. Taylor, from 'dynamite' to 'a damp squib'.[56]

Unknown to Churchill, Lloyd George had told Curzon, on 3 December, that neither Churchill nor Northcliffe would be in the new government. It was not until the day Asquith resigned that Aitken revealed this to Churchill after a dinner at F.E. Smith's house. Aitken had just returned from a meeting with Lloyd George, who had offered him a minor appointment, which he had declined. In possession of the news that Churchill was not to be in the government he felt he should offer some kind of hope to his friend. He told him 'The new Government will be very well disposed towards you. All your friends will be there.' Churchill 'blazed into righteous anger', turned to Smith and said 'Smith, this man knows I am not to be included in the new Government' and walked out into the street.[57]

No doubt Lloyd George felt guilty at excluding Churchill, but he had no choice since Bonar Law had insisted his party would not join a coalition which included him. Lloyd George asked Riddell to explain the situation to Churchill and reassure him that he would try to find him a post 'such as Chairman of the Air Board' after the publication of the Dardanelles Commission report.[58] When Riddell delivered this message, Churchill asked him to tell Lloyd George 'I will take any position which will enable me to serve my country. My only purpose is to help defeat the Hun, and I will subordinate my own feelings so that I may be able to render some assistance.'[59]

To be once more excluded from office was one more brutal blow for Churchill. As he told Sinclair, it was 'the downfall of all my hopes and desires'. Lloyd George, he complained, had given way to the press, which was still very hostile towards him. The result was a feeble and untried government.

In the midst of this personal despair, Churchill found the energy to write a deeply felt letter of sympathy to Katherine Asquith on the death of her husband Raymond. He recalled when they last met 'on the old ramparts in bright sunshine' at Montreuil they had 'talked about war, about the coming offensive, about his son, about all sorts of things'. Raymond, he said, was one of 'these gallant charming figures that flash and gleam amid the carnage ... disdainful of death and suffering'.[60]

In January 1917, when Churchill wrote to congratulate Fisher on his seventy-sixth birthday, he told him that 'I am simply existing.' They were both, he wrote, 'quite powerless', which was a pity since 'a descent on the German coast, the bringing in of Denmark and the entry and domination of the Baltic would secure a decisive victory for the allies.'[61]

There were other moments when Churchill's despair and anger erupted. In February, Riddell drove home with Churchill after an Other Club dinner. He found Churchill 'very bitter' about Lloyd George and did not wish to see the Prime Minister except to receive 'some definite proposal'. He had had enough 'mealy-mouthed promises and expressions of good will'.[62]

All now depended on the report. Would it clear Churchill's name?

CHAPTER 13

RETURN TO POWER

We have not yet invented an unsinkable ship, we have discovered the unsinkable politician. – *Morning Post*

A WELCOME PUBLICATION

The moment that Churchill had waited for since May 1915 finally arrived on 9 March 1917 when the Dardanelles Commission published its first report. This covered operations up to 23 March 1915 and concentrated on how the decision to carry out the attack had been made. Three aspects of this received particular attention: how decisions had been arrived at in the Admiralty; the role of the naval and military experts attending the War Council; and how the Council reached decisions.

In considering the decision-making structure of the Admiralty, the Commission noted, but did not criticise, the fact that 'The Board of Admiralty sank into insignificance, its place being taken by the War Staff Group.' They discussed the complaint from some junior sea lords that they had not been consulted over the operation. Again, there was no criticism. Indeed, Wilson had told the Commission that the board was not in the habit of discussing operations and war orders. The Commission was, though, concerned that Sir Henry Jackson had not been adequately consulted over the Carden plan. As to Fisher having remained silent throughout the War Council meetings the Commission was adamant that, in doing this, he had effectively given his approval to the Council's decisions.[1]

No aspect of the naval campaign was more criticised than the way in which the War Council used (or did not use) the naval and military experts who attended. The Commission noted that 'the precise position assigned to the expert members' was far from clear. To a man, the members of the Council had assumed that the experts assented if they did not openly express dissent.[2]

The final general area that the Commission examined was the Council's procedural methods. They did not mince words when they criticised the 'vagueness and want of precision' in the Council's methods and the failure to read out the decisions reached at the end of each meeting. This was a clear condemnation of Asquith's methods.[3]

The Commission's sixteen conclusions did not amount to much, but they were all founded on their view that everyone on the War Council would have preferred a joint military/naval attack from the start 'had not other circumstances led to a modification of the programme'.[4] This was an important conclusion for Churchill since it showed the Commission's determination to treat the Dardanelles operation as a corporate venture – not as one of Churchill's private stunts or even just an Admiralty operation. Their central criticism of the Council was that it failed to carry out a 'much fuller investigation' before giving authority for the operation at the meeting on 13 January. There then followed another conclusion that was of great value to Churchill. In the Commission's view, had the Council studied the plan in more depth 'we think it would have been ascertained that sufficient troops would have been available.'[5] Churchill, of course, had claimed that this was so at the time and always seemed to have had a better understanding of where various divisions were than did Kitchener. But, said the Commission, once the Council began to mass troops in the Mediterranean (from 16 February) there should have been 'an immediate and vigorous effort to ensure success'.[6] The hesitation had simply given more time for the Turks to prepare. Once again, the Commission supported what Churchill's line had been in early 1915. It was he who, on several occasions, urged more vigour in the troop concentrations.

In examining the conflict as a purely naval or a combined operation, the Commission drew attention to the fact that Grey, Asquith, Balfour and Wilson had all testified that they considered (up to 23 March) the operation to be naval, which could have been broken off at any time.[7] Additionally, both Asquith and Grey had testified that, despite the failure to reach Constantinople, the operation had been valuable and staved off 'untoward consequences'.[8]

Churchill was mildly criticised in two respects. Firstly, said the Commission, he should have asked Fisher to give his views explicitly at the meeting on 28 January, knowing that they were considerably at variance with his own. Secondly, the Commission concluded that 'Mr Churchill seems to have advocated the attack by ships alone ... on a certain amount of half-hearted and hesitating expert opinion.'[9] However, this statement was softened by the Commission noting that none of the experts had expressed dissent. And, very importantly for Churchill, the Commission recorded that 'Lord Kitchener, who occupied a commanding position at the time the decision was taken, was in favour of the project.'[10]

As Chairman, Asquith came in for criticism because he had failed to encourage the experts to speak up and ran the meetings in a vague manner. The deceased Kitchener was criticised on three counts: his 'unwillingness to impart full information even to members of the War Council'; that he 'did not sufficiently avail himself of the services of his General Staff'; and for not telling Churchill that he was withholding the 29th Division. This, the Commission declared, 'gravely compromised the probability of success'.[11] As for criticism of Fisher, he much resented the Commission's judgement that he had acted from 'a mistaken sense of duty' by not giving his opinion at the meetings. If the view held by Fisher and Wilson of the role of experts was to prevail this 'would exercise an extremely bad effect upon the general efficiency of the public services'.[12]

A short but accurate summary of the report was published in *The Times* newspaper. It stated:

> The whole story is a tragic record of drift, disorganisation, and ultimate disaster, for which the blame in chief must be placed on want of leadership in the head of the Government.

The newspaper was, though, less generous in the detail, where it described Churchill as the 'prime-mover' and the only person who was 'consistent when all the rest were vacillating'. It was, however, 'the consistency of a dangerous enthusiast, who sought expert advice only when he could be sure of moulding it to his own opinion'.[13] On the basis of the report this was perhaps fair comment. Had the newspaper had access to the evidence (see Chapter 12) it would have seen that Churchill consulted almost night and day over the Dardanelles operation.

Even Churchill's allies were able to read the report as inauspicious. Beatty told his wife, 'I should think from it that as far as Winston and Fisher are concerned, they are done.'[14] But, Beatty was overlooking the fact that Asquith, Kitchener and Fisher were, in the Commission's eyes, more culpable than Churchill. Churchill was censured for the minor fault of enthusiasm; the others for the major defect of incompetence. Riddell appreciated this when he wrote in his diary 'It is not good for Winston, but it is bad for Asquith and Kitchener. Winston does not come out black or white, he comes out grey.'[15]

Given the outcome, Churchill would have been wise to keep quiet and let the press and his critics move on to other things. But, Churchill never knew when to leave well alone. The day following the publication of the report, he asked Riddell to call on him. Riddell sat through a long tirade on the parts of the report that had been deleted (presumably for security reasons) and said he was going to demand to see a full copy of the evidence. Meanwhile, he told Riddell, he was going 'to fight and attack Northcliffe'.[16] Riddell advised against such a tactic but agreed to take a letter to Lloyd George, whom he saw daily. The letter declared that '[the] excisions ... are extremely injurious to me' and did not 'represent the evidence given before the Commission'.[17] Two days later, Churchill asked in the House which minister had been responsible for the deletions. Bonar Law neatly deflected the question by declaring that 'The Cabinet is responsible for the excisions.'[18]

Churchill was now unstoppable and, when the report was debated in the Commons on 20 March, he once more raised the question of the deletions. He complained that the Commission had used a narrative with 'a great number of clippings and snippings ... with the greatest patience and the greatest skill to form a connected narrative'.

He was outraged at such proceedings and went on to pronounce that 'it is the fundamental principle that if a document is quoted, if an extract from a document is taken, one should know what the context is, and if one answer of a witness is cited, that answer can only be judged in relation to the whole of his evidence.'

Having asked for the impossible – the evidence could not be published in wartime – Churchill next launched into a detailed account of his role in the Dardanelles campaign. He was, he said, 'determined to show, firstly, the great precision and thoroughness with which all our action was taken; and, secondly, that no one has a right to say that naval expert opinion was not marshalled, arrayed, and massed behind the Admiralty action'. As to the Commission's methods of searching for the culprits, these were 'pernicious in the last degree'.

On a more specific point, Churchill took objection to the Commission implying that there had been a 'terrible loss of life and vast expenditure of treasure'. He correctly pointed out that 'so far as the naval operations were concerned – and they are alone within the purview of this interim Report – there was very little loss of life and hardly any loss of treasure.'[19]

Having delivered his counter-evidence against Lloyd George and the Commons, Churchill then turned on Sir William Pickford, the Commission's chairman, who had replaced Lord Cromer on his death in January. In a letter to Pickford of 1 May, Churchill once again condemned the Commission's use of 'brief extracts and quotations', which, he said, 'in some cases are actually misleading'. Churchill then dealt with items that he felt were serious inaccuracies. There was the statement that he 'strongly advocated the adoption of the Dardanelles enterprise' on 28 January. He continued: 'There was no necessity for me to add "strong advocacy" to the general chorus of approval.'[20] On this point, the minutes confirm Churchill's version. Hardly had he started to speak before the others enthusiastically pressed forward the operation, while he was still warning of the risks. His letter continued to give other examples where the Commission's report implied that he was carelessly enthusiastic, while memoranda and letters show that he had warned of risks, losses and uncertain outcomes. (It is regrettable that space does not allow us to take note of the many inaccuracies in the Commission's version of the naval campaign.)

LEADER OF THE OPPOSITION

While Churchill waited for the Commission's report to work its magic and return him to power, he remained the most vocal and influential opposition member in the Commons. If he could not shape the war by making policy, he was determined to shape it through criticism.

Although the Commission's report dominated Churchill's thoughts during February and March, he kept up his interest in naval and military affairs. In February, during a naval estimates debate, he was most supportive of Lord Carson (First Lord since 16 December 1916) over his handling of the U-boat crisis. He could not, though, resist adding that there had been no good reason why Carson's measures 'should not have been adopted, not in January and February, 1917, but in the similar months of 1916'. There was praise too for Beatty's 'war mind' and Fisher's ungrudging service at the Board of Invention.[21] Yet, for all his goodwill, Churchill was as mistaken as everyone else over the Admiralty's response to the U-boat threat. The work he was praising – Jellicoe's vigorous anti-submarine campaign – was a total disaster, based as it was on attempting to locate U-boats in the vastness of the open sea. Only when convoys were introduced in April 1917 did the Admiralty finally bring the U-boat depredations within acceptable limits.

On 5 March, Churchill made a long and varied contribution to the army estimates debate. When the Liberal MP Mr William Pringle attacked 'the useless and wasteful adventure at Salonika', Churchill leapt at the opportunity to re-justify the Dardanelles campaign. 'In 1915,' he told the Commons, 'great and dazzling opportunities' had existed in the Eastern Mediterranean when 'decisive results' had been possible with the resources available. But, 'from the moment that Bulgaria entered the struggle against us [October 1915]' Germany had had an open route through to Constantinople. 'It ought to have been frankly recognised that our successful amphibious intervention in this theatre on a great scale had passed, and that this method of influencing the main decisions of this war was no longer open.'[22]

Next Churchill turned to India. Now was the time for that nation to take 'a notable part ... in this great world-struggle', he declared and should be given the chance 'to share our burdens, to share our fortunes, and to share our counsels'. He gave no explanation as to why it might appeal to Indian nationals to travel thousands of miles to face death in the mud of Flanders.

More practically, Churchill once more turned to the subject of the cavalry in particular, and horses in France in general. Transporting the fodder and bedding for these animals was as much strain on merchant shipping as would be needed 'to conduct the Salonika expedition'. (From 1915, the transportation of forage for horses and mules required more shipping than any other item.)[23] He mocked the idea that the cavalry would ever be of use:

Of course, if the orthodox military view should prove to be correct, and that at some moment in the future great masses of Cavalry will gallop through a gap in the lines, leaping trenches and barbed wire, scrambling over the shell-holes and craters, making a way through the Artillery barrages, and gaining open country beyond – or what is assumed to be open country beyond – and, having got there, are able to achieve permanent and decisive results, then we shall all frankly admit that all this expense will have been justified.[24]

In more serious vein, Churchill pointed out that what the army needed most was railways, not horses. Finally, Churchill returned to his 'machines not men' theme. Arguing against 'vast offensives' the sole purpose of which was the attrition of men, he called for 'frugality' in the use of manpower.

> Machines save life, machine-power is a substitute for man-power, brains will save blood, manœuvre is a great diluting agent to slaughter, and can be made to reduce the quantity of slaughter required to effect any particular object.[25]

A bill to allow the military authorities to recall previously wounded men provided Churchill with his next chance to harass the government on 20 March. He reiterated his view that it was more just to call up fit men over forty years old than to recall 'the recovered invalids and recovered wounded who have gone back to their homes, who have taken up civil work, and who are reunited with their families'. He argued that if the Bill were amended to include 300,000 to 500,000 older men, this would permit 'a less severe scrutiny' of the ex-servicemen. He called on all members of the House to remember their responsibility to 'their constituents in thousands of little cottages and little homes' rather than simply to 'let these matters go' on the grounds of it being wartime.[26] When the government persisted with this proposal in the following month, Churchill lashed out at what he called a 'really extraordinary' proposal. How could the War Office, he asked, be so out of touch with 'the real sentiments of the people of this country' as to consider recalling 'these totally disabled people … and put them through the mill again with a view to seeing how many of them are to be sent out to France'.[27]

These debates marked the peak of Churchill's virulent and powerful opposition to Lloyd George's handling of the war. Some historians have argued that Churchill 'needed to criticise the government enough to make sure that Lloyd George would want to neutralise him by giving him a job'.[28] This is difficult to accept. In all the conversations that Riddell had with Lloyd George, the latter *never* made any comment to suggest that a troublesome Churchill had to be silenced by giving him office. As we shall shortly see, Lloyd George desperately needed both Churchill's war-making skills and the psychological support of a soul mate.

PLAYING THE COUNTRY SQUIRE

In March 1917, the Churchills purchased Lullenden, a Tudor manor with seventy-seven acres of land, near Lingfield in Surrey. With a great hall and nine bedrooms the house was a fittingly grand wartime home for his and his brother's family. Clementine quickly turned the house into a place for entertaining his many visitors and then they both began the task of transforming the garden. When the house was put up for sale in 2001, potential buyers were told they would acquire 'Churchill's wild white cherry trees, white magnolias, crimson Japanese azaleas and blood-red Britannia rhododendrons'.[29]

At first the families only spent weekends there, but as the air raids intensified on London, Lullenden became their main home and the children attended a local school. After enjoying romping around the spacious house, the children were soon banished to a barn in the grounds. For all the children's noise, Lullenden was a haven for the Churchills where, for a few precious hours, they could escape the hostility of Whitehall, the press and the Commons. The escape was not total, though. Randolph, on asking a boy at the local school whether he would be his friend, received the reply: 'No. Your father murdered my father' – at the Dardanelles![30]

RAPPROCHEMENT

The months of April to July were a period of reconciliation between Churchill and Lloyd George as they were manoeuvred into meetings by Addison, Guest and Riddell, while an audience of hostile Tories bayed from the sidelines.

After three significant speeches in the Commons, all of which he thought had been 'vy well received', Churchill began to feel more optimistic. He was particularly pleased with the Dardanelles debate which, he told Sinclair, had been 'vy successful to me personally'. Mistakenly, he thought that he now had 'strong bodies of public opinion between me & the malevolence of the Tory Press'. In fact he was, over the next three months, to be the victim of some of the most poisonous gossip and innuendo that any senior politician has ever suffered.

Whatever Churchill thought was the public mood it was still the case that he had almost nothing to do, and so it is no surprise that he reported to Sinclair that 'The war weighs heavy on us all … with death so ubiquitous & life so harsh, I find a difficulty in setting pen to paper.'[31] Things were no better a month later when C.P. Scott found him 'bitter' about the isolation forced on him by Lloyd George. He had 'a sort of hungry look about him'.[32]

Churchill, without knowing, had good reason to be personally optimistic. Christopher Addison, then Minister of Munitions, was working behind the scenes to find a role for him on the supply side at the ministry. But Addison was perplexed as to just how to make use of Churchill's 'exuberance and keenness' without causing 'friction with groups of other important supply services'.[33] It was not yet obvious that the solution would be for Churchill to take Addison's job.

Churchill waited for what he hoped was his imminent return to power. In the Commons on 4 April, during a debate he managed to turn a question towards a request for more secret sessions. The question came from the Liberal MP Sir Charles Henry, who was concerned that Parliament was being ignored during the war as the executive assumed more and more powers. This, he said, 'threatens to become a menace to our Parliamentary life'. Churchill did not agree. The war, he told the Commons, had taught the government two lessons: the need for 'the concentration of power in a few hands and the integrity of executive action'. Ministers had to be freed from consuming 'their strength and energy in arguing and convincing others'. When 'every hour is of the utmost consequence' they had to be left to get on with the job. No doubt Churchill meant every word of this, but such a policy left ordinary members, such as him, out of the key debates. This may explain why he seized this moment to ask for more secret sessions – not a logical way to free ministers from having to appear in the House to justify their actions. Nevertheless, Churchill defended such sessions on the grounds that 'I or other hon. Members [should] have the opportunity of speaking to our fellow Members in the House of Commons on some of the great, vital, urgent questions of the hour, without having it all printed in the *Berliner Tageszeitung* and the *Hamburger Nachrichten* two days later.'[34]

By the first week of May 1917, the worst was past for Churchill. On 9 May, Frederick Guest, Churchill's cousin, but also the Liberal Chief Coalition Whip, began to prepare the ground for his return. Both Guest and Lloyd George were alarmed at the signs that Churchill was about to use a forthcoming secret session to stress 'the terrible importance of a reunion of all parties and the inclusion of Asquith in his Cabinet'. Guest's promotion of Churchill left Montagu astounded at his apparent enthusiasm for Churchill who was now 'a brilliant, self-sacrificing, self-effacing, far-seeing, [and] courageous statesman'.[35] From some later comments by Addison, it seems that Guest had both initiated the campaign and pushed it farther and harder than Lloyd George considered wise. In early June, some Tories were complaining to Addison about Guest's 'pro-Churchill campaign' and, at one point, Lloyd George became quite angry at Guest's aggressive style.[36]

When the secret session that Churchill had requested took place on 10 May, once again Asquith's group of Liberals refused to open the debate, leaving the Speaker free to call Churchill. His status as the unassailable leading opponent of the government was growing by the day.

There is, of course, no verbatim record of this session, but the issues Churchill raised can be pieced together from diaries, letters and memoirs. The veteran Tory MP Sir Robert Sanders' own recollection describes Churchill as saying: 'we would do no real good at present on the West Front in view of the Russian trouble and that our sound policy was to wait till next year when the US could give really effective help on land'. On the whole the speech was well received. Sanders called it 'a very good speech';[37] Montagu described it as 'a wonderfully good speech';[38] and even Lloyd George found it 'excellent'.[39] No doubt this was, in part, because Churchill made no mention of calling back Asquith. While there is no evidence that the day had been stage-managed, it had worked out perfectly for all the main players. Churchill had demonstrated his statesmanlike side with his moderation and his loyalty by refraining from mentioning Asquith. Guest and Lloyd George, on the other hand, had tested the waters by allowing Churchill to have his secret session. No damage had been done and now the way was clear for Lloyd George to bring Churchill back. Only the day and the post remained to be decided.

A week later, Churchill was lunching with Lloyd George at Walton Heath, but on this occasion the faithful Riddell could not attend so there is no record of what was said, but we know what Churchill told Riddell that he would say. He intended, recorded Riddell, to advocate Asquith's return. As to the men who were in Lloyd George's Cabinet, Churchill hardly had a good word for any of them. In particular, he criticised Milner and Curzon and declared that 'LG was fighting the battle practically single-handed.' It was his fault, though, since 'He made a terrible mistake cutting himself adrift from me.' This was a typically naive Churchill remark since, had Lloyd George not cut himself off from Churchill in 1916, he would never have become Prime Minister in the first place.[40]

After the lunch, Lloyd George confided his thoughts to Stevenson, who duly recorded them in her diary. Churchill was to come back because Lloyd George 'wants someone in who will cheer him up and help & encourage him, & who will not be continually coming to him with a long face and telling him that everything is going wrong … Bonar Law not the least of them'. Stevenson noted that Lloyd George had been meeting Churchill recently and assumed that 'they have talked things over'.[41]

Towards the end of May, Churchill went to France to visit the Front and old friends. Lloyd George gave the visit his blessing, requesting the French Prime Minister to give Churchill 'every facility' to see the operations of the French army.[42] Haig was annoyed at Churchill asking for Lloyd George's help over the visit; he would gladly have arranged matters himself, he told Churchill.

The visit does not seem to have had any particular purpose. Churchill met his 'old friend' General Émile Fayolle, he dined with General Philippe Pétain (now Chief of the General Staff), lunched with Viscount Esher and General Wilson, met the French Prime Minister Painlevé, and also the British Ambassador Lord Bertie. Churchill told his wife that Bertie was worn out, which is exactly the impression one gets from reading the tired and opinionated entries in his diary. Haig welcomed Churchill like an old friend then after lunch he had a private talk with him and found him 'most humble'. Churchill reiterated his view that there should be no great offensive before 1918, while Haig 'urged the necessity of dealing a powerful blow *at the present time*'.[43] Churchill made much the same points to Esher, who recorded them in a letter which testified to the strength of Churchill's vision at this time:

> At the moment he is captured by the picture of what 1918 may bring forth in the shape of accumulated reserves of men and material, poured out from England in one great final effort, while at the same time a million Americans sweep over Holland on the German flank.[44]

SCOTLAND FOR EVER

By early June, it was common knowledge in the coalition that Lloyd George was trying to find a place for Churchill at the Air Board. Curzon's reaction was typical: 'some of us … only joined LG on the distinct understanding that W Ch was not to be a member of the Govt,' he told Law.[45]

Churchill's opponents made sure that the press was well briefed against him, scoring a great victory when the *Sunday Times* newspaper hit out against Churchill returning to power. His presence in the government 'would constitute a grave danger to the Administration and the Empire as a whole' the paper pontificated. 'Nothing would tend to more effectively damn Mr. Lloyd George's Government in the eyes of the whole country than the co-option of Mr. Churchill.'[46] By now Addison was pressing hard for Churchill's reintegration. Aware that there would be Tory opposition, he advised Lloyd George to hasten the appointment since 'the more it is talked about the more opportunity there is for opposition to gather'.[47]

After the South African General Jan Smuts (a member of Lloyd George's Imperial War Cabinet) enthused about the proposed appointment, he was asked by Guest to put the offer to Churchill. Smuts told Churchill that, in his view, Munitions was now 'routine' while 'Air offered great scope to his constructive ability and initiative'.[48] These arguments did not move Churchill from his preference for Munitions, but he would take Air if it were offered.

The reaction came on 8 June, when Lloyd George received a flood of letters of protest. Lord Derby, Secretary of State for War, declared that, at best, Churchill should only be the deputy at Air and, in any case he was not to attend War Cabinet meetings or to see War Office telegrams. All this hardly mattered, though, since Derby thought that Churchill's appointment would bring the government down. Meanwhile, Sir George Younger, Chairman of the Unionist Party, told Lloyd George that the appointment 'would strain to breaking point the Unionist Party's loyalty to you'.[49] Curzon declared that Churchill would be 'an active danger in our midst'.[50] The row was even taken out of the confines of Whitehall when the National Unionist Council passed a resolution which declared that Churchill's return would be 'an insult to the navy and the army'.[51]

Another voice of dissent came from one of Churchill's old adversaries: Admiral Lord Beresford. On 2 June, he wrote to Law to inform him that 'if Winston Churchill is appointed, I have a small Committee of well known and influential men, we intend holding meetings all over the country calling attention to Winston Churchill's career … I have papers and proofs which I shall make public, and we will stop at nothing.'[52] It was a typically foolish intervention and had Beresford stopped to think, he would have realised that Law had sat on the Dardanelles Committee with Churchill from May to November 1915 and had therefore had plenty of opportunity to form his own judgement of his then Cabinet colleague. In July, Beresford was to repeat his attack on Churchill at the Queen's Hall after Churchill had been appointed to the Ministry of Munitions. While saying that he did not wish to be personal, he denounced Churchill's appointment on the grounds that 'his past official career stamped him as entirely unfitted for his present or any other position in the Government'. He claimed that he had received 'hundreds of letters protesting against Mr. Churchill's return to office'. [53]

Nothing had prepared Lloyd George for this wave of hysterical comment. People were 'more excited about his appointment than about the war', he remarked. It 'surpassed all my apprehensions' and reached '[the] dimensions of a grave ministerial crisis which threatened the life of the Government'. [54]

It may have been this outburst of Tory anger that led to Churchill being offered the Duchy of Lancaster – not the Air Board – on 18 June. Unsurprisingly he declined the offer, telling Guest that he wished either to be in the War Cabinet or to have a war department. In reporting this to Lloyd George, Guest revealed that he now had good evidence that the Tories were no longer a threat to him. They were stepping back from the brink.

In a sense, Lloyd George also stepped back since there was no significant action on the appointment until 16 July when, without consulting his Cabinet colleagues, he offered a choice of posts to Churchill. In practice, it was a reshuffle as Carson was relieved of the Admiralty in order to join the War Cabinet, Eric Geddes (a businessman) went to the Admiralty, Montagu became Secretary of State for India and Churchill went to Munitions, vacated by Addison, who was to set up a new Ministry for Reconstruction.

Knowing that the Tories would have caused no end of trouble had they been consulted, Lloyd George had called on 'Max' Aitken (who had become Lord Beaverbrook on 2 January 1917) to assist him in the mechanics of the change. He asked him whether it was his view that Churchill should join the government. It was, said Beaverbrook, and he would support the appointment. On hearing this, Lloyd George asked Beaverbrook to go next door to No. 11 Downing Street and inform Bonar Law that he (Lloyd George) had just sent a communiqué to the press to announce that Churchill was now Minister of Munitions.

The reaction of the various newspapers was predictably based on their political affiliations. The *Morning Post*, owned by the eccentric Countess Bathurst and the die-hard Unionist H.A. Gwynne, declared that Churchill was a 'Meddlesome Matty' who should be 'imprisoned in an empty sea-mine, and anchored off the German coast'.

A biographer of Lloyd George noted 'Never did a minister take office amid such widespread ill-will.' [55] The Tories fumed. Long was infuriated that he had not been consulted, while Derby felt he ought to resign. Arthur Lee, a Conservative MP who was very close to Lloyd George, was so outraged by the behaviour of his own party that he was tempted to resign his post as Director-General of Food Production. Lloyd George talked him out of this, saying:

You see I have got back Winston. That was not easy – for other reasons – but *I have had my way*, and I mean to do so more in the future. There are still certain men, chiefly Unionists, whom I mean to get back and you come *first* amongst them.[56]

To compensate for the barrage of hate from Churchill's Tory opponents, there was a chorus of cheers from his friends and admirers. Robert Donald, editor of the *Daily Chronicle*, was 'glad to see you back', while the retired Major General John Brabazon was 'delighted', as was C.P. Scott.[57]

There was still the question of Churchill being re-elected in his constituency as was required of ministers taking up Cabinet office. (The earlier Acts of June 1915 and June 1916 to suspend such elections were no longer in force; the Act of December 1916 had suspended elections only for the two months of December 1916 and January 1917.) Churchill could be sure that he would not be opposed by official candidates from the coalition parties, but could equally expect some less conventional opponents. One such man was none other than H.A. Gwynne of the *Morning Post*. In private, writing to Bathurst, Gwynne said that he felt he had to prevent Churchill taking office and would therefore 'fight Winston Churchill at Dundee'. He realised that 'time is horribly short' but assured Bathurst that he was doing his utmost to stand. It would be worth it since 'If we can beat him at Dundee then we shall avoid an enormous danger. If he stays, the Government is doomed.'[58] In the event, Gwynne either thought better of his scheme or simply ran out of time since his name never appeared on the ballot paper. There was still a contest, however, since a Dundee man, Mr Edwin Scrymgeour, stood as the prohibitionist candidate.

So, despite having a war to win and munitions to produce, Churchill had to travel to Dundee to fight his election campaign. His address warned against 'domestic controversy' in wartime and praised Russia for her part in the war. There was praise, too, for Scotland. Churchill was 'confident' that his constituents would use their votes 'to back our Armies, to inspirit our Allies, and to confound our Prussian foes'.[59]

At his first meeting in Dundee, Churchill improbably told his audience that 'I harbour no resentment of any kind against those who endeavoured to prevent me from returning to office.'[60] A few days later, speaking in an industrial area of the city, he told his electors that the only issue at this election was 'the prosecution of a righteous war to an unmistakable victory'. People should 'forget everything except the country and the danger in which we stood'. As for his opponent, he accused Scrymgeour of proposing 'to seek peace with Germany in order to suppress the liquor traffic in Scotland'.[61]

At his next meeting, Churchill warned his electors that 'if the majority for the Government should be seriously reduced' people would say 'The U-boat is telling in Scotland.' Turning to war aims he declared that 'we are not fighting for booty' but to restore 'the harmony of Europe'. What was needed was 'an unmistakable victory' leading to 'the total loss of confidence of the German people in their present ruler and system of government'. This exclamation brought cheers from the crowd. Anticipating the task that he was to take up on returning to London, Churchill told his audience that the army would be 'supplied with shells, guns, tanks, aeroplanes, in numbers larger than have ever before been used'. He concluded: 'Scotland for ever. Pray for our righteous cause, and vote as you pray.'[62]

When the polls opened on 30 July, voting was slow. Without motorcars to ferry voters to and from the polling stations the streets were almost deserted, but 7,302 constituents turned out to give Churchill their vote, while Scrymgeour had to be content with 2,036.[63] Churchill was now both Minister of Munitions and Member of Parliament.

CHAPTER 14

MACHINES, NOT MEN

Events have proved the utility of Tanks. – Haig, June 1917[1]

SETTLING IN

As Churchill made the transition from member for the opposition to war minister, Riddell found him in a relaxed mood at Lullenden, where he was painting in the garden, and he noted the progress that Churchill had made in his new hobby. Later, Churchill showed off his new potato field which, he claimed, 'he had helped to plant and cultivate'. Turning to the war, Churchill confided to Riddell that he thought that 'the war is going badly for the Allies and that they should mark time until next year.' It was best to wait until the Americans could enter the fray.[2]

A few days later, this scene of rural contentment was nearly brought to an abrupt end when the Churchills' motorcar was in a collision at a crossroads in the nearby village of Dormansland. Although the vehicle was tipped on its side, Churchill and his wife were no more than shaken and continued their journey in another vehicle.

The Munitions Department had been in existence for two years when Churchill arrived. Its organisation reflected its founder's personality: Lloyd George had cut red tape, discarded regulations and dissolved restrictive practices. The energy, dash and enthusiasm that he had released had driven the ministry to unimaginable heights of production. But, in the wake of his methods had come muddle, confusion and duplication.

Churchill later described the culture of the ministry at that time when he joined: 'Whatever was needed for the fleets and armies had only to be ordered ... Megalomania was a positive virtue.' But, after a period in which 'to add a nought, or a couple of noughts, to almost any requisition ... would have constituted an act of merit' it had become clear that, however much Munitions produced, the armies consumed it all.[3] It was time for consolidation, priorities and clear thinking.

Churchill's task was complicated by the extraordinary position of the Admiralty, which was free of any restrictions on the use of materials and labour: 'The Board ... was the sole judge. Theirs was the first claim upon materials and skilled labour of all kinds,' he later wrote.[4] He cited the case of skilled men 'being withdrawn from making rangefinders for anti-aircraft guns' to make 'potato-peeling machines for the Grand Fleet'.[5] Meanwhile, his ministry was short of steel, short of skilled labour, and short of shipping. He was now to spend eighteen months fighting against a rapacious and uncontrolled Admiralty and a Commander-in-Chief who preferred to strip the munitions factories of men and march them towards machine guns, rather than use them to produce the weapons of war. Churchill seemed to be alone in regarding men as a precious commodity to be conserved at all costs: 'machines, not men' was to be his motto.

On 24 July, Dr Addison, Churchill's predecessor at the ministry, introduced him to the senior staff. Harold Bellman, a principal assistant in the ministry, later recalled that 'many of the controllers of important branches made no secret of their intense dislike of the appointment'. At his initial meeting, Churchill neatly penetrated the cold and hostile atmosphere by declaring that 'he started from scratch in the popularity stakes'. After he had outlined his plans for swifter production 'the atmosphere changed perceptibly'. Bellman concluded: 'Those who came to curse remained to cheer. The courage and eloquence of the new minister dispelled disaffection … it was a personal triumph at a critical juncture.'[6]

Riddell had already warned Churchill that 'the leading men are in a state of mutiny, and that resignations are imminent'.[7] Churchill quickly grasped the source of their discontent. The ministry employed 12,000 officials, arranged in some fifty departments, each with its own head, and 'each claiming direct access to the chief'.[8] He immediately took up Riddell's advice to create a council and streamline the managerial structure. This took some time to set up. Meanwhile, Churchill turned his attention to a range of pressing matters.

Convinced that steel and skilled labour were going to be his two most serious concerns, Churchill asked his Parliamentary Secretary, Sir Laming Worthington-Evans, and the Chairman of his Advisory Committee, Sir Arthur McDougall Duckham, to provide him with details of the demand for 'steel, skilled labour, ball bearings, stampings and castings, etc.' In typical Churchill fashion, he asked for this information to be presented 'with short tables showing the main features on each side'.[9]

One of Churchill's first actions was to seek Curzon's support in limiting the Admiralty's use of steel. Their ammunition stocks, he wrote, are 'out of all proportion to what would be necessary to sink the German Fleet'.[10]

As well as dealing with the finance and mechanics of production, Churchill took care of the man who mattered most: Haig. On 26 July, he wrote to tell him that he hoped to 'study your wishes and sustain your efforts' and asked him for his suggestions to 'improve the liaison' between the army and the ministry.[11] Haig replied, telling Churchill that 'We are now very well off for ammunition … except 6-inch Howitzer.' There was, though, a continuing shortage of guns, the supply of which had not yet reached the level that he had requested in 1916. And, although it was often rumoured that Churchill was not welcome at the Front, Haig ended by cordially inviting him to visit 'whenever you can spare the time'.[12]

Another issue that Churchill had to face was the removal of weaker officials. He quickly realised that Sir Albert Gerald Stern, who was Secretary of the Landships (tanks) Committee, was not capable. The tank supply, Churchill told Lloyd George, was 'in a very bad condition'.[13] Stern was removed in October and replaced by Rear Admiral Archibald Moore. There were also problems with Churchill's other Parliamentary Secretary, Frederick Kellaway MP. 'He is clearly not up to the task,' Churchill complained as he asked Lloyd George to replace him with John Hills MP.[14] The change was not made, presumably because of political complications that Lloyd George wished to avoid. Churchill was more successful in his desire to remove the Controller of Inventions, Colonel H. Goold-Adams, who was dismissed in January 1918.

On 18 August, Churchill announced the formation of his new Munitions Council. This was to consist of his Financial Secretary (Worthington-Evans), Kellaway and the heads of his ten new departments. He later wrote, 'The relief was instantaneous. I was no longer oppressed by heaps of files … Instead of struggling through the jungle I rode comfortably on an elephant whose trunk could pick up a pin or uproot a tree with equal ease.'[15] The three key men on the council were his Vice Chairman, Sir James Stevenson, a businessman, who dealt with ordnance; Sir Arthur Duckham, an engineer, who was an expert on coal-derived chemicals; and Professor Walter Layton, the statistical adviser to the Ministry of Munitions.

There was one man whom Churchill particularly wanted at his side: Sir William Greene, the Permanent Secretary at the Admiralty, with whom he had worked for many years. By chance, the Admiralty was making several board changes at the time and so felt able to agree to Greene's transfer in the first week of August. Greene would not have been surprised at Churchill's memoranda setting out his office requirements for the new council. These included a room 'not too distant from my room' and telephone connections to all the members: 'I shall want at least 20 switches on my table.'[16]

Addison noted in his diary, in early September, that Churchill's changes had upset some of the officials at Munitions and two had been moved to the Admiralty. But he correctly forecast that 'it will settle down as they get to know Winston better'.[17] Riddell shared Addison's confidence, noting at the end of July that 'He [Churchill] has evidently been working hard to master the work of his new Department and displayed considerable knowledge of the situation.'[18]

The initial reservations over Churchill's appointment soon disappeared. His energy, his determination to remove obstacles to increased production, and his interest in the work of all departments quickly won over his staff. Even though '[he] made heavy demands on all branches' his staff rose to the challenge. But, as Bellman recalled, he had no time for inefficiency or incompetence. On receiving a wordy, ill-phrased and lengthy paper Churchill flung it back 'with the endorsement in red ink across the corner of the first folio: "What *does* the damn fool mean? W.S.C."'[19]

Although he was very demanding, Churchill was also solicitous of his staff's welfare. In his first days at the Ministry, he asked Duckham and Stevenson to make sure that all heads of department had '10–14 days off in the summer and autumn'.[20] A week or two later, Churchill had commissioned the writing of a staff welfare handbook. It was to be 'short, simple and practical' and laid out using 'special types and plenty of spacing'.[21] He also set up a luncheon club for the senior staff so that they could 'meet in twos and threes in *quiet* and agreeable surroundings'. His intention was that they would get to know each other. There should, he said, 'be no crowding and no hustle'.[22]

CONFLICTS WITH WORKERS

Churchill arrived at the ministry only days before the first infantry attack at Passchendaele on the first day of the Third Battle of Ypres. Munitions workers had laboured for long hours in often dangerous factory conditions to despatch ever-greater quantities of arms and ammunition to battlefields. But nothing appeared to have changed. The fighting at Passchendaele would result in another 250,000 British losses and yet the end of the war would be no nearer. At home, Churchill found ever growing discontent among the weary munitions workers, with the threat of strikes never far away. Speaking to a meeting of shipbuilding and engineering employers he identified three causes of unrest: fatigue, pay differences between semi-skilled and skilled workers, and the much disliked 'leaving certificates'. Munitions workers were not allowed to leave their jobs without one of these certificates, which authorised them to move to another munitions manufacturer. The certificates were a deep source of discontent.

As Churchill was entering office, George Barnes MP, a Labour member of the War Cabinet since May 1917, had reported on the outcome of a series of studies on labour unrest. The most pressing cause was the rise in food prices, coupled with the suspicion that some people were profiting from these increases. Other causes included delays in settling disputes and trade union fears that practices they had renounced for the duration of the war would not be reinstated after the conflict.[23] Two of these practices directly affected Churchill's work: dilution (the use of women and other non-traditional workers to take up the jobs of enlisted men) and leaving certificates.

But the issue that caused most trouble in the autumn was the comparative pay for piece-rate and skilled work. Endless informal wage deals had resulted in skilled men being paid less than unskilled pieceworkers. At the War Cabinet (which Churchill attended by invitation only) on 12 October, he proposed the abolition of leaving certificates and a fifteen per cent bonus to certain workers. The issue was referred to a committee of Barnes, Churchill, Milner and the Minister of Labour.

When the issue came back to the War Cabinet, on 13 October, they accepted the committee's recommendation of a twelve and a half per cent increase for around 250,000 skilled workers. Also, leaving certificates were to be abandoned with effect from October 1915. At the end of November, Colonel F. Hall MP asked a string of questions in the Commons about the costs to Munitions of the increase. Churchill first explained that the increase had come from Barnes' committee and had been approved by the War Cabinet. The increase, he said, was inevitable following the abolition of leaving certificates. Without it 'large numbers' of skilled men would have moved to less skilled but more highly paid piecework. He estimated that the increase affected around 300,000 men and would cost £6.5 million in a full year. Then Churchill revealed that this settlement would lead to further wage demands from 'semi-skilled and unskilled time-workers' who were now free to move to other jobs. In consequence, the War Cabinet had extended the increase 'to all time-workers on engineering work, on munitions, and in the shipyards'. This would add another £7.5 million to the Munitions budget.[24]

The end of this saga came in January 1918, when Barnes, in a speech to a Rotary Club luncheon, accused Churchill of having 'butted in' with his extended offer. He complained that Churchill had 'made himself responsible for dealing with an anomaly … Mr Churchill did not know that that anomaly had been very largely adjusted by other means.' Barnes added that Churchill's action 'encouraged men to go on the old lackadaisical system of working by time. The time fetish was a stupid fetish. Piecework gave a man an added interest in his work.'[25] In his memoirs, Barnes claimed that he had spoken in the heat of the moment: '[when] I said, Churchill had "butted in" … I meant no attack on Churchill'. He had simply used his name to represent 'all of us who had by then endorsed his proposal'.[26] His explanation lacks credibility, but we can assume that Barnes was somewhat embarrassed by his intemperate attack on a colleague.

CONFLICTS WITH COLLEAGUES

While Churchill had been battling with the workers, the worst fears of the Tory members of the government had been realised: Churchill had dared to give his opinion unasked at a War Cabinet meeting. The row began on 15 August, when Churchill was present at the meeting, as usual by invitation. The meeting arrived at a discussion on sending heavy artillery to the Russians. According to Lord Derby, the War Minister, 'Mr Winston Churchill over-stepped his province by giving his views and voting on the policy to be pursued.'[27] If we turn to the War Cabinet minutes we find that Churchill (a) presented figures to show that the wastage of guns on the Western Front was lower than forecast; (b) there were already too many guns in Flanders for the amount of ammunition available. No vote was taken on the decision to send two batteries of guns to Russia.

How did this innocent intervention result in a row that nearly led to the resignations of both Geddes and Derby? Perhaps a clue lies in the way the discussion went. A Major General Poole had urged that the guns be sent; Robertson and General Furse opposed this, arguing that the guns were needed in Flanders; Derby said he would support the military view; Milner, who had been to Russia, said it was politically imperative to send the guns; Balfour argued that the guns should be sent to keep Russia in the war. It is clear from this that the decision was made on the *political* grounds of needing to support a weakened ally. Derby was overruled and so vented his anger on the innocent Churchill. (Anyone reading the minutes can clearly see that Milner and Balfour were the only two voices that carried any weight that day.)

Derby then enlisted General William Robertson, Chief of the Imperial General Staff, in a joint letter of protest to Lloyd George. They told him that Churchill, in addition to giving his departmental views on the gun supply, 'took an active part in the discussion of policy, and even voted'. This behaviour was 'quite irregular' since 'he is not a member of the War Cabinet'. The two men objected to 'interference on questions of military policy' by 'Ministers who do not happen to be in the War Cabinet'. They concluded by asking the Prime Minister to ensure that there should be no 'similar incident' in future.[28]

Geddes also found fault with Churchill, who he accused of interfering in Admiralty business in mid-August. The incident that upset Geddes occurred at a second meeting of the War Cabinet on that same day when, yet again, Churchill was present by invitation. A discussion was opened on finding guns to arm merchant ships. Somebody (not identified in the minutes) suggested that the Admiralty might have a number of guns available. Since there was no representative from the Admiralty present, the War Cabinet set up a committee under General Smuts to look into the matter. The committee comprised of Smuts, Churchill, and one representative from both the War Office and the Admiralty. When Geddes heard of this he was furious. This and other recent actions by Churchill, he told Lloyd George, showed that 'he contemplates an extension to his functions ... and an infringement of mine'. If this continued 'the whole structure of departmental responsibility is destroyed'. He too asked Lloyd George to ensure that Churchill did not exceed his powers in future.[29]

That these two ministers were near to resignation over such minor incidents only demonstrates the deep hatred that they had for Churchill. After Geddes had been to see Hankey both to complain and to threaten resignation, Hankey brought the whole thing down to earth in his diary, writing 'All because Churchill ... had dared to say that Haig was better off than had been calculated for as regard [*sic*] 6" howitzers ... "What right has he to express an opinion? He is only an ironmonger."'[30] Hankey quietly advised Lloyd George that Churchill should 'let the clutch in gently' to avoid Geddes' resignation.[31]

Not that Churchill had any intention of slowing his pace. In a letter to Lloyd George, on 19 August, he vigorously defended the right of the Minister of Munitions to 'review & examine the whole of our resources and to express his convictions as to the best use that can be made of them'.[32] He did, though, have the discretion not to send this letter.

THE STEEL SHORTAGE

By mid–August, Churchill was ready to develop his priorities for 1918. In a departmental memorandum, which he phrased largely as a set of questions, he set out some ideas for consideration. He thought artillery would be 'a fairly constant factor' but anticipated 'a gigantic expansion of trench mortars'. He talked of 'an expansion in "short range artillery" 10 or even 20 times as great as anything yet witnessed'. Then there was the question of very long-range guns and his plan for a huge growth in aeroplane production. He feared that the demands of a trench mortar programme and 'an enormous aerial bombing programme' would outstrip the supply of explosives. He concluded that 'the manufacture of explosives should be pushed to the extreme limit'.[33] These bold imaginings were soon to be challenged by problems in the supply of steel and nitrates.

Throughout Churchill's time at Munitions, steel remained in short supply. By the end of August, he was trying to locate enough merchant shipping to transport over 700,000 tons from the United States. Although this steel was destined for France, its delivery would reduce demands on his own sources.

Soon after voicing his first thoughts on increased production, the supply of steel was threatened by a strike of Cumberland miners over the employment of men from outside their district. Turning to his statistician, Walter Layton, he asked what damage the strike had done in terms of ships not built and wheat not imported. He stated that the strike 'has inflicted more injury on our shipping and food supply next year than all the efforts of the German submarines have been able to inflict in 1, 2 or 3 months'.[34] (Churchill liked to play the strike theme both ways. When it suited him, it was a serious threat to the war effort. When attacked in the Commons in February 1918 over the ministry's strike record, he dismissed it as negligible. The days lost in the previous six months were 'one-fourth of one per cent' … Is not that an amazing figure?' he asked. 'Such a percentage in any business in the world would be considered almost negligible, and hardly to come within the range of business calculation.'[35])

A few weeks later, Churchill heard rumours that some people in the steel trade were denying that the supply was 'a very urgent matter'. He wrote to the chairman of each steel manufacturing company to stress the importance. 'This is a steel war,' he told them. Steel was 'the foundation upon which all our chances of Victory stand' and was needed 'to hurl at the enemy' and 'to build the cargo ships'. In a flood of rhetoric he told the chairmen:

> The ships which feed ourselves and our armies, the shells and guns our soldiers fire, the rifles they wield, the loop-holes through which they fire, the dug-outs which afford them shelter and protection, the light railway lines that bring up food and ammunition, all depend on Iron and Steel.

Churchill concluded by advising the chairmen that they could post a copy of his letter on their company notice board if they wished.[36]

WITH THE GENERALS

Churchill knew that the secret of running a large manufacturing organisation was to stay close to the customer. His 'customers' were fighting in France and he spent much of his time, up to the end of the war, on visits to that country. His munitions visits began when he and 'Eddie' Marsh arrived there on 12 September. It was, wrote Marsh, 'a perfect day' with 'the smoothest possible crossing'. They lunched at Calais on French bread and Gruyère cheese and were served by a waiter who recognised Churchill and expressed his pleasure at seeing him again. After lunch, they were greeted by Captain Desmond Morton, ADC to Haig. Morton (who was to be a personal assistant to Churchill in the Second World War) took his two visitors out through wrecked villages and old battlefields until they reached Wytschaete Ridge, where they put on steel helmets. As they walked around what was supposed to be a relatively safe area, they came under fire from German artillery and hurriedly departed by road for Haig's HQ at St Omer. Marsh described it as 'an ugly modern chateau, in nice green grounds with a pond and a little river'. He noted that there was no champagne, the house was cold and there was no lock on the back door.[37]

At dinner, Marsh observed that Haig was 'not a talking animal'; he only livened up when the discussion turned to tanks.[38] Churchill must have been delighted when Haig described a recent operation where he would have expected 600 to 1,000 casualties, but tanks had reduced that number to just fifteen. Haig noted with satisfaction in his diary that Churchill was now 'all in favour of concentrating our efforts against the Western Front'.[39]

While at dinner, news came that a new French government had just been formed and the Minister of Munitions whom Churchill was to have met was now out of office. His successor Louis Loucheur was an unknown quantity.

On 13 September, Churchill had talks about strategy with Haig and Lieutenant General Sir Launcelot Kiggell, Haig's liaison officer with the French. Perhaps unwisely, Churchill revealed to Haig that Lloyd George doubted that the Allies could beat the Germans on the Western Front. This irritated Haig and merely reinforced his low opinion of the Prime Minister. Then Churchill and Marsh moved on to visit John Churchill at the 1st Anzac Corps HQ. On their return to Haig's HQ they passed a column of soldiers, who cheered and waved as they recognised Churchill.

The next day when Churchill and Marsh were still at GHQ, F.E. Smith arrived unexpectedly for lunch. Haig, abstemious himself, provided an appropriate spread at which Smith consumed 'several glasses of wine, port and old brandy'. It was now Smith's turn to reveal more than he should, telling Haig that 'he, Lloyd George and Winston Churchill dine regularly together once a week'. Haig was shocked, particularly since 'he (Smith) is not in the War Cabinet'. All these men had Lloyd George's ear while he, Haig, was left out of the discussions of his war.[40]

There were more talks between Churchill and Generals Sir James Birch (artillery adviser) and Richard Butler (a staff officer) in the afternoon. In the early evening, the two men left for Amiens. After they had departed, Haig wrote in his diary 'I have no doubt that Winston means to do his utmost (as Minister of Munitions) to provide for the army, but at the same time he can hardly help meddling in the larger questions of strategy and tactics.'[41]

This was not the only caustic comment that Haig made of Churchill, but it does not adequately represent their relationship. Haig was jealous and wary of *all* politicians – even those who did their utmost to help him. A taciturn and reserved man, he was defensive even with those who had his well-being at heart. When he let the barriers down he could be more open, as Marsh noted after their visit: 'He and W. seemed to warm to one another as the visit went on, and at our last luncheon Haig was quite genial and cracked several jokes.'[42]

On 15 September at 10.15 a.m., Churchill and Marsh left for Arras, passing German prisoners of war working on repairs to the road. At Albert, they noted the statue of the Fallen Virgin on the top of the Basilica of Notre-Dame, which Marsh found 'curiously moving'. Beyond Albert, 'coarse grass and weeds' now covered the old battlefields, across which were scattered 'nameless white crosses'.[43] They visited the HQ of the 15th Army Corps, where Churchill had talks with the commander, General Sir Henry Thuillier, and the Adjutant General, Lieutenant General Sir George Fowke and finally left at 4.15 p.m. Marsh's account continued:

> And we hadn't gone far before he was attracted by the sight of shells bursting in the distance. This, we were told, was a daylight raid on Chérizy – irresistible! – out we got, put on our steel helmets, hung our gas-masks around our necks, and walked for half an hour towards the firing – there was a great noise, shells whistling over our heads, and some fine bursts in the distance, but we seemed to get no nearer, and the firing died down, so we went back after another hour's delay. W's disregard of time, when there is anything he wants to do, is sublime.

The two men finally arrived in Paris at 10.30 p.m., Marsh 'as tired as I've ever been', where dinner at the Ritz with Freddie Guest, Spiers and Layton awaited them.[44]

The following day, Churchill had talks with General Ferdinand Foch, Chief of the French General Staff, in the morning and the then Prime Minister Paul Painlevé in the afternoon. The day ended with dinner at the *Ambassadeurs*.

On 17 September, Churchill and Marsh met the new French Minister of Munitions, Louis Loucheur – 'a brisk little man with a spaniel's button nose, very business-like and capable' – for the first time. Later, at dinner with a Mr Drexel and two Americans 'W. was very eloquent on the necessity of bringing over every possible American soldier … Drexel much impressed'.[45] The next day, Churchill and Marsh motored to Amiens where they dined with Asquith and his private secretary Maurice Bonham-Carter. The conversation turned to jokes too rude for Marsh to even record. Much shocked, Churchill steered the discussion back 'to more decorous lines'.[46]

On 20 September, their last day in France, Churchill and Marsh lunched with General Sir Tom Bridges (liaison officer with the American forces), while a band played Elgar's variations on 'Three Blind Mice'. Churchill was keen to stay the night, but the army HQ overruled him. He may have owed his life to this decision since the following day the HQ was shelled and General Bridges was seriously wounded.

MANAGING MUNITIONS

Almost immediately after Churchill had returned to London, a crisis arose over the supply of guns. It occurred due to German aircraft penetrating the defences of London, on 1 October, despite the heavy anti-aircraft barrage. Churchill warned that such a barrage could not be sustained because the guns were rapidly wearing out and ammunition supplies were low. He had, though, already arranged with Smuts to repair twenty guns each month. In addition, the War Cabinet had ordered the immediate installation of four guns destined for merchant shipping and the re-allocation of all the 3-inch gun production in the next month to Home Defences.

This arrangement was, of course, a temporary expedient achieved by diverting guns destined for both shipping and the Western Front. The inadequacy of this arrangement became clear the next day, when Haig sent an urgent appeal to Derby for 6-inch howitzer shells. 'Recent successes,' Haig wrote, 'have been due to a large extent to an ample supply of ammunition.' The proposed reduction in supplies 'will seriously hamper present offensive operations'.[47]

In a telegram of 9 October, Churchill informed Northcliffe (then Head of the British War Mission to the United States) of the 'grave anxiety' over the fear of a reduced supply of 6-inch howitzers. 'The supply of this nature of ammunition,' he wrote, 'is of vital importance to the common Allied cause.'[48] The continuing crisis over gun shortages led the War Cabinet, on 9 October, to set up a committee of Curzon, Balfour, Derby and Churchill 'to consider the allocation of guns in relation to the demands put forward by our armies and by those of the Allied Governments'.[49] Churchill was ready to search out every available gun, even looking as far afield as India. On 19 October, he wrote to Montagu enquiring as to whether the 9.2-inch guns at Bombay and elsewhere 'could be liberated'. 'Even half of them would be a very useful contribution.'[50] Two weeks later, Churchill was disappointed to find that the output of guns and gun carriages was below target. Output in October was lower than that of September and '*repaired* guns are far below the estimate'. 'What is the cause of this?' he asked his Director General of Shell and Gun Manufacture.[51]

In October, despite his heavy workload, Churchill still found time to make two morale-boosting speeches. The first, early in the month, was given to the Aldwych Club, where he told his audience how his ministry laboured 'from morn to night' in their attempt to ensure 'a decisive victory'. He attacked the evils of Prussian militarism but declared that there would be no peace until the Allies' 'vital objects were achieved'. There was praise for 'the check of the German submarine campaign' but, said Churchill, it was too soon 'to say that it had been defeated'. (Merchant shipping losses had peaked at 900,000 tons in April and fallen to 350,000 tons in September, following the introduction of convoys.) He claimed that Britain was 'the most experienced of the allies', and declared that the outcome of the war was now 'squarely on our shoulders. If we failed, all failed.'[52]

On the second occasion, two weeks later, Churchill addressed the American Club in London. He told them that 'Germany had made many mistakes' in the war and the two greatest of these were to assume 'that Britain would not enter the struggle' and 'that America would not fight'.[53]

No detail of his ministry's work seemed to escape Churchill's attention. In early November, he issued a memorandum on the need for air-raid shelters at munitions factories. He pointed out that private companies were installing these and that the ministry had to accept a fall in output during the construction work. Not content with identifying the need, he then provided a detailed technical specification on depth, ventilation and materials. Yet another memorandum was circulated on the following day with more details of construction methods ('all kinds of odd material can be worked in') and advising that 'A deep narrow zigzag trench in an open field is extremely good protection.'[54] On 5 October, he reported to the War Cabinet, confidently telling his colleagues that the work would be completed in ten days.

An unexpected difficulty arose, in late October, when Churchill found to his surprise that a Select Committee on War Expenditure had been investigating various ministries. At least in the case of Munitions, neither the ministers nor the senior officials had been informed nor consulted. The first that Churchill knew about the committee was when he read in *The Times* newspaper that his ministry showed 'very serious instances of lack of financial control'. His financial section was unable to determine whether the national factories (purposely built for the war) 'are wisely used or not'. The committee accepted that it was not reasonable for the Minister of Munitions to attend to such details and recommended 'that one of the Parliamentary Secretaries should be charged with the Finance of the Ministry and be responsible to Parliament' and that one member of the Council should be designated as the Finance Member.[55]

Churchill took the suggestion of the lack of consultation calmly and simply wrote to Lloyd George to request that an additional financial secretary be appointed. Clearly, Lloyd George was not too bothered about the report since he took no action until January, when he declined the additional appointment. The role was then added to the workload of Sir Laming Worthington-Evans.

When it came to protesting to the chairman of the committee about its discourteous methods of procedure, Churchill was more forthright. On 3 November, he told Herbert Samuel (an ex-Home Secretary) that large parts of the report were clear quotations from people who had been left off the new council. It was wrong of the committee, he continued, to base its report on the comments of junior staff. In an unkind gibe at Samuel, Churchill pointed out that many of the problems noted in the report related to the time when they had both been in Cabinet.

CRISIS AT CAPORETTO

On 27 October, when he was at Lullenden, Churchill received an urgent telegram commanding him to go immediately to Lloyd George's house at Walton Heath. Churchill recalled 'He showed me the telegrams, which even in their guarded form revealed a defeat of the first magnitude.'[56] These telegrams told of the disaster at the Battle of Caporetto, where the Austrian Army had scored a massive victory. The Italian Army was in full retreat, leaving behind thousands of dead and hundreds of guns. By the time Churchill met General Alfredo Dallolio, the Italian Undersecretary of State for Munitions, in Paris on 17 November the Italians had lost over 3,000 guns. Replacements for these – and almost every other type of munitions – were desperately needed.

After talks with Dallolio, Churchill telegraphed to London. He informed Lloyd George that Italy's needs were most urgent, but were modest and could be met without damage to supplies destined for the Western Front. (The core of the Italian request was 150,000 rifles, 2,000 machine guns and 600 artillery pieces.) The French government had agreed to contribute, so Churchill now sought Lloyd George's approval for him to negotiate the details.

On 21 November, the War Cabinet discussed Churchill's telegram and the sensitive Derby was horrified to find that once more Churchill was trampling over his territory.

He told his colleagues that he would accept anything that Churchill negotiated, provided it had the approval of Furse (now Master-General of the Ordnance). The War Cabinet endorsed this view and Churchill's proposal for a conference on Italian munitions. (His attempt to open negotiations to reduce the shipping tonnage used by the French was firmly refused, as this was a matter for Milner's shipping committee.) Directly after the meeting, Derby despatched General Furse to oversee the wayward Minister of Munitions.

While the disaster at Caporetto was unfolding, the French Parliament was in turmoil over secret contacts for a compromise peace settlement. On 13 November, Painlevé resigned and three days later the seventy-six year old Georges Clemenceau became Prime Minister. His reputation for ruthless and authoritarian leadership had led to his sobriquet of 'Tiger'. Although Churchill does not appear to have commented on Clemenceau's appointment, he must have welcomed the arrival of a man in his own mould at the very moment when the war was approaching a perilous climax: Italy in defeat; Russia collapsing; the French exhausted; and the Americans not yet on the scene.

CHAMPIONING THE TANK

While tanks had been in use since April 1917, the Battle of Cambrai, which opened on 20 November, is often cited as their first significant deployment. This is a convenient point to review the history of the tank and Churchill's role in its development.

The first person to envisage a bullet-proof machine in war was the novelist H.G. Wells in his short story *The Land Ironclads* published in 1903. He gave no technical specification and, at one hundred feet in length, his machines offered no practical blueprint for the War Office in 1914. At the end of that year, Hankey suggested the construction of a wire-crushing machine with huge rollers; a few days later, Churchill offered his strong support and urged that the idea be researched 'with vigour'.[57] Following a demonstration of caterpillar tracks in February 1915, Kitchener supported further development of the as-yet-unnamed machine. His instructions disappeared into the files of the War Office and no more was heard about them. Meanwhile, Churchill was running a 'freelance' operation at the Admiralty and by the end of March 1915 had placed an order for eighteen landships. When Balfour took over from Churchill at the Admiralty, he authorised his staff to continue work on the landships and welcomed Churchill to the project committee. Shortly after, the War Office decided to join in and the Landships Committee became a joint operation between the two ministries. In February 1916, the first tank was demonstrated at Hatfield Park. A week later, Haig wrote to the War Office to say that he believed that '"Tanks" can be usefully employed in offensive operations'.[58] The tank had been born.

At every key point in the story so far, Churchill had been present. In 1919, his contribution was recognised by the *Report of the Royal Commission on Awards to*

Inventors which stated that 'it was primarily due to the receptivity, courage and driving force of the R. Hon. Winston Spencer Churchill that the general idea of the use of such a machine as the "Tank" was converted into practical shape.'[59]

It was natural that when Churchill arrived at the Ministry of Munitions, one of the first things that he asked for was a briefing on the state of tank development. In October, he realised there was a lack of urgency in tank design and production. He gloomily reported to his friend Lord Hugh Cecil that tank development had been halted for the previous twelve months.

Ten days later, Churchill wrote a paper for the War Cabinet attacking the policy of attempting to defeat the Germans by 'pure attrition'. What was needed was 'the concentration of all our methods of attack upon the enemy simultaneously at the decisive period'. He recognised that the Allies could not rely on 'numerical superiority in men'. They must use 'war machinery'. He then considered the merits of artillery, air power, railways, trench mortars, tanks and gas. His fundamental point was that the Allies required something that 'could advance continuously *and at a sufficient speed* on a front of twenty or thirty miles'. That ruled out artillery which, although it had 'blasting power', had no 'moving power'. All this reads as if Churchill were preparing the case for massed tanks, but in fact the paper ended with a call for the development of (unspecified) means of mechanical movement on the battlefield. Such a method could inflict 'a decisive defeat'.[60]

But, since tanks were as yet the only mobile machine on the battlefield, Churchill was to press for ever greater numbers in the following year. Meanwhile, as the year drew to a close, Haig – a strong believer in tanks – saw a more complex picture. He realised that the collapse of Russia was imminent. With the eastern border no longer under attack, Germany would be free to transfer vast armies to the west. It was time for the Allies to switch into defensive mode. On 4 December, Haig ordered: 'The employment of the British Army in 1918 was to be a defensive one … The role it had taken in 1917 was, therefore, to be reversed.'[61] For all the merits that Churchill's tanks possessed, they had so far only been proved in an offensive role. His own plans for the mass building of tanks and for more 'mechanical movement' on the battlefield were now in direct opposition to the plans of the Commander-in-Chief.

THE DISAPPEARING SHIPPING

At the beginning of November, Churchill circulated his draft 1918 budget for munitions to the War Cabinet. His opening sentence neatly summarised his difficulties: 'The foundation of the Munitions Budget is Tonnage; the ground floor is Steel; and the limiting factor is Labour.'[62] Everywhere he looked he found obstacles. Labour was being taken from him just when he most needed more workers. A lack of merchant shipping was restricting iron ore imports, while the army was asking for an almost fifty per cent increase in the supply of aeroplanes. The Air Board wanted to treble production. Yet Churchill still claimed that if the resources of munitions were used to their fullest efficiency, he could meet all the requirements of the army.

In the area that was most important personally to Churchill – tanks – he had accepted Haig's insistence that he could not provide the men for vast numbers of machines. While noting that 'Tanks have never yet been used in numbers under conditions favourable to their action' he bowed to Haig's limit of a Tank Corps of 18,500 men and budgeted to build 1,080 tanks.

He closed by reminding the War Cabinet of what needed to be done to meet his production targets. Firstly, shipping tonnage for non-military purposes 'must be cut down', even to the extent of reducing some food imports. Secondly, the Admiralty should find labour for shipbuilding from its current manpower. Third, 'the dormant man-power of the units in the Home army must be made effective as an aid to transport, industry and agriculture'. And finally, 'the business of supply must be properly co-ordinated' to reduce waste.[63]

Having resolved his budget at the beginning of November, Churchill was faced with an alarming piece of news at the end of the month. The Shipping Controller, Sir Joseph Maclay, had re-allocated two million tons of shipping to supply food to the French and Italians. One and a half million tons had been found from shipping previously allocated to munitions. Writing to Maclay, Churchill said that he would be compelled to suspend shipments of steel products to the two countries. The losses to munitions would be crippling. He was particularly annoyed because it had been agreed to construct concrete barges (which saved on steel) to relieve the problem, but so far only seventy had been ordered.

That same day Churchill wrote to Loucheur to tell him the bad news. 'The whole steel situation in Great Britain has however been revolutionised,' he told him. He would have to reduce the weight of ammunition sent to France 'by between half a million and 750,000 tons'. French arms production would suffer too since he would no longer be able to supply the promised 40,000 tons of steel. All he could do was to ask Loucheur to press for a reduction in the tonnage that had been allocated to food for France.[64]

Having established just how serious his position was, Churchill now put his creative mind to work. On 23 November, he wrote to the oddly named Clamping Committee, and suggested that there must be 20,000 tons of metal in the Hyde Park railings. 'The weight of metal in the area of the London streets must be enormous,' he continued. And what of the '700,000 or 800,000 tons of shell-steel lying about on the Somme battlefields'? He recommended setting up a smelting plant there.[65]

Overnight, Churchill's brain continued to work on creative solutions to his tonnage problem. On 26 November, he sent the committee twelve suggestions for relieving the steel shortage. These centred on restricting the weight of a shell fired in 1918 to the same as in 1917 and reducing the use of trench mortars. But, he also recommended increasing the output of tanks and aeroplanes.

This dreary correspondence continued for several weeks, lightened only by a typical Churchillian quip: Maclay admitted that concrete barges had been 'in the air for some time'. Churchill replied 'With regard to concrete barges, you say they have been "in the air" for a long time. My anxiety is that they should be in the water in a short time.'[66]

And then, just as suddenly as the tonnage had been withdrawn, it was given back on the last day of the year as the U-boat threat continued to diminish. While the tonnage crisis turned out to be a non-event, it had allowed Churchill once more to demonstrate his extraordinary capacity to rise to the occasion.

ALL MUST BE READY, ALL MUST BE THERE

By early December, the tank was slowly proving its value. Churchill looked forward to large-scale production despite Haig's reservations about manning. In a paper for the War Cabinet, he argued that tanks saved lives, ammunition and money. In recent actions without tanks, '54 square miles had been gained and 300,000 men killed or wounded, at a cost of £80 million'. He contrasted this with the Battle of Cambrai, where '42 square miles had been gained, fewer than 10,000 men killed or wounded and only £6,600,000 spent on ammunition'.[67]

This passage on tanks appeared in a long paper on manpower which Churchill wrote for the War Cabinet on 8 December. His overall theme was the urgent necessity to increase the army 'to the highest possible strength'. In saying this he was following the conventional view of Haig and his generals. He departed from this consensus when he added that these men 'once raised … must be husbanded and not consumed'. Until the Americans arrived, the Allies had to adopt a defensive holding operation. 'This army must be an army crouched and not sprawled … an army sustained by every form of mechanical equipment, including especially tanks and aeroplanes.' In this way, Churchill reconciled his support for more men with his plea for 'machines not men'. In a competition for resources between tanks and aeroplanes on the one hand and men on the other, he came down firmly on the side of the machines.

As to finding the men, Churchill had his own suggestions to make. Geddes' figure of a deficit of 645,000 could be met, he suggested, by a series of measures. A defensive stance in Flanders would yield 120,000; the navy could find 90,000; Munitions could offer 100,000; the home garrisons could release 210,000; and mines and railways would supply a further 60,000. In total Churchill estimated there were 600,000 men readily available.[68] Another source of men, not mentioned in the paper, was the cavalry. Even as late as March 1918, thousands of cavalrymen were standing by to charge through gaps in the line made by the infantry. Churchill had proposed that these men be retrained to operate the tanks, but Haig clung to his cavalry. In the meantime, Churchill advised his friend Sinclair to ask for a posting to tanks.

Having set out his views on the war in 1918, Churchill then repeated the exercise in the form of a morale-boosting speech at Bradford on 11 December. Of all the war leaders, only Lloyd George could have matched this remarkable oration as Churchill wove together a message of peril, noble war aims, ambitions for an honourable peace and imaginative use of the military machine. It can be seen as the first of his many great war speeches, mixing as it did realism and aspiration.

His opening was blunt: 'The country is in danger. It is in danger as it has not been since the battle of the Marne … The future of the British Empire, and of democracy, and of civilization, hang … in a balance.' It was, Churchill argued, 'impossible … to conceal these facts from ourselves'. He then turned to Britain's war aims, which had not changed since 'that breathless night in August [1914] … when we knew that the Belgian frontier had been crossed'. He could not have known it, but with his next words he was to define the focus of his life and energies for the next twenty-seven years:

> Our sole war aim is this – that those who have committed crimes too numerous for one to recount shall not profit by them and shall not emerge from the struggle stronger than when they began it … that Prussian militarism shall go out of the conflict abased.

But, much as he longed for peace, there were to be no 'specious peace terms'. No peace could be based on 'weakness and war weariness on the part of the Allies'. Only victory could bring an 'honourable' peace.

While the War Cabinet wrestled with strikes and manpower shortages, Churchill had no problem in telling his audience that 'I have absolute confidence in the loyalty and the resolve of the people of this island … Our reserves of manhood are still large.'

Having underlined the peril, justified the continuance of the war and flattered the British people, Churchill then sought to drive them forward. More men were needed: 'We must raise the strength of our army to its highest point. A heavier strain will be thrown upon that army than it has ever had to bear before. We must see that it is stronger than it has ever been before.' Speaking of the new recruits, Churchill pleaded 'Husband their lives, conserve and accumulate their force'. To this end, he appealed for 'Masses of guns, mountains of shells, clouds of aeroplanes – all must be ready, all must be there.'[69]

That these masses of munitions would soon be needed was confirmed on 3 March 1918 when the defeated Russia signed the Treaty of Brest-Litovsk with the Central Powers. Germany's two-front war was now to become a one-front war. In 1917, the Allies were able to deploy much greater numbers of men on the Western Front than the Germans, with a comfortable ratio of three Allied men to every two Germans. Now the odds were reversed as Germany massed 190 divisions to face 173 Allied divisions.

On a visit to France in February 1918, Churchill worried about his wife and children sleeping at 41 Cromwell Road when the moon was full and the night sky clear. He suggested to his wife that she send the children to the country. Meanwhile, he was to meet General Sir Reginald Barnes (57th Division) for discussions on munitions.

On 18 February, business in the Commons forced Churchill to return to London to deal with a hostile parliamentary question about the wage increases agreed in the previous year. On 22 February, he returned to France and spent the day sightseeing, which gave him the chance to meet Jack Churchill and to revisit Ploegsteert: 'everything has been torn to pieces ... all my old farms are mere heaps of bricks and mouldering sandbags.' But he was pleased to find that the dugout that he had ordered to be built at Laurence Farm was still being used. Lunch was a social occasion with General William Birdwood (Australian Corps commander) and Jack; later there was dinner at Barnes' HQ. In the midst of his reminiscing and socialising, Churchill continued to work as bags of government mail passed between London and France. His shorthand writer at his side, Churchill dictated memoranda and letters while he roamed the battle areas. His visits included Ypres, which he had last seen in 1915. Now 'it has largely ceased to exist'. As for the countryside, there was 'nothing except a few tree stumps in acres of brown soil'. After five hours of walking on the battlefields, Churchill poignantly told his wife 'Nearly 800,000 of our British men have shed their blood or lost their lives here during 3½ years of unceasing conflict! Many of our friends & my contemporaries all perished here.'[70]

After spending some time with the Cavalry Corps and enjoying Sinclair's company once more, Churchill went to Paris on 26 February. In the evening, there was dinner in the Ritz with Sir Charles Ellis (Scientific Adviser to the Army Council) and Lord Bertie the Ambassador. Bertie reported back to Lord Stamfordham that Churchill 'talked a lot of rot at and after dinner to the effect that as we did not go to war to obtain Alsace Lorraine for France it ought not to be continued a single day beyond what might be necessary to obtain from Germany the evacuation of Belgium'. He was shocked to find that Churchill did not rule out Germany's colonies being restored after the war, reporting Churchill as having said 'the war is a European war to settle the fate of Europe'. So bizarre did Bertie consider Churchill's views that he wondered if, post-war, Churchill planned to become leader of a Labour-Pacifist Party with eventual Premiership. He was fifty per cent right![71]

THE 1919 PROGRAMME

Soon after returning from France, and daily expecting the inevitable German spring offensive on the Allied line, Churchill turned his mind to 1919. On 5 March, in a paper for the War Cabinet, he argued that 'the year 1918 is settled for good or ill' and it was now time to ask 'How are we going to win the war in 1919?'

There was only one answer: 'offensive action'. He then sharply rephrased this question by asking 'If you cannot starve out your enemy, if you cannot bear him down by numbers or blast him from your path with artillery, how are you going to win?' Answering his own question, he replied by *a means of continuing forward progression*. There were four means to do this: aeroplanes, tanks, gas, and machine guns.

Churchill went on to argue that aeroplanes and machine guns were already being vigorously used but tanks and gas were only 'on a miniature and experimental scale'. Gas favoured the Allies, since the prevailing wind was from the west. In the development of the tank, the Allies were far ahead of the Germans in technical knowledge and engineering skills. And it was tanks that were at the heart of his paper. He wanted to see '150,000 to 200,000 fighting men … carried forward certainly and irresistibly on a broad front and to a depth of 8 or 10 miles in the course of a day'.[72] Geddes, Hankey and Wilson all welcomed the paper, which they clearly found inspiring. But Haig would not have agreed had he seen it. His priorities for further production of mechanical aids to war were, first the increased use of aeroplanes, second light railways and then tanks. The common limiting factor in supplying these was engines, which meant that there was no way tanks could be produced in the numbers that Churchill proposed without a reduced output of aeroplanes and light railway locomotives.

While Churchill was busy with grand strategy he was forced to find time to deal with an order from the Surrey War Agricultural Committee to improve the cultivation of his land at Lullenden. Churchill told their representative, a Mr H.E. Cooke, that he was willing to extend his cultivation, but the German prisoners that he had been offered had not been satisfactory. He had not been able to get the hay in before it rotted and the only labour he now had was 'one gardener, one very old and crippled man and two boys'.[73]

The next stage in Churchill's proposed 1919 tank programme was to take the discussions to France. On the morning of 19 March 1918, he arrived at Montreuil to meet Furse, Kiggell and others. He then went on to lunch with Haig, who recorded in his diary that 'C. has written a paper urging the reorganisation of the army so as to employ mechanical appliances to take place of men, because we are lacking in manpower. He stated that with the approval of the War Cabinet, he was proceeding with the manufacture of a large number of tanks (4,000).' This had been done 'without any consideration of the manpower situation and the crews likely to be available to put into them'.[74] Somewhat surprisingly, on the very day that Haig was disparaging Churchill's plan for 4,000 tanks, Wilson was telling the War Cabinet that 'the fastest way of winning the war would be to achieve a breakthrough on a broad front using around 8,000 tanks'.[75]

From Haig's HQ, Churchill went to see General Tudor at Nurlu: 'We arrived after dark upon a tranquil front lit rarely by a gun-flash.'[76]

The next day, Churchill was struck by how quiet it was at the Front. Although Tudor knew that the German attack could not be far away, he happily took Churchill on a tour of his positions. Churchill later recalled that everything possible had been done to resist an attack. As he retired to bed, Tudor told him that the latest intelligence showed that out in the darkness, not more than half a mile distant, there were eight German battalions ready to attack. Could Churchill's munitions and Haig's army withstand the coming onslaught?

CHAPTER 15

THE LAST PUSH

Winston a real *gem* in a crisis. – Sir Henry Wilson[1]

GERMANY'S LAST OFFENSIVE

The date 21 March 1918 was one that Churchill would never forget. He had woken at 4.00 a.m. to a total silence – an unusual experience near the front line. Some time later he heard a number of very heavy explosions in the distance: 'And then … there rose in less than one minute the most tremendous cannonade I shall ever hear … Far away to the north and to the south, the intense roar and reverberation rolled upwards to us.'[2] The time was 4.40 a.m. and the last great German offensive had begun. The British front line was under attack from 6,000 guns and 3,000 trench mortars. By the end of the day, German infantry had overrun the British lines and, in places, advanced four and a half miles. Churchill's hope that the Allies could hold a defensive line until the Americans arrived had been shattered.

Lloyd George did not realise just how serious the position was until the morning of 23 March. When Riddell arrived at Walton Heath, he found the Prime Minister anxiously waiting for him. '"I must go back to London at once," he said. "The news is very bad. I fear it means disaster. Come with me!"'[3] The telegram that Lloyd George had received informed him of the retreat of the Third and Fifth Armies. In London, he called a meeting of the War Cabinet at 4.00 p.m. to discuss sending reinforcements. They considered calling on the French for assistance and the possibility of bringing troops from Mesopotamia, Salonika, Palestine and Italy. Churchill was not listed as being present, but he must have been there since Wilson noted in his diary that 'Winston helped like a man' when the former pressed the case for conscription.[4]

Two men remained resolutely cool in the crisis. One was Churchill, who in a telegram to the Australian *Sunday Times* newspaper declared 'We have only to endure to conquer.' Now was the hour 'for Britain to show the cool and dogged tenacity which in every foreign country is recognised as the great characteristic of our race'.[5] The other was Hankey. To him the War Cabinet's decision to send 50,000 young men to France was a sign of panic.

Whatever Churchill's role had been on 23 March, he met Lloyd George on the following day. He had gone to the War Office to be briefed by General Wilson who, 'with the gravest face showed me the telegrams and his own map'. The two men then walked over to Downing Street, where they found Lloyd George sitting in the garden and talking with Lord French. After a few minutes, Lloyd George called Churchill to one side and asked how, if the British had been unable to hold the strongly fortified front line, they could hope to hold the new defensive lines. Churchill reminded him that all offensives lose their impetus as the line is extended. Having reassured the Prime Minister, Churchill repeated the exercise that night when he and Wilson dined at Churchill's house in Eccleston Square. (Sir Edward Grey's tenancy at No. 33 had ended and the Churchills had taken back the house for their own use.) Wilson was worried over the loss of 1,000 guns, but Churchill confidently told him that they could easily be replaced. At the end of the day, Wilson summed up how the principal players had responded to the crisis: 'LG has, on the whole, been buoyant, BL *most* depressing, Smuts talked much academic nonsense, Winston a real *gem* in a crisis, & reminded me of Aug: 1914.'[6]

That night, Churchill wrote a long letter to Lloyd George, urging action in all directions. Although the letter was never sent, it is important for the way it reveals Churchill's capacity to think creatively under the pressure of events. He urged the Prime Minister to send out 50,000 naval men and most of the marines; the conscription age should be raised to fifty-five, with Ireland being treated as the rest of Britain; the Americans, not yet able to form in divisions, should be inserted into the British and French armies; and, finally, King George V should be allowed to visit France. Lloyd George, Churchill argued, was to pay no attention to the War Office's insistence that no more than 10,000 men could be shipped across the English Channel each day: the navy would find the means to transport more men. All that Lloyd George needed to win was 'courage and a clear plan … now is the time to risk everything'.[7]

But Churchill had more than good advice to offer. He had munitions. Just three days after the German onslaught, Churchill was able to promise 2,000 guns and 230 million rounds of ammunition for delivery by 6 April. (In the event, only 1,200 guns had been lost.) Churchill's munitions were seemingly inexhaustible.

It was on this same day that Lloyd George succeeded in bringing about a single point of command to co-ordinate the British and French war fronts. The War Cabinet approved the arrangement on the following day and Wilson noted in his diary that Haig was 'greatly pleased'.[8]

Churchill's munitions output could only be maintained by epic efforts of workers in the factories. He urged the munitions workers 'to speed up the completion and dispatch' of critical items. To achieve this there were to be no Easter holidays: 'Now is the time to show the fighting army what the industrial army can achieve,' he told them.[9]

LLOYD GEORGE'S ENVOY

Once the first shock of the German offensive had passed, Lloyd George turned his attention to appealing for aid from the French and Americans. In his eyes there was only one man to whom he could entrust this task: Churchill. This appears to have been the Prime Minister's own decision, reached without consulting colleagues. Although he told Clemenceau that he '& the War Cabinet' were sending Churchill to France, there is no mention of this in the War Cabinet minutes. Writing to the French Prime Minister, Lloyd George informed him that Churchill would go to Foch's HQ, where he would be available to assist the general.[10] Later that day, Derby and Wilson independently heard of the arrangement and each asked Lloyd George to cancel. Churchill was to see Clemenceau and no one else. The Prime Minister acceded to their demands. A message was sent to Churchill advising him to stay in Paris and not at Foch's HQ. That evening, Leo Amery, an assistant secretary to Hankey, found Churchill soaking in a hot bath at the Ritz Hotel and in good humour.

Churchill was overwhelmed by the warm reception he received from Clemenceau on 29 March, who was determined not only that his visitor should see everything but that he, Clemenceau, would personally escort him. The next day Churchill, Clemenceau, his personal general and other officers set off in 'five military motor-cars, all decorated with the small satin tricolours of the highest authority'. Two hours later, after a ride in which the cars had 'leapt and bounded on the muddy roads' the party reached the French HQ at Beauvais.

At Beauvais, they met General Foch and Brigadier General Maxime Weygand, the French representative on the new Supreme War Council. They were all ushered into a room which had a huge map on the wall. Foch used this to support a breathless and heroically optimistic account of how the Allies would push back the Germans in five days. In the stunned silence that followed the speech, Clemenceau rose from his chair, walked up to Foch and silently hugged him in a huge embrace. Next was a visit to Rawlinson's HQ, now completely surrounded by shell craters from a recent bombardment by German artillery. Rawlinson was struggling to re-group the shattered Fifth Army and apologised because he could only offer his guests bread, pickles and some meat. On hearing this, Clemenceau produced a stack of sumptuous chicken sandwiches to fortify the meal. Haig then arrived and he and Clemenceau went into another room. When they returned, Clemenceau turned to Churchill and said 'It is all right. I have done what you wish. If your men are tired and we have fresh men near at hand, our men shall come at once and help you.' Churchill had achieved the first half of his mission. Having settled his business, Clemenceau asked to be taken to the battlefield. Rawlinson protested at the danger but the indomitable French Prime Minister insisted. As they neared the British lines, Churchill took over as guide. They approached as close as possible to the artillery lines until the German shells began falling very close to the group. Ignoring the danger, Clemenceau joined

Churchill in getting out of the car and climbing a small rise to get a better view of the battle. It was with the greatest difficulty that Churchill persuaded Clemenceau, who was deep in conversation with troops coming back from the front line, to return with him in the car.

From the battle area the two men moved on in the evening to Pétain's HQ in a number of railway coaches located in a siding at Beauvais. There they found the general in the highest spirits as he described his grand plans for bringing up more guns and ammunition and building new roads. After a light lunch with Rawlinson, the party welcomed the 'simple but excellent dinner … served in faultless style' in one of Pétain's 'sumptuous saloons' of his mobile HQ.[11]

We have already read the malicious comments that Bertie was in the habit of making about Churchill. On the very day that Clemenceau was so royally treating the Minister of Munitions, Spiers' wife noted in her diary that Bertie had been briefing Clemenceau against Churchill. This attempt by the ambassador to blacken Churchill's name clearly had no success.

During the day of 29 March, Churchill sent Lloyd George two telegrams and then spoke to him on the telephone. He told him how impressed he was by what he had seen in Flanders, where the British army was holding its ground, but he asked for marine gunners to be sent as reinforcements. As to the French, Churchill doubted that they would be able to counterattack in the short term but the plans that he had seen were 'worthy of the French Army … Clemenceau of course a tower of strength and courage'. What worried Loucheur – and hence Churchill – was the million additional men that the Germans had available from the Russian front. Unless the Americans arrived quickly, 'the conclusion is inevitable', he told Lloyd George.[12]

This conveniently led to Churchill's second mission, which was to persuade Clemenceau to back Lloyd George's appeal to President Woodrow Wilson to expedite the despatch of American troops. He passed Lloyd George's telegram to Clemenceau requesting him to give it his full support and to add his own message to President Wilson. (Lloyd George had conveyed the telegram in this manner partly because no one else in London had seen it – not even General Wilson. Churchill was the only colleague whom he trusted in his appeal to the Americans.) Writing on the following day, Churchill reported to Lloyd George that the Germans were still making gains and the French lacked artillery. Also the French troops were exhausted and war-weary, while many areas of the front were very sparsely manned.

Lloyd George's faith in Churchill as a trusty and forceful envoy had proved justified. But old jealousies had been aroused once more, this time in Lord Milner, who told General Wilson that the despatching of Churchill to France had been 'a direct snub' to him. Milner claimed to have told the Prime Minister that he would quit the government unless 'full confidence' was shown in him.[13] And full confidence was shown just a few weeks later when he became Secretary of State for War, displacing Lord Derby.

THE MUNITIONS MIRACLE

While the scale of the disasters on the British and Italian fronts was beyond anyone's imaginings, the scale of munitions that Churchill offered for the fight back exceeded anyone's expectations. Within two weeks of the March attack, Churchill was able to assure General Dallolio that all needs could be met. Output in the first two months of 1918 was massively up on the output for the same period in 1917. The highest increase was in the manufacture of aero engines, which were up 245 per cent; aeroplane output had increased by 233 per cent; tank production was up thirty per cent; and medium guns increased by fifty-seven per cent. During 1917, the munitions industry had released over 100,000 men to the army, their place being taken in the main by women. In 1914, the industry had employed 70,000 women which had now increased to 750,000.

When Churchill reported to the Commons on the supply of munitions, *The Times* described his achievement as a 'triumph'.[14] He had told the House that, despite the recent heavy losses, the munitions supply was 'slightly to the good'. These losses had amounted to some 1,000 guns and up to 5,000 machine guns. Ammunition dumps lost amounted to two or three weeks' output. But there were now 'more serviceable guns ... than when the battle began'. The Air Board had been able to meet all the army's demands for aeroplanes, while all the tanks lost would be replaced by new models as fast as the army could take delivery.[15] After the war, Lloyd George said that this achievement 'was entirely due to the tremendous energy of Mr Churchill'.[16] The King was similarly appreciative, but spread his praise more widely when he asked Churchill to pass on his personal thanks and congratulations to the munitions workers. By 8 May, Churchill felt sufficiently in control to send a memorandum to the munitions factories expressing the hope that workers would be able to take a Whitsun holiday. (The Ministry did not directly control all the munitions factories, so had no power to guarantee the holidays.)

In early April, the French Minister of Munitions indicated that France intended to give up the use of gas shells if the Germans would do the same. Churchill, a most determined supporter of gas, was strongly against the proposal. In any case, he refused to trust any promise by the Germans to abandon the use of gas. When the War Cabinet discussed the issue ten days later, they fully supported Churchill's view, echoing his distrust of German promises.

One of the schemes that Churchill was working on, in May, was the development of long-range guns that could be used to shell German towns. Current British artillery had a maximum range of twenty-two miles. Having drawn up a list of German towns within sixty-two miles of the French front line, Churchill commissioned work to begin on a 16-in gun with a range of sixty-eight miles. (The Germans were already using such guns to bombard Paris. Their largest gun – the Paris gun – had a reputed range of eighty-one miles.) Later in the year, he told the Air Minister, Sir William Weir, that he wanted to develop long-distance bombing aeroplanes. It was time, he told Weir, to make the German experience 'something of the havoc he has wrought in France and Belgium'.[17]

The year 1918 was the year of Lloyd George and Churchill. It was they who drove the strategy and provided the munitions to fight the war. In 1914, Asquith had twice mentioned to Venetia Stanley that Lloyd George lacked courage. (No one, of course, ever accused Churchill of that fault.) And Asquith was probably right in the sense that Lloyd George had never *shown* any courage in the war-like sense of the term. But, by April 1918, he had found courage of a high order – in part, no doubt, because he had fallen under the spell of Churchill. When the Prime Minister looked round his War Cabinet, he found no inspiration, but when he looked outside, he saw Churchill striding over difficulties, driving forward vast programmes and bouncing back from defeats. What he saw, he liked, and as the war progressed he took on more and more of Churchill's characteristics by challenging orthodox military opinion while creatively seeking ways past the latest impossible obstacle. The two men also shared another characteristic: a love of coalition. *All* of Lloyd George's time as Prime Minister was in a coalition, and *all* Churchill's first premiership was similarly spent (except for a few weeks before the 1945 general election) as a coalition leader. Neither man was a natural party political animal. But there were still occasional tensions. For example, in April, Churchill resented the fact that Austen Chamberlain was in the War Cabinet. Meanwhile, Lloyd George was ever ready to believe rumours that Churchill was trying to keep in with Asquith.

Another important relationship during the last six months of war was the Churchill-Haig connection. At times, Haig complained about Churchill interfering in matters that did not concern him, but fundamentally he trusted Churchill as a man who could deliver. Towards the end of April, when Haig could see how smoothly the losses of March had been replaced, he noted in his diary that '[Churchill] is doing very well at the Munitions Department. 54,000 tons are to be shipped weekly of ammunition.'[18] Haig clearly found Churchill's many visits to the various HQs and to GHQ during 1918 to be useful. And when Churchill requested that Haig provide him with a place in France this was quickly arranged.

The accommodation was a number of rooms in a chateau at Verchocq that, as Churchill recalled, was set 'amid wonderful avenues of trees'. The location was ideally convenient since he could reach it in two hours from Hendon Aerodrome. As he put it, '[I] could upon occasions work at the Ministry of Munitions in the morning and follow the course of a great battle in the afternoon ... I managed to be present at almost every important battle during the rest of the war.'[19]

DOUBTS AND FEARS ON THE HOME FRONT

Although Churchill thought that the war would last long into 1919, it did not stop him thinking about post-war politics. His own position was dependent on the patronage of Lloyd George. If Parliament returned to party politics after the war, he would be in a difficult position. The Tory Party would surely attempt to push him out once more, as it had in 1915. The Liberal Party was also a dubious proposition, since Churchill had been, as he saw it, betrayed by Asquith. It was time for him to begin building a political base – something he could not do as long as there was no 'regular Cabinet'. On 15 April, he disingenuously wrote to Lloyd George advising him that 'you wd be wise to form a regular Cabinet'. This was in his (Lloyd George's) interest since 'the Irish question cannot be faced without a political organisation of the Govt'. He went on: 'On even wider grounds I think the present system is condemned. It is quite right to have a War Council for the day to day settlement [of running the war] ... But the high policy of the State ought not to be settled by so narrow & unrepresentative a body.'[20] This was followed by a muddled letter which declared that he would not take on 'any political responsibility without recognised regular power'.[21] But Lloyd George saw no need to change his councils in the height of a war.

In May, the National Society of Amalgamated Brassworkers passed a resolution to thank their 'fathers, brothers and sons' for their 'heroic bravery on land and water'. This provided Churchill with another opportunity to issue a morale-boosting message. 'Although the crisis is grave,' he said, 'I have profound confidence that we shall not be beaten down.' He declared that the Germans did not have sufficient reserves to match their ambitions even though they were ready to 'squander the blood of a million Germans'. Declaring his conviction that the Allies would win, victory, he said, would end 'the cruel system which has let loose these horrors on the world'.[22]

On 31 May, Churchill was at the Harrow Road Register Office to witness his mother's third marriage. Her first marriage to his father had lasted from 1874 until Lord Randolph Churchill's death in 1895. In 1900, she had married George Cornwallis-West, but they divorced in 1914. Her third husband was Mr Reginald Porch. The Times newspaper described him as 'Resident in the Nigerian Civil Service and a lieutenant in the Nigerian Regiment, West African Frontier Force'.[23] He was three years younger than his newly acquired stepson. How the marriage might have developed we shall never know since three years later Mrs Porch died from complications following a broken ankle.

In June, Churchill paid a ten-day visit to the Western Front, but he does not appear to had many meetings. Derby, who was now British Ambassador to France, noted in his diary that 'Winston cannot have much to do in his office ... as far as I can see [just] joy-riding'.[24] But then Derby (a Tory) felt a great antipathy towards Churchill at all times. Also, he may have been unaware of the prodigious quantities of work that Churchill could do when other people were asleep in bed.

Visits to France were one thing. Spain proved to be another in early June. King Alfonso XIII of Spain had informed the Duke of Westminster that he would like to receive a visit from Churchill. Barely had this news reached London before the British Ambassador to Spain, Sir Arthur Hardinge, had written to Balfour and advised against the visit, saying that it might give the impression that Britain was trying to bring Spain into the war. Hardinge was correct to advise caution, as Churchill was not above seeking new allies.

REBELLION AT HOME

On 26 June, a strike began at the works of The Alliance Aeroplane Company at Acton near London, following the dismissal of a shop steward. His offence had been to blow a whistle to halt production and then call a union meeting during working hours, having previously been disciplined for the same action. Negotiations were opened to settle the strike and the union agreed to resume work on 4 July in return for an arbitrator being appointed. But when the arbitrator arrived, the workers still refused to resume work. On 9 July, Churchill declared the strike, unauthorised by the unions, to be illegal. This was the beginning of a wave of unofficial strikes at munitions factories over the next three weeks.

Churchill moved in to take command and, after a series of meetings on 10 July, he concluded that the workers at the factory had prevented 'the legitimate development of the shop steward and ship committee programme'. He ordered that the factory be taken over by the Ministry of Munitions. The shop steward – a Mr Rock – would be reinstated prior to a full inquiry into the circumstances of his dismissal. A report in *The Times* declared Churchill's action to be 'entirely novel'. There was, it continued, 'no precedent for such a measure'. Against this apparently swift and decisive action, the factory owners issued a statement accusing the ministry of having failed to act when they were first asked. The details of the case are of no importance, but Churchill's action demonstrated that he was prepared to do whatever was necessary to keep munitions in production.[25]

A few days later, Churchill appealed to the War Cabinet for their support in his taking even more drastic action 'against persons conspiring against the State'. He told his colleagues that 'It was absurd to comb out men from workshops for the army and to allow others to walk out of the shops and remain immune while engaged on a strike.' His solution was to withdraw the protection certificates from workers who refused to return to work. Without these certificates the men could then be conscripted. On 16 July, the War Cabinet readily agreed to this action.[26]

In mid-July, a series of strikes were declared in Coventry. The principal cause was more subtle, being driven by two factors: selecting skilled workers for the army and the abolition of leaving certificates. These two actions had resulted (as anticipated) in a shortage of skilled labour. Employers had reacted by retaining skilled workers, with the result that some employers had more than the ministry considered to be their fair share. To counteract this, the ministry had introduced a rationing system for skilled labour, which involved compelling some employers to release some men.

In turn, some of these sacked men claimed that they could not find other work. Strikes based on the problems arising from the rationing of skilled labour were declared by Churchill to be those which did not arise from a trade dispute. To incite such strikes, he said, was a 'grave' matter. If the dispute were not settled quickly it would 'lead to grave consequences'.[27]

On 22 July, notices were posted in Coventry warning 'all workmen' that the threatened strikes were not 'an ordinary Trade Dispute' and that taking part or inciting others to take part could lead to 'very serious penalties under the Defence of the Realm Act'.[28] The following day, workers in Coventry suspended their threat to strike. Meanwhile, strikes appeared to be imminent in Manchester, Birmingham, Glasgow and many other manufacturing centres.

By 24 July, there were 60,000 workers on strike in Birmingham, including 5,000 women. The ministry was now more active at local level, distributing leaflets to explain the skilled labour rationing scheme. The leaflet included questions such as 'Is the embargo of general application?' Answer: it only applied to some one hundred companies. And, 'Is it true that the trades unions have not been consulted?' Answer: 'They had the scheme fully explained to them this spring.'[29]

That same day, Churchill briefed the War Cabinet on the situation. There were 7,000 men still on strike at Coventry and he advised the War Cabinet to act immediately by issuing a 'declaration that men on strike would have their exemption certificates withdrawn'. The strikers, he argued, were not engaged in an industrial dispute but were seeking to 'oppose conscription and dilution'. The War Cabinet withheld any action, advising Churchill to remind the Trade Union Advisory Committee of government policy and to give them an opportunity to settle the strikes.[30]

Lloyd George gave the strikers a few more days to pull back but they made no conciliatory moves. On 27 July, he issued the government's ultimatum, which *The Times* neatly summarised as 'work or fight': 'all men wilfully absent from their work on or after Monday, 29 July, will be deemed to have voluntarily placed themselves outside the area of munitions industries. Their protection certificates will cease to have effect from that date.'[31]

The day after the ultimatum took effect, Churchill was able to report that at Birmingham there had been 'a considerable resumption' of work and a mass meeting at Coventry had voted to resume work that night. He expected a general resumption of work on the following day. He was to set up a Committee of Inquiry, but he gave no details of its remit.[32]

THE FIGHT BACK AT AMIENS

The Allies had been on the defensive in France since 21 March. German forces had taken large areas of territory from the Allies, but at a huge cost in men and resources.

When writing to Sinclair in July, Churchill had rightly predicted that the final decisive phase of the war was near and the day came just four weeks later. With over-extended supply lines, an exhausted and depleted German army faced the British at Amiens on 8 August. Rawlinson's Fourth Army, fighting alongside the French and Canadians, advanced up to seven miles on the first day of the battle and there were to be similar gains on the following day. It was clear to both sides that the war had turned in the Allies' favour.

In *The World Crisis* Churchill recalled being at the War Cabinet when General Wilson announced the attack and that he decided to take a break in order to witness the battle. In fact, there was no War Cabinet meeting on that day and Churchill was not at any other of its meetings around that time. He went on to claim that he was on the battlefield on 9 and 10 August, but there is uncertainty as to the exact days involved. His first call was at Rawlinson's HQ, but his arrival was 'much delayed by enormous columns of German prisoners which endlessly streamed along the dusty roads'. Churchill noted how 'The woe-begone expression of the Officers contrasted sharply with the almost cheerful countenances of the rank and file.' Summoning up his great powers of imagination he described how 'All had passed through a severe experience, the crashing bombardment, the irresistible on-rush of the tanks spurting machine-gun bullets … the catastrophe of surrender [and] the long march from the battlefield.' The maker of the mighty weapons of victory had not lost his magnanimity.[33] His own role in this victory did not go unrecognised as Haig wrote on 9 August to thank him for his 'energy and foresight' which had 'rendered our success possible'.[34]

What Churchill had witnessed was the beginning of the end of the German menace. General Erich von Ludendorff recognised the hopelessness of his situation, naming 8 August as 'the black day of the German army'.[35] He called for his men to go on the defensive while Germany sued for peace.

While Churchill may have been happy in 1927 to have described this visit as a holiday, he had actually kept on working and thinking about munitions. On 10 August, he wrote to Lloyd George to express his concern about various shortages. The Germans, he noted, had longer-range shells, in part because a false nose cone had been developed. (British engineers had said this was impossible.) There was a lack of mustard gas and the high-powered aeroplanes were not performing well. Perhaps his greatest disappointment was the tank. For this he blamed Admiral Moore, who had had charge of production after Stern had been removed in late 1917. As he wrote of his plans for a tank corps of 100,000 men to be in place for June 1919, Churchill showed that he had not yet realised the significance of the Amiens victory. He concluded by inviting the Prime Minister to spend some time at Verchocq: 'it is a very beautiful place, with the most lovely trees'.[36]

By 14 August, Churchill was back at work with conferences and meetings. The following day he was stuck in one meeting after another while outside the summer sun was shining. Generals and ministers from America, Britain, France and Italy sat in deliberation on arms deliveries both for their own needs and those of the smaller Allies. Churchill, Louis Loucheur and Edward Stettinius, American Secretary of State for War, met separately to discuss how to supply the American Third Army. On the whole, Churchill got on well with Stettinius, he told his wife, but there was one serious problem: the Anglo-American tank factory at Châteauroux. This had been a project of 'that foolish Colonel Stern', which Churchill had reluctantly agreed to accept. Now it was 'an international scandal' since there was no French labour available. Everything was ready to start the production of the desperately needed tanks.[37]

On 18 August, Churchill had dinner with the new ambassador, Lord Derby, Sir William Weir, Bonham Carter and General Bridges. Derby, still trying to find his way around the unfathomable French military and political system, and still angry following his removal from the War Office, was in an unusually mellow mood. For once 'Winston was really most amusing … He is a great admirer of tanks and wants to make thousands of them and comb out the army in every way to man them.' When Churchill launched a bitter attack on the navy's selfishness, he found a ready audience. Weir was fretting as materials and manpower went to a more than strong enough navy; and Derby himself said he knew 'from painful experience' the sacrifices that the army had made for the navy.[38]

After Churchill's strange exchange of correspondence with Lloyd George, in April, about the need for a 'regular cabinet', nothing more was heard of party politics until early September. During the first week of that month, Churchill, Rothermere and Riddell were staying at Danny House near Hurstpierpoint. (Riddell had rented this house for three months to provide Lloyd George with a country retreat.) When the talk turned to the merits of a general election, Churchill and Rothermere showed no interest. A week later, Derby recorded in his diary that Lloyd George was keen on an election, which he expected to return him with a large majority. By late October, Riddell was noting that Churchill was 'busy intriguing'.[39] While he gave no details of the precise direction of the intrigue, Churchill was undoubtedly trying to play safe. Should he fall in with Asquith, whose star had faded but was by no means burnt out? Or would the self-effacing and apparently apathetic Andrew Bonar Law finally take over as leader of the largest party in the Commons? Or perhaps he should simply cling to his saviour, Lloyd George.

On 8 September, after a day on the beach at Overstrand with his family, Churchill flew to France. On his first day there he lunched with Haig, who told him of the low level of morale in the German army. Churchill was not entirely convinced –

after all, the politicians had spent four years listening to Haig's forecasts of the imminent collapse of the German forces – but he hoped that this time Haig was right. Dinner that night was with Jack Churchill, General Tudor and the Adjutant General Fowke.

On the same day, Churchill had also visited the battlefront with the fearless and professional Major General Louis Lipsett, who commanded the Third Canadian Division. (Seven weeks later Lipsett was to be the last British general to be killed in the war.) He noted how the troops were supported by tanks and how the Allied soldiers had walked freely and captured Germans in their thousands. But beyond that line he found a burial ground for several hundred Canadians killed in the battle. This demonstrated the eternal problem of trench warfare: how to sustain a penetration of the enemy's line. Only tanks could do that, he told Lloyd George.

On 12 September in Paris, Churchill wrote to his wife and in amongst family news he confided to her that 'I am trying to arrange to give the Germans a good first dose of the Mustard gas before the end of the month. Haig is vy keen on it. Their whining in defeat is gratifying to hear.' That day was the anniversary of their marriage, which set Churchill thinking of their ten years together. 'I reproach myself for not having been more to you.' He continued: 'Do you think we have been less happy or more happy than the average married couple?'[40]

Three days later, he was able to tell Clementine that 'The hamper of mustard gas is on its way. This hellish poison will I trust be discharged on the Huns to the extent of nearly 100 tons by the end of this month.' There was also the good news that the Americans had accepted his offer of 2,000 guns, which he was sure they would need in 1919. In a relaxed mood, Churchill went on to describe his office arrangements in France, where 'the work arrives in steady consignments, & the telephone & aeroplane keep me in closest touch'. He was, he said, 'thoroughly contended'.[41] Clementine was less so and she scolded him for being away for (with a short break) nearly a month: 'you bad Vagrant'.[42]

In July, General Wilson had circulated a paper which predicted the decisive defeat of the Central Powers in 1919. In early September, Churchill responded with his own paper laying out his plans for *Munitions in 1919*. He set out nine actions to support a victory. These included the requirement to bring over as many American troops as possible. This done, there would be a need to 'arm, equip and clothe them'. In the construction field any project that would not provide a benefit in the climax period should be abandoned. The winter was to be used to accumulate munitions on the largest possible scale. In the early spring, it would be possible to begin releasing coalminers to the army – at the same time munitions production could be reduced. And, in a flight of typically creative Churchillian-style thinking, he had a solution to Haig's insistence that he had not the resources to man mass tank units: the navy could supply the men for 'the last 2,000 British tanks to be completed before the battle'.[43]

RALLYING THE WORKERS

In October, Churchill went on a morale-boosting campaign in the main munitions areas in Scotland and the north of England. At a lunch on 7 October, he revealed his doubts as to victory coming that year. Then at a War Aims meeting attended by 5,000 people (including a number of hecklers) he talked about the need for a decisive victory: 'We must not,' he told his audience, 'allow ourselves to be cozened by smooth words out of the victory which our men had deserved by their blood and our women by their tears.'[44] He was perhaps alarmed at the fact that Germany had appealed to President Woodrow Wilson for armistice terms. Churchill wanted peace but only peace with victory.

On 8 October, he was in Glasgow where, during a private meeting with shipbuilders and engineers, he was deluged with demands to restore pre-war working practices, complaints about arbitration tribunals and concerns about pay and inflation. These were all signs of the increasing difficulty in keeping the millions of munitions workers under relentless pressure to produce more and more. After a visit to a shell-filling factory, Churchill made a speech from the top of a motorcar, where he declared 'we are going to win'. He praised the enterprise of the munitions factories and the women who had worked in them. At a Glasgow Corporation luncheon, he extolled the 'overwhelmingly powerful' navy and the valiant army. But more needed to be done: 'It was the last spurt which would give us decisive victory' – but in 1919.[45]

After a brief visit to Newcastle, where he visited the famous Elswick factories, Churchill arrived in Leeds on 10 October. There he talked of the 'unequalled' achievements of the British army. There was no other army that 'has suffered such grievous losses on the Allied side' or 'taken captive so many combatants of the enemy'. But it was a 'crafty enemy', which attacked its 'peaceful neighbours' and which should not be allowed to escape the consequences of its crimes. He warned against the danger of accepting a peace in which the Germans simply retreated to their own territory. That still left the menace of the submarine. The only safe peace was one based on 'effective guarantees'.[46]

At Sheffield, on the following day, Churchill could afford to be honest about the disasters of the last four years. He told his audience that 'in the last few months ... a total transformation of our fortunes has taken place' after 'four years of war uncheered [sic] by great successes either by land or sea'. But the dangers were not at an end and the Germans still showed no sign of repentance. The war had to go on, but Churchill did not want to demand 'unconditional surrender' since 'no nation should be denied a reasonable assurance as to its future'. What he did want was to '[make] sure that our men's lives have not been sacrificed in vain, and that we shall not be confronted with a renewal of the struggle'.[47] It would never have occurred to him that the Allies' failure in this respect would later lead to his own 'finest hour'.

Churchill ended his tour by visiting the munitions factories at Manchester on 14 October. At a luncheon given by the Manchester and District Armaments Output Committee, he spoke about the text of Germany's reply to President Woodrow Wilson's fourteen point plan which had appeared in the morning newspapers. (Wilson had put these forward as a 'possible basis of a general peace'.[48]) While Germany appeared to accept Wilson's stipulations, the statement was somewhat vague. Churchill told his audience that there must be 'no relaxation of effort' until there were 'adequate safeguards and guarantees'. He feared that the Germans would use an armistice to 'recover their breath'. As to specifics, it was imperative for Germany to 'right the wrong of 1871' and return Alsace-Lorraine to France.[49]

SENSING THE END

On 25 October, soon after completing his tour of the munitions factories, Churchill travelled again to France. After lunch with Haig's Chief of Staff, Churchill and Marsh departed for Verchocq. This time their travels were aided by the loan of a 1914 Rolls-Royce Silver Ghost motorcar. But due to the poor condition of the French roads, a tyre burst. This happened in a very narrow lane and Churchill's driver refused to reverse, resulting in a rare outburst of anger as Churchill started swearing profusely at the man. Despite these problems they were only thirty minutes late for dinner at the chateau with Sinclair. With just seventeen days of war remaining, Churchill received the welcome news that Sinclair was to be appointed as liaison officer between the Ministry of Munitions and the army at the Front.

The swearing incident and the events of the next day suggest that a general air of irritation and weariness was setting in on the Front. The day started well for Marsh when he slipped out of the chateau before breakfast to walk along the famous avenue of trees. He returned to breakfast 'quite uplifted'. But once back on the road, tempers frayed. At the checkpoint to enter the battle area, the sentry muddled the passes and had to ask to see Churchill's pass twice. Churchill was not pleased. After lunch at Cateau he had nothing to do, so they all went for a trip in the motorcar. When they reached a damaged bridge a furious row broke out between Churchill and Sinclair. The latter had been trying to leave the party all morning in order to get back to his colonel. Churchill finally 'sulkily' conceded that they must turn back. After delivering Sinclair, Churchill snapped 'I shall take no more interest in him.'[50] The next day, Churchill and Marsh were on the road again to visit the newly liberated Lille and lunch with General Barnes.

They had come to Lille for the ceremonial entry of the British troops into the city. General Birdwood led the march past of infantry. Marsh noted how they were 'majestic in their serious and serene faces ... their uniforms splendidly brushed up ... there wasn't a smiling face'.[51] Next was lunch with Major General Tudor in a house only recently vacated by German officers. The blood-stained floor testified to the death, a week earlier, of the last German officer in the town. They were in a relaxed mood as Tudor took the party towards the Front, but reality soon returned when, while using the belfry of a ruined church to get a better view, the smell of mustard gas drifted towards them. The party rapidly returned to the safety of Tudor's HQ for the night.

Despite all Churchill's warnings against optimism during his tour of the factories, in Flanders the evidence of a German collapse was everywhere. Not surprisingly, Clementine thought Churchill had done enough and should return home. Writing from 3 Tenterden Street, she pointed out that 'even if the fighting is not over yet, your share of it must be'.[52] The new address signalled the now 'homeless' state of the Churchills as they had once again re-let 33 Eccleston Square and taken to short-term rentals for their own accommodation. (Number 3 Tenterden Street belonged to an aunt of Churchill.)

On what was to be Churchill's last day in France during the war, his life nearly ended on the battlefield. He and Marsh were once more motoring round when they arrived at a destroyed bridge over the River Lys. They turned back, mistook the direction of the Front, and began to drive directly towards the German lines. Only when shells began to fall on each side of the road did they realise their mistake. The following day, 30 October, they flew back to England to the welcome news that Turkey had surrendered. Churchill must surely have thought back to his struggles to push Turkey out of the war nearly four years earlier.

MORE DOUBTS ON THE HOME FRONT

The rapid collapse of the Western Front prompted Churchill once more to consider his future. He wrote to his election agent in Dundee to warn him that he expected an election 'almost immediately' and asked him to suggest dates for speaking engagements in the city. He assumed that the coalition government would be asking for a mandate for 'reconstruction and demobilisation'.[53]

Lloyd George, also, had an election on his mind and, on 6 November, asked his Liberal ministers whether they would continue to work with him after the war. Churchill, assuming that Lloyd George was to continue with his existing Cabinet arrangements, sulked. Only when he discovered that the Prime Minister intended to re-establish full Cabinet government did he perk up. The next day, Churchill sent an equivocal letter to Lloyd George. While willing to handle the closure of his ministry he was not ready to take any 'far reaching political decision' without knowing 'the character & main composition' of Lloyd George's next government. His pretext for this odd letter was his avowed desire 'not to be an embarrassment to you', but we can assume that the real issue was who was to get the plum jobs. His fear was that they would all go to the Tories.[54]

Lloyd George's reply was long and pained. Churchill's letter, he said, had been 'an unpleasant surprise'. He was hurt to hear that Churchill was preparing to leave the government solely because of 'an apparent dissatisfaction with your personal prospects'. Lloyd George then declared: 'If you decide to desert me … the responsibility must be yours.'[55] In reply, Churchill said that he had been misunderstood. But when he declared that he feared 'office without real responsibility' and would prefer to be a private member, he merely proved that Lloyd George had understood him all too well.[56]

WAR'S END

By 6 November, the headlines in the British newspapers were all variations on 'Germans in full retreat'. On 8 November, the German High Command sent a wireless message to ask for the safe passage of a courier and two staff officers through the Allied lines. The following day, the Kaiser abdicated and fled to Holland. Meanwhile, reports of a revolution were emerging from Germany. The final surrender came at 5.00 a.m. (French time) on 11 November when Germany signed the armistice terms.

At 11.00 a.m. – the moment the armistice came into effect – Churchill was standing at the window of his office, waiting for Big Ben to strike the eleventh hour. As the sound rang out over the quiet street there was not a soul in sight; then the doors of the numerous offices and hotels opened and a joyous crowd of workers poured onto the street. Soon the street was a solid mass of humanity, pushing its way westwards down the Strand to go to Buckingham Palace and cheer the King.

By now, Clementine had arrived and the two of them decided to go to Downing Street to congratulate Lloyd George. As soon as they got into Churchill's car, a number of people jumped on the running boards as the loaded vehicle nudged its way through the throng.

It was typical of Lloyd George that there was no great celebration party that night at Downing Street, just a quiet dinner with Wilson, Churchill and F.E. Smith. One might have expected an evening of reminiscences, but they mostly discussed the forthcoming election.

The diners made no attempt to discuss the staggering achievements of the years of Lloyd George's premiership and Churchill's time as Minister of Munitions. Had they done so, Churchill could have drawn attention to his own astonishing success. He had raised aeroplane output by 117 per cent from 14,748 to 17,270 units; tank production had increased twenty-two per cent from 1,110 to 1,359; artillery by fifty-seven per cent from 5,137 to 8,039; machine guns by fifty-two per cent from 79,700 to 120,900; and trench mortar units rose by eight per cent. At the same time, coal output, iron ore production and steel production all *fell*, as did the size of Churchill's workforce.[57] (No doubt the tank output would have been much higher had Churchill

not agreed with Stern's Châteauroux factory idea.) Only one other man in the
government could have achieved all this: Lloyd George.

—————⇒➤●◄⇐—————

Churchill did not desert Lloyd George and nor did Lloyd George desert Churchill.
At the general election, on 14 December, they both stood as Liberals in support of
the coalition government. Lloyd George's coalition won 478 seats – a majority of 325
over the opposition. Churchill was returned with a massive majority of 15,365. Lloyd
George asked him whether he would like the Admiralty or the War Office and he
expressed a strong preference for the Admiralty. On 9 January 1919, Churchill joined
the new government but as Secretary of State for War and Air.

EPILOGUE

Churchill went into the First World War as a retired cavalry man; he came out with the mind and attitudes of a theatre of war commander. At Omdurman in 1898, he had learned to charge an ill-armed enemy with headlong abandon. In the war, he had learned when to attack and when to pause; where to attack and where to defend.

The war ruined the reputations of dozens of generals and many high politicians. Yet it raised two men to unimaginable heights: Lloyd George and Churchill. Although Churchill's post-war political career progressed, first as Secretary of State for War (1919-22) under Lloyd George and then as Chancellor of the Exchequer (1924-29) under Prime Minister Stanley Baldwin, his enemies refused to forget his joining the Liberals in 1904. No longer restrained by issues of national security, they began to write the history that, in many ways, has remained to this day. The Bacchantes? Churchill's stupidity by overruling his staff. Antwerp? A fool's errand carried out against all military opinion. Dardanelles? A one-man operation supported by no one else in the War Council. Gallipoli? All Churchill's fault.

I hope that this book has shown both how these ludicrous accusations arose and just how baseless they are. The truth is that Churchill was one of the few men who grew with the war and learned from it. Not everything he tried worked, but he never made the mistake of repeating the same failed tactic over and over again. Had he been a front-line general, he would not have spent four years sending men to walk into machine-gun fire – his search for different means of offensive is proof of that. And, at the level of conjecture, had he remained at the Admiralty it is unthinkable that, year in, year out, he would have failed to try convoys and failed to search for better means of defence against submarines. But two First Sea Lords (Jackson and Jellicoe) and two First Lords (Balfour and Geddes) did just that.

⸺⸻⸺

Given the vilification that Churchill suffered during the war, and given the endless attempts to blacken his name afterwards, his return to office in the Second World War seems almost inexplicable. Until, that is, we look back at his experience twenty years earlier. The more we examine those four years of war the more we can see that they were his preparation for the great office of wartime Prime Minister.

Churchill's introduction to modern, mechanised large-scale war had taught him the importance of seven factors: the role of combined operations; the value of science and technology; the need for integrated command systems; the necessity of a genuine coalition; the vital role of a very small War Cabinet; the need for honest morale boosting; and the prize of code breaking. All but the last of these had been Asquith's responsibility in 1914-16. He failed in each and every one. All were Churchill's responsibility in the following war. He rose to the challenges that each set him.

Churchill was the first person (along with General French) to identify the value of combined operations when, in 1914, they developed their proposal for clearing the Belgian coast. French's army, under the cover of Churchill's naval guns, would have worked its way along the shore with the aim of driving the Germans from their ports and submarine bases. One reason why the War Council failed to develop this project was its failure to recognise Britain's greatest strength: its amphibious capacity. Alone of all the powers in the war, Britain had naval fleets and squadrons which were able to land men and guns on almost any approachable beach. Yet, not once did the Council ask itself the question 'How can we use our greatest asset?' Instead, it built on its weakest factor: a very small army. But Churchill, in part because he was as much an Admiralty man as a soldier, comprehended this unique power to land and fight where Great Britain chose. In the next war, this power would be exploited to the full – sometimes disastrously, as at Operation 'Jubilee', Dieppe, in 1942; sometimes gloriously, as in Sicily, Italy and the D-Day landings at Normandy.

No man in the First World War did more than Churchill to promote the use of science and technology to save the lives of soldiers while destroying an enemy's army. Also, it was Churchill when he was at the Admiralty who set up the Landships Committee. Yet even in 1918, he was still grappling with generals who kept faith with the obsolete cavalry and refused to retrain those men to fight in tanks. When Churchill became wartime Prime Minister, all this experience came flooding back as he surrounded himself with scientists, engineers and statisticians. Even before the war, he was secretly visiting the engineers who were working on radar, offering them encouragement and backing their calls for more funding. The memoirs of men such as E.G. Bowen,[1] Sir Robert Watson-Watt,[2] and R.V. Jones[3] testify to Churchill's capacity to see the potential of some rudimentary equipment rigged up on a workshop bench. This was no more than Churchill applying what he had learnt in the First World War.

The art of code breaking was another technical side of war that Churchill encouraged. When the German naval code books were captured it was by his direction that the resulting intelligence was exploited. The code-breaking system 'Ultra', in the Second World War, was modelled on his Admiralty experience of 1914-15. Only a privileged few knew what went on behind the anonymous door with the 'Room 40' sign on it. Those inside kept quiet when outside, and the precious decodes were cautiously shared. Officers at sea were never told of the existence of the decoding team – even Jellicoe was not informed. All that the admirals were told was 'according to a reliable source ...'.

The years 1914-17, were littered with failings and disasters which arose from the lack of an integrated command structure. Churchill first became aware of this when he heard how the French armies were retreating on both of Sir John French's flanks, leaving his army exposed. For almost all of the war, British generals cursed the French for lack of co-operation, while the French likewise cursed the British. It was Lloyd George who finally forced through an integrated command structure – a lesson that Churchill did not forget when it became his turn to subordinate British forces to General Eisenhower.

During the First World War, Churchill had seen, under Asquith, first the problems of running a great war without a coalition, and then the problems of living with a sham one. Until May 1915, Asquith's government lacked the moral authority for modern war – that is a war which mobilises the home front as well as that overseas. In May 1915, during a moment of personal weakness he gave in to a coalition while never really believing in that style of government. He brought in weak men and threw out the strong individuals precisely because he could not accept the challenge of those who took the war seriously. When it came to Churchill's time to choose his coalition, he sought a true war-winning team, assembled from across all the main parties. His deputy was the leader of the Labour Party, Clement Attlee; one of his three chancellors was an independent MP (Sir Kingsley Wood) and one a Labour man (Hugh Dalton); his Home Secretary was Herbert Morrison, another Labour man. Despite the great powers that he took into his own hands (including being the War Minister), he chose as his First Lord of the Admiralty the Labour politician A.V. Alexander. At the same time as maintaining an inclusive government, Churchill acknowledged the importance of a small War Cabinet and his first (1940-42) had just five members.

We have seen that Churchill played an active part in morale-boosting during the First World War, whether he was in or out of office. His early speeches were clumsily phrased and jingoistic in tone. Slowly he learnt to use a more assertive style and to deal honestly with the strains and difficulties of war. None of his speeches at this time rose to the heights that he would achieve twenty years later, but his First World War endeavours were the basis of splendours to come.

Churchill was not alone in realising that the First World War was only a dress rehearsal. Many biographies testify to men and women who, on hearing the terms of the Treaty of Versailles, predicted that the German armies would march again. But one alone amongst them rose from the First World War formed and ready to fight the second.

KEY PLAYERS

With some exceptions, titles, ranks and posts are given only for 1914-18.

Note on unusual titles
First Lord was the government minister in charge of the navy.
First Sea Lord was the admiral in charge of naval administration.
Chancellor of the Exchequer was the government minister in charge of finance.
Chancellor of the Duchy of Lancaster was a non-departmental ministerial post.

Addison, Christopher. 1914 Parliamentary Secretary to the Board of Education; 1915 Parliamentary Secretary to the Ministry of Munitions; 1916 Minister of Munitions; 1917 Minister without portfolio.

Aitken, William Maxwell 'Max'. See Beaverbrook.

Asquith, Herbert Henry MP. 1914-16 Prime Minister and leader of the Liberal Party; remained party leader until the party split at the end of 1918.

Asquith, Katherine. *Née* Horner. Wife of Raymond Asquith.

Asquith, Raymond. Eldest son of Herbert Asquith; 1904 Barrister; 1914 Enlisted; 1916 Killed in Battle of the Somme.

Asquith, Violet. Daughter of Herbert Asquith.

Balfour, Arthur MP. An ex-Prime Minister; 1915-16 First Lord of the Admiralty.

Barnes, George MP. An ex-Labour Party leader; 1916-17 Minister of Pensions; 1917-20 Minister without portfolio.

Battenberg, Admiral Prince Louis Alexander. 1912-14 First Sea Lord.

Beatty, Vice Admiral David. 1913-16 Commander of First Battlecruiser Squadron; 1916-19 Commander-in-Chief, Grand Fleet.

Beaverbrook, Lord. Formerly Aitken, 'Max'. 1910-1916 MP; 1917 Lord Beaverbrook.

Beresford, Admiral Lord Charles MP. 1910-16 MP; 1916 Created Lord Beresford of Metemmeh and of Curraghmore in the County of Waterford.

Bertie, Sir Francis. 1905-18 British Ambassador to France; 1915 Created Lord Bertie.

Bonham-Carter, Violet. See Asquith, Violet.

Callaghan, Admiral Sir George. 1911-14 Commander-in-Chief, Home Fleet; 1914-18 Commander-in-Chief, The Nore.

Callwell, Major General Sir Charles. 1914-15 Director of Military Operations and Intelligence at the War Office; 1916-18 Liaison duties with Allies.

Carden, Vice Admiral Sackville. 1914-15 Commander of Mediterranean Squadron.

Carson, Sir Edward MP. 1910-21 Leader of the Ulster Unionist Party; 1915-16 Attorney General; 1916-17 First Lord of the Admiralty; 1917-18 Minister without portfolio.

Cavan, Major General Lord. 1914-15 Commander of 4th Guards Brigade; 1915-16 Commander of Guards Division; 1916-18 Commander of XIV Corps; 1918 Commander-in-Chief of British forces on the Italian Front.

Churchill, Clementine Spencer-. *Née* Hozier; wife of Winston Churchill.

Churchill, Gwendoline 'Goonie'. *Née* Bertie; wife of John Churchill.

Churchill, Major John Spencer-. Churchill's brother; 1914-18 variously on the staff of French, Hamilton and Birdwood.

Churchill, Mary Spencer-. Churchill's fifth child. Later, as Mary Soames, wrote extensively on her parents.

Clemenceau, Georges. 1917-20 Prime Minister of France.

Cradock, Rear Admiral Christopher. 1914 Commander of 4th Squadron of the Royal Navy.

Cromer, Lord. Unionist member of the House of Lords; 1916-17 Chairman of the Dardanelles Commission; died 29 January 1917.

Curzon, George, First Marquis Curzon of Kedleston. Ex-Viceroy of India; 1916-17 President of the Air Board; 1916-19 Lord President of the Council.

Dallolio, General Alfredo. 1915-18 Italian Undersecretary of State for Munitions.

de Robeck, Rear Admiral John. 1914 Commander of Second Cruiser Squadron; 1915 Second-in-command at Dardanelles; 1916-19 Commander Second Battle Squadron of Grand Fleet.

Derby, Lord. 1916-18 Secretary of State for War; 1918-20 Ambassador to France.

Esher, Viscount. Courtier; 1914-18 Undisclosed intelligence activities in France.

Fisher, Admiral Lord John. Ex-First Sea Lord; 1914-15 First Sea Lord; 1915-18 Chairman of the Board of Invention and Research.

Foch, General Ferdinand. 1914 French army officer. 1914 Command of XX Corps; 1914 Command of Ninth Army; 1914 Commander-in-Chief; 1915-16 Command of Northern Army Group; 1916-17 Italian command; 1917 French representative on Supreme War Council; 1918 Co-ordinator of Allied armies in France; 1918 Marshal of France.

French, General Sir John. 1914-15 Commander of the British Expeditionary Force; 1915-18 Commander-in-Chief of the British Home Forces; 1918-21 Lord Lieutenant of Ireland.

Gibb, Captain Andrew. 1915-16 Served with Churchill in Sixth Battalion Royal Scots Fusiliers.

Goodenough, Admiral Sir William. 1913-16 Command of Second Light Cruiser Squadron.

Grey, Sir Edward. 1905-16 Foreign Secretary.

Guest, Captain Frederick MP. 1912-15 Treasurer of the Household; 1914-15 ADC to Sir John French; 1916 Service in East Africa; 1917-21 Parliamentary Secretary to the Treasury; 1917-21 Chief Whip of Coalition Liberal Party.

Guest, Ivor – see Lord Wimborne.

Haig, Field Marshal Douglas. 1914-15 Command of First Army Corps; 1915-18 Commander of the BEF.

Haldane, Viscount. 1912-15 Lord Chancellor.

Hamilton, General Sir Ian. 1914-15 Command of Home Defence; 1915 Commander of the Mediterranean Expeditionary Force.

Hankey, Colonel Maurice. 1912-1938 Secretary of the Committee of Imperial Defence.

Hobhouse, Charles MP. 1914-15 Postmaster General.

Jackson, Admiral Henry. 1913-15 Chief of the Admiralty War Staff; 1915-16 First Sea Lord.

Jellicoe, Admiral John. 1914-16 Commander-in-Chief of the Grand Fleet; 1916-17 First Sea Lord.

Joffre, General Joseph. 1911-16 Commander-in-Chief of the French army.

Keyes, Rear Admiral Roger. 1914-17 Commander of the battleship *Centurion*; 1917-18 Commander of Fourth Battle Squadron; 1918 Commander of the Dover Patrol.

Kiggell, Lieutenant-General Launcelot. 1914-15 Director of Home Defence; 1915-18 Haig's Chief-of-Staff.

Kitchener, Lord. 1914–16 War Minister. Died 5 June 1916.

Lambert, George MP. 1905–15 Civil Lord to the Admiralty.

Law, Andrew Bonar, MP. Leader of the Conservative Party. 1915–16 Secretary of State for the Colonies; 1916–19 Chancellor of the Exchequer.

Layton, Professor Walter. 1917–18 statistical adviser to Ministry of Munitions.

Lloyd George, David MP. 1908–15 Chancellor of the Exchequer; 1915–1916 Munitions Minister; 1916–22 Prime Minister.

Long, Walter, MP. 1916–19 Secretary of State for the Colonies.

Loucheur, Louis. 1917–18 French Minister of Munitions.

Marsh, Wilson 'Eddie'. Private Secretary to Churchill.

Milne, Admiral Sir Archibald. 1912–14 Commander-in-Chief, Mediterranean Fleet.

Milner, Lord. 1916–18 War Cabinet member; 1918 Secretary of State for War.

Moore, Rear Admiral Archibald. 1912–14 Third Sea Lord; 1914–15 Commander of Second Battlecruiser Squadron; 1915–17 Commander of Ninth Cruiser Squadron; 1917–19 Controller of Mechanical Warfare Department at Munitions.

Nicholas, Grand Duke. 1914–18 Commander of the Russian armed forces.

Nicolson, Sir Arthur. 1910–16 Permanent Secretary in the Foreign Office.

Northcliffe, Lord. Press baron. 1916 Director for Propaganda.

Painlevé, Paul. 1917 Prime Minister of France.

Paris, General Archibald. 1914 Commander of Royal Marine Brigade; 1914–16 Commander of Naval Division at Antwerp, Dardanelles and in France.

Pétain, General Philippe. 1914 Commander of Sixth Division of French army; 1914 Commander of 23 Corps; 1915 Commander of Second Army; 1917–18 Commander-in-Chief of French army.

Rawlinson, General Henry. 1914–16 Commander of IV Corps; 1916 Commander of Fourth Army; 1917–18 Additional Command of Second Army.

Richmond, Captain Herbert. 1913–15 Assistant Director of Operations at Admiralty; 1915 Liaison officer with Italian fleet; 1915–18 Sea-going commands.

Riddell, George. Newspaper proprietor.

Robertson, General William. 1914–15 Quartermaster General of BEF; 1915–18 Chief of the Imperial General Staff.

Samson, Commander Charles. 1914 Commander of Three Squadron RNAS; 1916 Commander of HMS *Ben-my-Chree*; 1917 Commander of an aircraft group at Great Yarmouth.

von Scheer, Admiral Reinhard. German admiral. 1914 Commander of Second Battle Squadron; 1915 Commander of Third Battle Squadron; 1916 Commander of High Seas Fleet; 1918 Chief of Naval Staff.

Scott C.P. Editor and proprietor of the *Manchester Guardian*.

Seely, Colonel 'Jack'. 1912–14 Secretary of State for War; 1914–18 Commander of the Canadian Cavalry Brigade.

Sinclair, Archibald. 1914–18. With the Guards in France.

Souchon, Rear Admiral Wilhelm. 1914 Commander of Kaiserliche Marine's Mediterranean squadron; 1914–17 Commander-in-Chief of the Ottoman Navy; 1917 Commander of the Fourth Battleship Squadron of the High Seas Fleet; 1918 Commander of the Imperial Navy base at Kiel.

von Spee, Vice Admiral Maximilian. 1912–14 Commander of German East Asia Squadron.

Speyer, Sir Edgar. Financier and philanthropist.

Spiers, Captain Edward. 1914–15 Captain in Eleventh Hussars; 1915–16 Liaison officer with French Tenth Army; 1917–20 Head of British Military Mission to Paris.

Stamfordham, Lord. Private Secretary to King George V.

Stanley, Venetia. Daughter of Edward Lyulph Stanley, 4th Baron Sheffield; married Edwin Montagu July 1915.

Stern, Albert. 1914 Lieutenant in the Royal Naval Volunteer Reserve; 1916 Head of Mechanical Warfare Supply Department; later transferred to the army.

Stevenson, Frances. Lloyd George's secretary.

Sturdee, Vice Admiral Frederick. 1913-14 Chief of the Admiralty War Staff; 1914 Commander of Squadron in South Atlantic; 1916-18 Commander of Fourth Battle Squadron.

Thuillier, General Sir Henry. 1915-16 Commander of Second Infantry Brigade, BEF; 1916-17 Director of Gas Services; 1917 Commander of Fifteenth Division; 1917-1918 Ministry of Munitions; 1918-19 Commander of Twenty-third Division, Italy.

Troubridge, Admiral Ernest. 1913-14 Commander of Mediterranean Cruiser Squadron; 1915 Head of the British naval mission to Serbia; 1915-18 Miscellaneous services in the Balkans.

Tyrwhitt, Commodore Reginald. 1913-18 Command of destroyers of Home Fleet (the Harwich Force).

Warrender, Vice Admiral George. 1912-15 Commander of Second Battle Squadron; 1916 Commander-in-Chief at Plymouth; 1916 Retired.

Weir, Sir William 1915 Director of Munitions, Scotland; 1916 Member of the Air Board; 1917 Member of the Air Council; 1918 President of the Air Council.

Wemyss, Admiral Rosslyn. 1914 Commander of the Twelfth Cruiser Squadron in the Channel Fleet; 1915 Various duties at Dardanelles and Gallipoli; 1916 Commander of the East Indies & Egyptian Squadron; 1917 Second Sea Lord; 1917-19 First Sea Lord.

Wilson, Admiral of the Fleet Sir Arthur. Retired admiral and ex-First Sea Lord.

Wilson, General Sir Henry. 1914 Sub-Chief of the General Staff to BEF 1914; 1915 Chief Liaison Officer with the French army; 1916-18 Commander of Four Corps; 1918-22 Chief of the Imperial General Staff.

Wimborne, Lord. 1914 On staff of 10th Irish Division; 1915-18 Lord Lieutenant of Ireland.

WORKS CONSULTED

Churchill College Archives
The Papers of 1st Lord Fisher of Kilverstone.

The National Archives
ADM 116/1336 Miscellaneous papers and telegrams 1914-15
ADM 116/3486 First Lord (Mr Winston Churchill's) miscellaneous papers 1907-16
ADM 116/1351 War Operations and Policy. Naval and Military 1914-18
ADM 116/1322 Formation of Naval Brigades 1914-16
ADM 116/1681 Miscellaneous Private Office papers 1913-20
ADM 116/3454 Admiral Lord Fisher's personal papers 1914-17
ADM 116/3491 Dardanelles operations 1915-16
ADM 137/50 Home Waters telegrams, July 1914-February 1915
ADM 137/96 Dardanelles telegrams, part 1, 21 September 1914-18 February 1915
ADM 137/110 Dardanelles telegrams III, 8 March-24 April 1915
ADM 137/452 Seizure of Advanced Base
ADM 137/1089 Dardanelles, January-April 1915
AIR 1/2326/223/53/1 The final report of the Dardanelles Commission on the conduct of operations
CAB 19/33 Dardanelles Committee Proceedings
CAB 22 War Cabinet Minutes 1914-16
CAB 23 War Cabinet Minutes 1916-39
CAB 37/121 Cabinet Papers

Published works
Addison, C., 1934. *Four and a Half Years*, 2 vols. London: Hutchinson.
Arthur, Sir G., 1920. *Life of Lord Kitchener*, 3 vols. London: Macmillan.
Aspinall-Oglander, C.F., 1951. *Roger Keyes.* London: Hogarth Press.
Asquith, H.H., 1928. *Memories and Reflections 1852-1927*, vol. II. London: Cassell.
Asquith, H.H., 1923. *The Genesis of War.* London: Cassell and Company.
Asquith, H.H. (Ed. Brock), 1982. *Letters to Venetia Stanley.* Oxford: Oxford University Press.
Bacon, Admiral Sir R.H., 1929. *The Life of Lord Fisher of Kilverstone, Admiral of the Fleet*, 2 vols. London: Hodder and Stoughton.
Bacon, Admiral Sir R.H., 1936. *The Life of John Rushworth Earl Jellicoe.* London: Cassell.
Baring, M., 1922. *The Puppet Show of Memory.* London: Heinemann.
Barnes, G.N., 1924. *From Workshop to War Cabinet.* London: Herbert Jenkins.
Beaverbrook, Lord, 1928. *Politicians and the War 1914-1916*, vol. I. London: Thornton Butterworth.
Beaverbrook, Lord, 1932. *Politicians and the War 1914-1916*, vol. II. London: Thornton Butterworth.
Beesly, P., 1982. *Room 40: Naval Intelligence 1914-18.* London: Hamish Hamilton.
Beiriger E.E., 1997. *Churchill, Munitions and Mechanical Warfare: The Politics of Supply and Strategy.* New York: Peter Lang Publishing.

Bellman, Sir H., 1947. *Cornish Cockney*. London: Hutchinson.

Bertie, Lord (Ed. Lennox), 1924. *The Diary of Lord Bertie of Thame 1914-1918*. London: Hodder and Stoughton.

Birkenhead, Earl of, 1989. *Churchill 1874-1922*. London: Harrap.

Black, N., 2009. *The British Naval Staff in the First World War*. Woodbridge: The Boydell Press.

Blake, R. (Ed.), 1952. *The Private Papers of Douglas Haig*. London: Eyre & Spottiswoode.

Blake, R., 1955. *The Unknown Prime Minister*. London: Eyre and Spottiswoode.

Bonham-Carter (Ed. Pottle), 1998. *Champion Redoubtable: The Diaries and Letters of Violet Bonham Carter 1914-1945*. London: Weidenfeld and Nicolson.

Bonham-Carter M. (Ed.), 1962. *The Autobiography of Margot Asquith*. London: Eyre & Spottiswoode.

Bonham-Carter, V., 1963. *Soldier True*. London: Frederick Muller Ltd.

Bonham-Carter, V., 1965. *Winston Churchill as I Knew Him*. London: Eyre & Spottiswoode and Collins.

Bowen, E.G., 1987. *Radar Days*. Bristol: Adam Hilger.

Brett. M.V. (Ed.), 1934. *Journals and Letters 1903-1910*. London: Ivor Nicholson and Watson.

Brett. M.V. (Ed.), 1938. *Journals and Letters 1910-1915*. London: Ivor Nicholson and Watson.

Bridges, Sir T., 1938. *Alarms and Excursions*. London: Longmans Green & Co.

Brough, C., 2003. *Galloper Jack*. London: Macmillan.

Buczacki, S., 2007. *Churchill and Chartwell: The Untold Story of Churchill's Houses and Gardens*. London: Frances Lincoln.

Callwell, C.E., 1919. *The Dardanelles*. London: Constable.

Callwell, C.E., 1920. *Experiences of a Dug-Out 1914-1918*. London: Constable and Co.

Callwell, C.E. (Ed. Edward), 1927. *Field-Marshal Sir Henry Wilson: His Life and Diaries*. London: Cassell & Co.

Campbell, J., 1983. *F E Smith First Earl of Birkenhead*. London: Pimlico.

Chalmers, W.S., 1951. *The Life and Letters of David, Earl Beatty*. London: Hodder and Stoughton.

Churchill, R.S., 1967. *Winston S Churchill*, vol. II. London: Heinemann.

Churchill, R.S., 1969. *Winston S Churchill*, vol. II Companion Part 3. London: Heinemann.

Churchill, R.S., 1959. *Lord Derby 'King of Lancashire'*. London: Heinemann.

Churchill, W.S., 1923a. *The World Crisis 1911-1914*. London: Thornton Butterworth Ltd.

Churchill, W.S., 1923b. *The World Crisis 1915*. London: Thornton Butterworth Ltd.

Churchill, W.S., 1927. *The World Crisis 1916-1918* Part II. London: Thornton Butterworth Ltd.

Churchill, W.S., 1932. *Thoughts and Adventures*. London: Thornton Butterworth Ltd.

Churchill, W.S., 1941a. *Great Contemporaries*. The Reprint Society.

Churchill, W.S., 1941b. *The World Crisis 1914-1918* Abridged ed. Macmillan.

Churchill, W.S., 1948. *Painting as a Pastime*. London: Odhams Press.

Clark, A. (Ed.), 1974. *A Good Innings: The Private Papers of Viscount Lee of Fareham*. London: John Murray.

Coates, T. (Ed,), 2000a. *Defeat at Gallipoli: The Dardanelles Part II 1915-1916*. London: The Stationery Office.

Coates, T. (Ed.), 2000b. *Lord Kitchener and Winston Churchill: The Dardanelles Part I 1914-1915*. London: The Stationery Office.

Colvin, I., 1936. *The Life of Lord Carson*, vol. III. London: Victor Gollancz Ltd.

Corbett J.S., 1920. *Naval Operations*, vols I and II. London: Longmans, Green and Co.

D'Este, C., 2008. *Warlord: A Life of Churchill At War, 1874-1945*. London: Allen Lane.

David, E. (Ed.), 1977. *Inside Asquith's Cabinet: Diaries of Charles Hobhouse*. London: John Murray.

De Groot, G.J., 1993. *Liberal Crusader: The Life of Archibald Sinclair*. London: Hurst & Co.

Dutton, D. (Ed.), 2001. *The War Diary of The British Ambassador, The 17th Earl of Derby*. Liverpool: Liverpool University Press.

Edmonds, J.E., 1925. *Military Operations: France and Belgium 1914*. London: Macmillan.

Egremont, M., 1980. *Balfour*. London: Collins.

Fisher, Lord, 1919. *Memories*. London: Hodder and Stoughton.

French, Sir J., 1919. *1914*. London: Constable and Co.

George, D.L., 1933. *War Memoirs of David Lloyd George*, 6 vols. London: Ivor Nicholson & Watson.

Gibb, Captain A.D., 1924. *With Churchill at the Front*. London: Gowans and Gray Ltd.

Gilbert, M., 1971. *Winston S Churchill*, vol. III, 1914-1916. London: Heinemann.

Gilbert, M., 1972a. *Winston S Churchill*, vol. III, Companion Vol. 1. London: Heinemann.

Gilbert, M., 1972b. *Winston S Churchill*, vol. III, Companion Vol. 2. London: Heinemann.

Gilbert, M., 1975. *Winston S Churchill*, vol. IV 1916-1922. London: Heinemann.

Gilbert, M., 1977. *Winston S Churchill*, vol. IV, Companion Part 1 Jan 1917-June 1919. London: William Heinemann Ltd.

Gretton, Vice-Admiral Sir P., 1968. *Former Naval Person*. London: Cassell.

Grey, Viscount, 1928. *Twenty-Five Years 1892-1916*, vol. II. London: Hodder and Stoughton.

Halpern, P.G. (Ed.), 1975. *The Keyes Papers*, Vol. I 1914-1918. London: Navy Records Society.

Hamilton, Sir I., 1920. *Gallipoli Diary*, 2 vols. 1920. New York: George H. Doran. (Unpaginated online version cited in this text.)

Hamilton, Sir I., 1944. *Listening for the Drums*. London: Faber & Faber.

Hankey, Lord, 1961. *The Supreme Command 1914-1918*, 2 vols. London: George Allen and Unwin Ltd.

Harris, J. P., 1995. *Men, Ideas and Tanks*. Manchester: Manchester University Press.

Harris, K., 1982. *Attlee*. London: Weidenfeld and Nicolson.

Hart, L., 1930. *A History of the World War 1914-1918*. London: Faber & Faber.

Hassall, C., 1959. *Edward Marsh Patron of the Arts*. London: Longmans.

Hicks Beach, Lady V., 1932. *Life of Sir Michael Hicks Beach*, vol. I. London: Macmillan.

Holmes, R., 1981. *The Little Field-Marshal: Sir John French*. London: Jonathan Cape.

Hyde, H.M., 1953. *Carson: The Life of Sir Edward Carson, Lord Carson of Duncairn*. London: Heinemann.

James, Admiral Sir W., 1955. *The Eyes of the Navy*. London: Methuen & Co.

James, Admiral Sir W., 1956. *A Great Seaman: The Life of Admiral of the Fleet Sir Henry F. Oliver*. London: Witherby Ltd.

Jenkins, R., 1964. *Asquith*. London: Papermac.

Joliffe, J. (Ed.), 1987. *Raymond Asquith: Life and Letters*. London: Century.

Jones, R.V., 1978. *Most Secret War*. London: Hamish Hamilton Ltd.

Kerr, M., 1934. *Prince Louis of Battenberg*. London: Longmans, Green and Co.

Keyes, R., 1939. *Adventures Ashore and Afloat*. London: Harrap.

Keyes, Sir R., 1934. *The Naval Memoirs of Admiral of the Fleet Sir Roger Keyes*. London: Thornton Butterworth Ltd.

Lee, J., 2000. *A Soldier's Life*. London: Macmillan.

Lee, Viscount (Ed. Clark), 1974. *A Good Innings: The Private Papers of Viscount Lee of Fareham*. London: John Murray.

Lees-Milne, J., 1986. *The Enigmatic Edwardian: The Life of Reginald, 2nd Viscount Esher*. London: Sidgwick & Jackson.

Lennox, Lady A. (Ed.), 1924. *The Diary of Lord Bertie of Thame 1914-1918*, 2 vols. London: Hodder and Stoughton.

Mackay, R.F., 1973. *Fisher of Kilverstone*. Oxford: Oxford University Press.

Magnus, P., 1958. *Kitchener: Portrait of an Imperialist*. London: John Murray.

Marder, A.J., 1952a. *Fear God and Dread Nought*, vol. I, 1854-1904. London: Jonathan Cape.

Marder, A.J., 1952b. *Portrait of an Admiral*.

Marder, A.J., 1956. *Fear God and Dread Nought*, vol. II Years of Power 1904-1914. London: Jonathan Cape.

Marder, A.J., 1959. *Fear God and Dread Nought*, vol. III, 1914–1920. London: Jonathan Cape.

Marder, A.J., 1961. *From Dreadnought to Scapa Flow*, vol. I. London: Oxford University Press.

Marder, A.J., 1965. *From the Dreadnought to Scapa Flow*, vol. II. London: Oxford University Press.

Marsh, E., 1939. *A Number of People*. London: William Heinemann.

Massie, R., 2003. *Castles of Steel*. New York: Random House.

Masterman, L., 1939. *C.F.G. Masterman: A Biography*. London: Nicholson and Watson.

Maurice, Sir F., 1928. *The Life of General Lord Rawlinson of Trent*. London: Cassell & Co.

McEwen, J.M., 1986. *The Riddell Diaries*. London: The Athlone Press.

Miller, G., 1996. *Superior Force*. Hull: University of Hull Press.

Milne, Sir A.B., 1929. *The Flight of the 'Goeben' and the 'Breslau'*. London: Eveleigh Nash Co.

Murfett, M.H. (Ed), 1995. *The First Sea Lords: From Fisher to Mountbatten*. London: Praeger.

Naylor, L.E., 1965. *The Irrepressible Victorian*. London: MacDonald.

Nicolson, H., 1952. *King George the Fifth: His Life and Reign*. London: Constable.

Osborne, E.W., c2006. *The Battle of Heligoland Bight*. Bloomington: Indiana University Press.

Owen, F., 1954. *Tempestuous Journey: Lloyd George His Life and Times*. London: Hutchinson.

Padfield, P., 2009. *Maritime Dominion*. London: John Murray.

Patterson, A.T., 1966. *The Jellicoe Papers*. London: Navy Records Society.

Powell, E.A., 1915. *Fighting in Flanders*. London: William Heinemann.

Ramsden, S. Baron (Ed.), c1984. *Real Old Tory Politics*. London: Historians' Press.

Ranft, B.M. (Ed.), 1989. *The Papers of Admiral Sir John Fisher* (2 vols). London: Navy Records Society.

Ranft, B. McL. (Ed), 1989. *The Beatty Papers*. Aldershot: Scolar Press for the Navy Records Society.

Riddell, Lord, 1933. *War Diary 1914-1918*. London: Ivor Nicholson and Watson.

Roskill, S., 1970. *Hankey, Man of Secrets*, Vol. 1 1877-1918. London: Collins.

Roskill, S., 1977. *Churchill and the Admirals*. London: Collins.

Roskill, S., 1980. *Admiral of the Fleet Earl Beatty*. London: Collins.

Rumbold, Sir H., 1940. *The War Crisis in Berlin July-August 1914*. London: Constable.

Sassoon, S., 1945. *Siegfried's Journey*. London: Faber.

Seely, J.E.B., 1931. *Fear, and Be Slain*. London: Hodder & Stoughton.

Soames, M., 1979. *Clementine Churchill*. London: Cassell.

Soames, M., 1998. *Speaking for Themselves*. London: Doubleday.

Swinton, The Earl of, 1966. *Sixty Years of Power*. London: Hutchinson.

Taylor, A.J.P. (Ed.), 1971. *Lloyd George: A Diary by Frances Stevenson*. London: Hutchinson.

Taylor, A.J.P., 1965. *English History 1914-1945*. Oxford: Oxford University Press.

Thompson, J.L, 2000. *Northcliffe: Press Baron in Politics 1865-1922*. London: John Murray.

Toye, R., 2007. *Lloyd George and Churchill*. London: Macmillan.

Waley, S.D., 1964. *Edwin Montagu: A Memoir and an Account of His Visits to India*. London: Asia Publishing House.

Watson-Watt, Sir R., 1957. *Three Steps to Victory*. London: Odhams Press Ltd.

Wemyss, Lady W., 1935. *The Life and Letters of Lord Wester Wemyss*. London: Eyre and Spottiswoode.

Wilson, K. (Ed.), 1988. *The Rasp of War*. London: Sidgwick & Jackson.

Wilson, T., 1970. *The Political Diaries of C.P. Scott 1911-1928*. London: Collins.

Woollacott, A., 1994. *On Her Their Lives Depend*. Berkeley: University of California Press.

Young, K., 1966 *Churchill and Beaverbrook*. London: Eyre & Spottiswoode.

NOTES

Abbreviations used in endnotes

AJB Arthur Balfour
BL Bonar Law
CSC Clementine Churchill
EG Sir Edward Grey
EM Eddie Marsh

HHA Herbert Asquith
JF John Fisher
LG Lloyd George
PL Prince Louis of Battenberg
VS Venetia Stanley
WSC Winston Churchill

PRELUDE

1   The political head of the navy and with a seat in the Cabinet.

CHAPTER 1

1   Corbett 1920, Vol I p. 185.
2   Corbett 1920, Vol I p. 185.

CHAPTER 2

1   HC Deb, 13 May 1901 vol. 93 cc1483–579.
2   *The Times*, 29 June 1914.
3   Wilson, 1988, p. 15.
4   Churchill, 1941, p. 109.
5   WSC to CSC, 23 July 1914 in Soames, 1998, pp. 93–4.
6   HHA to VS in Asquith, 1982, p. 123.
7   Rumbold, 1940, p. 126.
8   Churchill, 1941, pp. 110–12.
9   JF to Esher, 29 Apr 1912 in Marder, 1956, p. 459.
10   PL to WSC 13 Aug 1915 in Gilbert, 1971, p. 6.
11   HHA to VS, 28 Jul 1914 in Asquith, 1982, pp. 126 and 129.
12   HHA to VS, 2 Aug 1914 in Asquith, 1982, p. 146.
13   Marder, 1965, p. 4.
14   WSC to CSC, 28 July 1914 in Soames, 1998, p. 96.
15   Churchill 1941, p. 124.
16   HHA to VS, 1 Aug 1914 in Asquith, 1982, p. 140.
17   HHA to VS, 1 Aug 1914 in Asquith, 1982, p. 140.

18   Churchill, 1941, p. 127.
19   WSC to CSC, 2 Aug 1914 in Soames, 1998, p. 98.
20   Corbett, 1920, p. 28.
21   Churchill, 1941, p. 128.
22   Churchill, 1941, pp. 131-2.
23   Wemyss, 1935, p. 158.
24   David, 1977, p. 180.
25   The spelling at that time.
26   HC Deb, 3 August 1914 vol. 65 cc1809-32.
27   Churchill, 1931, p. 135.
28   HHA to VS, 4 Aug 1914 in Asquith, 1928, pp. 20-1.
29   WSC to EG & HHA, 3 Aug 1914 in Gilbert, 1972a, pp. 12-13.
30   *The Times*, 4 Aug 1914.
31   Gilbert, 1971, p. 31.
32   *The Times*, 4 Aug 1914.
33   BBC News website.
34   Bacon, 1936, pp. 199-200.

CHAPTER 3

1   Hankey, 1961, pp. 185-6.
2   Miller, 1996, Chapter 1.
3   Churchill, 1923a, pp. 222-3.
4   Churchill, 1923a, p. 224.
5   *The Times*, 12 July 1939.
6   Churchill, 1923a, p. 224.
7   Marder, 1965, p. 33.
8   Corbett, 1920, pp. 67-8.
9   HC Deb, 26 February 1919 vol. 112 c1717.
10   *The Times*, 5 Aug 1914.
11   Soames, 1979, p. 89.
12   French, 1919.
13   *Manchester Guardian*, 8 Aug 1914.
14   HC Deb, 7 August 1914 vol. 65 cc2153-6.
15   *The Observer*, 9 Aug 1914.
16   TNA ADM 137/452.
17   Marder, 1952, p. 96.
18   Marder, 1952, p. 98.
19   ODNB.
20   HHA to VS, 9 Aug 1914 in Asquith, 1982, p. 161.
21   Marder, 1952, p. 100.
22   Beatty to his wife, 20 Sept 1902 in Ranft, 1989, p. 11.
23   Marder, 1965, p. 9.
24   Marder, 1959, p. 52.
25   David, 1977, p. 183.
26   Hassall, 1959, p. 120.
27   Hassall, 1959, pp. 130-1.
28   Taylor, 1965, p. 7.
29   David, 1977, p. 188.

30   David, 1977, p. 184.
31   *The Times*, 28 Aug 1914.
32   Asquith, 1982, p. 29.
33   Gilbert, 1971, p. 58.
34   ODNB.
35   Massie, 2003, p. 98.
36   *The Times*, 29 Aug 1914.
37   Osborne, 2006, p. 105.
38   Beatty to his wife, 29 Aug 1914 in Roskill, 1980, p. 84.
39   Massie, 2003, p. 116.
40   *The Times*, 7 Sept 1914.
41   Clark, 1974, p. 135.
42   Gilbert, 1972a, p. 66.
43   Beresford to Bellairs, 4 Feb 1906. McGill Bellairs archive.
44   Clark, 1974, pp. 135-6.

CHAPTER 4

1   Haldane to WSC, 3 Sept 1914 in Gilbert, 1972a, p. 79.
2   *Manchester Guardian*, 5 Sept 1914.
3   ODNB.
4   *The Times*, 12 Sept 1914.
5   *The Observer*, 20 Sept 1914.
6   *The Times*, 22 Sept 1914.
7   *Manchester Guardian*, 22 Sept 1914.
8   Holmes, 1981, p. 199.
9   David, 1977, p. 187.
10   French, 1919.
11   Holmes, 1981, p. 367.
12   Churchill, 1923a, pp. 278-9.
13   French, 1919.
14   Churchill, 1941, p. 70.
15   Gilbert, 1971, p. 64; Gilbert, 1972a, p. 79; Churchill, 1923a, pp. 279-80.
16   Haldane to WSC, 3 Sept 1914 in Gilbert, 1972a, p. 79.
17   Gretton, 1968, p. 39, fn.
18   David, 1977, p. 188.
19   *The Times*, 8 Sept 1914.
20   *The Times*, 7 Sept 1914.
21   Hankey, 1961, pp. 196-7.
22   French, 1919.
23   Churchill, 1923a, pp. 323-4.
24   Corbett, 1920, p. 176.
25   *The Times*, 23 Sept 1914.
26   HHA to VS, 22 Sept 1914 in Asquith, 1982, p. 253.
27   *The Times*, 3 Jul 1916.
28   Hankey, 1961, p. 180.
29   Black, 2009, p. 110.
30   James, 1956, pp. 129-30.
31   HHA to VS, 17 Sept 1914 in Asquith, 1982, pp. 244-5.
32   French, 1919.

33   HHA to VS, 3 Oct 1914 in Asquith, 1982, pp. 259-60.
34   EG to Villiers, 3 Oct 1914 in Gilbert, 1972a p. 156.
35   Powell, 1915, p. 316.
36   Churchill, 1923a, p. 345.
37   Bonham-Carter, 1965, p. 318.
38   Beaverbrook, 1928-32, p. 54.
39   HHA to VS, 5 Oct 1914 in Asquith, 1982, pp. 262-3.
40   HHA to VS, 5 Oct 1914 in Asquith, 1982, pp. 262-3.
41   Powell, 1915.
42   Churchill, 1923a, p. 355.
43   Maurice, 1928, p. 104.
44   HHA to VS, 6 Oct 1914 in Asquith, 1928, p. 42.
45   Gilbert, 1972a, p. 175.
46   David, 1977, p. 189.
47   HHA to VS, 8 Oct 1914 in Asquith, 1982, pp. 257-8.
48   Corbett, 1920, p. 185.
49   Bonham-Carter, 1965, p. 340.
50   BL to unknown, 14 Oct 1914 in Blake, 1955, p. 235.
51   Miss Stevenson referred to Lloyd George as 'C' in her diary – an abbreviation for 'Chancellor of the Exchequer'.
52   Taylor, 1971, p. 6.
53   HHA to VS, 13 Oct 1914 in Asquith, 1982, pp. 275-6.
54   *Manchester Guardian*, 15 Oct 1914.
55   HHA to VS, 10 Oct 1914 in Asquith, 1982, pp. 270-1.
56   Aspinall-Oglander, 1951, p. 264.
57   Hart, 1930, p. 91.
58   EG to CSC, 7 Oct 1914 in Soames, 1979, p. 114.
59   LG to WSC, 7 Oct 1914 in Toye, 2007, p. 131.
60   Hankey, 1961, pp. 207-8.
61   Gilbert, 1972a, pp. 212-3.
62   HHA to VS, 27 Oct 1914 in Asquith, 1982, pp. 287-8.
63   *The Times*, 14 Nov 1918.
64   Taylor, 1971, p. 8.
65   JF to Mrs McKenna, 3 Oct 1914 in Marder, 1959, pp. 60-1.
66   *Manchester Guardian*, 30 Oct 1914.
67   Hay to *The Times*, 31 Oct 1914.
68   Formerly Lambton.
69   PL to WSC, 28 Oct 1914 in *The Times*, 30 Oct 1914.
70   Birkenhead, 1989, pp. 324-5.
71   Gilbert, 1972a, pp. 224-5.
72   WSC to PL, 29 Oct 1914 in *The Times*, 30 Oct 1914.
73   HHA to VS, c20 Oct 1914 in Asquith, 1928, pp. 45-6.

CHAPTER 5

1   HHA to VS, 2 Nov 1914 in Asquith, 1982, p. 305.
2   Lees-Milne, 1986, p. 270.
3   Marder, 1959, p. 80.
4   *Manchester Guardian*, 16 Feb 1915.
5   *Manchester Guardian*, 11 Dec 1915.

6 Beatty to Lady Beatty, 2 Nov 1914 in Chalmers, 1951, pp. 160-1.
7 *The Times*, 31 Oct 1914.
8 Uncle of the eponymous novelist.
9 Fisher, 1919, pp. 88-9.
10 Fisher, 1919, pp. 55 and 58.
11 HHA to VS, 2 Nov 1914 in Asquith, 1982, p. 305.
12 Adm to Cradock, 14 Sept 1914 in Corbett, 1928, p. 309, fn 1.
13 HHA to VS, 4 Nov 1914 in Asquith, 1982, p. 309.
14 HC Deb, 16 November 1914 vol. 68 c193.
15 Churchill, 1923a, p. 428.
16 HC Deb, 11 November 1914 vol. 68 cc5-36.
17 Jellicoe to Adm, 12 Nov 1914 in Patterson, 1966, pp. 83-6.
18 WSC to Jellicoe, 12 Nov 1914 in Patterson, 1966, pp. 86-8.
19 Jellicoe to Adm, 14 Nov 1914 in Patterson, 1966, pp. 90-1.
20 Churchill, 1923a, p. 451.
21 Duff to EG, 3 Dec 1914. TNA ADM 116/1336.
22 Duff to Nicolson, 3 Dec 1914. TNA ADM 116/1336.
23 HC Deb, 27 November 1914 vol. 68 cc1600-16.
24 Addison, 1934, p. 47.
25 WSC to French, 26 Oct 1914 in Holmes, 1981, p. 260.
26 French, 1919.
27 French, 1919.
28 War Council Minutes, 1 Dec 1914. TNA CAB 22/1.
29 War Council Minutes, 1 Dec 1914. TNA CAB 22/1.
30 WSC to JF, 21 Dec 1914 in Marder, 1959.
31 War Council Minutes, 7 Jan 1915. TNA CAB 22/1.
32 WSC to JF, 10 Dec 1914 in Marder, 1959, p. 91.
33 Hankey to JF, 10 Dec 1914 in Marder, 1959, p. 92.
34 Churchill, 1941, p. 257.
35 Addison, 1934, p. 50.
36 JF to Jellicoe, 17 Dec 1914 in Patterson, 1966, p. 106.
37 *The Times*, 21 Dec 1914.
38 HHA to VS, 21 Dec 1914 in Asquith, 1982, p. 334.
39 Magnus, 1958, p. 306.
40 HHA to VS, 19 Dec 1914 in Asquith, 1982, p. 330.
41 HHA to VS, 20 Dec 1914 in Asquith, 1982, p. 325.
42 Gilbert, 1972a, pp. 331-2.
43 WSC to JF, 21 Dec 1914 in Marder, 1959, p. 105.
44 WSC to HHA, 29 Dec 1914 in Marder, 1965, p. 185.
45 Asquith, 1928, p. 52.
46 Churchill, 1923a, p. 322.
47 James, 1956, pp. 137-8.
48 JF to Jellicoe, Nov? 1914 in Gretton, 1988, pp. 198-9.
49 CSC to WSC, 19? Sept 1914 in Soames, 1998, pp. 104-5.

CHAPTER 6

1 Bonham-Carter, 1998, p. 177.
2 *Manchester Guardian*, 25 Jan 1915.

3   Patterson, 1966, pp. 118-9.

4   Taylor, 1971, p. 23.

5   Asquith, 1982, p. 390.

6   JF to WSC, 4 Jan 1915 in Marder, 1956, p. 124.

7   Gilbert, 1971, p. 232.

8   Magnus, 1958, p. 310.

9   Kitchener to French, 2 Jan 1915 in Holmes, 1981, pp. 262-3.

10   WSC to Carden, 3 Jan 1915. TNA ADM 137/96.

11   JF to WSC, 3 Jan 1915 in Marder, 1959, pp. 117-8.

12   WSC minute, 3 Jan 1915 in Gilbert, 1972a, pp. 365-6.

13   Patterson, 1966, vol. 1, pp. 122-4.

14   Marder, 1952, pp. 134-5.

15   Black, 2009, p. 113.

16   War Council Minutes, 7 Jan 1915. TNA CAB 22/1.

17   WSC to Jellicoe, 3 Mar 1915 in Patterson, 1966, pp. 150-2.

18   Asquith, 1928, p. 54.

19   War Council Minutes, 7 Jan 1915. TNA CAB 22/1.

20   Gilbert, 1972a, pp. 396-7.

21   Gilbert, 1972a, pp. 401-2.

22   War Council Minutes, 13 Jan 1915. TNA CAB 22/1.

23   Carden to WSC, 5 Jan 1915. TNA ADM 137/96.

24   WSC to Carden, 6 Jan 1915. TNA ADM 137/96.

25   Black, 2009, p. 122.

26   War Council Minutes, 8 Jan 1915. TNA CAB 22/1.

27   TNA ADM 137/96.

28   War Council Minutes, 13 Jan 1915. TNA CAB 22/1.

29   Hankey, 1961, pp. 265-6.

30   WSC to Carden, 15 Jan 1915. TNA ADM 137/96.

31   JF to Jellicoe, 19 Jan 1915 in Marder, 1959, p. 133.

32   Asquith, 1928, p. 57.

33   Gilbert, 1972a, p. 458.

34   Marder, 1959, p. 147.

35   WSC to JF, 28 Jan 1915 in Marder, 1959, p. 149.

36   War Council Minutes, 11.30 a.m. 28 Jan 1915. TNA CAB 22/1.

37   War Council Minutes, 11.30 a.m. 28 Jan 1915. TNA CAB 22/1.

38   Bonham-Carter, 1998, p. 177.

39   War Council Minutes, 6.30 p.m. 28 Jan 1915. TNA CAB 22/1.

40   Gilbert, 1972a, pp. 447-8.

41   HC Deb, 15 February 1915 vol. 69 cc919-79.

42   War Council Minutes, 9 Feb 1915. TNA CAB 22/1.

43   Asquith, 1928, p. 62.

44   HHA to VS, in Asquith, 1982, p. 429.

45   War Council Minutes, 16 Feb 1915. TNA CAB 22/1.

46   Brooke to Violet Asquith, 18 Feb 1915 in Bonham-Carter, 1998, p. 22.

47   War Council Minutes, 19 Feb 1915. TNA CAB 22/1.

48   Carden to WSC, 20 Feb 1915. TNA ADM 116/3491.

49   WSC to Carden, 25 Feb 1915. TNA 116/3491.

50   Carden to Adm, 26 Feb 1915. TNA ADM 116/3491.

51   Carden to Adm, 27 Feb 1915. TNA ADM 116/3491.

52   Asquith, 1982, p. 453.

53 Gilbert, 1972a, p. 587.
54 Carden to Adm, 28 Feb 1915. TNA ADM 116/3491.
55 Asquith, 1982, p. 454.
56 Gilbert, 1972a, pp. 591-2.
57 Marder, 1965, p. 240.
58 David, 1977, p. 224.
59 Bonham-Carter, 1965, p. 369.
60 WSC to Kitchener, 4 Mar 1915 in Gilbert, 1972a, pp. 628-9.
61 WSC to Carden, 4 Mar 1915. TNA ADM 116/3491.
62 Carden to Adm, 6 Mar 1915. TNA/ADM 116/3491.
63 WSC to Carden, 8 Mar 1915. TNA ADM 116/3491.
64 Gilbert, 1972a, pp. 656-8.
65 Gilbert, 1972a, pp. 659-60.
66 War Council Minutes, 10 Mar 1915. TNA CAB 22/1.
67 Carden's report, 10 Mar 1915. TNA ADM 116/3491.
68 Gilbert, 1972a, pp. 676-7.
69 Churchill to Carden, 11 Mar 1915. TNA ADM 116/3491.
70 Carden to Adm, 13 Mar 1915. TNA ADM 116/3491.
71 Churchill to Carden, 13 Mar 1915. TNA ADM 116/3491.
72 Beesly, 1982, p. 81.
73 Carden to WSC, 14 Mar 1915. TNA ADM 116/3491.
74 Carden to WSC, 14 Mar 1915. TNA ADM 116/3491.
75 WSC to Robeck, 17 Mar 1915. TNA ADM 116/3491.
76 Hamilton, 1922.
77 Robeck to Adm, 19 Mar 1915. TNA ADM 116/3491.
78 War Council Minutes, 19 Mar 1915. TNA CAB 22/1.

CHAPTER 7

1   JF to WSC, 27 Mar 1915. Marder, 1959, pp. 172-4.
2   French, 1919.
3   War Council Minutes, 19 Mar 1915. TNA CAB 22/1.
4   Not the same vessel as the liner *Queen Elizabeth*.
5   WSC to Robeck, 20 Mar 1915. TNA ADM 137/110.
6   Vice Adm E Med to Adm, 21 Mar 1915. TNA ADM 137/110.
7   JF to WSC, 20 Mar 1915 in Marder, 1959, p. 167.
8   Asquith, 1928, p. 67.
9   Hamilton Diary, 1920. Entry for 15 Mar 1915.
10 Malta to Adm, 23 Mar 1915. TNA ADM 116/3491.
11 HHA to VS, 23 Mar 1915 in Asquith, 1982, pp. 500-1.
12 WSC to Robeck, 24 Mar 1915. TNA ADM 137/110.
13 Vice Adm Med to Adm, 25 Mar 1915. TNA ADM 116/3491.
14 Hamilton to HHA, 25 Mar 1915. Marder, 1965, p. 245.
15 McEwen, 1986, p. 103.
16 Asquith, 1928, p. 68.
17 JF to Jellicoe, 26 Mar 1915 in Marder, 1959, p. 169.
18 JF to WSC, 28 Mar 1915 in Marder, 1959, pp. 175-6.
19 HHA to VS, 30 Mar 1915 in Asquith, 1982, p. 520.
20 TNA ADM 137/110.

21 Hamilton Diary, 1920. Entry for 31 Mar 1915.
22 JF to WSC, 31? Mar 1915. Marder, 1959, p. 179.
23 Kitchener to Hamilton, 3 Apr 1915. TNA ADM 116/3491.
24 JF to Jellicoe, 4 Apr 1915. Marder, 1959, p. 186.
25 Montagu to Hankey, 22 Mar 1915 in Asquith, 1982, p. 184.
26 Hobhouse Diary, 7 April 1915 in David, 1977, p. 234.
27 WSC to JF, 8 Apr 1915 in Gilbert, 1972a, p. 782.
28 Sea Lords to JF, 8 Apr 1915 in Marder, 1959, pp. 188-9.
29 JF to Sea Lords, 8 Apr 1915 in Marder, 1959, pp. 190-1.
30 WSC to JF, 11 Apr 1915 in Marder, 1959, pp. 193-4.
31 JF to WSC, 12 Apr 1915 in Marder, 1959, pp. 194-5.
32 Jack C to WSC, 11 Apr 1915 in Gilbert, 1972a, pp. 790-1.
33 Hamilton to Kitchener, 13 Apr 1915. TNA ADM 116/3491.
34 Hamilton Diary, 13 Apr 1915.
35 JF to WSC, 16 Apr 1915 in Gilbert, 1972a, p. 799.
36 HHA to VS, 16 Apr 1915 in Asquith, 1982, p. 544.
37 HHA to VS, 16 Apr 1915 in Asquith, 1982, p. 545.
38 Hankey, 1961, p. 302.
39 WSC to Mrs Brooke, c24 Apr 1915 in Hassall, 1959, p. 329.
40 Jack C to WSC, 5 May 1915 in Gilbert, 1972b, pp. 844-5.
41 Hamilton Diary, 23 Apr 1915.
42 JF to Jellicoe, 23 Apr 1915 in Marder, 1959, pp. 201-2.
43 Hamilton Diary, 27 Apr 1915.
44 JF to Jellicoe, 28 Apr 1915 in Marder, 1959, p. 206.
45 HHA to VS, 28 Apr 1915 in Asquith, 1982, p. 574.
46 Riddell, 1933, p. 82.
47 *Morning Post*, 23 Apr 1915 in Marder, 1959, p. 259.
48 HC Deb, 4 May 1915 vol. 71 cc968-9.
49 Bertie, 1924, p. 159.
50 Bertie, 1924, pp. 161-2.
51 *East Anglian Daily Times*, 9 May 1915.
52 Adm to VA E Med, 9 May 1915. TNA ADM 116/3491.
53 JF to WSC, 11 May 1915 in Marder, 1959, pp. 215-18.
54 WSC to JF, 11 May 1915. CCA FISR 991.
55 Hankey, 1961, p. 314.
56 Gilbert, 1972b, p. 865.
57 JF to Asquith, 12 May 1915. CCA FISR 993.
58 HHA to JF, 12 May 1915. CCA FISR 994.
59 HHA to VS, 12 May 1915 in Asquith, 1982, p. 593.
60 HHA to VS, 5 May 1915 in Asquith, 1982, p. 584.
61 HHA to VS, 12 May 1915 in Asquith, 1982, p. 593.
62 WSC minute, 13 May 1915. TNA ADM 116/3491.
63 JF to Robeck, 13 May 1915 in Gilbert, 1972b, p. 872.
64 Riddell, 1933, p. 86.
65 JF to Asquith, 13 May 1915. CCA FISR 996.
66 Churchill, 1923b, p. 350.
67 Gilbert, 1971, p. 446.
68 Gilbert, 1971, p. 433.
69 War Council Minutes, 14 May 1915. TNA CAB 22/1.
70 WSC to HHA, 14 May 1915 in Churchill, 1923b, pp. 353-4.

71   Gilbert, 1971, p. 436.
72   JF to WSC, 15 May 1915. CCA FISR 1004.
73   Taylor, 1971, p. 50.

CHAPTER 8

1   Tyrwhitt to Keyes, early June 1915 in Halpern, 1975, pp. 144-5.
2   Bonham-Carter, 1965, p. 385.
3   Jenkins, 1964, p. 365.
4   Churchill, 1923b, pp. 358-8.
5   Bonham-Carter, 1998, p. 51.
6   Today the Wharf is in Oxfordshire.
7   WSC to JF, 15 May 1915. CCA FISR 1006.
8   JF to WSC, 16 May 1915. CCA FISR 1010.
9   Churchill, 1923b, p. 364.
10   McKenna to JF, 16 May 1915 in Marder, 1959, p. 232.
11   Lloyd George, 1933, vol. I, pp. 227-9.
12   BL to Asquith, 17 May 1915 in Blake, 1955, p. 246.
13   Taylor, 1965, p. 30.
14   Churchill, 1923b, p. 365.
15   Brett, 1938, p. 236.
16   Hobhouse Diary, 17 June 1915 in David, 1977, p. 247.
17   Asquith, 1928, pp. 95-6.
18   Bonham-Carter, 1998, p. 52.
19   HHA to JF, 17 May 1915. CCA FISR 1017.
20   Churchill, 1923b, p. 366.
21   CCA FP 5486.
22   *Daily Express*, 18 May 1915.
23   *Evening Standard* and *St James' Gazette*, 18 May 1915.
24   Churchill, 1923b, pp. 366-70.
25   Beaverbrook, 1928-32, p. 125.
26   HHA to BL, 18 May 1915 in Asquith, 1928, p. 98.
27   *The Times*, 19 May 1915.
28   Churchill, 1923b, pp. 371-2.
29   McEwen, 1986, p. 114.
30   Taylor, 1971, p. 52.
31   HC Deb, 19 May 1915 vol. 71 cc2392-3.
32   Clark, 1974, pp. 129 and 141.
33   Violet Bonham-Carter Diary, 19 May 1915 in Bonham-Carter, 1965, pp. 402-3.
34   McEwen, 1986, pp. 115-16.
35   Gilbert, 1972a, p. 459.
36   WSC to BL, 21 May 1915 in Beaverbrook, 1928-32, pp. 126-7.
37   BL to WSC, 21 May 1915 in Blake, 1955, p. 252.
38   WSC to HHA, 21 May 1915 in Gilbert, 1972b, p. 926.
39   HHA to WSC, 21 May 1915 in Gilbert, 1972b, pp. 926-7.
40   Jack C to WSC, 20 May 1915 in Gilbert, 1972b, pp. 916-7.
41   French to WSC, 20 Mar 1915 in Gilbert, 1972b, p. 918.
42   Hamilton Diary, 1920, 20 May 1915.
43   Marlborough to WSC, 24 May 1915 in Gilbert, 1972b, p. 940.

44 McEwen, 1986, p. 114.
45 Hobhouse Diary, 23 May 1915 in David, 1977, p. 247.
46 Egremont, 1980, p. 268.
47 McEwen, 1986, p. 119.
48 Hassall, 1959, pp. 340-1.

CHAPTER 9

1 WSC to Jack C, 19 Nov 1915 in Gilbert, 1972b, pp. 1279-80.
2 Churchill, 1941a, p. 300.
3 CCA FISR 1007.
4 Bonham-Carter, 1998, p. 54.
5 Marder, 1965, p. 260.
6 Moore to WSC, 1 Dec 1915 in Gilbert, 1972b, pp. 1298-8.
7 *Morning Post*, April 1915.
8 Bonham-Carter, 1998, p. 177.
9 Marder, 1965, p. 260.
10 Keyes, 1934, p. 275.
11 Gilbert, 1972b, p. 936.
12 Shuttleworth to WSC, 31 May 1915 in Gilbert, 1972b, p. 973.
13 Hassall, 1959, pp. 346-7.
14 WSC to Seely, 12 June 1915 in Gilbert, 1972b, pp. 1016-7.
15 WSC to Jack C, 19 June 1915 in Gilbert, 1972b, pp. 1041-3.
16 Soames, 1979, pp. 125-6.
17 Churchill, 1948, p. 17.
18 WSC to Jellicoe, 1 June 1915 in Marder, 1965, p. 289.
19 *The Times*, 2 Jun 1915.
20 WSC to Jack C, 19 June 1915 in Gilbert, 1972b, pp. 1041-3.
21 McEwen, 1986, p. 128.
22 Churchill, 1923b, pp. 385-91.
23 Hamilton to WSC, 30 June 1915 in Gilbert, 1972b, pp. 1064-5.
24 *The Times*, 7 June 1915.
25 WSC paper, 9 June 1915 in Gilbert, 1972b, p. 999.
26 WSC to Seely, 12 June 1915 in Gilbert, 1972b, pp. 1016-7.
27 Churchill, 1923b, p. 404.
28 Hankey to Esher, 23 June 1915 in Gilbert, 1972b, pp. 1050-1.
29 AJB to WSC, 8 July 1915 in Gilbert, 1972b, pp. 1082-3.
30 JF to Pamela McKenna, 12 July 1915 in Marder, 1959, p. 278.
31 Keyes to his wife, 17 July 1915 in Halpern, 1975, p. 163.
32 Hankey Diary, 17 July 1915.
33 WSC to CSC, 17 July 1915 in Soames, 1998, p. 111.
34 Hamilton to WSC, 5 Aug 1915 in Gilbert, 1972b, pp. 1117-18.
35 WSC to HHA, 12 Aug 1915 in Gilbert, 1972b, pp. 1030-1.
36 EG to WSC, 18 Aug 1915 in Gilbert, 1972b, p. 1139.
37 Dardanelles Committee Proceedings, 27 Aug 1915. TNA CAB 19/33.
38 Taylor, 1971, pp. 59-60.
39 Addison, 1934, pp. 122-4.
40 Addison, 1934, p. 130.
41 Wilson, 1970, p. 140.

42 Dardanelles Committee Proceedings, 14 Oct 1914. TNA CAB 19/33.
43 Jenkins, 1964, pp. 376-7.
44 McEwen, 1968, p. 136.
45 WSC to HHA, 11 Nov 1915 in Gilbert, 1972b, p. 898.

CHAPTER 10

1 *Manchester Guardian*, 16 Nov 1915.
2 *Manchester Guardian*, 13 Nov 1915.
3 *The Times*, 15 Nov 1915.
4 *The Times*, 17 Nov 1915.
5 *Manchester Guardian*, 17 Nov 1915.
6 *The Times*, 16 Nov 1915.
7 Blake, 1955, p. 272.
8 *The Observer*, 21 Nov 1915.
9 Bonham-Carter, 1965, p. 428.
10 *The Times*, 16 Nov 1915.
11 *Manchester Guardian*, 16 Nov 1915.
12 HL Deb, 16 November 1915 vol. 20 cc336-7.
13 *The Times*, 13 Nov 1915.
14 *The Times*, 16 Nov 1915.
15 *Manchester Guardian*, 16 Nov 1915.
16 *The Times*, 19 Nov 1915.
17 Violet Asquith recalls the occasion as being a lunch: Bonham-Carter, 1965, p. 429.
18 Beaverbrook, 1928-32, p. 74.
19 Bonham-Carter, 1965, p. 430.
20 *Manchester Guardian*, 19 Nov 1915.
21 *The Times*, 17 Nov 1915.
22 Joliffe, 1987, p. 218.
23 Buck to Blumenfeld, 21 Nov 1915 in Toye, 2007, p. 156.
24 WSC to CSC, 25 Nov 1915 in Soames, 1998 pp. 118-19.
25 Hart, 1930, p. 219.
26 CSC to WSC, 15 Dec 1915 in Soames, 1998, p. 134.
27 Margot Asquith's brother.
28 *The Times*, 17 Dec 1915.
29 Blake, 1952, p. 117.
30 WSC to EM, 1 Dec 1915 in Hassall, 1959, p. 377.
31 Blake, 1952, p. 117.
32 Gilbert, 1972b, p. 1345.
33 Gibb, 1924, pp. 7-9.
34 Gibb, 1924, p. 19.
35 Gibb, 1924, pp. 21-3.
36 Gibb, 1924, p. 39.
37 WSC to CSC, 8 Jan 1915 in Gilbert, 1972b, p. 1364.
38 WSC to CSC, 13 Jan 1916 in Soames, 1998, pp. 152-3.
39 In command of the artillery of 1st Division in France.
40 WSC to CSC, 18 Jan 1916 in Soames, 1998, pp. 155-6.
41 WSC to CSC, 19 Jan 1916 in Soames, 1998, p. 156.

CHAPTER 11

1   WSC to CSC, 10 Apr 1916 in Soames, 1998, pp. 198-9.
2   WSC to CSC, 27 Jan 1916 in Soames, 1998, pp. 163-4.
3   Gibb, 1924, pp. 72-3.
4   Gibb, 1924, p. 59.
5   Gibb, 1924, p. 47.
6   Gibb, 1924, p. 97.
7   Gibb, 1924, p. 93.
8   Gibb, 1924, pp. 81-8.
9   Gibb, 1924, p. 89.
10 Gibb, 1924, p. 92.
11 CSC to WSC, 27 Jan 1916 in Soames, 1998, pp. 162-3.
12 WSC to CSC, 20 Jan 1916 in Soames, 1998, pp. 157-8.
13 Campbell, 1983, p. 428.
14 Blake, 1952, pp. 126-7.
15 WSC to CSC, 1 Feb 1916 in Soames, 1998, pp. 166-7.
16 Gibb, 1924, p. 62.
17 WSC to CSC, 6 Feb 1916 in Soames, 1998, pp. 169-70.
18 WSC to CSC, 8 Feb 1916 in Soames, 1998, pp. 171-2.
19 WSC to CSC, 14 Feb 1916 in Soames, 1998, pp. 175-6.
20 Gibb, 1924, pp. 74-5.
21 JF to BL, early Feb 1916 in Marder, 1959, pp. 294-5.
22 JF to Lambert, 11 Feb 1916 and JF to Jellicoe, 12 Feb 1916 in Marder, 1959, pp. 303-7.
23 JF to Garvin, 19 Feb 1916 in Marder, 1959, pp. 315-16.
24 Wilson, 1970, p. 187.
25 Wilson, 1970, p. 187.
26 Wilson, 1970, p. 188.
27 JF to WSC, Mar 1916 in Gilbert, 1972b, pp. 1440-1.
28 Wilson, 1970, p. 189.
29 HC Deb, 7 March 1916 vol. 80 cc1401-46.
30 HC Deb, 7 March 1916 vol. 80 cc1401-46.
31 *The Times*, 8 Mar 1916.
32 *National Review* in Marder, 1965, pp. 399-400.
33 Addison, 1934, p. 180.
34 Margot Asquith to AJB, 8 Mar 1916 in Gilbert, 1972b, pp. 1443-4.
35 Wilson, 1970, pp. 190-1.
36 Wilson, 1970, p. 191.
37 JF to WSC, 11 Mar 1916 in Marder, 1959, pp. 323-3.
38 WSC to CSC, 13 Mar 1916 in Soames, 1998, pp. 185-6.
39 WSC to CSC, 17 Mar 1916 in Soames, 1998, p. 191.
40 Gibb, 1924, pp. 75-7.
41 WSC to CSC, 19 Mar 1916 in Soames, 1998, pp. 191-2.
42 WSC to CSC, 22 Mar 1916 in Soames, 1998, pp. 192-3.
43 God willing.
44 CSC to WSC, 24 Mar 1916 in Soames, 1998, pp. 193-4.
45 WSC to CSC, 28 Mar 1916 in Soames, 1998, pp. 196-7.
46 WSC to F.E. Smith, 8 Apr 1916 in Birkenhead, 1989, p. 427.
47 Churchill's successor as Chancellor of the Duchy of Lancaster.
48 WSC to HHA, 12 Apr 1916 in Gilbert, 1972b, pp. 1487.

49   *The Times*, 26 Apr 1916.

50   Gibb, 1924, pp. 109 and 111.

CHAPTER 12

1   Wilson, 1970, p. 234

2   Wilson, 1970, pp. 204-5.

3   WSC to JF, 14 May 1916 Gilbert, 1972b, p. 1502.

4   HC Deb, 09 May 1916 vol. 82 cc472-620.

5   HC Deb, 10 May 1916 vol. 82 cc699-739.

6   HC Deb, 17 May 1916 vol. 82 cc1545-72.

7   HC Deb, 23 May 1916 vol. 82 cc2003-69.

8   HC Deb 01 June 1916 vol. 82 cc2953-3050.

9   Wilson, 1970, p. 212.

10   Hankey's Diary, 3 June 1916 in Hankey, 1961, p. 518.

11   Hankey's Diary, 5 June 1916 in Hankey, 1961, p. 518.

12   Callwell, 1920.

13   McEwen, 1986, p. 158.

14   Wilson, 1970, p. 213.

15   *The Times*, 8 June 1916.

16   Hamilton, 1944, p. 254.

17   Wilson, 1970, p. 212.

18   His term for 'depression'.

19   Wilson, 1970, p. 220.

20   HC Deb, 26 June 1916 vol. 83 c532.

21   Riddell, 1933, p. 196.

22   McEwen, 1986, p. 162.

23   Riddell, 1933, p. 196.

24   HC Deb, 18 July 1916 vol. 84 cc850-60.

25   HC Deb, 20 July 1916 vol. 84 cc1236-91.

26   McEwen, 1986, p. 166.

27   *The Times*, 22 July 1916.

28   HC Deb, 24 July 1916 vol. 84 cc1360-427.

29   WSC memo, 1 Aug 1916 in Gilbert, 1972b, pp. 1534-9.

30   Blake, 1952, p. 157.

31   WSC to Seely, in Gilbert, 1972b, pp. 1542-3.

32   Birkenhead, 1989, p. 434.

33   JF to Lambert, 21 Aug 1916 in Marder, 1959, pp. 365-6.

34   HC Deb, 22 August 1916 vol. 85 cc2505-57.

35   HC Deb, 11 October 1916 vol. 86 cc91-2W.

36   *The Times*, 11 Sept 1916.

37   TNA CAB 19/33, p. 74.

38   TNA CAB 19/33, p. 74.

39   TNA CAB 19/33, p. 75.

40   TNA CAB 19/33, p. 82.

41   TNA CAB 19/33, p. 84.

42   TNA CAB 19/33, p. 85.

43   TNA CAB 19/33, p. 86.

44   TNA CAB 19/33, p. 86.

45 TNA CAB 19/33, p. 103.
46 TNA CAB 19/33, p. 111.
47 Gilbert, 1971, pp. 811-12.
48 TNA CAB 19/33, pp. 291-2.
49 TNA CAB 19/33, pp. 293.
50 Montagu to WSC, in Gilbert, 1972b, pp. 1580-1.
51 HC Deb, 8 November 1916 vol. 87 cc249-368.
52 Beaverbrook, 1932, pp. 102-7.
53 HC Deb, 16 November 1916 vol. 87 cc1043-168.
54 Wilson, 1970, p. 234.
55 Wilson, 1970, pp. 234-5.
56 Taylor, 1965, p. 73.
57 Beaverbrook, 1932, pp. 289-91.
58 Riddell, 1933, p. 232.
59 Riddell, 1933, p. 232.
60 Joliffe, 1987, p. 15.
61 Marder, 1959, p. 423.
62 McEwen, 1986, p. 185.

CHAPTER 13

1   TNA WO 106/33, para 37-68.
2   TNA WO 106/33, para 17-27.
3   TNA WO 106/33, para 70 and 28.
4   TNA WO 106/33, para 121b.
5   TNA WO 106/33, para 121c.
6   TNA WO 106/33, para 121i.
7   TNA WO 106/33, para 76.
8   TNA WO 106/33, para 118.
9   TNA WO 106/33, para 112.
10 TNA WO 106/33, para 121f.
11 TNA WO 106/33, para 121j.
12 TNA WO 106/33, para 91.
13 *The Times*, 9 Mar 1917.
14 Beatty to his wife, 12 Mar 1917 in Ranft, 1959, p. 409.
15 McEwen, 1986, p. 186.
16 McEwen, 1986, p. 187.
17 WSC to LG, 10 Mar 1917 in Gilbert, 1977, pp. 42-3.
18 HC Deb, 12 March 1917 vol. 91 cc709-10.
19 HC Deb, 20 March 1917 vol. 91 cc1753-831.
20 WSC to Pickford, 1 May 1917 in Gilbert, 1977, pp. 50-9.
21 HC Deb, 21 February 1917 vol. 90 cc1359-98.
22 HC Deb, 5 March 1917 vol. 91 cc81-182.
23 Hart, 1930, p. 62.
24 HC Deb, 5 March 1917 vol. 91 cc81-182.
25 HC Deb, 5 March 1917 vol. 91 cc81-182.
26 HC Deb, 20 March 1917 vol. 92 cc636-715.
27 HC Deb, 3 April 1917 vol. 92 cc1139-211.
28 Toye, 2007, p. 176.

29   *Daily Telegraph*, 24 Oct 2001.
30   *Daily Telegraph*, 24 Oct 2001.
31   WSC to Sinclair, 22 Mar 1917 in Gilbert, 1977, p. 45.
32   Wilson, 1970, p. 285.
33   Addison, 1934, p. 167.
34   HC Deb, 4 April 1917 vol. 92 cc1363-98.
35   Toye, 2007, p. 177.
36   Addison, 1934, p. 167.
37   Ramsden, 1984, p. 84.
38   Toye, 2007, p. 179.
39   McEwen, 1986, p. 189.
40   McEwen, 1986, p. 189 and Riddell, 1933, p. 251.
41   Taylor, 1965, p. 158.
42   LG to Painlevé, in Gilbert, 1977, p. 61.
43   Haig's journal, 2 June 1918 in Blake, 1952, p. 234.
44   Esher to Haig, 30 May 1917 in Brett, 1938, p. 121.
45   Curzon to BL, 4 June 1917 in Gilbert, 1977, p. 68.
46   *Sunday Times*, 3 June 1917.
47   Owen, 1954, p. 411.
48   Smuts to LG, 6 June 1917 in Gilbert, 1977, p. 69.
49   Sir George Younger to LG, 8 June 1917 in Gilbert, 1977, p. 70.
50   Curzon to LG, 8 June 1917 in Gilbert, 1977, p. 72.
51   Owen, 1954, p. 413.
52   Beresford to BL, 2 June 1917. PA BL/82/1/3.
53   *The Times*, 26 July 1917.
54   Owen, 1954, pp. 410 and 413.
55   Owen, 1954, p. 414.
56   Clark, 1974, p. 170.
57   Donald to WSC, 18 July 1917 in Gilbert, 1977, p. 100; Brabazon to WSC, 18 July 1917 in
      Gilbert, 1977, p. 100; and C.P. Scott to WSC, 18 July 1917 in Gilbert, 1977, p. 101.
58   Gwynne to Lady Bathurst, 20 July 1917 in Wilson, 1988, p. 221.
59   WSC to Electors of Dundee, 26 July 1917 in Gilbert, 1977, pp. 115-16.
60   *The Times*, 23 July 1917.
61   *The Times*, 28 July 1917.
62   *The Times*, 30 July 1917.
63   *The Times*, 31 July 1917.

CHAPTER 14

1   Harris, 1995, p. 97.
2   Riddell, 1933, p. 258.
3   Churchill, 1927, p. 294.
4   Churchill, 1927, p. 295.
5   Churchill, 1927, p. 311.
6   Bellman, 1947, pp. 65-6.
7   Riddell, 1933, p. 257.
8   Churchill, 1927, p. 298.
9   WSC to Evans and Duckham, 26 July 1917 in Gilbert, 1977, p. 111.
10   WSC to Curzon, 26 July 1917 in Churchill, 1927, pp. 551-3.

11   Churchill, 1927, p. 551.
12   Haig to WSC, 29 July 1917 in Gilbert, 1977, pp. 116-17.
13   WSC to LG, 9 Sept 1917 in Gilbert, 1977, pp. 157-9.
14   WSC to LG, 9 Sept 1917 in Gilbert, 1977, pp. 157-9.
15   Churchill, 1927, p. 300.
16   WSC to Greene, 20 Aug 1917 in Gilbert, 1977, p. 143.
17   Addison, 1934, p. 426.
18   Riddell, 1933, p. 258.
19   Bellman, 1947, p. 67.
20   WSC to Duckham and Stevenson in Gilbert, 1977, pp. 111-12.
21   WSC to Newman, 5 Aug 1917 in Gilbert, 1977, pp. 125-6.
22   WSC dept minute, 3 Nov 1917 in Gilbert, 1977, p. 191.
23   *The Times*, 23 July 1917.
24   HC Deb, 28 November 1917 vol. 99 cc2011-5.
25   *The Times*, 16 Jan 1918.
26   Barnes, 1924, p. 171.
27   Derby note, 18 Aug 1917 in Churchill, 1959, p. 283.
28   Derby & Robertson to LG, 15 Aug 1917 in Gilbert, 1977, pp. 133-4.
29   Geddes to LG, 16 Aug 1917 in Gilbert, 1977, pp. 134-5.
30   Gilbert, 1977, pp. 136-7.
31   Roskill, 1970, p. 425.
32   WSC to LG, No. 1, 19 Aug 1917 in Gilbert, 1977, pp. 140-1.
33   WSC memo, 15 Aug 1917 in Gilbert, 1977, pp. 131-2.
34   WSC to Layton, 23 Aug 1918 in Churchill, 1927, p. 557.
35   HC Deb, 18 February 1918 vol. 103 cc544-66.
36   WSC to Chairmen of Steel Cos, 10 Sept 1917 in Gilbert, 1977, pp. 160-1.
37   Marsh, 1939, pp. 252-4.
38   Marsh, 1939, p. 254.
39   Blake, 1952, p. 254.
40   Blake, 1952, p. 254.
41   Blake, 1952, p. 254.
42   Marsh, 1939, p. 256.
43   Marsh, 1939, p. 257.
44   Marsh, 1939, pp. 259-60.
45   Marsh, 1939, p. 261.
46   Marsh, 1939, p. 262.
47   Gilbert, 1977, p. 172.
48   WSC to Northcliffe, 9 Oct 1917 in Gilbert, 1977, p. 172.
49   War Cabinet Minutes, 9 Oct 1917. TNA CAB 23/4.
50   WSC to Montagu, 19 Oct 1917 in Gilbert, 1977, p. 180.
51   WSC to Sir Glynn West, 5 Nov 1917 in Gilbert, 1977, p. 191.
52   *The Times*, 4 Oct 1917.
53   *The Times*, 20 Oct 1917.
54   Gilbert, 1977, pp. 169-70.
55   *The Times*, 27 Oct 1917.
56   Churchill, 1927, p. 340.
57   WSC to HHA, 5 Jan 1915 in Harris, 1995, p. 17.
58   Haig to War Office, 9 Feb 1916 in Harris, 1995, p. 56.
59   Harris, 1995, p. 33.
60   Churchill, 1927, pp. 304-9.

61   Harris, 1995, pp. 136-7.
62   Churchill, 1927, pp. 315-22.
63   Churchill, 1927, pp. 315-22.
64   WSC to Loucheur, 25 Nov 1917 in Churchill, 1927, pp. 325-6.
65   WSC to Clamping Committee, 25 Nov 1917 in Churchill, 1927, pp. 326-7.
66   WSC to Maclay, 15 Nov 1917 in Gilbert, 1977, pp. 196-7.
67   Churchill, 1927, pp. 378-84.
68   Churchill, 1927, pp. 378-84.
69   *The Times*, 11 Dec 1917.
70   WSC to CSC, 23 Feb 1918 in Soames, 1979, pp. 205-6.
71   Bertie to Stamfordham, 28 Feb 1918 in Gilbert, 1977, pp. 254-5.
72   Churchill, 1927, pp. 394-403.
73   WSC to Cooke, 15 Mar 1918 in Gilbert, 1977, pp. 269-70.
74   Blake, 1952, p. 294.
75   Harris, 1995, p. 164.
76   Churchill, 1927, p. 410.

CHAPTER 15

1   Gilbert, 1977, p. 275.
2   Churchill, 1927, p. 411.
3   McEwen, 1986, p. 223.
4   Gilbert, 1977, p. 273.
5   Gilbert, 1977, pp. 271 and 273.
6   Gilbert, 1977, p. 275.
7   WSC to LG – not sent. Gilbert, 1977, p. 276.
8   Wilson Diary, 26 Mar 1918 in Gilbert, 1977, pp. 279-80.
9   *The Times*, 27 Mar 1918.
10   LG to Clemenceau, 28 Mar 1918 in Gilbert, 1977, p. 281.
11   Churchill, 1932, p. 177.
12   WSC to LG telegram, No. 2, 29 Mar 1918 in Gilbert, 1977, pp. 284-5.
13   Wilson Diary, 30 Mar 1918 in Gilbert, 1977, p. 287.
14   *The Times*, 26 Apr 1918.
15   HC Deb, 25 April 1918 vol. 105 cc1139-254.
16   Toye, 2007, p. 187.
17   WSC to Loucheur, 18 Aug 1918 in Gilbert, 1977, pp. 377-8.
18   Blake, 1952, p. 306.
19   Churchill, 1927, p. 481.
20   WSC to LG, 15 Apr 1918 – not sent. Gilbert, 1977, pp. 302-3.
21   WSC to LG, 4 May 1918 in Gilbert, 1977, pp. 309-10.
22   *The Times*, 8 May 1918.
23   *The Times*, 3 June 1918.
24   Derby, 2001, p. 44.
25   *The Times*, 11 July 1918.
26   War Cabinet Minutes, 16 July 1918. TNA CAB 23/7.
27   *The Times*, 20 July 1918.
28   *The Times*, 22 July 1918.
29   *The Times*, 25 July 1918.
30   War Cabinet Minutes, 24 July 1918. TNA CAB 23/7.
31   *The Times*, 27 July 1918.

32   *The Times*, 30 July 1918.
33   Churchill, 1927, pp. 506-8.
34   Haig to WSC, 9 Aug 1918 in Gilbert, 1977, p. 367.
35   Hart, 1930, p. 479.
36   WSC to LG, 10 Aug 1918 in Gilbert, 1977, pp. 370-1.
37   WSC to CSC, 15 Aug 1918 in Gilbert, 1977, pp. 374-5.
38   Derby, 2001, p. 152.
39   McEwen, 1986, p. 243.
40   WSC to CSC, 12 Sept 1918 in Soames, 1998, p. 214.
41   WSC to CSC, 15 Sept 1918 in Soames, 1998, pp. 214-15.
42   CSC to WSC, 17 Sept 1918 in Soames, 1998, p. 216.
43   War Cabinet paper, 5 Sept 1918 in Churchill, 1927, pp. 519-20.
44   *The Times*, 8 Oct 1918.
45   *The Times*, 9 Oct 1918.
46   *The Times*, 11 Oct 1918.
47   *The Times*, 12 Oct 1918.
48   World War I Document Archive http://wwi.lib.byu.edu/index.php/Main_Page
49   *The Times*, 15 Oct 1918.
50   Hassall, 1959, pp. 450-1.
51   Hassall, 1959, pp. 452-3.
52   CSC to WSC, 29 Oct 1918 in Soames, 1998, pp. 216-17.
53   WSC to Ritchie, 5 Nov 1918 in Gilbert, 1977, pp. 406-7.
54   WSC to LG, 7 Nov 1918 in Gilbert, 1977, pp. 410-11.
55   LG to WSC, 8 Nov 1918 in Gilbert, 1977, pp. 408-10.
56   WSC to LG, c9 Nov 1918 in Gilbert, 1977, pp. 410-11.
57   Broadberry, S. and Howlett, P., 'The United Kingdom During World War I: Business as
      Usual?' 2003. http://www2.warwick.ac.uk/fac/soc/economics/staff/academic/broadberry/
      wp/wwipap4.pdf

EPILOGUE

1   Bowen, 1987.
2   Watson-Watt, 1957.
3   Jones, 1978.

INDEX

Ranks and posts have generally been omitted since they changed so frequently during the war.

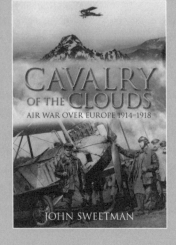
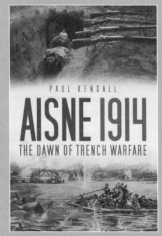
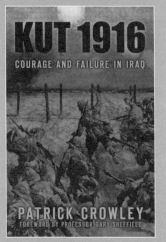
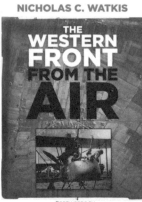